PUBLIC OPINION AND POLITICS IN EIGHTEENTH CENTURY ENGLAND

Public Opinion and Politics in Eighteenth Century England

TO THE FALL OF WALPOLE

By

WILLIAM THOMAS LAPRADE

Professor of History in Duke University

GREENWOOD PRESS, PUBLISHERS
WESTPORT, CONNECTICUT

DA480
· L3
1971

60-861-832

Originally published in 1936
by The Macmillan Company, New York

First Greenwood Reprinting 1971

Library of Congress Catalogue Card Number 70-114538

SBN 8371-4806-5

Printed in the United States of America

To
NANNIE CALFEE LAPRADE

CONTENTS

viii   CONTENTS

PUBLIC OPINION AND POLITICS IN EIGHTEENTH
CENTURY ENGLAND

CHAPTER I

THE HERITAGE FROM THE PAST, 1700

> Though you cannot make that time present which is past, yet in imagination and reflection . . . place yourselves in the midst of that state of things which belonged to that period. Cease for once to know what is; and blot out of your memories all that has passed in the whole intermediate space. . . . In doing this . . . though you can in supposition frame that former scene to be now first present, you cannot frame that inward feeling or passion . . . nor can words or art raise any image of it within you, but what will be like a shadow or a ghost, faint and languid, compared with what was once really felt.
>
> BISHOP HOADLY, recalling the Revolution in the
> *London Journal,* November 2, 1723.

ENGLISH adults awake at twelve o'clock, midnight, December 31, 1700, like those at any moment of time, looked backward to a past they understood little and forward to a future they foresaw less. Officially it was not the beginning of a new year and a new century. Though Englishmen were embarking upon generations of unpremeditated experiment, the past was with them in a way the future could not be.

Octogenarians still alive had lived in every reign since Queen Elizabeth's, but were proud of no successful monarch since her time. In troubled years no Stuart king had learned her art of rallying the English people to a common cause. A lad of eight in the third year of Charles I might well have heard his elders talk of Wentworth and of Buckingham and the petition which the Parliament forced the King to sign. Coming of age, he scarcely understood the bitter fight between the same King and another Parliament. At twenty-nine, among the crowd, he saw the axe deprive the royal body of its head and felt emotions that he could not formulate.

As a man he watched with anxious hopes and fears changes

1

and failures of succeeding months. He read the pamphlets that appeared by scores and pondered them. He had no other time to live, but in those days his world held little of stability. At thirty-seven he saw a giant pass and wondered if another arm could draw the bow of Oliver. At thirty-nine he watched Monck's army come to town. At forty in another crowd he saw the King return and thrilled with hope renewed. Soon he shook his head again. Absent courtiers did not understand how people felt in years they were away. He saw the Church, restored, making some of Laud's mistakes. He saw Dissenters driven forth. He felt again the fear of Rome. He saw excesses in the royal court. He heard dark rumors that the King was traitor to the country and was making terms with France. Although the Duke of York was openly a Roman Catholic, he feared the violence of an exclusion bill.

At fifty-eight he did not easily accept the plot of Titus Oates, but saw the people surge at Godfrey's bier. The heads of men he knew began to fall. The King was helpless in the terrors of the hour. At sixty he read Filmer's *Patriarcha,* published on the Stuart side. The next year saw two Parliaments dissolved. Louis of France agreed to pay his cousin's bills. Roger L'Estrange began to ply the people with *Observators.* The Tower found a place for Shaftesbury. Dryden published *Absalom and Achitophel.* The axe was now in other hands. An aging man of sixty-three saw Russell and then Sydney die.

When he was sixty-five another reign began. The foolish James, unmindful of the lessons that his brother learned, began to make his throne untenable. Monmouth came to claim the crown and lose his head; Jeffreys presided at the trials of his followers. Unwittingly, the King aroused the deepest fear that England could be taught to feel. Churchmen and Dissenters were impelled to join a common cry. At sixty-eight a man still older looked through windows into City streets alive with mobs that cheered the bishops on their way to find a lodgment in the Tower.

Ensuing months were tense and tried an old man's nerves. Things were done that seemed incredible. A king was frightened from his throne without a loss of life. A foreigner with

an army of the hostile Dutch by patient, artful moves assumed
the crown discarded by the father of his wife. It was a harder
thing to win the favor of the people he agreed to rule. He
brought them wars they did not wish. With him were foreign
friends who claimed rewards for help they gave.

Parliament pledged him by a Bill of Rights. It learned to
grant him year by year the power and means to raise the army
it could not withhold in war. It granted toleration to Dissenters who had helped. It pledged itself for interest on a debt to
pay expenses of the war with France, and with these bonds
set up a bank to market credit as the need arose. When peace
was made, it took the army from the King. It took back lands
that he bestowed on favorites. It threatened to impeach his
ministers. It seemed to look suspiciously on all he did.

And thus an aged man of eighty years found things as little
settled as when life began. There was no army; but, a war
in sight. There was no unity against an exiled claimant of
the crown upheld by France. A frantic King, who scarcely
hoped to keep the throne and helpless saw the peril that his
native country faced, now found the power of Spain about to
fall into his rival's hands. Perhaps it was as well that life was
almost spent.

Men were not wanting who had reached this age. John Eve-
lyn, the diarist and pundit in the Royal Society, was such a
man. On New Year's Eve in 1700 he could look backward four
score years and still had left a span of six years more. Other
younger notables who lingered on had meanwhile had their
day. Sir Christopher Wren walked, a man of sixty-eight, amid
a city he had helped to build anew and served the reigning
monarch as Surveyor General of the Royal Works. John Locke
at the same age had left the Board of Trade. His memory for
four years more could cherish stirring times with Shaftesbury.
His books were handy arsenals from which the journalists on
whatever side in generations just ahead would draw their arguments.

Sir Isaac Newton, ten years younger, had completed work
that would insure his lasting fame and now was Master of the
Mint. One year older, Thomas Rymer had for seven years

been working on the *Foedera*. Dryden had not lasted out that year. Frequenters of Will's Coffee-House would miss his figure in the chair. He had lamented Cromwell's death in verse, had greeted and supported Charles, had drawn his pen upon the side of James, and now in William's reign had died in peace just short of threescore years and ten.

At Clapham in retirement Samuel Pepys at sixty-seven, with only his allotted three more years to live, now mused with fewer thrills upon his shorthand jottings than when he set them down as fresher memories. None yet foresaw his double fame in time to come. Roger L'Estrange, a stronger man, though eighty-four would outlive Pepys. Remembering many services to both the first and second Charles, he had been prisoner and exile in their cause. Lately he tried his pen on safer tasks, works of antiquity.

Richard Cromwell at a quiet country house lived as an obscure old man of seventy-four. Few recalled that he had tried a little while to fill his father's place. He was to linger on for yet another dozen years. Titus Oates, a younger man of greater fame, at Wapping preached occasionally to dissenting groups. At sixty-nine the Earl of Danby still attended Parliament as the Duke of Leeds and gave the King advice when called upon. He knew the strength and weakness of the English crown. The Church had been his bulwark as chief minister. Amid a feverish fear of Rome he had gone helpless to the Tower. Even now a listener might not understand the tale he had to tell.

Though ten years younger, Laurence Hyde, the Earl of Rochester, recalled his father as chief minister of the King, later an exile on the Continent, and his own sister as the heir apparent's bride. A niece, until her death, had been the royal consort of his present Majesty. Another niece was heir apparent to the crown. Through the friendship of his wife and services rendered by himself, John Churchill, Earl of Marlborough, had won the favor of the latter niece. Her private nickname for the King was "Caliban." Churchill's sister had been mistress of the exiled King. Her son, the Duke of Berwick, was an officer of France. Perhaps Churchill had just grounds to think that William made no haste to use his military talents in the field.

But age would soon deprive him of his opportunities. His family was growing up. He needed to make haste. Recently he and William were more friendly than before. Two of his daughters were already matched with men whose fathers could not be ignored. Reluctantly in that very month the King accepted Sidney, the first Earl of Godolphin as his minister. Five years Churchill's senior, that Lord had been a page and then a minister to Charles II and had adhered to James almost unto the last. The shrewd and charming Robert Spencer, Earl of Sunderland, at sixty had now almost lived his life. William had taken his advice as kings before had done. Though out of office, he had not yet ceased to count. His son, a widower and aristocratic radical, took for a second wife that year Marlborough's second daughter, Anne. Henrietta, the elder sister, had married Godolphin's only son two years before.

In Parliament were able lesser men. Christopher Musgrave at sixty-six still sat for Oxford, a consistent sympathizer with the Church. So was Sir Edward Seymour, one year older, who sat for Exeter. Though sixty-nine, Henry Guy was to outlive them both. He had been early in the favor of King Charles II. A Secretary of the Treasury in the last years of that King and through the reign of James, he had served William four years in the office too. Few in his time knew better how men got their seats in Parliament. He had been in the Tower a little while. He had another decade yet before he died, bequeathing wealth to William Pulteney, now a youth of just sixteen. Paul Foley, sometime Speaker of the lower house, had died the previous year. Robert Harley, husband of Foley's niece, had learned some of the latter's art of politics and was an abler leader on his own account.

Some of the men who helped to make the Revolution were now in middle age. They never would be unimportant in their time. William Bentinck, Earl of Portland, the King's Dutch lieutenant, had been born in 1649. John Somers, two years younger, now a peer, had given up the great seal in that year. He was learned in the law and a chief author of the Bill of

Rights. Two years younger still, Edward Russell, Earl of Orford, had quit the Admiralty the year before. Thomas, the first Marquess of Wharton, patron of the turf, now fifty-two, had entertained the King at Woburn in his fiftieth year. He liked elections when the opposition made a fight. He was reputed publisher of the famous song that helped to raise the nation against James II, for which Henry Purcell wrote the air. Wharton was Comptroller of the Household throughout William's reign. Charles Talbot, Duke of Shrewsbury, had quit his place that year to go to Rome in search of health and quieter scenes. Charles Montague, at thirty-nine, had just become the Baron Halifax. As founder of the Bank and a promoter of the national debt, he had already made a name, though life still seemed to him to lie ahead.

Thomas Tenison had written against Hobbes in Charles the Second's reign, had ministered to Monmouth at his death, had preached the funeral sermon for Nell Gwyn. (Members of her profession did not live so long.) His was a moderating voice, and hence at sixty-four he had been half a dozen years Archbishop of Canterbury and would be so for half a generation yet to come. Gilbert Burnet, historian of the Reformation, historian also of his time, had found the courage to reproach a king, had kept his head amid the Popish Plot, had ministered to Russell when he died, had been outlawed by James II, and now at fifty-seven as Bishop of Salisbury was advocate in the House of Lords of a tolerant king and Church.

Because Sir William Temple had not lived the century out, Jonathan Swift at thirty-three, thus early disappointed in his hopes, had to return to Ireland and try to be contented with preferments there. Joseph Addison at twenty-eight with a pension of three hundred pounds a year was traveling on the Continent preparing for diplomacy, which it transpired was not his career. Captain Richard Steele at even age had written mourning verses for the Queen and got a child by Richard Tonson's daughter, but as a recompense would publish *The Christian Hero* through her father's brother, Jacob, the next year. In authors with patrons of repute booksellers had to tolerate some things they might not like. As secretary of the Kit-Cat

Club, Jacob Tonson drew for mutual help his men of talent to associate with men of station, family, or means.

These men and others of like kind made up the English ruling class. Each had ambitions of his own: a thirst for power, a zest for life, material stakes, prestige of birth, acquired skills, and thus a little game to play. Each had lieutenants of the lesser folk and hangers-on. Each looked for help to family or friends. Each strove for power, or place, or fame, or wealth, or combinations that appealed. Each might have justly said, he had the country's good at heart. And thus they strove among themselves, aspiring to achieve ambitions that might grow with each success.

The king was a contender in this strife. Although the saying was already old, that English kings could do no wrong, it merely meant, the king was both an institution and a man. But the office and the man were merged in one, and royal favor was a major prize for which men strove. The king with a substantial group to help was irresistible. Power and honors were his gifts. Rivals had to intimidate or to conciliate his will.

True, men alive had helped to bring kings to account, but this had not been lightly done, and the restored monarch was given rights above the claims of later kings. Though in the face of clamorous fears these claims might be ignored, they were embedded deep in many loyal hearts and had to be regarded by one who wished to win the favor of the English populace.

A paradox, the Church was both the greatest bulwark of this feeling toward the king and the most potent rival of the royal will. None could resist the cry of "Church and King." United, the Church alone was perhaps stronger than the king. But it involved too many hopes and interests to stay united long. Only immediate, overwhelming fear would move it singly in a common cause. The fear of Rome was likeliest to have this scope and easiest to arouse. This ghost had not been laid since the Pope's bull against Elizabeth. Time added incidents to give persistent life. The slightest provocation now would call it forth to stalk the streets and galvanize the English factions into one. The Popish Plot taught Charles II the power of the English Church. Failure to understand it drove his brother from the throne.

But the Revolution left the Church less united and more fearful than before. Some indeed thought its existence insecure. The Commonwealth had suppressed it; the royal family brought it back. Simple gratitude and a will to live thus combined to merge the interests of the Church and the legitimate ruling house. Rationalizing arguments derived the power of both from a divine, common source. Supporting statutes were passed in early Restoration years. In consequence, when James adhered to Rome, a thoughtful subject's heart was torn between the loyalties to King and Church. These two conflicting feelings stirred deeply but unevenly in many English breasts.

Bishops and clergy who had joined the Revolution, moved by fears of Rome, were also faithful to the hereditary line and would not take the oaths prescribed to William as their king. This caused a cleavage in the Church. Places were vacant on the bench for sympathizers with the new régime. But lesser clergy, having cure of souls in smaller parishes, could not afford this sacrifice and thus kept on their work with a suppressed loyalty to him they thought to be the rightful king.

These latter had themselves within the generation past been shaped somewhat by souls of whom they had the cure. The forms of worship were prescribed; familiar rites had been restored with the King. But ministers to the English common people bred in the mid-decades of the seventeenth century could not ignore the popular, lingering loyalties: the Scriptures as the revelation of God's will, formal piety, an holy Sabbath day, salvation in a world to come which each sought for himself by individual acts and attitudes. Priests of the restored Church took from superiors the polity and ritual of the martyred King. But in their parishes they found a stubborn heritage from the Puritans. A prudent priest permits conforming men to find their several ways to God. Hence in some measure the restored priests themselves learned to conform to what their people felt.

This was more true perhaps in rural than in urban parishes. In the populous localities Dissenters, having substance and numbers sufficient, established chapels of their own. The Toleration Act allowed them liberties and made of them a faction to be reckoned with. Objecting to restrictions on these liberties, they joined in agitation for repeal. Remembering the past, and seeing this, churchmen began to fear Dissenters all the more. Accordingly, churchmen and Dissenters both were forces of which a politician took account. Feelings that these two groups shared jointly—the fear of Rome and loyalty to a pious mode of life—were factors that no leader could ignore.

Outside the circle of the Restoration court, religion and the Church aroused in Englishmen of that time emotions more intense, more widespread in extent, than any other stimuli to which they gave response. Partly on that account perhaps, hard pressed, thoughtful leaders began to seek respite by questioning the bases of this prevailing mood. But by its very nature the progress of this work was hazardous and slow. Conventional piety, intrenched, fought back and easily held its ground everywhere except in circles of urban intelligentsia. Clever scoffers had their fling. Learned skeptics made their points and left their works to generations yet unborn. A ruler of England in that time might use their facile pens, might even share their views himself, but seldom dared oppose the latent force of narrow piety, fearing its power if aroused.

Parliament reflected or responded to moods and feelings of the populace and ruling class. Leaders in the House of Lords had made the Revolution, had staked their lives and all on its success, had preached its causes to their followers, had pledged their wealth to carry on the war it brought. They disagreed among themselves on many policies, but on this major point they had a common will. The exiled King still lived in France, a threat endangering their lives and property. Unless they rallied England to their side, the things they held might pass into the waiting hands of France and Rome. The City merchants shared these fears and had invested in the bonds for William's war.

The House of Commons was uncertain yet. In calmer times, if calm should ever come again, the king and a substantial faction in the Lords could manage it. Some of its members were lieutenants of the larger landed men. Some, having purely local interests, were apt to find it prudent to support the minister in power. Many with local interests had to fight to hold their ground. The parsons had influence that could not be defied. They made appeals to hopes and fears a layman could not match. Under the Triennial Act there was not time between elections to justify too great expenditure in nursing many borough interests. In part there had to be dependence on the feelings of the hour. Therefore an election might become a fearful time. One was in progress when the century closed.

Struggles for power, whether in province or in Parliament, were largely personal. Parties were ephemeral. Observant writers had begun to predicate that they were not then what they had been hitherto. In fact, they never were. Yet there was general and effective use of party names. A man professing loyalty to *Whig* or *Tory, King* or *Church* or *Commonwealth,* if summoned by the name professed, might stand and vote in shire, borough, or in Parliament. But parties were not national in scope and lacked a membership on which to count. A group in Parliament would club and dine to wage a session's fight, but these alliances might not outlive the year. Men or factions were allied or not as circumstances changed.

Always there was an opposition and a ministry. Shrewdly, in times of stress, the former affected to support the "country" as against the "court." The "court" at any given time merely meant the men in power and their friends; the "country" consisted of disgruntled men left out. Leaders or factions readily changed sides, but seldom or never was one group wholly substituted for another in the seats of power. Leaders and factions were realities to count upon; parties were scarcely more than annuals.

Because the king was still the source of power, his favor was a prize for which men strove. He might change his mind or die. He had fears himself on which his courtiers might play, hopes and wishes they might utilize. Also he usually had an heir apparent on whom a leader out of power might base a hope deferred. The heir apparent, too, might feel the disappointed longings of a human heart. The heir apparent's court thus was—and long would be—a rallying place for rivals of the men in power.

But opposition leaders did not like to wait. The danger was, that they might die before the king. A king might be induced to change his ministers. A minister might be driven from the service of the king. Politics had thus become a sort of game; the stakes, the offices of power. But such a game required rules of sportmanship, or else it risked the safety of the country as a whole. These rules were not yet made, and thus the fight for power was stark and real. The issue might be desperate. The winner had his little day at court. The loser might retire to the Continent, take an apartment in the Tower, or lose his head to give the mob a holiday. If he had following and wit enough, he might survive at home to strive for what he lost.

Men recalled that in the previous century kings had had to fight to get or keep the crown. One had lost his head. Two received the scepter with the help of arms. Another now in exile craved a heritage for his son of which he felt that he had been deprived by force. Therefore the favor of the king, important though it was, might not decide unless his people willed to have him rule. Even thoughtful leaders scarcely knew what they expected from a king.

Management of the army was a case in point. Surely, the hand that ruled the country should have responsibility for its defense. But Cromwell with his army had seemed to justify the fears of Parliament when it withheld the force from Charles I. William had brought an army to defend the country against the fear of military power and Rome. More recently, he had been disarmed by Parliament. Given an army, any king, it seemed, might take away his subjects' liberties.

Nevertheless, there was no substitute for a king. He was a part of any government the English people understood. So were Lords and Commons. Experiments in Cromwell's time but emphasized the wish for an hereditary ruler and for a legislature of the sort that England knew.

It was the business of the king in Parliament to deliberate in secret and decide. And yet the mass of adult people had a part. They gave importance to the rest. They were the ruled; they did the work; they carried arms; they sailed the seas in ships; they paid the bills; they could not be ignored. At times, in divers groups, they had to be induced to vote.

There was variety in their response. Their fears had diverse roots. Their loyalties were numerous. The Church, the reigning king, conventional piety, the royal house, the country—all these made appeal. More direct was the pull of local leadership. Some cherished still an earlier cause's shibboleths or party names. A single issue seldom stirred decisive groups to act, but various feelings could be mobilized to serve a single, simple cause.

Appealing for potential followers, each contending leader strove to magnify his weight. Perhaps he had a local landed interest enhanced by the connections of his family. Upon this base he built alliances with other leaders or with lesser families. He learned the art of winning men by the emotions that they felt, by sharing loyalties that they confessed. Upon occasion it was helpful to intimidate, not by direct use of force, but rather by arousing fears upon a question mooted at the time. The "passions" of the multitude, as they were called, were factors no aspiring leader dared neglect.

Oral appeals were not made to crowds. There was no adequate police. A crowd became a mob. The social cement could not stand the strain. The safety of life and property was involved. Only on formal occasions or under official auspices with patronage from the ruling class could an assembly meet. Almost constant was the fear of mobs and violence, ready weapons for the hands of those who wished to overthrow the men in power.

But they were dangerous weapons too, and leaders tempted to their use were fearful for the social stakes they held themselves. Yet seldom absent from the minds of those in place was the fear, these weapons might be used. This fear intimidated all their thoughts and made them hesitate to project change. The problem was, to keep the power in their hands, pursuing peace in hopes of calm till cherished institutions could be rooted in the soil.

This was no easy task, because they claimed the right of revolution for themselves if pushed too far, a right which other men might claim as well. Contending leaders had not learned to take a vote and then abide by the result until they could arouse the people for another count. Hence men in power who were afraid that rivals would dislodge them from their seats were more afraid of the results in time should they themselves lack weapons that they feared the most.

The urban district of the capital was the most frequent scene of fateful party strife. To avoid it, Charles II summoned his last Parliament to meet at Oxford. Even a prosy gazetteer [1] thought of London and Westminster as two cities "now reduc'd" to "one, . . . the Metropolis of England, the Seat of the British Empire, the Epitome and Glory" of the kingdom. It was a "City which for Greatness, Beauty, Conveniency, Plenty of Provisions, Trade, and Riches" was "inferiour to None beyond the Sea," being a "Magazine of all Sorts of Commodities, either for Use or Pleasure" and the "great Rendezvous of Men and Women of all Professions and Degrees." From this center emotions with propelling force enough radiated to the provinces until the noise was heard throughout the land.

The press was used in many ways to make appeals. The Licensing Act had lapsed five years before. News had become a vendible commodity. The trade was thriving, but still in its infancy. Thrice weekly several papers were made ready when the posts went out. George Ridpath, Abel Roper, and Abel Boyer had begun their long careers. There was no demand for dailies yet. A timid bird still had to learn its wings. Readers were few. Domestic news was chiefly spread by other means. Rumors flew about the streets. Gossip flourished everywhere. Men abroad or in the provinces subscribed to written news-letters which could be had from confidential hands to suit the taste. But even pamphleteers addressed a larger audience than those who read.

Within the memories of men a novel engine had appeared

[1] Guy Miege, *The New State of England under Our Present Monarch, King William III* (third ed., 1699), Pt. I. 184.

and had achieved a rôle none had foreseen. Merchants had introduced the tea and coffee of the Orient and sugar from the other hemisphere. But men accustomed to a native brew had to be taught to like these alien drinks. A chilly passer-by might stop to toast his shins beside the cheerful fire that kept the kettles hot. Tables were placed with chairs about in which a lingerer might rest. The longer he remained, the more he drank, the greater was the profit of the "coffee-man."

News or comment on the topics of the week might stimulate a group to talk when papers, pamphlets, or news-letters on the tables had tempted them to come and read. Coffee-houses thus became supporting patrons of the press by taking papers in. A ready reader found an audience. Perhaps he added comments as he read. Hearers questioned him or made reply. And thus the group, forgetting time, might drink and talk the hours away.

The number of the houses multiplied, and kindred spirits went to those most likely to afford congenial company. An author with a name, or wishing one, might there display his talents to the world. With fame achieved, he might himself, as Dryden and John Trenchard did, become the chief attraction of a coffee-house, drawing others in to hear him talk, perhaps to share reflected honor in his company. No group of men with common interests but had its favorite resort. Some, more select, might take a private chamber in which to club and dine. But in the public rooms the pulse beats of the city's life were seen. To sense the feelings of the crowd one lingered there. Substantial men met there with bluff democracy.

Rapidly these shops increased by scores till hundreds lined the city streets, and they became the foci of the nation's public life. Ministers and opposition leaders had "levees" to make themselves accessible. From them their henchmen went to spread or glean the gossip of the day. The way was thus direct from the "great men" to the coffee-houses and on occasion thence to city mobs who might be easily induced to march. "Runners" learned the art of stirring up these groups and went from place to place to guide the conversation to the point desired.

Pamphlets were anonymous, but whispers that the author was a great man of the time or had one's patronage would cause assembled groups to lend an ear and ask the inner meaning of the piece. Paragraphs untutored readers might have overlooked were given explanation with enhanced effect because not clear except to the initiate. Mindful of this audience, authors slyly clothed their thoughts in mystery. They did not write for hurried readers in impatient haste to reach the point, but for those with time and taste to linger till the meaning was made clear.

These techniques were the stock in trade of those who studied how to make appeals in efforts to arouse the crowd. Pamphlets there were, and paragraphs in the news; runners to spread reports by word of mouth; agents to guide the mob if one was wished, to give it drink and thus increase the noise, to find it effigies to burn, to furnish cries to make the points desired, if possible perchance to get it safely broken up. The object was to mobilize and intensify, when an occasion came, as many as possible of the latent loyalties the people felt. Amid this clamor Parliament sat; the king and ministers had to work. Sometimes the latter tried to make a counter noise. But to defend was harder than to criticize; the volume of noise seldom equaled that of an attack. Successful leaders had to sense when it was prudent to give way and when the noise could be defied.

All of this was an experiment. Men of the previous generations had not learned to ride the storms they raised. The problem was to give cohesion to society by compromise, to find the routine for a quiet time, to teach contending leaders when to strive and when to cease their strife in order to achieve the common good. The passing century bequeathed this heritage.

CHAPTER II

WILLIAM'S LAST VICTORY, 1700–1702

Men easily admit the force of an Argument which tends to support
Notions that it is their Interest to diffuse, and readily find Wit and
Spirit in Satire pointed at Characters which they desire to depress. But
to the opposite Party, and even to themselves when their Passions
have subsided and their Interest is disunited from the Question, those
Arguments appear only loud Assertions or empty Sophistry; and the
Wit which was clamorously praised discovers itself to be only Impudence or low Conceits.

ROBERT WALPOLE in the House of Commons, 1741.

THROUGH the gray Christmas of 1700, disillusioned but determined, William III waited for the dawn of the new century and the coming of the Parliament summoned to meet February 6. Before that eventful year began, urged by Trenchard's pamphlet,[1] Parliament disarmed England, sending home ungratefully his Dutch guards. The death of the electoral Prince of Bavaria (January, 1699) reopened the dispute with Louis XIV over the dominions of the dying King of Spain. Thereupon (March, 1700), William signed secretly a second partition treaty, making what terms he could without an English army. In April, unaware of this venture, Parliament deprived some of his friends of estates granted in Ireland and threatened to impeach others in office. To prevent it, he prorogued the scurvy assembly without the courtesy of a speech and sought consolation among the Dutch. In late autumn he dissolved the Parliament after his return.

In the summer of 1700 the Emperor objected to the second Partition Treaty and the little Duke of Gloucester resigned a game in which he was never more than an important pawn. November 1, Charles II of Spain died leaving a will which

---

[1] John Trenchard, *A Short History of Standing Armies in England,* 1698.

16

Louis XIV accepted in a fortnight. William's work was all to do over, but he knew that the sands of his life were falling fast. Was there time to win his long duel with Louis? To do it, he must make haste, and he could no longer indulge the personal feelings that had moved him in the previous spring.

Perhaps he could at least keep James and his son from the English throne; even that would depend upon the temper of the new Parliament. Considering the happenings since the Treaty of Ryswick, the English would scarcely make war again under his command. But the eleven years he had worn the crown of this rent and troubled island had taught him much. This people could not be driven; perhaps it might be led. Not easily would its great men act together. Who should have power was the perpetual question in their strife. Why not add the prestige of his own name to the faction stronger for the time?

To try this experiment, William had taken the great seal from Somers after proroguing Parliament to prevent his impeachment. Robert Harley seemed to know how to manage the House of Commons. A more reasonable man, he might prove to be, than the older bickering nobles. Recent events showed that little could be done without him. Through him it might be possible to accomplish more. The affection of the mass of the people for the Church, the King now saw, was deeper than he had thought. To let the lesser clergy meet again in Convocation might conciliate friends of the Church in the House of Commons. It might even win some of the clergy, who had been difficult for him since the death of his wife. The clergy counted greatly with the mob, especially outside of London, and the City was now divided by the two East India companies. Not much could be done in England against the clergy and the mob. Harley understood these matters, which was part of his strength.

If English leaders would only cease their endless quarrels with each other and join the fight against Louis, the day might be won. One faction cared as little for England as another. Each strove to serve its own purpose. Daniel Foe was trying to turn the laugh on these boasted "True-born Englishmen."

How did he put it?

> Why civil Feuds disturb the Nation more
> Than all our Bloody Wars have done before.
> The grand Contention's plainly to be seen,
> To get some Men put out, and some put in.

Who were the English, that they should be contemptuous of others, even of the Dutch, who brought them help in a time of need?

> The silent Nations undistinguished fall,
> And Englishman's the common Name for all.
> Fate jumbl'd them together, God knows how;
> Whate'er they were, they're True-Born English now.
> The Wonder which remains is at our Pride,
> To value that which all wise Men deride.
> For Englishmen to boast of Generation
> Cancels their Knowledge and lampoons the Nation.
> A True-Born Englishman's a Contradiction,
> In Speech an Irony, in Fact a Fiction:
> A Banter made to be a Test of Fools,
> Which those that use it justly ridicules;
> A Metaphor invented to express
> A Man akin to all the Universe.[2]

A man with such wit might be useful. He must pay attention to the fellow. The late Queen had known him. He had published more than once against France in the war; there was greater need of publication now. A satire on Englishmen would not help much with the mob. It might not hurt, but Englishmen would not be laughed into fighting Louis. Whithersoever they might have come, these English had feelings an outsider did not share. Usually hot against each other, they could at times unite against a foreign foe.

Louis might still be defeated if the war against him should become an English cause, overshadowing the petty disputes that had lately vexed him and taken his time. Somers, Montague, and Wharton would enlist for the fight. Could he win

---

[2] Of course there is no certainty that William saw these lines before their publication in January, 1701.

Harley, the House of Commons, Rochester, Seymour, Nottingham, and the Church? There was also the stubborn, pious Anne who would follow him. That meant John Churchill, Lord Marlborough, and his irrepressible wife. Why not, if they would help against Louis? Marlborough had military talent; he might be the man. Fate and Anne were with him. Better have him against than for Louis. The new century promised no easy days, knowing life was short.

Robert Harley was in his fortieth year that Christmas. At Brampton Castle he mourned the recent death of his father. Along with notes of condolence came letters from Henry Guy and others saying that the King's new ministers would have a friendly Parliament. With William's favor, Harley would count for more in that Parliament than in the last. Blood of noblemen of old ran in his veins. Given a chance, he would restore the name of his family to the roll of the great. A pity his father had not lived to see an achievement almost in sight. He would have to play secondary rôles a while yet, indispensable though he was. Soon others would find out what he already felt himself of his ability to steer the country through troubled seas.

If, without proscribing any, the King would seek counsel from moderate men, time would bring calm. Somers, Montague, and Orford, from whom his Majesty parted with regret, preferred another commonwealth to the restoration of the Stuarts after Anne. They would oppose Rochester, Seymour, Musgrave, Nottingham and such men to the bitter last. He could not be easy in his own mind at the prospect of the son of James II on the throne. To continue the quarrels of the preceding years ran that very risk. The King should say, "A plague o' both your houses!" The succession should be fixed by law. Sophia of Hanover might be the best candidate, but no foreigner should come to the throne again without a provision that Continental obligations would not obscure the pursuit of English interests. Eleven years of William had taught the necessity of this safeguard. Leaders whose help must be had if the succession was to be settled would not do without it.

Harley relished the antics of the hot churchmen as little as the King. But he recognized that many men whose help must be had were wedded to the Church. Antagonizing the Church would lose their support and make of churchmen an embittered faction too strong for any other party to oppose. Conciliation was an easier way. Better commit churchmen to Hanover in advance in order that in a critical time they would be less tempted by the lure of the old house.

Peace and quiet were needed above all things, and war was to be avoided at any reasonable cost. A war would increase the danger of the French King accomplishing his will. Injustices of the moment should be endured for the sake of a peaceful succession to the crown. William, it was true, wanted war. But a war not supported by all English factions would imperil the Protestant succession. The King himself had come to see that the English would not fight with effect unless they could be brought to embark on a war with enthusiasm.

Election reports still straggled in when a letter from Godolphin offered the nomination to the speakership, which Seymour had declined.[8] Be it the speakership then; it would be more thereafter. The House of Commons just elected, unless he mistook it, would respond to his leadership, speaker or not. A ruler of England could not neglect that house. Harley could not do without Godolphin yet; but neither could the Lord Treasurer do without him. To stand well at court was necessary. He and William understood each other, but after William would come Anne with Marlborough and perhaps Godolphin. In a court the game had to be played with pieces suiting the fancy of a king—or queen. The House of Commons not so long ago had made and unmade kings. The speakership was not to be despised.

D. Foe, writer of verses and pamphlets, maker of pantiles and brick, one time hose factor and accountant to the commissioner of the glass duty, spent Christmas seeing through the press a reply in verse to John Tutchin's *The Foreigner.* His blood boiled that so many Englishmen so soon forgot their

---

[8] Historical Manuscripts Commission, *Reports on the Manuscripts of the Duke of Portland,* contain the bulk of Harley's correspondence, IV. 14.

obligations to their King and deliverer and to the Dutch. As proprietor of a substantial business and as a Protestant Dissenter he shared William's fear of the King of France. Earlier in the year he had published a pamphlet[4] advocating war. The hot churchmen were as dangerous to toleration and the Protestant succession as were the open Jacobites and friends of Louis. At a time when Englishmen should unite against France and Rome it was a shame for the King to lack the services of the Lords Somers and Halifax. For the English and the Dutch to quarrel would be a crime. A mixture of banter and downright truthtelling might rally men to the old standards and help bring a Parliament to Westminster in a mood to speak the voice of the nation. Testifying of his own will to help were pamphlets appealing to the electors and one dedicated to the King on *The Danger of the Protestant Religion Considered from the Present Prospect of a Religious War in Europe.*[5]

Others besides Foe sharpened their pens in the campaign in favor of William and a war with France. A writer publishing about the middle of January went to the heart of the matter. "The whole Art of Government," he asked, "has consisted so long in making use of Factions, how is it possible on the Sudden to come to the Art of putting an End to them?"[6] The answer was easy. This art would no more be discovered in a Parliament managed by the King's new allies than in one led by their rivals, as long as the factions chiefly tried to discredit each other.

Harley was easily placed in the chair when Parliament met

---

[4] *Two Great Questions Considered.*

[5] The poems of both Tutchin and Foe are in *Poems on Affairs of State,* II. 1ff. For Defoe see William Lee, *Daniel Defoe; His Life and Recently Discovered Works,* I. xxxviiiff., and Paul Dottin, *The Life and Adventures of Daniel Defoe,* translated by Louise Ragan, pp. 74ff.

[6] *An Account of the Debate in Town Concerning Peace and War. In a Letter to a Gentleman in the Country,* 1701, reprinted in *State Tracts,* III. 76ff. In the same collection see *The Present Disposition of England Considered* (III. 67ff.); *The Duke of Anjou's Succession Considered as to its Legality and Consequence* (III. 22ff.); *Anguis in Herba; or the Fatal Consequences of a Treaty with France* (III. 312ff.). See in *Somers Tracts* (Sir Walter Scott's edition), XI. 195ff., George Stepney, *An Essay upon the Present Interests of England.*

in February. In the lower house of Convocation, which assembled for business at the same time, Francis Atterbury enjoyed the first fruits of his efforts to extend the powers of that body in Church and State. But Archdeacon Nicholson of Carlisle expressed the view of others besides himself in the remark, that "if there should happen to be a majority of his [Atterbury's] kidney, he'd as soon hope to have the Church's peace established by a Convocation of English bull dogs." [7]

William invited the new Parliament to consider the disputed succession to two of the most important crowns in Christendom, those of England and Spain. After the Commons reassembled in their own house, the Speaker in the conventional phrase announced that "to prevent mistake" he had got a copy of the King's Speech, wherein it was urged that the loss of the Duke of Gloucester made "absolutely necessary" a "further Provision for the Succession to the Crown in the Protestant Line" and that the "Death of the late King of Spain, with the Declaration of his Successor . . . made so great an Alteration of Affairs abroad" that Parliament ought "very materially to consider their present State."

Pamphlets were already out urging limitations on the powers of sovereigns of the new house and the peril of the country from France. "That we are in the greatest Danger," said one, "of losing our Trade, our Liberty, and our Religion will hardly be deny'd by any Man who will seriously reflect on the Consequences likely to attend the present Union of France and Spain." The King himself sent to Parliament and caused to be published an intercepted letter purporting to reveal French activity in behalf of James II.[8]

In order to procure the passage of the Act of Settlement William accepted reluctantly limitations with which Parliament hedged the new house. At least the country was committed against James and Louis. But Parliament wished to see any treaties the King had signed since the last war before

---

[7] Norman Sykes, *Edmund Gibson, Bishop of London,* has a good account of the controversy about Convocation and quotes Nicholson's remark, p. 33.

[8] *Commons Journal,* XIII. 332, 335, 338; *State Tracts,* III. 154ff., 381ff.; *Somers Tracts,* XI. 192ff.; *Harleian Miscellany,* X. 478ff.

considering the "balance of Europe." Learning thereby the circumstances of the signing of the second Partition Treaty, the Commons proceeded to impeach first Portland and then Somers, Halifax, and Orford. A resolution (April 25) requested the King to remove these four "from his presence forever." Old accusations concerning Captain Kidd's ventures were revived to give impetus to the prosecution, and William was urged to hasten proceedings against that pirate. Without something to prevent it, English factions seemed likely to spend on each other energy needed against enemies abroad. That Louis XIV meant business, he had proved in February by seizing the barrier towns.[9]

The atmosphere of London was usually congenial for operations such as William's supporters now began, but City factions were still at odds. Therefore, four days after the address of the Commons against the accused peers, William Colepepper, chairman of the grand jury at the Maidstone quarter sessions in Kent, applied to by some other gentlemen, agreed that it was the "proper work of the grand jury to present the grievances of the country." The Chairman, three and twenty justices, and as many freeholders as the parchment would contain signed a petition which was soon ready. Colepepper and four other influential men of the county went forthwith to present it to Parliament.

Thomas Hales, one of the county members, told them when they reached town (May 6) that is was too late to submit the petition that day; but it was not too late for Hales to borrow it to show to Seymour among others of the Church faction. Discovering the spirit that would greet it, Hales refused to present the petition. His colleague, Meredith, reluctantly performed the office when Colepepper, paraphrasing Luther, announced that if "every tile upon Saint Stephen's was a devil" he would persist until he had fulfilled his mission.

Half an hour after presenting the petition, the five men from Kent were asked at the bar of the House to acknowledge

---

[9] *Commons Journal*, XIII. 333; *Parliamentary History*, V. 1248ff.; *A Full Account of the Proceedings in Relation to Captain Kidd*, reprinted in *State Tracts*, III. 231ff.

the document they had brought. Soberer members tried to persuade the five to profess penitence for their deed, but followers of Seymour fanned the foolish anger with which they soon inflamed themselves. The men of Kent would accept no statement that would do, bluntly insisting, "we will have no sorry." They were first held in custody by the sergeant of the House and later, refusing exorbitant demands of that official for money, were committed to the Gatehouse prison.

Colepepper's brother, one of the five, returned to Kent on parole to reassure his wife. Rumors were soon afloat of dire things that might ensue. On the day he returned to custody the Speaker of the House received a paper from Daniel Foe, disguised as a woman it was said, speaking the mind of the King's friends in terms indicated by its concluding words:

Thus Gentlemen, you have your Duty laid before you, which it is hoped you will think of; but if you continue to neglect it, you may expect to be treated according to the Resentment of an injured Nation; for Englishmen are no more to be Slaves of Parliaments than to a King. Our Name is Legion, and we are Many.

Supporting the "Kentish Petition," the "Legion Paper" further urged the House to cease its inquiries to no national purpose and to take measures that "the French King be obliged to quit Flanders, or that his Majesty be addressed to declare War against him."

The Kentish Petition itself, which desired the House to "have Regard to the Voice of the People; that our Religion and Safety may be effectively provided for; that the loyal Addresses of the House may be turned into Bills of Supply; and that his Majesty may be enabled powerfully to assist his Allies before it is too late," was voted to be "scandalous, insolent, and seditious; tending to destroy the Constitution of Parliament and to subvert the established Government of the Realm."

But the intimidated Commons found excuses for failure to prosecute the impeachments, requested the King to take steps to protect himself against his people, voted him supplies for the year, and were prorogued (June 23). Freed by the prorogation, the men of Kent were entertained at dinner in the Mercers' Hall with Foe in their midst. Many sympathizers and friends came to meet and greet them on their way.

William and Marlborough went to the Continent seeking definite alliances against Louis. The King's supporters at home redoubled their efforts to arouse the country. Foe's plain-spoken *History of the Kentish Petition* soon appeared and a more ambitious pamphlet from the pen of Somers. The latter began: " 'Tis a melancholy Reflection to consider how universal a Dissatisfaction the Management of the House of Commons has this Sessions caused the People of England," probably more a statement of the author's wish than an actual fact, though there were indications that it might have a basis of truth. Before the prorogation the Lords ordered the publication of the letter from the States-General asking the help against France promised to the Dutch in the treaty of 1678.[10]

By the end of the first week in September William and Marlborough had arranged a treaty, with England, Holland, and the Emperor as parties. For two months they were to seek from France a peaceful settlement of disputed points. But James II died at St. Germains ten days after the treaty was signed. Louis XIV, visiting the dying man in his last hours, recognized his son as King of England.

William made haste to profit by this act of his rival. On the advice of Somers he dissolved Parliament again, calling a new one to meet December 30. "An exact Account of the Sickness and Death of the Late King James II, as also the Proceedings at St. Germains thereupon" was published as *A Letter from an English Gentleman in France to his Friend in London*. Another pamphlet proclaimed *The Dangers of Europe from the Growing Power of France with some Thoughts on Remedies, and particularly on the Cause of our Divisions at Home*. Swift offered a pointed Classical analogy, *A Discourse of the Contests and Dissensions between the Nobles*

---

[10] Somers' pamphlet is reprinted in *State Tracts*, III. 257ff. See also *Somers Tracts*, XI. 242ff.; *Commons Journal*, XIII. 518ff.; *Parliamentary History*, V. 1250ff.; Lee, *Defoe*, I. 51ff.; Hist. Mss. Com., *Portland*, VIII. 90ff.; Philip Yorke, Earl of Hardwicke, *Miscellaneous State Papers*, II. 436ff.

*and the Commons of Athens and Rome, with the Consequences
they had upon those States.* With tracts and lampoons Foe
kept up his work.[11]

On the day that the new Parliament was to meet a news-
paper proclaimed the success of William and his friends, attributing it to the "unparallel'd Affront to his Majesty and an
Insult to our very Constitution," by which Louis had "rous'd
up the universal Indignation of the whole Nation against a
Faithless Crown." Harley was chosen Speaker of the new
House by the narrow majority of four, and he was soon persuaded of the necessity of war. In a speech written by Somers
William asked Parliament to fulfill the expectations of Europe.
"Let me urge you," he said, "to disappoint the only hopes of
our enemies by your unanimity. I have shown and will always
show how desirous I am to be the common father of all my
people. Do you in like manner lay aside parties and divisions.
Let there be no distinction heard of amongst us for the future
but of those who are for the Protestant religion and the present establishment, and of those who mean a Popish prince and
a French government." An enthusiastic pamphleteer emphasized the King's appeal by bearing witness that, "Whatever
Names may have been formerly coin'd to distinguish Parties
here in England, there is at present neither Whig nor Tory,
Williamite nor Jacobite, nor any real Distinction but between
those that are in a French and those that are in an English
Interest, . . . there is no other real Distinction among us,
but those who care for the Protestant Religion and the present
Establishment, and those who mean a Popish Prince and a
French Government." [12]

Encouraged by evidence of his success, William made cautious changes in the ministry, replacing Godolphin with Carlisle as First Lord of the Treasury and Hedges with Manchester as Secretary of State. Parliament attainted the son of
James II, ever afterwards known as the *Pretender,* and required holders of places in Church and State to abjure him.

---

[11] *State Tracts,* III. 343ff.; *Somers Tracts,* XI. 339ff.; Hardwicke, *State
Papers,* II. 452ff.
[12] The *Postman,* Dec. 27–30, 1701; *State Tracts,* III. 373ff.

This act passed the lower house by a bare majority. William approved it by commission in the last moments of his life, which ended in the late winter of 1702, before his measures against Louis began to bear fruit in the field.

The abjuration had repercussions throughout the country. Young Robert Walpole, having interrupted his education on the death of his father to become head of the family and a member of the new Parliament, had seconded the motion for the passage of the act. His brother, Horace, wrote from St. John's College, Oxford, that Robert was more likely to be "excommunicated" for this offense than himself to suffer expulsion for "staying too long." The "master, tutor, pupils, sophs, batchelors, and all" were angry at his "speeching it against them and their little dapper king the other side of the water." A prescient journalist hailed the new century as

so far from Promising less than the Preceding, that it seems as if designed to outdoe it in Events and Revolutions. If we may judge of the Future by the Past, within the Space of a Twelvemonth, what is there of Wonderful that we may not expect? There needs no more than to cast but one Glance of an Eye upon the present Position of Europe to see that there is no Revolution which we may not have Reason to fear, or cause to flatter our Hopes withal.[13]

William was learning in his last days how to win to compliance with his will those who depended upon his favor. Otherwise, the political alignment was much the same. Why did rival factions now find it expedient to enlist under him against Louis? Was the transformation within the year due to the King's art or, as historians are wont to say, to the unwitting blunder of his rival? For most of the questions that matter in a history of public opinion there are no certain answers. We cannot know what would have happened without the work of William, Defoe, and the men of Kent or French support of the Pretender's claim.

[13] William Coxe, *Memoirs of the Life and Administration of Sir Robert Walpole,* II. 3; *Present State of Europe* (Jan., 1702), XIII. 3.

CHAPTER III

CHURCH AND QUEEN, 1702–1709

In all states that possess any portion of public freedom, the appeal to parties is always made to the people. Though the body of the nation enjoy but a very small share of any government, they make up with their weight and numbers what they want in authority as individuals. The candidates for office endeavour to gain their favours by applying to their principles, but oftener to their prejudices; and those succeed best who impose with the most address upon their credulity and fears. The good opinion of a people is therefore the citadel, if the expression may be used, to which factions direct all their irregular attacks; and when a party happens to possess themselves of that stronghold, they overawe their antagonists and govern at discretion the roisy populace by whose suffrages they have ascended to power. The domestic history of the present reign [that of Anne] contains little more than a continued series of such political hostilities.

JAMES MACPHERSON, *History of Great Britain*, II. 635.

I

HARLEY TO THE RESCUE

THE accession of Anne was a triumph for the Church, though the victory was not clear at first. The Church party, already powerful, gained the support of the ruling monarch. Anne's devotion to the Church was the most positive and genuine element in her character. Thereby she found solace for revolt against her father. But the war with France bequeathed by William claimed her first attention. He had largely succeeded in making it England's war. By a clever stroke, it was also Marlborough's and in a sense Anne's war. Consequently, the Church had to wait until the war was launched.

Marlborough took charge where the war was concerned, leaving to his wife the more personal matters of the Queen's court. A skilled diplomat, one of the Queen's chief ministers, and commander of her troops, his place was one that only an emergency could justify. Godolphin was persuaded to become Lord Treasurer again. Harley, still a capital figure in the House of Commons, had to be consulted. Daniel Finch, Earl of Nottingham, and Sir Charles Hedges became the Secretaries of State. The problem was to enlist for the Queen's government the support of as many factions as might be had.

To the extent that William had aroused the nation against France, Anne inherited his strength by adopting his policy. "Too much cannot be done," she said to Parliament, "for the encouragement of our allies, to reduce the exorbitant power of France." She urged the union of England and Scotland to strengthen the country for the fray. Making a bid for the support of William's opponents, she protested that her "Heart" was "entirely English," and promised a "careful and diligent administration for the good of all." She concluded these reflections on her predecessor with the assurance, "you will always find me a strict and religious observer of my word." To prove her interest in the war, she allotted for its expense a hundred thousand pounds from the Civil List. She reassured the pious by a proclamation for the "Incouragement of Piety and Virtue, for the Preventing of Vice, Prophaneness, and Immorality, and for Restraining the Spreading false News and Printing and Publishing of Irreligious and Seditious Papers and Libels."

The names of the impeached lords were omitted from the list of her Privy Council. Therefore, they would oppose the ministers, though they might support the war. Rochester, on the other hand, received as little consideration and thus opposed the war, encouraging the Church party of which he was a leader to insist upon immediate compliance with its demands. Little wonder the Queen and her ministers, in her farewell speech to the Parliament inherited from William, revealed their pressing fear:

> I shall always wish that no differences of opinion among those that are equally affected to my service may be the occasion of heats and animosities among themselves. I shall be very careful to preserve and maintain the Act of Toleration, and to set the minds of

all my people at quiet; my own principles must always keep me entirely firm to the interests and religion of the Church of England and will incline me to countenance those who have the truest zeal to support it.

The most agile walkers of a political tight rope could not have preserved the unity of the nation long. The Lords were busy before the prorogation with several current pamphlets. In a thirtieth of January sermon Charles I was compared favorably with Christ. Dr. James Drake alleged in his *History of the Last Parliament* that Somers, Halifax, *et al.* had "mounted their own Beast, the Rabble, and driven the sober Part of the Nation like Cattle before them" in the hope of setting up another commonwealth in which they might rule. Godolphin had no taste for such questions. Marlborough, who held Godolphin to his task, was immersed in the war. Harley had the needed talent, but he was merely Speaker and depended upon his colleagues for the favors necessary to be dispensed in the maintenance of substantial power.[1]

The Lord Treasurer soon found himself in need of Harley's help. A new Parliament friendly to the ministry was elected in the atmosphere that produced such pamphlets as Defoe's *New Test of the Church of England's Loyalty* on one side and Drake's reply, *Some Necessary Considerations Relating to all Future Elections of Members to Serve in Parliament.* Henry Sacheverell, a fanatical, eloquent Oxford clergyman, insisted in a sermon upon "the dependence of Government on Religion in General, and of the English Monarchy on the Church of England in Particular," urging a "bloody Flag" and "Banner of Defiance" against enemies of that Church. Supporting a contrary view, John Dennis published *The Danger of Priestcraft to Religion and Government.*[2]

After the meeting of Parliament in autumn, the tired Godolphin was soon at his wit's end. The Queen wished Marlborough to be voted a substantial sum for life and her own ineffective husband to have assurance of a hundred thousand

---

[1] *Parliamentary History*, VI. 18ff.; Abel Boyer, *History of the Reign of Queen Anne digested into Annals*, I. 35ff.
[2] *Somers Tracts*, XIII. 198ff.; Lee, *Defoe*, I. 61ff.

pounds a year in case of her death. Churchmen insisted that Dissenters no longer be permitted to qualify for office by taking occasionally the sacrament according to the rites of the national establishment. The Archbishop of Canterbury warned that trouble was brewing in Convocation. "Does anybody think," asked Godolphin impatiently (December 10), "England will be persuaded that the Queen won't take care to preserve the Church of England? And do they forget that not only the fate of England but all Europe depends upon the Appearance of our Concord in the dispatch of our Supplies?" [3]

The creation of four new peers relieved slightly the tension in the House of Lords, though not the embarrassment of ministers in the service of a Queen devoted to the Church who needed the support of wealthy Dissenters to finance the war. When churchmen pushed through the House of Commons a bill to prevent occasional conformity, the ministers evaded the question for a year by so amending it in the Lords as to arouse a controversy between the two houses and thus obscure the issue. Godolphin confessed to Harley, however, that in both houses the "Queen's servants" were "vying" who could be "maddest," while the heat out of doors reached a point not easy to cool.

Churchmen argued with faultless logic that "occasional" was no less sinful than habitual conformity. Since "Schism" was "certainly a spiritual Crime," and occasional conformance proved that "a Man's Conscience" would "let him conform," in "such a Man Nonconformity" was "Wilful Sin." The logic of Defoe's *Shortest Way with Dissenters* may have been as sound. With an irony overlooked by some of the serious minded churchmen and little appreciated by those he tried to help, he suggested a way to end the whole vexing question. The Lords made public their proceedings, but the Commons (February 25) after complaining of the writings of Dyer in his news-letters and ordering Defoe's pamphlet to be burnt by the hangman, forbade the "Clerk or any other Person whatsoever" to publish the "Votes and Proceedings" of their house.

The Queen prorogued Parliament two days later. She still

[3] Hist. Mss. Com., *Portland*, IV. 54ff.

hoped to preserve "toleration" and to "take care of the interests of the Church," but she thought it might have been for the public service to have had some further Laws for restraining the great License . . . assumed of Publishing and Spreading scandalous Pamphlets and Libels." Under the laws as they were, she hoped members would do their "Duty" in their "respective Stations to Prevent and Punish such Pernicious Practices." Above all other things, she recommended "Peace and Union" among themselves as "the most Effectual Means" of discouraging and defeating the "Designs" of "Enemies." [4]

Existing laws easily convicted Defoe, who was put in prison and stood in a pillory. His *Hymn to the Pillory* won the sympathy of the London mob, but left him handicapped both in attending to personal affairs and in serving the country. Aimed at Sacheverell and similar fanatics, his shafts had gone astray. "I had engaged a Party and embroiled myself with the Government," he said. He had no taste for the rôle of martyr, though obliged to play it for the time. Dissenters in whose favor he ventured gave little sympathy in his trouble. His conviction helped as little the cause of the Queen and her ministers.

Simon Harcourt, an ambitious lawyer of the Church party, complained a fortnight after Parliament was prorogued that his friends were "growing infidels" for lack of evidence of good will towards them. By midsummer Godolphin reflected pessimistically, "we are running headlong into all the same steps for which we blamed others and which gave us a handle to their disadvantage; but unless one will serve particular ends and particular turns, endeavouring to serve the public will not support one." [5]

Friends of Harley suggested that he claim the credit himself if he undertook to save the ministry from its threatened fate. Perhaps a way would open. Before the end of summer he learned that John Tutchin, who thundered semi-weekly

[4] *Commons Journal*, XIV. 207ff.; *Parliamentary History*, VI. 145; Boyer, *Annals of Anne*, I. 180ff.; Hist. Mss. Com., *Portland*, IV. 57ff.

[5] Keith Feiling, *History of the Tory Party, 1640–1714*, pp. 330ff., is much the best narrative account of the political events of the time. See also Lee, *Defoe*, I. 65ff.; Hist. Mss. Com., *Portland*, IV. 6, 58, 65.

against churchmen in his *Observator,* might be "heard of at
Allon's Coffee House near Charing Cross." Through the Lord
Treasurer, Defoe was released to help allay the heat of factions, though Godolphin confessed wearily, "as to the talk of
hot men of either party, perhaps I have not that due regard
for it which I ought to have, because I am really so extremely
indifferent as to any consequences of it relating to myself; but
I am not so in what concerns the Duke of Marlborough" and
the war. He expected, when he returned to town in October,
"to see the whole government torn to pieces." It was agreed
ten days later that Hedges should receive "instructions" from
Harley; Seymour would gradually be dropped; Marlborough,
Godolphin, and Harley would meet twice a week or oftener
to place matters in a proper train.[6]

Team work was needed. A second bill against occasional
conformity was beaten with difficulty in the House of Lords,
since Marlborough and Godolphin thought it prudent to vote
for it as a concession to the Queen. Out of doors Harley inspired Dr. Charles Davenant to write against it and for "moderation." In London, just after the bill was lost (December
16), Swift thought it to be "the warmest reign of party and
faction" he "ever knew or read of." He "observed the dogs
in the streets much more quarrelsome than usual; and the
very night before the bill went up, a committee of Whig and
Tory cats had a very warm and loud debate upon the roof"
of the house where he lodged.

Lords and Commons quarreled at even greater length over
the famous case of Ashby versus White, involving the imprisonment of the men of Aylesbury and a long canvass of
fundamental constitutional points. On Christmas day (1703)
Godolphin greeted Harley with a pathetic desire to help do
something during the holidays to calm the people. It was no
easy task. Davenant's plea for moderation inspired a bitter
poem, *Faction Display'd.* The author's confessed purpose
was to trace traitors "thro' every dark Disguise . . . pene-
trate Intriguing Statesmen's Hearts, Their deepest Plots, and
all their wily Arts." Answering another pamphlet, *Moderation*

[6] Hist. Mss. Com., *Portland,* IV. 68, 75; VIII. 109.

a Virtue, Charles Leslie, a nonjuring clergyman, offered *The Wolf Stript of Shepherd's Clothing,* to which Defoe, in turn, responded in *The Dissenter's Answer to the High Church Challenge.*[7]

Reassembling in January, 1704, the House of Commons proceeded against Tutchin as a stirrer of sedition. He absconded, but kept on writing. Defoe interposed *An Essay on the Regulation of the Press;* and Tindal, *Reasons against Restraining the Press.* Defoe began (February 19) in his *Review* a long labor in behalf of moderation and peace. Since the immediate point was to turn attention from domestic strife to the foreign enemy, his original title was the *Weekly Review of the Affairs of France.* In an effort to conciliate churchmen, the Queen had sent to Parliament twelve days before an offer to contribute the arrears of the Tenths for the relief of the poorer clergy.

But the two houses were readier for discord than harmony. They were still at odds on both the Aylesbury election and a proposal to investigate the state of the public accounts. When the Lords appointed a committee to consider a reputed Jacobite conspiracy, the Commons besought the Queen (February 29) "to reassume the just Exercise of her Prerogative and take to herself" the task. This bickering was ended by the prorogation, April 3. Shortly thereafter Defoe tried with less success an earlier trick in *Legion's Humble Address to the Lords,* urging that house to support the interests of the country, neglected by the Commons. Nottingham and others disposed to make the cause of the Church paramount naturally tended to draw away from the ministry.[8]

In order to bear the increasing burden of leadership both out of doors and in the House of Commons, Harley needed the prestige of office. Accordingly, without giving up the speakership, he was admitted to the Privy Council in April and be-

---

[7] *Parliamentary History,* VI. 153ff., 178ff.; Boyer, *Annals of Anne,* II. 171ff.; Hist. Mss. Com., *Portland,* IV. 77; F. E. Ball, *Correspondence of Jonathan Swift,* I. 38f.; *Poems on Affairs of State,* IV. 79ff.; Lee, *Defoe,* I. 81ff.

[8] *Commons Journal,* XIV. 326ff.; *Parliamentary History,* VI. 377ff.; *Somers Tracts,* XI. 272ff., 462ff.; Boyer, *Annals of Anne,* III. 6ff.

came Secretary of State in May with his protégé, Henry St. John, Secretary at War. Defoe, as the confidential agent of the new minister, went on preaching moderation in the *Review*. On the very day that Harley received from the Queen through Godolphin the warrant for his pardon, that grateful subordinate was suggesting an intelligence office to keep the Minister in touch with all parts of the country. John Tutchin had offered his services also, boasting "concerns with all the secretaries of state for several years past." Leslie, on the other side, imitating L'Estrange, began in his *Rehearsal* to reply to Tutchin's *Observator*. The method of the ministry, as he satirized it, was to "Huff and Ding, and appear greater, if not in Number, yet in Noïse." That, Leslie said, "carries it with the Mobb. And having the Mobb in London, we appear to have the Nation." [9]

The political skill of Harley began to count. In late autumn a friend flattered him as "entirely master of two opposite parties." Both thought him "to be theirs" and trusted him "to promote their several different interests." Favors to either side did not "lessen" his "esteem in the other party," but were "ascribed to a depth of policy . . . peculiar" to himself rather than to a "leaving of the party." Both sides thought that "at a proper time and occasion" he would show himself "entirely in their distinct interest." This letter was written amid the celebration of Marlborough's victory at Blenheim, which helped the cause of the ministers, though opponents tried desperately to lessen the effect by including where possible the name of Sir George Rook in addresses of congratulation.

Machinery was set up for the distribution of the Queen's bounty, but Sacheverell, on the other hand, suggested that Dissenters be prohibited from training their children in their own faiths. In an effort to pacify Atterbury, he was made

---

[9] Leslie went on to complain (August 5–12) that friends of the Church knew "not the Mystery of Caballing and Carrying on their Business by Joint Concert and a Common Purse." Hist. Mss. Com., *Portland*, IV. 86, 106; *Bath*, I. 61; Lee, *Defoe*, I. 91; Boyer, *Annals of Anne*, III. 1ff. Students interested in topics involving the newspaper and periodical press in England in the eighteenth century are greatly indebted to R. S. Crane and F. B. Kaye for *A Census of British Newspapers and Periodicals, 1620–1800* and to [J. G. Mudidiman] for the *Tercentenary Handlist of English and Welsh Newspapers*.

Dean of Carlisle, though Nicholson, now Bishop in that diocese, objected, preferring his own peace to this small contribution toward that of the ministers and inspiring in Godolphin the thought that "a discreet clergyman" was "almost as rare as a black swan." Leslie alleged that the intention was to "have none but true Blue Whiggs" in the "Ministry or in any Command either by Sea or Land" in order to deprive "Churchmen" of credit for "Victories." Harley had need of ambidexterity and seemed likely to be busy enough. His colleague, Hedges, caused the publisher of a pamphlet written by one of his agents to be prosecuted.[10]

In the last days of October Anne exhorted Parliament in her usual sermon:

> I cannot but tell you how essential it is for attaining these great ends abroad of which we have so hopeful a prospect, that we be entirely united at home. . . . It is plain our enemies have no encouragement left but what arises from their hopes of our own divisions. It is therefore your concern not to give the least countenance to their hopes.

But Spencer Compton had urged Robert Walpole to be on hand for a political move if Harley should resign the speakership. Leslie and Tutchin hammered at each other and the populace. Harley heard that "Popish writers" as "usual" had engaged "coffee-men and their other customers." His informant reported also a "universal desire both in city and country to know the Commons' debates" as soon as possible. Since this information would go forth in any case, why not repeal the restrictions of the previous session and resume the publication by authority of the *Votes?* It might be well to appoint both writers and publishers. A few days later Defoe reported the probability that extremists on both sides would unite against Harley and suggested the revival of the occasional conformity bill by the ministers themselves in order to divide this opposition. Later, they could defeat it.[11]

[10] Hist. Mss. Com., *Portland*, IV. 118, 126, 130, 140; *Bath*, I. 63; Boyer, *Annals of Anne*, III. 100ff.; *Rehearsal*, Sept. 23–30, 1704.
[11] *Parliamentary History*, VI. 356; Coxe, *Robert Walpole*, II. 5; Hist. Mss. Com., *Portland*, IV. 146ff.; VIII. 156. The best accounts of the war in these years are in George Macaulay Trevelyan, *Blenheim*, and Winston Churchill, *Marlborough, His Life and Times, 1702–1705*.

Harley kept the speakership. Perhaps he had no need to try Defoe's trick if he had had the inclination. Godolphin complained within a week of a hundred and fifty members of Parliament at the Fountain Tavern resolving that the money bills of the year should wait on that to prevent occasional conformity. He reproached Harley that the "Queen's servants" might have hindered the introduction of the bill and that to reject it in the Lords would cause criticism. Sponsors of the measure helped the ministers by tacking it to a money bill. The House of Lords had a standing order against tacking, which afforded a way of escape without a vote on the question itself.[12]

The general election of 1705 interrupted the interminable proceedings concerning the Aylesbury men and set every faction to mending its emotional fences. Defoe in the *Review* interrupted his essays on trade, because he "saw with Concern the Variety of Wheels and Engines set on Work in the Nation, and the Furious Methods to form Interests on either Hand . . . with so much Animosity and Party Fury" that he had "terrible Apprehensions of the Consequences." Said a pamphleteer in Harley's pay: "If the Whigs have their *Observator,* have not the Tories their *Rehearsal?* The *Review* does not take more Liberties than the *Whispering Post.*" He omitted the *Post Boy,* the *Flying Post* and Samuel Buckley's *Daily Courant;* the last was begun in the initial year of Anne's reign as England's first successful daily newspaper. There were pamphlets defending "tackers" and "anti-tackers," "high" Church and "low."

The loudest cry was from friends of the Church, that it was in "danger." Their most notable piece, *The Memorial of the Church of England's Loyalty,* probably the joint composition of Drake and others, alleged that bishops and the ministers had conspired to ruin God's cause. Edmund Gibson, later Bishop of Lincoln and London, replied in *Presbyters not always an Authoritative Part of the Provincial Synod,* which, Atterbury complained to Harley, was meant to cause strife in Convoca-

---

[12] *Parliamentary History,* VI. 359ff.; Boyer, *Annals of Anne,* III. 172ff.; Hist. Mss. Com., *Bath,* I. 64. There were whispers nevertheless that Harley inspired the revival of the question.

tion. Matthew Tindal contributed a *Memorial of the State of England*. Defoe said bluntly: "The Danger of the Church is from Men of Heat and Passion . . . from such as these all our Ruin has proceeded, Occasional Bills, Imprisoning Electors, denying the Benefit of the Law to Englishmen, Addressing the Queen to extend her Prerogative and to deny Justice." Lord Poulett advised Harley from Hinton that in Dorset, Somerset, Devon, Cornwall, and Exeter the clergy preached "nothing but the Church being now in the greatest danger." The Bishop of Exeter was often named in the pulpit as an "enemy to the Church." As the canvass went on, the *Observator* remarked (May, 23–26) that Dissenters were standing by the Queen's friends in spite of the activity of the clergy. To explain ministerial successes, Leslie remarked (May 26–June 2) that those "against the Church and Crown" had "all agreed to carry on a general Cry that Papists" were "on the Side of the Church." This "with the Mobb, if Believed," would "Determine the Cause at once," since "whatever side the Papists" were on "must be Naught," proving at any rate that he knew the popular mood.[18]

John Smith, seconded by Walpole, was elected Speaker of the new House of Commons in October. Harley voted for Smith against William Bromley, the candidate of the Church faction, though he relished it little. Against Anne's wishes, Nathan Wright was replaced as Lord Keeper by William Cowper, now raised to the peerage, who did not sympathize with the extreme churchmen. The Queen suggested that the best way to preserve the Church was to prosecute the war, but opponents of the ministers hit upon the unexpected alternative of inviting Sophia to England.

This move was too clever to be sound. It seemed to impale the ministers on one or the other horn of a dilemma; they would have to choose between Sophia and Anne. But Harley refused to be caught. He appeased the Queen by advising that it was inexpedient for the Electress to come. He met

[18] Hist. Mss. Com., *Portland*, IV. 155, 176, 177, 188ff.; *Somers Tracts*, XII. 218ff., 475ff., 482ff., 504ff.; Boyer, *Annals of Anne*, IV. 14; Lee, *Defoe*, I. 103ff.; *Review*, Preface, April 17, 1705.

the friends of Hanover more than halfway by an act providing for a regency on Anne's decease, making sure that the succession would be managed by Hanoverian nominees. Friends
of the Church had to support this measure or risk the charge
of favoring the Pretender, which the ministerial faction was
more and more inclined to say was the case.[14]

Other rapids ahead were not so easy to navigate. Defoe
spent the summer and autumn traveling over England to
observe conditions, and reported that "in all parts the greatest hindrances to the forming the people into moderation and
union next to the clergy" were "the justices." Where they
were "moderate," the people lived "easy," and "the parsons"
had "less influence." That was matter enough. Neither parsons nor justices were easy to change.

Godolphin complained indignantly of "several insolences
of the clergy" which he thought "really insupportable and
next door to open rebellion." But Harley knew how impolitic
it was to embody "gentlemen (country gentlemen I mean)
against the Queen's service." At the instigation of Godolphin
he did remind the Attorney General that writers had "come
to that height as to leave nothing without marks of their
rage and fury." But he was wary, needing all of his own
friends, some of whom were beginning to say that the Lord
Treasurer favored too much those "vile wretches the Whigs."
Harley explained that Godolphin had not deserted the churchmen; they had left him. And even the Lord Treasurer found
it to be a delicate matter in September to trouble Anne with
the presentment by the grand jury of Drake's pamphlet and
hoped the *Gazette* would not carry it. Nerving himself the
next day to tell her, he hoped that people would feel "there
needs to be no more done in the matter."[15]

But people were not easily satisfied. After the hot churchmen lost the favor of the Queen by their foolish proposal, the
ministers, on the motion of Halifax, carried a solemn parlia-

[14] *Parliamentary History*, VI. 355ff.; N. Hooke, *Narrative of the Duchess of
Marlborough*, p. 159; Gilbert Burnet, *History of His Own Time* (1823 ed.), V.
218; Boyer, *Annals of Anne*, IV. 236ff.; Hist. Mss. Com., *Portland*, IV. 154.
[15] Hist. Mss. Com., *Portland*, IV. 256, 261, 269ff.; *Bath*, I. 73, 74, 76.

mentary vote that the Church was "under the happy reign of her Majesty in a most safe and flourishing condition, and whosoever" went "about to suggest and insinuate that the Church" was in "danger under her Majesty's administration" was an "enemy to the Queen, the Church, and the Kingdom." Supporting this resolution, Anne issued a proclamation in which she mentioned Drake's pamphlet, recited other notorious propaganda for arousing the fears of the timid, and announced that she would proceed with the full severity of the law against the "authors and spreaders of the said seditious and scandalous reports." Reassembling in January, 1706, the House of Commons became indignant against the publisher of *The Memorial,* though the author was left in safe obscurity. Having thus squelched the churchmen, the ministers rested for a moment on laurels won by Marlborough in the field. He was made a Duke and granted the manor of Woodstock. The two houses of Convocation were left to their quarrel over words proper to convey to the Queen their joint sentiments concerning the danger of the Church.[16]

II

A BREACH IN THE MINISTRY

This interlude of comparative quiet revealed the disagreement between Harley and his chief on political strategy. Harley wished to hold an even keel between rival Church factions. "I cannot," he wrote to Godolphin, "but apprehend danger from both sides in the extreme, and I am humbly of opinion to increase the number of those who would devote themselves to the Queen's and your [Marlborough's and Godolphin's] service would be best." Godolphin wished to be friends with Harley, though not fully aware of the extent of his dependence on the Secretary of State, but had lost patience with the hot churchmen. He estimated that of the 450

[16] Concerning the war see Trevelyan, *Ramillies and the Union with Scotland. Parliamentary History,* VI. 479ff.; Hist. Mss. Com., *Portland,* IV. 274, 279; Boyer, *Annals of Anne,* IV. 172ff., 203ff., 254ff.; *Observator,* Nov. 14–17, 1705; Dec. 29–Jan. 2, 1706.

present when the Speaker was elected there were in the new House of Commons, "Tories 190, Whigs 160, Queen's servants 100." At the close of the first session he thought the question was, "whether it be more likely or more easy to keep the 160 which with the Queen's true servants will always be a majority, or to get from the 190." The "160" seemed to him the better prospect. The clergy admitted, he said, that the Queen could have their support once they were "thoroughly satisfied which" was the "right way to preferment." "I mind only what men do, not what others say they do," he went on, concluding: "I take it our business is, to get as many as we can from the 190 without doing anything to lose one of the 160." It transpired that keeping the "160" involved appointing one after another of their leaders to office, which caused the loss of all of the "190" and some of the Queen's servants as well. More important, it alienated first Harley and then the Queen.[17]

Before this breach took place, Harley and Godolphin working together rendered perhaps their most memorable service to their country. The story of the union of England and Scotland to form a new nation, Great Britain, needs a volume instead of a paragraph. Those who carried the measure felt the immediate fate and future of the island to be at stake.

By good management, the opposition in England was restrained from debate until the Scots approved. Only those taking actual part in Scotland knew the difficulties they met. Defoe and William Paterson among others went thither to keep the English ministers informed and to help with propaganda for the union. Defoe scarcely exaggerated amid the turmoil when he wrote to Harley: "There is an entire harmony in this country, consisting of universal discords." Sir David Nairne in London, desiring to have the pamphlets on the question, was told by the Earl of Mar that he would have to await the chance of sending bulky parcels, which would then not be worth the trouble. "Only you will see how mad people are and what false grounds and views are put upon it." Nairne could not understand why friends of the union did

<hr />

[17] Hist. Mss. Com., *Portland,* IV. 291; *Bath,* I. 107, 109.

not obtain "counter addresses from some places" to balance active opposition out of doors. Mar explained that if Nairne were in Scotland he would be surprised that they went so fast. "I am not very timerous," he said, "and yet I tell you that every day we are in hazard of our lives. We cannot go on the streets but we are insulted." There were, he confessed, sound reasons for doubt "whether two nations independent in their sovereignties, that have their distinct Laws and Interests, and what I cannot forget their different forms of Worship, Church Government, and Order shall be united into one kingdom."

This end would never have been achieved, even after the ratification of the act in England (March, 1707), without the skill of the politicians, of whom Harley was perhaps chief, and the art of a multitude of lieutenants who, following the example of Defoe in his *Review*, substituted the term "British Nation" for England and took "frequent occasion to make Title and Subject correspond." [18]

Meantime Marlborough complained of criticisms in Tutchin's *Observator*. If he could not "have justice," he would find some friend to "break his and the printer's bones." A few weeks after this appeal was made to St. John and Harley, the journalist was set upon and beat so that he died. Thereupon Leslie became bolder in his *Rehearsal*, supporting extreme claims of the Church. "There was reason," he said (November 5, 1707), "for my Engaging with Tutchin, DeFoe, &c at the Beginning, that I might gain myself to be heard when I came to speak of serious Matters, which was not to be done without a little Fooling at first to draw on those Unthinking People who are pleased with Nothing else." [19]

Harley was already intrenching himself in the Queen's closet.

---

[18] The title of Defoe's publication became (March 8, 1707) *Review of the State of the British Nation*. See the Preface to Vol. V., and Boyer, *Annals of Anne*, V. 75f., 341ff., 442ff.; *Parliamentary History*, VI. 552ff.; Hist. Mss. Com., *Portland*, IV. 254ff., 278ff., 326ff., 343, 424, 468; *Mar and Kellie*, pp. 301ff., 319f., 328, 335; Hume Brown, *Union of England and Scotland;* James Mackinnon, *Union of England and Scotland;* A. V. Dicey and R. S. Rait, *Thoughts on the Union between England and Scotland*.

[19] Hist. Mss. Com., *Portland*, IV. 338; *Bath*, I. 82ff., 105; *Observator*, Sept. 24–27, Sept. 27–Oct. 11, 1707.

He did this not wholly, perhaps not chiefly through his relative, Abigail Hill, who by a private marriage which Anne graced became the wife of Samuel Masham that year. A more important clue to the dramatic events about to follow was the agreement of Harley and the Queen on essential politics. She opposed the appointment of Cowper as Lord Keeper in 1705. She resented even more the campaign to replace Hedges with Sunderland as Secretary of State in 1706. Both she and Harley understood that surrender on this point meant yielding in the end to the faction led by Somers, known as the "Junto." Neither Harley nor Anne thought it good for the country that any faction should triumph. The Queen was equally devoted to her prerogative and to the Church. Harley was concerned chiefly in preserving the Queen as the center of the ministry and himself as its guiding power.[20]

Yoked together, Queen and Church would be irresistible, and Anne was far from being pliable clay in the hands of favorites.[21] She preferred the congenial Abigail and finally excluded the termagant Sarah from her presence largely because one was docile and inclined to agree, while the other had a persistent will of her own. Godolphin and Marlborough

---

[20] William Coxe, *Memoirs of John, Duke of Marlborough*, II. 137, 147. In letters to Godolphin, September 10 and 21, 1706, Anne stated her views on the appointment of Sunderland: "I am of opinion, that making a party man secretary of state, when there are so many of their friends in employments of all kinds already is throwing myself into the hands of a party, which is a thing I have been desirous to avoid. . . . All I desire is, my liberty in employing and encouraging all those that concur faithfully in my service, whether they are called whigs or tories. . . . Why, for God's sake, must I, who have no interest, no end, no thought, but for the good of my country, be made so miserable as to be brought into the power of one set of men?" "As to my other difficulties concerning Lord Sunderland, I do fear for the reasons I have told you, we shall never agree long together; and the making him secretary, I can't help thinking, is throwing myself into the hands of a party. They desire this thing to be done, because else they say they can't answer that all their friends will go along with them this winter. If this be complied with, you will then, in a little time find they must be gratified in something else, or they will not go on heartily in my business. . . . Why, for God's sake, may not I be gratified as well as other people?" Again, she consented to admit Sunderland to the "Cabinet Council," but not as secretary of state. "This is a thing I have so much at my heart, and upon which the quiet of my life depends, that I must beg you for Christ Jesus's sake, to endeavour to bring it about."

[21] On this point see especially W. T. Morgan, *English Political Parties and Leaders in the Reign of Queen Anne, 1702–1710*, with whom the better subsequent writers have agreed.

were themselves frequently unable to keep promptly promises made in behalf of the Queen, never having her completely under control. She was grateful for their services to the country and herself and appreciated their weight at home and abroad due to the success of the war, but her consent to their advice had to be won and was not a matter of course. Harley after them was to discover that he could go no further or faster than he could persuade her grudging will.

Both the Duke and the Lord Treasurer felt the weight of years. Marlborough longed for the rising splendors of Blenheim and uncertain quiet in the society of a beloved wife. Godolphin, when vexed, imagined that he chiefly wished to go to Newmarket and to be let alone. Jointly they felt themselves to be the center about which the Grand Alliance revolved, the indispensable cement to hold it together until the humiliation of France should be complete. They were willing to humor any faction, adopt any reasonable expedient likely to serve that end.

Harley looked farther ahead. He saw a real danger that the passing of Anne would risk trouble over the succession to the crown. Against that event, he desired a favorable end of the war and a union in the ministry of as many men of all factions as could be induced to join. He agreed with the Queen that Marlborough and Godolphin were indispensable for the moment and the appointment of Sunderland unwise. But he felt greater confidence than she had as yet in his own ability to manage the kingdom without the Lord Treasurer and, if the worst came, without the Duke.

The appointment of Sunderland in December, 1706, to prevent threatened resignations by Marlborough and Godolphin fulfilled Anne's prophecy. Six months later Marlborough was suggesting that the Lord Treasurer, taking Harley with him, call upon the Queen and induce her to bestow ecclesiastical preferment in a way to promote her "true interests." The discouraged Godolphin had to reply: "Mr. Harley does so hate and fear lord Somers, lord Sunderland, and lord Wharton that he omits no occasion of filling the Queen's head with their projects and designs." That being true, wrote the Duke, let

Godolphin speak plainly to Harley, "for if he continues in doing ill offices upon all occasions to Lord Somers, Lord Sunderland, and Lord Wharton, it will at last have so much effect upon the Queen, whose inclinations are already that way, it must occasion that no measure will be followed."

When Sarah in the waning summer of 1707 reported a likelihood that Anne would go entirely over to Harley, the husband replied, very well then, but let the Queen depend wholly upon her senior Secretary of State and dispense with the services of Godolphin and himself. He admonished Anne pointedly (September 15) that the Lord Treasurer could not serve her effectively if "thought to have power when he has it not." Furthermore, she might expect trouble at the approaching session of Parliament if she did not remedy matters in advance. To Sunderland the Duke confessed that Godolphin might perhaps better retire, since he would "unavoidably be mortified and consequently not be able to serve England" with his previous "success." [22]

Informed by Harley about the same time that the meeting of Parliament would disclose discontent with happenings abroad, the Lord Treasurer replied in despair, "if we who have the honour to serve the best Queen in the world can't agree upon the proper measures for her service at home, whatever we do abroad will signify very little." The Secretary of State emphasized his own loyalty to his colleagues. He would "go along with the company . . . if they should say Harrow on the Hill or by Maidenhead were the nearest way to Windsor," if not obliged to "swear it." But he insisted that a ministry supported on any other ground than loyalty to Anne, Marlborough, and Godolphin would be a mistake. He dreaded to think of "running from the extreme of one faction to another . . . the natural consequence of party tyranny." In that case the government would be like a "door which turns both ways upon its hinges to let in each party as it grows triumphant." In mid-October he reminded Marlborough that he had foretold the year before events now taking place, but still professed a wish to serve

[22] Coxe, *Marlborough*, II. 265ff., 341ff.

the duumvirs in "their own way." A week later Godolphin lamented that much ought to be said of domestic matters, "if talking would mend them." Harley's retort was barbed: affairs "never succeed so well as when . . . directed. The people will follow somebody, and if your Lordship will not think fit to employ your thoughts, others will make use of your authority." [23]

Harley was beginning to think that the burden of rescuing the Queen and the country from the political doldrums might rest upon him. He foretold to Marlborough his own dismissal, adding "as soon as I am gone depend upon it, my Lord, the stream will run too high to be stemmed, and there are not (whatever may be pretended) heads of either party who are able to govern them. I heartily desire you would take care to have a true account of the temper of all sorts in England and the opinions and notions they have fixed as to affairs at home and abroad. And I wish that it does not prove that embracing some persons close and making others desperate do not end in truth in holding a handful of sand, the harder it is squeezed, the less it is and slips through the fingers."

When the Duke returned in November to attend the first session of the first Parliament of Great Britain he discovered conditions to be fully as dark as painted. Extreme men in both factions were attacking the ministers, complaining of the defeat in Spain and of the failure to protect trade. Lord Haversham stated the point bluntly: "I take the root of all our Misfortune to lye in the Ministry, and without a Change of Ministry in my Opinion, no other Remedy will be effectual." Some of the new friends of the ministry found fault with Marlborough's brother at the admiralty and with his pathetic chief, the Queen's husband. By inducing Anne to make a coveted appointment in the Church, the Junto was appeased for a moment. But matters took a more definite turn on the last day of the year, when William Greg, a clerk in Harley's office, was arrested for treasonable correspondence with France.[24]

---

[23] Hist. Mss. Com., *Bath*, I. 179f., 185f.
[24] Hist. Mss. Com., *Bath*, I. 186ff.; Boyer, *Annals of Anne*, VI. 253ff.; Coxe, *Marlborough*, II. 370ff.; *Parliamentary History*, VI. 594ff.

Marlborough and Godolphin were inevitably alienated from Harley as they came to depend more upon Somers and his friends. The Secretary of State applied to both of his colleagues in turn for explanations of their coldness. Godolphin answered from the Cockpit, January 30: "I have received your letter and am very sorry for what has happened to lose the good opinion I had so much inclination to have of you, but I cannot help seeing and hearing, nor believing my senses. I am very far from having deserved it from you. God forgive you."

Thenceforth the struggle was between Harley and his former colleagues. The latter examined Greg, seeking evidence to incriminate his superior. Anne resisted when told that she must choose between the Secretary of State and the Duke and Lord Treasurer. She was readier to give up Godolphin than Marlborough. But she and Harley were reconciled to giving up both at a Cabinet Council, February 9. To their discomfiture and surprise, the Duke of Somerset halted the meeting, saying: "I do not see how we can deliberate when the commander in chief and the lord treasurer are absent." They could not, since the Duke spoke for others of his colleagues.[25]

Harley's resignation two days later was followed by that of his friends, St. John and Harcourt. Anne found no pleasure in yielding and refused to appoint James Montague, brother of Halifax, attorney general. Godolphin and Marlborough rejoiced as little in the victory, knowing at what price it had been won. Or perhaps they did not yet understand their loss in adding Harley to the opposition, failing to appreciate fully what the Duchess of Marlborough later described as his "wonderful talent . . . in the supreme degree of confounding the common sense of mankind." He himself would have described it as a willingness to appeal to that same quality.[26]

While the contest over Sunderland's appointment raged, St. John suggested to Harley the prudence of conciliating the Church party. Leslie's diagnosis of the struggle was (November 22, 1707): "Other things as Religion, Liberty &c are

[25] Coxe, *Marlborough*, II. 387ff.; Hist. Mss. Com., *Bath*, I. 186ff.; Hooke, *Duchess of Marlborough*, p. 253.
[26] Ball, *Correspondence of Swift*, I. 75.; Hooke, *Duchess of Marlborough*, p. 218.

made the Pretence to stir up the People. But Power is the Mythologick Sence." Harley knew better than most men the art of wooing power. "News" was already described as "a Politick Medicine, made up so cunningly that it proves an Elixir to one side and a Poyson to the Other." Both Leslie and his opponents took seriously ranting in coffee-houses. "I tell you Masters," said one of that journalist's characters (March 3, 1708), "there's a great deal in Names. The most part of the World is governed with Words."

The same writer warned the Church that merely answering books and pamphlets was not enough. Weekly papers were more effective than books, since most people could not "read at all." However, they would "gather together about one" able to read and "listen to an *Observator* or *Review*" wherein they were taught "to banter Religion and the Holy Scriptures" and told "most Villainous Lies and Stories of the Clergy," which they sucked in "Greedily" and were "prejudiced past Expression." He was trying to fight these enemies with the same weapons, making "no Excuse for Stile." He wrote "for the Common People," desiring "only to be Plain . . . enabling Frequenters of Coffee Houses to carry the arguments in their Memories." [27]

Luckily for the ministers, the French decided at this juncture to promote an invasion of Scotland in the interest of the Pretender. The popular indignation that followed made it easy to obtain a flood of loyal addresses. Parliament was dissolved while this mood prevailed and a new one obtained, committed to the pursuit of the war until France was humiliated and the Protestant succession sure. But the Queen held back so much, among other things protesting against Somers as one of her ministers, that Sunderland and others of his friends were moved to distrust Marlborough and Godolphin and to try to make separate interests for themselves.

The Lord Treasurer and the Duke were, in fact, doing their best to manage the willful Queen, who fought with every weapon she had. Plaintively, she hoped that Marlborough

---

[27] Hist. Mss. Com., *Bath*, I. 121, 124; The *Weekly Comedy; or, the Humours of a Coffee-House*, Aug. 20–27, 1707.

would not help to force Somers upon her, "though lord treasurer tells me you will; for it is what I can never consent to." She yielded in the end, but not until the Duke threatened that not to do so would make her liable to the suspicion of sympathizing with her brother and would be "notice to everybody" that he and Godolphin no longer had credit with her and that she was "guided by the insinuations of Mr. Harley." The Lord Treasurer was reduced to the hope that Marlborough would perform "miracles abroad, and afterwards, that these" would "produce yet greater miracles at home." But domestic discontent hindered military success.

Harley did not abandon his purpose, though the abortive invasion and the ensuing elections obstructed his way. Anne resisted every step that her ministers took in an effort to gratify the natural demands of their new allies for a share in power. In consequence, the Duke despaired of serving the Queen or the country on the Continent, while Godolphin complained that he could not get through the autumn without the presence of his Grace in England. Marlborough sent in August the comforting thought that there was no chance of "washing a blackamoor white," and that they "must expect the next winter all the disagreeableness imaginable." In the same month he and Godolphin had again to threaten to resign in order to carry a point with Anne, who begged for help against the friends they sought to serve. The intention, she said, was "to tear that little prerogative the crown has to pieces; . . . to be short, I think things are come to, whether I shall submit to the five tyrannizing lords, or they to me." [28]

St. John, lacking a seat in Parliament, could only advise Harley (October 1, 1708):

There is no hope but in the Church of England party, nor in that neither on the foot it now stands, and without more confidence than is yet reëstablished between them and us. Why do you not gain Bromley entirely? The task is not difficult, and by governing him without seeming to do so you will influence them. . . . You broke the party, unite it again, their sufferings have made them wise, and

[28] Boyer, *Annals of Anne*, VII. 40ff.; Coxe, *Marlborough*, II. 418ff., 434f., 510, 517ff.

whatever pique and jealousies they may entertain at first will wear off, and you will have it in your power by reasonable measures to lead them to reasonable ends.

After the experience of the previous winter, the writer expected little help from the Queen in getting release from the "Egyptian bondage" into which they had fallen.

Harley, better informed, had more faith in Anne and had already applied to Bromley. The latter agreed that "the gentlemen and the clergy have everything to fear from some in power." Harley canvassed actively for Bromley as Speaker of the new House of Commons, assuring Harcourt in his enthusiasm that it would help to unite the party and might come near carrying.

The new allies of the ministers were relentless. Churchill left the Admiralty, and Somers entered the Queen's service. The death of the Queen's husband in late October opened the way for further demands. Orford was forced into the admiralty the next year, and Wharton was sent to Ireland as Lord Lieutenant. Swift, in England to seek for the Irish clergy the same bounty Anne had granted to the English, advised Archbishop King that the price of success would be acquiescence by the clergy in the removal of the sacramental test, which he hoped they were "prepared" for.[29]

The presence in the ministry of so many men they suspected made partisans of the Church uneasy. Leslie labored at length to prove 12 Charles II.c.30 to be not a mere statute, but part of the "Fundamental Laws of the Realm; . . . if it were repealed, that Repeal would be disputed, as being contrary to the Undoubted and Fundamental Law of the Realm." Parliament had not made this law; it "did not Enact, but Recognize and Declare what was the Undoubted and Fundamental Law of England from the Beginning." Invited to preach before the Lord Mayor, Atterbury advocated passive obedience so openly that the aldermen declined to thank him or to desire that he print the sermon. When the Convocation met, the ministers advised the Queen to prorogue it to prevent the

---

[29] Hist. Mss. Com., *Portland*, IV. 504; *Bath*, I. 191ff.; Coxe, *Marlborough*, II. 611ff.; Ball, *Correspondence of Swift*, I. 126f.

election of that fiery preacher as prolocutor of the lower house and the recurrence of the strife between the houses which was a fruit of his leadership.[80]

Lesser lights among the clergy lent a hand in sermons and pamphlets too numerous to cite. Most notable was Atterbury's friend, Sacheverell. An opponent thought him to be "the proudest priest that ever the Church was pester'd with since Arius." Through the Sheriff, George Sacheverell, a relative, he was invited (August 15, 1709) to preach the assize sermon at Derby. He supported the thesis that all who did not strictly adhere to the Church were heinous sinners, that moderate, tolerant churchmen were participants in sin. The published sermon, *The Communication of Sin,* was dedicated to the Sheriff, testifying that,

> When the *Principles* and *Interests of our Church and* Constitution *are so shamefully* Betray'd *and* Run Down, *it can be no little* Comfort *to all those who* Wish their Welfare *and* Security, *to see that notwithstanding the* secret Malice *and* Open Violence *they are persecuted with, there are still to be found such* Worthy Patrons *of both, who dare* Own *and* Defend *them as well against the* Rude *and* Presumptuous Insults *of the* One Side, *as the* Base, Undermining Treachery *of the* Other; *and who* Scorn *to* sit Silently by, *and* Partake in the Sins *of these* Associated Malignants.

Soon the preacher appeared on a larger stage. Notables of the City and the nation assembled, November 5, in St. Paul's to celebrate the escape from Guy Fawkes and the coming of William and listened to a long and frantic warning against *The Perils of False Brethren, both in Church and State.* The speaker felt the importance of the occasion. One who saw him then for the first time later wrote:

> I remember he sate directly against me during Prayers, and I was surpriz'd at the Fiery Red that overspread his Face, (which I have since seen fair and Effeminate enough) and the Gogling Wildness of his Eyes. And I may truly say, He was (if ever Man) transported with an Hellish Fury.

[80] *Rehearsal,* Oct. 13, 1708; Boyer, *Annals of Anne,* VII. 257ff.; *Political State,* I. 497ff.; Hist. Mss. Com., *Portland,* IV. 507.

This description was not by a friend, but it indicates the flavor of the sermon, in which the chief offense was by no means an epithet which the Lord Treasurer was later reputed to have applied to himself. Before he reached that term, which appeared in the plural, the man in the pulpit had denounced emphatically with a variety of expressions, in their very presence, political leaders who had failed to exorcise from Church and State all who would not strictly conform. He continued:

What a vast *Scandal* and *Offence* must it give to all Persons of *Piety,* and *Integrity,* to see Men of Characters and Stations thus *Shift* and Prevaricate with their *Principles,* and *Starting* from their *Religion* upon any occasion of *Difficulty* or *Tryal.* . . . To see Men's *Opinions set as* Loose about 'em as their Garments, to be put on or off for *Convenience?* What can *Unwary* Persons conclude from such *Tergiversation* and *Hypocrisy,* but that all Religion is *State-craft* and *Imposture?* That all *Godliness* is *Gain:* and that the *Doctrines* of the *Church* lie not so much in her *Articles,* as her *Honours* and *Revenues?* Without Doubt, this *Modern Latitude,* and infamous Double-dealing, as it can proceed from nothing but the *rankest Atheism,* so it must propagate it wherever it goes. . . . But this *Crime* . . . destroys all *common* Honesty, *Faith,* and *Credit* in the World, and in the Place of it, sets up an *Universal Trade* of *Cosenage, Sharping, Dissimulation,* and downright *Knavery.* For what Dependence can there be in a Man of no *Principles?* What Trust in *Equivocations, Evasions* and *Lies?* Nor indeed could any one be suppos'd so *Sottish,* as to place the least Confidence in these *Men,* did they not bait their *Hook* and *Cover* their *Treachery* with the *Sacred* and *Plausible Pretences* of *Friendship,* whereby they are capable of doing *much more Mischief,* than a *bare-fac'd* and *profess'd* Enemy. In what moving and *lively Colours* does the Holy Psalmist point out the *crafty* Insidiousness of such wilely Volpones? [31]

[31] In addition to the printed sermons see William Bisset, *The Modern Fanatick,* p. 14; Boyer, *Annals of Anne,* VII. 221; *Daily Courant,* Nov. 9, 1709; J. J. Cartwright, *The Wentworth Papers,* p. 99; Thomas Hearne, *Remarks and Collections,* II. 304, 313, 317. One of the antiquary's correspondents wrote, November 10, that the thirty clergymen who sat in the "quier" shook "at the terrour of" the preacher's "Inveterate Expressions." The sermon was "so violent" he did not think the Lord Mayor and aldermen would "desire him to print it." Another correspondent who heard the sermon, writing immediately afterward, said that it lasted an hour and a half and was "delivered with all the assurance and confidence that Violent Preacher is so remarkable for. I could not have imagined if I had not actually heard it myself, that so much Heat,

This language was scarcely to be borne, had there been no real danger that the fanaticism thus propagated would imperil the places of the ministers, the peace of the country, and the succession to the crown. The ministers knew the weakness of their position and the circumstances that determined the complexion of the new Parliament. They had to make their political hay in the sunshine of its power. Harley now made difficult paths he had formerly smoothed. Anne was perpetually resistant.

The victorious Marlborough returned that year to find his colleague still laboring to satisfy the Junto. People out of doors were more critical and exulted less in his triumphs. In desperation, he sought his office of Captain General for life as a means of relief from political brawls, only to discover that his new friends and some of his older ones would not trust him so far. In the confusions of the great, lesser men complained of neglect. Swift felt himself "used like a sober man with a drunken face." [32]

Sacheverell's sermon at St. Paul's was the climax of a campaign in behalf of the hereditary monarchy and the divine right of the Church. The ministers cast about for means of opposing this flood that seemed likely to engulf them. Having Parliament for the moment, they decided, by impeaching the preacher, to place it on record in favor of the Revolutionary settlement and against the subversive doctrines of which the sermon was a flagrant example. Sacheverell seemed to be an apt choice for their plan. His hot temper and extravagant language would probably alienate moderate men from a party accepting his support.

Harley sympathized even less with Sacheverell and his kind than he did with the new allies of Marlborough and Godolphin. But his old colleagues seemed to have won Anne in spite of her prejudice against their new friends. Denied access to the Queen, Harley had to work through the feeble Abigail. In

Passion, Violence, and Scurrilous Language, to say no worse of it, could have come from a Protestant Pulpit, much less from that pretending to be a member of the Church of England."

[32] *Parliamentary History*, VI. 744ff.; Boyer, *Annals of Anne*, VII. 277ff.; Ball, *Correspondence of Swift*, I. 128ff.; Coxe, *Marlborough*, III. 48ff.

August she had thought it dangerous for him even to write a letter to be shown to Anne, who "would be afraid of being examined about it." Nor could she make the marriage of Harley's daughter an occasion for seeing him herself, since the Queen would not excuse her attendance until the time ·of her approaching confinement. That Anne heard Harley's letter to Abigail "over and over" helped little, when she kept its recipient "in ignorance" and would not tell her "anything."

The expectant mother sent one ray of hope in mid-September before she left Windsor for Kensington. The Queen's "very sore eyes" were irritated by the news that the Duchess of Marlborough would come to her neighboring lodge for the rest of the season. Her Majesty would never consent that Sarah's daughter have the promise of the mother's office at court, though "her saying that" did not put Abigail at ease. Harley knew she had "made resolutions often" before and had been persuaded to "break them." Even this slender comfort was now interrupted until after October 22, when Samuel Masham announced the birth of a daughter.

St. John rusticated in enforced domesticity at Bucklebery, his wife's country estate. He was (September 21) "perfectly easy," but "with the same ease" would return to "the noise and business of active public life" if only his "friends" or his "country" would call. In October Harcourt wrote that "Pere Rivers," one of Harley's recent converts, wished to hear further. Harley himself was cultivating the Duke of Shrewsbury, just back from Italy with a wife whose ways did not commend her to the women of the court. The chief of the Talbots suited a court better than politics, wanting the power of decisive action in a storm. He and Harley agreed that the desire for peace might be exploited and increased when Parliament met, though Shrewsbury thought it would amount to little, considering the tendency of men to "change their minds" on going to London and to "submit to their leaders."

He could not foresee when he wrote that a preacher in St. Paul's would unwittingly open a way for a change in the public temper. Nor did any one foresee it. When Shrewsbury set out for London (December 1) a fortnight after Parliament met, urging Harley to follow as soon as the illness of his son would permit, the thought uppermost in his mind was the triumph of the Czar over Charles XII. Thomas Mansell in November had thought of nothing better than petty tactics on malt and land taxes, even taking pride in the public performances of Haversham.

Peter Wentworth, toward the end of August, reported to his brother the "town . . . very empty and no manner of news but a fresh talk of peace." There was gossip concerning the rivalry of Lady Sunderland and the Duchess of Somerset for the succession as groom of the stole if the Duchess of Marlborough should quit, though Peter thought it nothing but "town talk." In the middle of December he sent news of the "extraordinary way the house of commons" had resolved to proceed against Sacheverell "for his two Sermons." But he felt that "the Parsons need not be so angry, for they are the cause of it themselves for they have made their brags that before 'twas printed 'twas perused and examined by three able counsil in the law who has given their opinion that there's no law in being, either Ecclesiastical or Civil, that can be punisht for any of his expressions how sharp so ever they may be taken to be when apply'd to any perticulars." Dr. William Stratford, a zealous churchman of Oxford who did not like the preacher, admitted to Harley five days later that the prosecution might make "the Doctor and his performance much more considerable than either of them could have been on any other account." "It works more than I could have expected," he continued. "He is visited and presented by clergy and laity. Those whom he has used brutally forget their past resentments on this occasion and visit him. I hear Sir Simon Harcourt has promised to be one of his counsel." [33]

Had some one recalled to the father at Brampton at the bedside of his son the strange case of Titus Oates's famous plot, he might still not have foreseen the perilous ascent to power he was soon to begin. He had not wished to go that way. He had to depend upon Anne, who would act only when she could

[33] Hist. Mss. Com., *Portland*, IV. 424ff., 530; *Bath*, I. 197f.; Cartwright, *Wentworth Papers*, pp. 98ff.

be persuaded or felt inclined, which he did not mind so much as his dependence on the Church. If he should use it now, it would be only in order to thwart it in some degree in the end. In any case, he was needed in London.

CHAPTER IV

HARLEY'S CLIMB TO POWER, 1709-1711

Every Man speaks of the Fair, as his own Market goes in it. All are easily satisfied with themselves and their own Merit, though they are not so with their Fortune; and where they see others in better *Condition* whom they esteem less deserving, they lay it upon the ill Constitution of the Government, the Partiality or Humour of Princes, the Negligence or Corruption of Ministers.

Englishman's Journal, July 11, 1922.

I

THE FALL OF GODOLPHIN

NEITHER Anne nor Harley saw far ahead as they waited through the Christmas recess for Parliament to reassemble and try Sacheverell. With a shrewd opportunism that brought political success, Harley looked hopefully for his chance. Not for months would the way seem clear. The dogged Queen was resolved to contest every inch of ground with those who would encroach on her prerogative, preserving meanwhile a correct attitude toward the men in office.

She took more seriously than current makers of verse their references to her as "Augusta." She was grateful to Marlborough and Godolphin, who had won for her this large part in the drama of her time. She was profoundly grieved that they had lately turned against her, forcing her to yield one step after another until she was almost desperate. She refused to see Harley or to permit Abigail to see him for her, but she remembered his advice and loyalty when Somerset and the rest would not go on without the Lord Treasurer and the Duke.

The Earl of Essex died soon after Christmas, affording a

chance to attack Marlborough on a tender point, diminishing his prestige in the army and alienating him from Anne. It was a chance where Abigail could help. Essex had commanded a regiment and was Constable of the Tower. Mrs. Masham obtained the regiment for her brother, Colonel John Hill. The Tower required finesse.

At Harley's suggestion Lord Rivers solicited Marlborough's interest with the Queen. The Duke put him off, but agreed that in asking the place Rivers might say Marlborough had no objection to him. When the Captain General reached the Queen to give the advice which he imagined would be decisive, he found to his amazement that both places had been disposed. He sought aid from Sunderland and Somers and told Anne that giving the regiment to Hill would "set up a standard of disaffection to rally all the malcontent officers in the army." When the Queen would pay no heed, he and Sarah went off in high dudgeon to Windsor Lodge.

The Cabinet Council met and transacted business as usual, neither the Queen nor the Duke's colleagues referring to his absence. Some of the colleagues, at the Duke of Devonshire's (January 16), considered what ought to be done. Marlborough had written to demand that Anne dismiss either Abigail or himself and waited for the approval of friends to send the letter. Sunderland wished a vote of Parliament requesting the removal of the offending woman. Soberer politicians in the group, having launched the impeachment of a parson for a sermon, had no will thus to dignify a lady of the bedchamber. Their second thoughts made clear things that anger obscured to Sunderland and to his indignant parents-in-law.

A truce revealed the strategy of contending factions through the ensuing months. Harley tried to tempt Marlborough and Godolphin to quit their places in a way to give the impression of deserting the Queen and the country in a time of need, enabling him to acquire merit by coming to the rescue. A proper reply to this attack was for men in office to refuse to resign, insisting upon dismissal, thus giving an air of violence to the acts of the Queen and her new advisers. To pursue this strategy required no little patience and self-control on both sides. In an effort to persuade her to make concessions, Somers told Anne pointedly that Marlborough was "not to be considered merely as a private subject, because all the eyes of Europe" were "fixed upon him." This she could not deny; none knew it better than Harley. Consequently, Hill accepted a pension, and Marlborough returned to town to bestow the regiment upon another.

In Harley's circle, the outcome was represented as a triumph for the Queen. The Duke and his Duchess were said to have "made great submissions where they were due." Their mistress had not sent for them, saying: "No, they were gone upon their own affairs and might stay their own time." According to Peter Wentworth, upon the Duke's return, his friends reported all to be "well and right again." But later words of that correspondent (January 24) were more befuddled than usual. "Others talk," he said, "as if there was great matters in agitation such as the Queen can never consent to. 'Tis certain there's a great Hurly burly at Court but the perticular accations 'tis impossible for me to learn at least not saft for me to writ."

Three days later he heard that Marlborough and his friends denied the thought of asking Parliament to address the Queen to remove Abigail. But another three days of gossip and reflection made Peter doubt whether such heats among "great people" were easily allayed. Somerset had helped to eliminate Harley before; the current dispute was "carry'd much higher tho' in reality both" had "the same spring." There were rumors that Anne told the Duke that the nation wished peace and that Townshend at The Hague would thenceforth be directed by Somers instead of Marlborough. Considering these things, it was thought Sacheverell would "come off clear." [1]

The trial was to be a political and social event. The demand for tickets exceeded the number of seats it was possible to improvise in Westminster Hall. When Sir Christopher Wren appeared before the Lords to explain why he had left space without a scaffold, scorning the excuse that it was to save a

[1] Coxe, *Marlborough*, III. 142ff.; Cartwright, *Wentworth Papers*, pp. 102ff.; Hist. Mss. Com., *Portland*, IV. 531.

paltry three hundred pounds, they had to be told "plainly that the Q[ueen] was possitive she wou'd have no body over her head," whereat the "house laught coming so pat to what had been so lately the discourse of the town."

Before the trial, Marlborough was ordered by Parliament to be sent to the Continent to speed negotiations for peace. Some thought this to be a trick of Harley, to insure the Duke's absence when the case came up. In fact, like other consequential events, it was probably a fortuitous act precipitated by one who recked little of what he did. According to Peter Wentworth, Sir Gilbert Heathcote, a City Magistrate in the House of Commons, drew from his pocket a letter from a Dutch merchant saying that negotiation had begun afresh. He thought the Queen should be asked to send the Duke to care for England's interest. Bromley objected to taking so seriously news from one merchant to another. Another friend of Harley thought it exalting Marlborough's pride too much and setting him above the crown to prescribe that he be sent. To soften this, Walpole suggested that compliments to the Duke were compliments to his mistress as well, and thus the resolution passed.

Godolphin waited on Anne with a prepared answer describing Marlborough as "God Almighty's chief instrument" of her "glory" and of her "people's happiness," only to find that Walpole's enthusiasm had overshot the mark. Insisting that she had already given orders for the return, the Queen was grudgingly won to admit to Parliament: "I am very glad to find by this address that you concur with me in a just sense of the Duke of Marlborough's eminent services." The Duke posted off to Harwich. It mattered little that wintry winds and a stormy Channel delayed him there. The uncertainty of politics at home hindered the progress of negotiations abroad. While he waited the trial began.[2]

This spectacle entertained the town for several weeks and left an indelible impression on adults of that generation. Elderly women with long memories began to be afraid. Abi-

---

[2] Coxe, *Marlborough,* III. 159ff.; Cartwright, *Wentworth Papers,* pp. 110f.; *Parliamentary History,* VI. 893ff.

gail Harley wrote accounts of the trial to her nephew, Edward, Robert's son, at Oxford. Most of her information came from the father. At first, not having "read the sermon," she professed to have little concern. Detesting "unjust prosecutions from any side," she might be "partial to him," but would "never add a grain to his vanity." Anne, attending the trial (March 1), "appeared very pensive," though the "mob huzzaed her joining the Church and Sacheverell." The Harley family did not get to bed that night "till near morning."

After the trial was over, while awaiting the verdict, she moralized: "This business in all probability will break the Whigs; my foolish fears are it will raise the Tories to their old madness, the extravagance of every party is to be dreaded. If the clergy take up their old way of railing in the pulpits, as some already practice, this will certainly be one consequence, to empty the churches and fill the meeting houses." Reporting the verdict two weeks later, she lamented "the terrible animosities . . . raised throughout the kingdom, of which" she prayed "God avert the fatal consequences."

To her son on the Continent Lady Wentworth reflected as much of her own state of mind as of the trial. "Sacheverell," she said, "will make all the Ladys turn good huswives, they goe at seven every mornin . . . pray God send it ends well for this confution seems to me to be lyke the beginning of the lait troubles, I having laitly red Bakers Cronekles."

In the thick of the fight on the ministers' side, Defoe reflected in retrospect, closing the volume of the *Review* for the old calendar year in March, 1710:

We have had a most distracting turbulent time for the last two months of this year, occasioned by the Prosecution and Defence of a High-Flying Clergyman, who has undertaken in the teeth of a very Parliament, as well as of the Nation, to justifie and defend the exploded Doctrine of Non-Resistance.

This Defence has been carried on with all possible Riot, Fury, and Violence; and a strong Conjuncture of Papist, Jacobite, and High Church Mad Men has appeared in it, which has made them seem very formidable to the World—Rabbles, Tumults, plundering Houses, demolishing Meeting Houses, insulting Gentlemen in the Streets and honest Men in their Dwellings has been necessary Appendices of this Affair. And after all I might own, tho' the Man has been condemned, his Principles censured, and his Sermons burnt; yet it has not been without most fatal Consequences over the whole Nation, as it has reviv'd the Heats, Feuds and Animosities which were Among us, and which by the blessed Example and Exhortion of her Majesty began to be laid asleep in the Nation.

He had by him as he wrote "letters from Gentlemen of more Anger than Honour" who "faithfully promis'd . . . to come and kill" him "by such and such a Day." Friends had cited the fate of Tutchin and Godfrey. Thrice he had been waylaid. A little later he still shook a puzzled head:

> Would any Man that had seen the Temper of People in the Time of the late King James believe it possible, without a judicial Infatuation, that the same People should reassume their Blindness and rise up again for Bondage? Never since the Children of Israel demanded to go back and make Bricks without Straw and to feed on Onions and Garlick was any Nation in this World so sordid and so unwarrantably bewitched.[8]

Those who planned the prosecution and were careful to manage it circumspectly neither foresaw nor intended these results. The first of their four articles contained the crux of the point they tried to make. The purpose of the preacher's sermon was to "suggest and maintain, That the Necessary Means us'd to bring about the said Happy Revolution, were Odious and Unjustifiable; That his Late Majesty in his Declaration, disclaim'd the least Imputation of Resistance; and that to impute Resistance to the said Revolution, is to cast Black and Odious Colours upon his late Majesty, and the said Revolution." Four of the managers—Sir John Eyre, the Solicitor General; Sir Joseph Jekyll; Sir John Holler, the Comptroller of the Household; and Robert Walpole, Treasurer of the Navy—elaborated this point in their speeches to the Lords. Abbreviated excerpts stating their arguments succinctly were forthwith struck off and dispersed as a twopenny pamphlet.

The House of Commons, Sir Joseph said, had come to vindi-

[8] *Review,* VI. Preface; Hist. Mss. Com., *Portland,* IV. 532ff.; Cartwright, *Wentworth Papers,* p. 113; Lee, *Defoe,* I. 159ff.

cate the "Late Happy Revolution." Upon the law establishing the Protestant succession depended their "present Happiness and future Hopes." Could the "Pretender . . . have any Hopes, but in Avoidance of that Law?" Could it be thought proper to preach a "Doctrine in the Reign of the best of Princes" that would "be of no use but to the Worst?" The "Right Stating the Case of *Resistance* at the Revolution" would "be a Means of setting Men's Minds in the Love of Order and Regularity." It was a "Fundamental Rule that the Law is the only Measure of the Prince's Authority and the People's submission to it." Nothing was plainer than "that the Sense of the Law must be found out by the Law it self; and that Religion has nothing to do on that Occasion, but to enforce Obedience from the Consideration of higher Rewards and future Punishment." This speaker concluded: "Our Constitution was Received at the Time of the Restoration, when the Whole was Violated; and the Case of the Revolution is equal to it. . . . As the Nation agreed in the *Disease,* so likewise did they in the Remedy, by which the whole Frame of the Government was entirely Restor'd."

Eyre emphasized that the Revolution involved "Resistance." On it depended Anne's right to the crown and the "present Settlement of the Protestant Succession." If the "Resistance of the Revolution was not Legal, That Act of Settlement" could have *"no greater Force than an Act passed under an Usurper."* Hence the Commons thought it to be "of the greatest Consequence to maintain it . . . when her Majesty's most *implacable Enemies,* the Friends *of the Pretender,"* could "advance his Title on no other Pretence but that of Hereditary Right."

The Comptroller of the Household denied that the arguments of his colleagues implied that the "People are to be the Judges, when and how far they are to obey." Though the "Laws of Obedience, both Divine and Human," were "very express and positive," "Necessity" would "always make a justifiable Exception." So much depended "upon the Revolution" that the Commons were "highly Jealous of the Honour of it."

Walpole's clear perception of the immediate politics inspired an hortatory appeal:

When mercenary Scribblers are employ'd by a Party to vent their Malice, it may be fit to leave them to the course of common Justice. But when the Trumpet is sounded in Sion, when the Pulpit takes up the Cudgels, and gives the Alarm, and when those *bitter poisonous Pills* are gilded over with the *specious Name of Loyalty,* and People are taught to swallow them for their Souls and Consciences' Sake, the Commons cannot but think it high Time to put a Stop to the growing Evil. . . . The very Being of our present Government, is the Resistance that was necessarily used at the Revolution. . . . The Doctrine of unlimited passive Obedience is calculated for absolute Power. But if it cannot be an Advantage or Security to Her Majesty, who neither wants nor desires it, what can the Meaning of the Attempt be, but to prepare the People to be ready to embrace a Government in which it is like to be expected from them?

Defenders of Sacheverell walked as warily amid these delicate points. The preacher had left no recourse but to support the doctrine of passive obedience. For that purpose they offered a long list of passages from sermons and homilies by distinguished churchmen. Perhaps they quoted with greatest glee Gilbert Burnet, Bishop of Salisbury, soon to be active in his House against the prisoner at its bar. These quotations were mentioned by Sacheverell in his reply and given to the public in a pamphlet. His counsel denied that he had reflected on methods used at the Revolution, which was an exceptional case, not proper to be mentioned in a sermon dealing in generalities. In any event, the preacher had in mind resistance to "supreme authority," which meant in England a Parliament consisting of King, Lords, and Commons. Thus the Revolution was not a case in point.

The prisoner rode to his trial each morning in a carriage borrowed from a friend, enabling crowds to cheer his progress. The unsympathetic took offense. To one the "Doctor appear'd . . . to be Gay and Insolent." Seeing "that Triumphant Criminal," in a "Flaming and open Chariot, now and then Stopping, and then marching slowly in State to Westminster Hall," he felt resentful, thinking that he ought "as a Publick Enemy to his Church and Country" to have "been drawn upon a Sledge."

In person, the accused made his final appeal to the Lords. His speech was carefully prepared; some said it was the work of Atterbury; others, of Harcourt. It was addressed both to the assembly that heard it and to an audience at large. The latter had it at once at threepence the copy. The closing paragraph reflects the temper of the whole:

And so with all Humility and Resignation, I submit myself to your Lordships' Judgment, be it what it will. One thing I am sure it can never take from me: the Power of wishing and praying . . . for the Queen my Sovereign, for your Lordships my Judges, and for the Commons my Accusers; most earnestly beseeching Almighty God to deliver all Orders and Degrees of Men amongst us from all false Doctrines, Heresies and Schism, from Hardness of Heart, from Contempt of his Word and Commandment, from Envy, Hatred, and Malice, and all Uncharitableness.

A contemporary who tried to be fair observed that this "Studied, Artful and Pathetick Speech made no small Impression on Many of the Spectators and drew even Tears from some of the most tender-Hearted among the Fair Sex." But it had a "contrary Effect upon Others," who regarded it "as a Kind of sly Recantation of what the Doctor had advanced in his Sermon."

Riotous mobs expressed violent loyalty to Church and Queen by demolishing Dissenters' chapels as the Lords went to deliberate. Pamphlets were "thick upon the Compters of Westminster Hall." Partisans of the accused stopped their lordships on the way. Within the House, colleagues, ecclesiastical and lay, spoke on both sides. The speeches of four right reverend members were dispersed at large to such as had twopence to pay. The verdict pleased neither party. Speaker Onslow, a generation later, after examining the proceedings, was moved to note:

It was the great cause of the people and the constitution; and however unhappy in its effect at that time, and however impolitic it might then have been to have had such a prosecution, yet now we ought to rejoice that this memorial of the rights of the people is always to remain in the records of Parliament.[4]

[4] *The Speeches of Four Managers upon the First Article of Dr. Sacheverell's Impeachment; Collections of Passages Referr'd to by Dr. Henry Sacheverell in his Answer to the Articles of Impeachment; The Speech of Henry Sacheverell, D.D. upon his Impeachment at the Bar of the House of Lords in Westminster*

Through Abigail, Harley urged in vain that Anne take publicly the side of the accused. She attended the trial; she could not be blamed if the mob attributed a sympathy she did not express. The Duke of Shrewsbury, she said, advised her "not to meddle." That Duke himself intrigued with Somerset, Argyll, and Harley as the time for decision approached. Argyll was angry with Marlborough, but even St. John advised Harley that on the question of Sacheverell it would be wiser to "compound with" the head of the Campbells than "to insist much on convincing him." The Duke of Hamilton, appealed to by George Lockhart, noted the incongruity of voting for Sacheverell if one wished the support of Scot Presbyterians. But he wished the favor of the Queen and ultimately abandoned logic to follow his feelings. Argyll compromised, supporting the guilt of the prisoner, but exerting himself to lighten the punishment. The verdict carried, 62 to 59.

Defeated in his efforts to obtain an acquittal, with Argyll's help Harley was able to lessen the penalty proposed. Considering the forces on the side of Sacheverell, the wonder was, it was so severe. Wharton was reported as saying that he would "willingly submit to anything, even a fillip on the nose, so the Doctor might be found guilty." The Queen was quoted in the debate in the Lords as favoring leniency. In the end the accused was suspended from preaching for three years, and his sermons were ordered to be burnt. The proposal that he be ineligible for preferment during the time of his suspen-

---

Hall; [Sir John St. Leger] *The Managers Pro and Con; or, an Account of what is said at Child's and Tom's Coffee Houses for and against Dr. Sacheverell; The Bishop of Salisbury, his Speech in the House of Lords on the First Article of the Impeachment of Dr. Henry Sacheverell; The Bishop of Oxford, his Speech* etc.; *The Bishop of Lincoln's and the Bishop of Norwich's Speeches in the House of Lords* etc.; Boyer, *Annals of Anne*, VIII. 259ff.; Burnet, *Own Time*, IV. 538f.; *Parliamentary History*, VI. 805ff.; there were published immediately two editions of the *Tryal of Dr. Henry Sacheverell before the House of Peers, for High Crimes and Misdemeanors upon an Impeachment* which are the bases of the reports in the *State Trials* by Howell and others; F. Madan, *A Bibliography of Dr. Henry Sacheverell, extracted from the Bibliographer of 1883–4 with Additions*, lists many of the pamphlets. Not daunted by past experience, Defoe ventured again in satire: *The High Church Address to Dr. Henry Sacheverell for the Great Service he has done the Establish'd Church and Nation; wherein is shown the Justice of the Proceedings of those Gentlemen who have encourag'd the Pulling Down and Destroying of those Nurseries of Schism, the Presbyterian and other Dissenting Meeting Houses.*

sion failed by a margin of one vote; a friend soon offered a good living. Failing to obtain an acquittal, partisans indulged in bonfires and illuminations in an effort to make the lighter punishment appear to be a victory.[5]

During the trial the interest of the newly forming court circle was divided between the fate of the preacher and filling two vacant sees. The death of Chief Justice Holt brought another complication. Abigail was ready to despair concerning the episcopal candidates. She had told Anne, she informed Harley (March 10), that "her father never made a worse man bishop" than one of those suggested by the ministers still in office. She complained· further:

Nobody can serve her if she goes on privately doing these things every day, when she has had so much said to her as I know she has, both from myself and other people; and because I am still with her people think I am able to persuade her to anything I have a mind to have her do, but they will be convinced to the contrary one time or other. I desired her to let me see you, she would not consent to do that, and charged me to say nothing to you of what passed between us. She is angry with me and said I was in a passion, perhaps I might speak a little too warm but who can help it when one sees plainly she is giving her best friends up to the rage of their enemies?

The day before this outburst, St. John thought that "a Chief Justice whom we are jealous of, and two Bishops who will we are sure be against us, must turn all our schemes and those who go with us into a jest." He had just warned Halifax, Shrewsbury, and Somerset that he could not afford to accept again an office of no higher rank than that he had held before.[6]

Before the trial ended, Godolphin was sorry it had begun. Shrewsbury, Argyll, and Somerset were formidable enough without the secret help of Harley. The weary Minister tried to gain respite by proroguing Parliament and escaping to Newmarket. The anxious Captain General read listlessly the news from home. He regretted ever recommending Argyll to the

---

[5] *Parliamentary History*, VI. 887; Hist. Mss. Com., *Portland*, IV. 536ff.

[6] Hist. Mss. Com., *Portland*, IV. 535ff.; Coxe, *Marlborough*, III. 159ff. In the end Thomas Parker became Chief Justice, and the sees remained vacant until after the fall of Godolphin.

Queen. The behavior of Somerset, he thought to be a "true weathercocke." That of Shrewsbury indicated he knew he was making "his court to the Queen." In fact, at the moment Shrewsbury was the prospective great man, having as a peer the access to Anne that Harley was denied. He was the first to profit from the intrigue.

Before he left (April 5), Godolphin told Anne that in the future he could contribute little but "wishes" to her government. Disposed to find help where she could, she informed the absent Minister eight days later that Shrewsbury had expressed a "readiness to serve" her upon "all occasions" and a "willingness" to enter her service. She had decided to make him Lord Chamberlain, solacing the incumbent with a dukedom. She withheld the key and staff for a little, wishing to be the "first to acquaint" the Lord Treasurer with the change.

Little disposed to humor his opponents, Godolphin did not resign; instead, he expostulated with the Queen. Her action would cause every member of the "cabinet council except the Duke of Somerset to run away from it as they would from a plague." It would be fatal to the success of the war, leaving its conduct in the hands of those who would "like any peace the better the more it" left "France at liberty to take" her "time of imposing the Pretender upon the country." Personally, the writer would not obstruct any minister his mistress might employ. He wished permission to spend his remaining days "out of London" and that she would recur to his admonitions a year later to see whether the advice was sound. Forthwith he followed the letter, only to learn from Anne that she desired no further alterations in the ministry.

Shrewsbury meant to please. He would incur no blame if Marlborough and Godolphin should decide to quit. The Lord Treasurer added a postscript to his letter reporting the interview with the Queen, saying that he and most other people thought the Lord Chamberlain would "like very well to live easily" with the duumvirs. Indeed a few days later Godolphin found Shrewsbury "extremely full of professions" to himself, Marlborough, and Sarah. By "whatever door he came in," it was "always with an intention and a desire to live well" with those three and their friends. The Lord Treasurer repaid these compliments in kind and advised the Duke that their game for the time was to be friends with their new colleague.

The frantic Abigail lamented to Harley again that Anne would not let her see him. Thinking a conference necessary, she "had a mind to do it without her knowledge and so secret" that none but themselves would "know it."

Godolphin and Marlborough were not deceived. With a premonition where the next blow would strike, the Duke advised his Duchess to comfort Sunderland that "those are most happy who have least to do with courts." Unless Shrewsbury meant to desert his recent associates, his friendship would not last. But he still made professions when breaking the news that Anne might insist on the removal of Sunderland. Transmitting that notice, Godolphin reminded the father-in-law (May 12) of the strategy agreed upon.

The Lord Treasurer found friendship with Shrewsbury to be difficult in view of the absence of Marlborough and "Somerset's assiduity and inveterate malice join'd with the Queen's natural disposition and weakness." His conclusion on the "uneasy subject" was "that in general we must take care to keep our temper, and not suffer ourselves to be provoked by the injustices done us by others to make a wrong or unreasonable step ourselves; for that would not only be the greatest gratification to the duke of Somerset, lord Rivers, the duke of Argyle &c., but also draw the blame of any ill consequence upon ourselves, which otherwise would fall, as it ought to do, upon them." [7]

Younger men, such as Walpole and James Craggs, unaware of conditions behind the scenes, were indignant that no more was done to save the Duke's son-in-law. In fact, the jaded leaders plied the Queen with every art they knew. Marlborough resisted, though yielding in the end, the inclusion of Abigail's brother and brother-in-law among the promotions in the army. Another scheme was for Heathcote and a group of merchants to seek an audience with Anne in order to pro-

[7] Coxe, *Marlborough*, III. 165ff., 207ff.; Hist. Mss. Com., *Portland*, IV. 540.

test a change of ministers in general and the bruited dismissal of Sunderland in particular. The Dukes of Newcastle and Devonshire, heads of the powerful family interests of Holles and Cavendish, were to sponsor the audience. Devonshire was detained in the country and delayed the plan, though he sent a strong letter to be read in his name. Newcastle went on with the project, though Harley's son had already begun to seek his daughter's hand. The Queen dismissed Sunderland before the audience took place. To soothe the merchants' fears, she promised that no further changes would be made.

This vacant office was not the source of strength the schemers hoped. Poulett refused it, saying it should go to a member of the Church party, since the whole project depended upon its support. Harley still had to deal with Anne through Shrewsbury and Abigail. Somerset dallied in the country, hoping that Sunderland would be out before he returned. Back in town (May 24), he summoned courage, at Shrewsbury's request, to call on Harley after dark through the "back door."

Godolphin remonstrated with the Queen before the dismissal that it was an "act which must unavoidably make the Duke of Marlborough very uneasy" at a time when "the fate of all Europe" depended upon "his being encouraged and heartened." Anne's reply was shrewd: "The Duke of Marlborough is too reasonable to suffer a thing of this kind to do so much prejudice to himself and to the whole world, by taking it to heart; and surely nobody knows better than the Duke and yourself the repeated provocations which I have received from Lord Sunderland."

Inspired from home, the Duke himself wrote a letter to be shown to Anne, but this time carefully phrased so as not to be an ultimatum. He regretted that Sunderland was not "agreeable" to the Queen, but "his being at this time singled out" had no other reason but "that of being" his own son-in-law. For the sake of the public, he hoped the removal would at least be delayed to the end of the campaign. Somers (June 12) joined in a last effort to dissuade the Queen. Her reply in substance was the same as that she gave to the City group.

She meant to be rid of Sunderland, but she was "entirely for moderation" and did not intend to "make any farther alterations."

Perhaps she thought so at the time. To reënforce that resolution, Godolphin instigated through Marlborough and Lord Townshend on the Continent complaints from both the Dutch and the Emperor that further changes in the ministry would be unfortunate for the war. This was a delicate move, though England had set the precedent for the Emperor by a representation concerning Hungary. But when the Dutch followed their first appeal by a request that Parliament be not dissolved, Anne felt that her allies had overstepped the bounds.

Harley and his friends were not yet ready for bold action. They had to feel their way on the Continent, especially in Hanover. James Cresset, with whom Harley had discussed in April the choice of a confidential agent to that court, doubted whether "any mortal of tolerable worth and discretion" could be found willing to "undertake mysterious business during the present situation of affairs." With Sunderland out, Cresset himself was selected to go, though Somerset went to see Harley in a chair with drawn curtains to insist that the appointee be not notified until the Queen had opened the way with Henry Boyle, the Secretary of State.

From this welter of gossip, uncertainty, and backstairs intrigue few participants emerged with reputations unscathed. Yet none of the leading figures probably doubted his own integrity or good will to the public cause. Their trouble was, to know how the country should be served. The Queen had an undoubted right to change her ministers, but it was also important for Marlborough to command the army and keep his credit with the allies. It was impossible to foresee how the Duke would take the dismissal of his son-in-law. Partisans of the Lord Treasurer and the Duke would naturally press the Queen to keep their services, but in doing so it was not right to endanger the credit of the nation. Moreover, such men as Halifax, Somerset, and Newcastle, sensible of their own importance, were apt to think that the burden of saving the country rested on them if matters went too far.

Harley tried to deal tactfully wtih these grandees in the hope of winning them to his cause. To break suddenly with all of them would mean losing also Shrewsbury and the Queen, a humiliating experience he had no wish to repeat. The Church party, on the other hand, was already impatient with his Fabian tactics. A week after the dismissal of Sunderland, Harcourt wrote that the yielding by the Queen to the City group could not be "wiped off but by facts," which became "daily more necessary." Harley himself, the writer thought, was more "concerned than any one man living that something . . . be done to show the Queen's favour towards the Church of England" if there was "a real intention that way." But neither Harley nor Anne meant to yield entirely to the Church party if it could be helped, any more than they meant to take orders from the ministers in office. Harley was beginning to find out, too, that the Queen required no end of management and persuasion in making up her mind. Power was hers, and thus things slowly had to serve her will.[8]

With Sunderland out, Godolphin and his colleagues made their next stand on the dissolution of Parliament. So violent a step, they thought, would endanger the Queen's affairs at home and abroad. Both they and Harley knew the weakness of any alternative ministry in that House of Commons. More important, on this point most of the ministerial lords agreed. Indeed some of the peers that had thus far supported Harley were against the dissolution. Action would soon be necessary if Harley was to serve the Queen with any hope of success.

He was at pains to boast to the Duke of Newcastle as early as July 1 that he was in "almost daily attendance" on the Queen, though still at "unreasonable hours." Newcastle learned in the same letter that Cresset had kissed hands to go to Hanover. But before the end of the month Somerset summoned Shrewsbury and Harley on a hurry call to send another in the room of this envoy, suddenly deceased. The names of Poulett and these two dukes were passed by in turn for Rivers, who was to pause in Holland to smooth the way

---

[8] Coxe, *Marlborough*, III. 221ff., 254ff.; *Robert Walpole*, II. 11ff.; Hist. Mss. Com., *Portland*, II. 210ff.; IV. 542ff.; *Dartmouth*, p. 295.

for the enforced retirement of Godolphin if it should become necessary. In Hanover Rivers was to enlist the Electoral Prince to command the English army if Marlborough should retire. By this move the confederates hoped to show their loyalty to the Protestant succession and their unwillingness to lose the services of the Duke.

Marlborough felt keenly a proposal which he had vetoed in happier days. Now, on advice from home, he acquiesced. Cresset had been appointed without Godolphin's privity or consent, but he made no complaint when the instructions and papers of the deceased were sealed and delivered to Harley. He even permitted the payment of near a thousand pounds "equipage and advance money" on a memorial of the widow. Marlborough saw in the mission merely what he and his colleague must "expect."

Though Anne had ceased to consult Godolphin on public affairs, Shrewsbury told Halifax as late as July 12 that she was determined to reconcile Harley and the Lord Treasurer. Difficulties in the way were the Queen's resolution to have done with Sarah, Marlborough's devotion to his wife, and Godolphin's relations with both. "It is wonderful," commented Harley to Newcastle, "that the passion of a mad woman should so far influence public affairs and overrule a wise man." Pending the fate of Sunderland, Sarah had violated a promise made to both Anne and her husband by sending to the Queen a letter that might have offended a more tolerant woman.

Finally the thing was done. Godolphin had an audience (August 7) on routine business. He got the impression that the dissolution of Parliament was still "under a good deal of uncertainty." At a second conference later in the day he taxed the Queen with her recent conduct, asking point-blank: "Is it the will of your Majesty that I should go on?" Without hesitation, she answered, "Yes." On the following morning he got a note complaining of his recent conduct and suggesting that instead of returning his staff he break it, as easier for them "both."

Two notes written on the same day took the news to Marlborough. Anne assured him that the "Army" should "want for nothing." Godolphin was "chiefly concerned" that the Duke take the "matter in the manner . . . most advisable" for himself and "all the world besides." [9]

II

WATCHFUL WAITING

A friend to whom Harley had boasted sent playful congratulation: "You have got over the black gentleman. I always thought you a pretty good lad and a good raffler [rassler?]. You have often told me you would trip him in his heels, and now you have performed nobly." This view of the matter was too simple. The victor's hands were far from the white staff, and he despaired at times of getting it. Shrewsbury was currently regarded as "premier minister," though he refused to take the lead, admitting insufficiency. Poulett became First Lord of the Treasury. As Chancellor of the Exchequer Harley undertook to ride the financial storm which opponents had foretold would follow the fall of Godolphin. He knew that there would be efforts to make this prophecy come true.

There were large unfunded debts, some of them unauthorized. The Bank and agents of the Treasury made difficulties both at home and abroad. New machinery had to be improvised for raising money for the army and transmitting it to Holland. That Harley, assisted by John Drummond at The Hague, procured the funds in a disorganized market and met the country's obligations testifies to his capacity for affairs. Though Halifax, the Auditor of the Exchequer, lent a hand, this task alone was sufficient for a single man.

But Harley's chief concern through the long, hot weeks of that August and September was to preserve a united country as a means of making peace and insuring the Protestant succession. By emphasizing the Queen's right to choose her ministers and her treatment by Godolphin, Marlborough, and

[9] Coxe, *Marlborough*, III. 261ff.; Hist. Mss. Com., *Portland*, II. 211ff.; IV. 552ff.

Sarah, he hoped to keep the support of such men as Halifax, Newcastle, Somers, and Devonshire in addition to that of Shrewsbury and Somerset. He counted also on moderate friends of the Church. All depended upon the coöperation of Anne as actual head of the enterprise. She agreed, but the path she had to travel was uncertain, and neither she nor her advisers knew one day what ought to be done the next.

The dissolution of Parliament was the immediate point. On it Harley disagreed with the great lords whose help he craved. Godolphin, Sunderland, Wharton, and Walpole were busy. A further complication: since the close of the trial, Sacheverell had ridden in triumph through the country on a white horse. At places, though unsympathetic bishops tried to prevent it, partisans of the Church acclaimed him and made his coming the occasion for proposing candidates against a possible election. A presiding judge told the grand jury in Devon that "a wild Fire" was "running about, to the great Disturbance of the Peace."

Following this progress by the condemned preacher, churchmen sent addresses to the Queen from all parts of the kingdom supporting her hereditary claims, though usually with a prudent clause for Hanover. The other faction sent addresses too. The sheriff and grand jury of Chester "joyfully acknowledged" to Anne her "undoubted title, without presuming to distinguish between . . . Parliamentary and hereditary Right, much less to prefer that which" her "Glorious Predecessor, King William, had not" and the "illustrious House of Hanover most probably" would not have. More numerous were addresses from the Church's friends. The tense feeling moved Defoe to conclude in the *Review:* "If these things are the Sense of the Nation, we must acknowledge, it looks as if the Nation had lost its Senses."

The friendly great lords opposed to the dissolution pointed out to Harley that a general election amid this ferment would endanger his plans. But there was no alternative that did not leave Harley and the Queen at the mercy of these lords. Even with the support of Anne, Harley needed at least one house of Parliament that he could lead. Pressed by partisans of the

Church to make haste, he shrank from the necessity of choosing between them and the powerful lords. But there seemed to be no way to avoid a dissolution.

He sent advance information to Newcastle in mid-September that the proclamation would issue in a few days, Anne having "resolved" the question "in her own heart." St. John would replace Boyle as Secretary of State. Harcourt would be Attorney General, Halifax agreeing that his brother should retire. Devonshire and Cowper would hold on, he hoped, though Wharton, home from Ireland, joined with Somers in trying to persuade them to go out. As Wharton said to Harley's friend, William Legge, first Earl of Dartmouth, the issue was now clear: "If you have the majority, we are undone, if we have the majority, you are broke."

These plans came to grief. Even at Anne's entreaty, Cowper would not keep his seal. Harcourt reluctantly became Lord Keeper after he and Harley had tried in vain to induce Sir Thomas Trevor to change from Chief Justice of Common Pleas to the less certain chancery. Orford left the Admiralty. Ormond went to Ireland, replacing Wharton there. Rochester succeeded Somers. Walpole held on until dismissed, but to hinder, not to help. Somerset went to Petworth "in a Pet," not tarrying for a breakfast ready served. Thence he informed Newcastle (September 27): "I came hither yesterday to take care to keep out as many Tories and Jacobites in this new Parliament as I can."

The optimistic Halifax admitted to the same Duke the day before: "Our friends have quite gone off the stage, and those who were most reasonable and most disposed to set things right on the other side are not so much the masters of the field as they were; the auxiliaries they have taken in, whether by choice or by necessity . . . will have a share in the command." Newcastle himself held his post till death, but his henchmen worked against the ministerial candidates in Westminster.[10]

---

[10] Hist. Mss. Com., *Portland,* II. 219ff.; IV. 573, 598ff.; Boyer, *Annals of Anne,* IX. 179ff., 202ff.; Appendix, pp. 141ff.; *Review,* VII. 173ff.; Cartwright, *Wentworth Papers,* pp. 143ff.

Amid these crashing hopes, Harley needed to make an interest with the public if he was to avoid falling entirely into the hands of the Church. Mrs. Mary de la Rivière Manley had offered her services in May, "an unwarrantable intruder" moved by his "merit," "great capacity," and "zeal for the Church." She had published the year before two volumes of *Secret Memoirs and Manners of Several Persons of Quality of Both Sexes from the New Atlantis,* a familiar trick of alleging with elaborate details under veiled names violations of the moral code among the great. The curious soon had keys. Those accused could not reply without admitting the plausibility of the charges. The author had been arrested in the latter part of October, 1709; bailed on the day that Sacheverell preached his sermon; and discharged in February, 1710. In the same month that she proffered her services to Harley she published two further volumes of scurrility, later appearing as the third and fourth of *The New Atlantis.* It was possible to use her without approving of all she did.

An abler lieutenant renewed relations, departing no whit perhaps from the sincerity he ever claimed. "I have espoused an honest interest," he said, "and have steadily adhered to it all my days." Defoe had enlisted to serve the Queen. In his initial letter to Harley (July), he wrote: "I cannot but think that now is the time to find out and improve those blessed mediums of this nation's happiness, which lie between the wild extremes of all parties and which I know you have long wished for." Partisans of the Church always thought the *Review* to be a weapon of the enemy. Opponents of Harley at times denied that it reflected his real views. But it had an audience of its own, and its author could help in other ways.

Defoe's correspondents in different parts of the country enabled him to gauge its changing moods. He understood and sympathized with the Scots more than most Englishmen of the day. His knowledge of trade and finance, derived from observation and experience, commanded the respect of practical men. He had a journalist's knack of writing so that a layman could understand. He came to conferences through back doors at night and depended upon pittances disbursed almost as largess, but none was to serve Harley better in the years ahead.

The long title of his *Faults on both Sides; or, an Essay upon the Original Cause, Progress, and Mischievous Consequences of the Factions in the Nation, Shewing that the Heads and Leaders on both Sides have always imposed upon the Credulity of the Respective Parties . . . sincerely intended for the Allaying the Heats and Animosities of the People and Persuading all Honest, Well-Meaning Men to Compose their Party Quarrels and Unite their Hearts and Affections for the Promoting the Public Good and Safety of the Queen and Country* is sufficient evidence of the spirit of the piece. A second part later in the year was intended to show "the Original Cause, Progress, and Mischievous Consequences of the Factions in the Church" and that the clergy were "Ring Leaders and Beginners of Disturbances in Every State." Meanwhile, he had published an abler and more effective *Essay upon Publick Credit*, attributed then and long afterwards to Harley. Next came *An Essay upon Loans; a Vindication of the Faults on both Sides* and various pieces which did not interrupt the *Review* or other activities of its author in behalf of causes he supported with his pen.

Coincident with the fall of Godolphin, a new weekly appeared, instigated perhaps by St. John, addressed to the other wing of those supporting Harley. Dr. John Freind is said to have written for it; Matthew Prior lent a hand. Jacob Tonson's Kit-Cat Club, which had recently admitted Marlborough, dropped that poet from its roll. The new paper, the *Examiner*, tried to soothe the latter's wound. St. John himself sent a communication which gave the journal its place and was at once hailed as the program of the party. Cowper replied in a "Letter to Isaac Bickerstaff, Esq."; namely, Steele, who conducted his *Tatler* under that pseudonym. Both letters were reprinted and widely circulated as tracts.

The harping on nonresistance and passive obedience characteristic of the earlier numbers of the *Examiner* was as little likely to help the cause of Harley as the short-lived, satirical

Moderator, which was earlier in the field. But there was urgent need of a paper which he could inspire and control addressed to this audience. As by a miracle, an author with a hand of genius for the task appeared ready to make his market. Lacking Defoe's understanding of business and politics, he had more skill for invective and capacity for the prejudice by which it is inspired. Wearing the cloth and having already a reputation to conserve, he had to be approached with caution and paid with even greater care. The cost of his services only time would tell.

Jonathan Swift was sent to London (August, 1710) to solicit again the Queen's bounty for the Irish Church. His chief qualification for the mission was an acquaintance with great men in power. But Godolphin fell before he left Ireland, and he found London in a hubbub of uncertainty. For once he guessed right and appealed to the Queen through Harley instead of Shrewsbury. He was courted by friends out of or soon to be out of office, but was aggrieved that in prosperity they had not rewarded him according to what he thought were his deserts. In any case, if his mission was to succeed it was now foolish to consort with them. Harley learned through Erasmus Lewis that Swift felt himself to be ill used. The same agent brought the parson to the Minister, who straightway promised his interest with the Queen.

By early November Swift began to write for the *Examiner,* and the temper of the journal changed. The dangers of landed men from monied interests began to find a place. The need was emphasized of a paper to mediate between the *Review* and the *Observator* on one side and the *Rehearsal* on the other. Toward the end of November came an attack on Marlborough and his Duchess with an enumeration of their favors from the Queen. In order to cover as much as possible their relationship, Harley forbade the new recruit to attend his public levees, making a great favor of admitting him to the intimacy of his private circle. Lewis soon brought Swift into similar contact with St. John.

Never a hungry fish took more greedily tempting bait than the Irish parson yielded to the shrewd appeals of his new friends. They gave the sunshine of their company, the privilege to use his talents in their cause. To one ambitious to have a part in great affairs, that was much. But he was sometimes in straits for the pathetic materials with which he painted for the delectation of a fond woman in Ireland the picture of himself as one among the great. Had he foreseen acceptance of this record at face value by a credulous posterity, he might have had another bitter laugh at the expense of a world for which his contempt waxed as he was more convinced that he would be denied the place he wanted in his time.

The opposing side had a galaxy of writers. In June and July Walpole published *Four Letters to a Friend in North Briton upon the Tryal of Dr. Sacheverell* in the hope of stemming a tide already running toward the Church. The trial was necessary, he said, to save the Protestant succession. Steele enlisted for a while, and the *Tatler* was partisan. Addison's *Whig Examiner* gave place in October to the *Medley*. Arthur Mainwaring, John Oldmixon, and George Ridpath wrote with ready quills. The failing fortune of their patrons is no reflection on the ability of these writers or the quality of what they wrote. "We live in a Nation where at present there is scarce a single Head that does not teem with Politicks," observed the *Whig Examiner* (October 12).[11]

One reason why the great lords opposed the dissolution was their unreadiness for it. They had not anticipated an election until another year. Partisans of the Church were anxious to take advantage of the moment's mood. The result pleased Harley almost as little as it did those whom he had dislodged from power. Defoe reported from Scotland that all the High Church party there were Jacobites. Some of the elected peers were of that sort, but the Queen's name had been used openly for the list. Men elected were pledged to investigate Godolphin and the Duke. Even from England, those who came to

---

[11] In addition to citations in the text, see: Hist. Mss. Com., *Portland*, IV. 541; Hearne, *Collections*, II. 292, 297, 304, 389f.; Ball, *Correspondence of Swift*, I. 190ff.; Lee, *Defoe*, I. 172ff.; *Somers Tracts*, XIII. 2ff.; Swift, *Journal to Stella* (Walter Scott's ed.), II. 28ff.; [James Caulfield], *Memoirs of Celebrated Persons Composing the Kit-Cat Club*.

Westminster to support the change were bent on actions which would defeat the hopes of Harley and belie his promises.

Before the Parliament met, Drummond wrote that Rivers on his way to Hanover made the Dutch anxious from a fear of losing Marlborough. Drummond thought it possible and desirable for Harley and the Duke to work together. Harley professed a loyalty to the Queen inclining him to live with any man "her service or the public good" required. But Marlborough on returning home would "enter into the rage and animosity" of his friends. Meanwhile, the ministers cashiered several generals for drinking too enthusiastically to the Duke and to "damnation" for the other side. Harley knew also that the Queen would soon get rid of Sarah, who now threatened to publish some of the intimate correspondence of their happier days.

Greeting her new Parliament, Anne carefully promised to carry on the war and to "employ none but such as" were "heartily for the Protestant Succession in the House of Hanover." By a stratagem, the committee to prepare the Lord's address contained prominent Scot Jacobites. They had to declare themselves openly or to thank the Queen for "great care to transmit the blessings" of her reign to posterity "by securing the Protestant Succession in the House of Hanover." In the lower house, where Bromley was the Speaker now, the committee's draft referred to neither the House of Hanover nor the Pretender. When Walpole inspired Lechmere to offer an amendment remedying this omission, Harley himself made haste to second the move.

Marlborough returned, gritted his teeth, and called on Harley. A bitterer task, he took a letter from his wife, the which he had to beg the Queen to read, offering to submit in any manner prescribed if only she might keep her places as long as her husband should keep his command. But Anne was adamant, and said so frankly. In three days the husband returned to bring his wife's gold key. The Duchess of Somerset succeeded as Groom of the Stole; Abigail, as Cofferer. Marlborough was promised coöperation in the conduct of the war.

This Parliament was harder to manage than the one dissolved. A hundred and fifty members, organized as the October Club, began to eat together to plot means of hastening changes in the ministry and more severe measures against the men turned out. They had to be humored by an investigation of the failure of the war in Spain and of the alleged misuse of public funds. A veto by the Lords prevented them from reopening the question of land grants made in William's reign. A statute was passed requiring members of the House of Commons to have a substantial holding of land. On recommendation of the lower house of Convocation, the construction of fifty new churches was authorized for London and its environs.

Then, early in March, while the last measure pended, Count Guiscard, a French adventurer in English pay, in the presence of a Council assembled to examine him on the charge of treasonable correspondence, stabbed Harley with a penknife. The life of the wounded man was in danger for a while. Weeks of enforced retirement gave him time to think. The rumor was that his recovery would bring the white staff and a peerage. Others said that the Queen preferred the Earl of Rochester. Some stronger hand was needed at the helm, for the October Club, as though from sheer perversity, defeated a proposed leather tax, thus hindering the progress of the money bill.

His colleagues in the House resolved (April 11) that the Speaker should congratulate the wounded man upon his reappearance on the floor. But he went out too soon and was confined another fortnight. In that interval, news of the Emperor's death changed the face of things. Poulett wrote (April 18) to urge that Harley take the lead, reporting that Halifax "upon common talk which I told him you would not hear of, said he had power to assure you might command him, Somers and every Whig in England." "Anglesey and old Leeds," the writer went on, "say there will be no government if you do not resolve; only the cabinet councillors say nothing to me of it." Halifax in person asked that day for an interview, feeling the "conjuncture" to be "so extraordinary and so nice" that he thought there was "no medium between a vigorous asserting the Queen and her Government, or being lost forever." "Men's eyes," he said, "are turned toward you, expecting their safety from your interest and prudent management under the present difficulties." Even Rochester thought that the news of the Emperor made it necessary for Harley to meet with his colleagues, or they must come to him.

Before the convalescent reappeared in the House of Commons, a letter from Somerset asked his counsel on the question of "a new Emperor and a new King of Spain, for the same Person cannot nor must not pretend to both." Shrewsbury wrote (April 25) to say that Harley could not be "greater" than he wished him, but there would be other changes "upon which" it was "impossible to give an opinion unless one knew how far the Queen would go." Harley withheld his decision until he had piloted the revenue bill through the House of Commons and had sponsored another authorizing the founding of the South Sea Company as an agency for funding the naval debt inherited from Godolphin. While the last bill was in committee, the Earl of Rochester suddenly died.

Scarcely waiting for the funeral, Poulett advised that the vacant place be filled by a colorless peer such as the Duke of Buckinghamshire, rather than by Nottingham, who would succeed to the leadership of the Church party in the House of Lords. "You are the man alone," he urged, who has "the turning necessity at will upon others, and though you do wonders, if Lord Somers was as dead as Rochester, nobody would respect you a conjuror to raise either of them again to life." Somerset promised two weeks later (May 18) not to trouble much in the future since "you are and are to be very soon declared *le premier ministre*."

And thus it turned out. May 29, as Earl of Oxford and Mortimer, he finally received from the Queen the white staff as Lord High Treasurer, the last but one on whom she or any other English sovereign was to bestow that office. It was the anniversary of the Restoration. Her Majesty, said a contemporary gazetteer, "thought fit to pitch upon that Auspicious

Day for the Inauguration of a Prime Minister to whose Wisdom, Vigilance, and Dexterity the Restoration of the Publick Credit was principally owing." [12]

[12] Hist. Mss. Com., *Portland*, IV. 619ff., 674ff.; *Bath*, I. 201; Coxe, *Marlborough*, III. 336ff., 360ff.; *Parliamentary History*, VI. 928ff.; Cartwright, *Wentworth Papers*, pp. 159ff.; [Daniel Defoe], *Secret History of the White Staff*, Pt. II, sec. ed., pp. 17ff.; Boyer, *Annals of Anne*, IX. 318ff., 384; *Political State*, I. 369ff.; Ball, *Correspondence of Swift*, I. 235ff.; Swift, *Journal to Stella*, I. 369ff.

CHAPTER V

THE TRIUMPH OF OXFORD, 1711–1712

I am afraid that we came to court in the same dispositions as all parties have done; that the principal spring of our actions was to have the government of the state in our hands; that our principal views were the conservation of this power, great employments to ourselves and great opportunities of rewarding those who had helped to raise us, and of hurting those who stood in opposition to us. It is however true, that with these considerations of private and party interests, there were others intermingled which had for their object the public good of the nation, at least what we took to be such.

BOLINGBROKE in his *Letter to Sir William Wyndham.*

AFTER the success of the Church party in the general election of 1710 Harley had submitted to the Queen at Windsor a report on conditions, with a tentative plan for the future. She should send forthwith to foreign courts, especially to The Hague, the center of business and intelligence, men who would look to her instead of to Marlborough. She should determine before the Duke's return how she would greet him, and his future relations with her ministers, reserving to herself major appointments and promotions in the army.

The majority in the House of Commons needed "prudent conducting." "Pleasing the clergy, avoiding giving jealousies, and hopes of places after" would render the members easy for a session. Opposition was stronger in the Lords. Peers such as Peterborough, Mohun, and Haversham might be won. The Queen should let both factions of the clergy understand that she wished peace and should bestow preferment on some members of the High Church faction, lately slighted.

The popular mood was favorable, but "this bent and disposition of the people should be guided for the Queen's service and the public good, and not be at the disposal of particular persons." He advised "steady management" and "avoiding to give jealousies." Since "divisions at court" were the chief hope of the opposition, it would be serious if "by the behaviour of any of those" having "credit with the Queen there should be a pretence in either House to doubt what the Queen's mind" was. Anne herself was the "center of power and union"; her opponents would quickly enter a "breach" in her ministry. There was "one weak place where the enemy" might "attack"; namely, "the affair of the House of Hanover." Harley sought the "Queen's great wisdom to consider how to prevent it."

Sunderland agreed on this last point. He wrote to his father-in-law on the dissolution of Parliament in August: "The Affair of Hanover is, and must be our sheet anchor, and if it be rightly managed, you will be effectually revenged of all your enemies." It seemed to be the best game to play, but it might prove a long one for aging men whose course was almost run; the younger, such as the writer and Walpole, would have fresher hopes.

The Earl of Oxford and Mortimer would go again to pay his court at Windsor on the morrow. For thirty-one days he had fondled his white staff. Besides lying for a while at the point of death, he had done many other things in the past seven months, some of them according to his plan. But, as he saw it, a plan in politics was chiefly useful when rallying support. "Wisdom in public affairs was not," what was "commonly believed, the forming schemes with remote views; but the making use of such events as happen." He, Shrewsbury, Rochester, and St. John ran the government for some months as a sort of junto. Then Guiscard broke his knife and missed his mark. Death claimed as suddenly the Emperor and Rochester. Fate had saved him, opening a way to power at home and probably to peace abroad. But it was a tortuous way. His fate gave grudgingly. He had hard and dangerous work to do with dull and unsure tools.[1]

---

[1] Hardwicke, *State Papers*, II. 485ff.; Coxe, *Marlborough*, III. 297; Ball, *Correspondence of Swift*, I. 266; Hist. Mss. Com., *Portland*, V. 28ff.; Gilbert Parke, *Letters and Correspondence of Bolingbroke*, I. 84, 94, 136, 151, 157, 190.

Shrewsbury, out of the secret though still at court, would not help or hurt much. Somerset attended cabinets no longer, but Anne insisted on his Duchess—another "heifer to the plow." God send that she pull in a team with Abigail. At worst, she was better than Sarah. Newcastle was friendly and might be bound closer by a family alliance. Marlborough would be easier to manage, now that his wife was out. The Queen could not do without him while the war went on, and it would probably last for at least another year; but neither could the Duke afford to desert the Queen. St. John disagreed here.

But with all his flashy brilliance, would St. John ever mature into a statesman? The fruits of success might never ripen for one with eager hands. He would rashly make opportunities rather than wait for and improve them. He had even claimed the uncertain merit of Guiscard's enmity, though escaping the pain of the wound. Perhaps that was merely a countermove against the report that he had broken his sword and run away, frightened in the melee, but it left an ill taste in the mouth of a friend.[2]

[2] Harley's family circle had it that St. John, seeing the wounds inflicted on Guiscard by the swords of Newcastle and Ormond, broke his own and, after grappling with the assailant, "ran out, called for the surgeon . . . and without a sword in the utmost confusion ran away to St. James's, went to Mrs. Masham's lodging in the fright" and thence to the Queen's physician and the Queen to tell the news (Hist. Mss. Com., *Portland,* IV. 670). Swift's account amid the excitement to Archbishop King was that St. John immediately on the attack drew his sword and stabbed Guiscard in the breast. Other members of the Council followed this example until interrupted by Poulett's request that the assailant be spared for the hangman. Thereupon, "Mr. St. John's sword was taken from him and broke"; a footman came and bound Guiscard (Ball, *Correspondence of Swift,* I. 238ff.). When Guiscard died Swift explained to Stella that the coroner attributed the death to a bruise in order to "clear the Cabinet Counsellors from whom he received his wounds." In the *Examiner* of March 15, written while the recovery of Harley was uncertain, the same author, after alleging the responsibility of the previous ministry for the presence of Guiscard in the country, related that the "murderer confessed in Newgate, that his chief design was against Mr. Secretary St. John, who happened to change seats with Mr. Harley for more convenience of examining the criminal: and being asked what provoked him to stab the Chancellor? he said, that not being able to come at the Secretary, as he intended, it was some satisfaction to murder the person whom he thought Mr. St. John loved best." Swift afterward noted that St. John read this passage before publication and did not change it. At any rate, after Harley began to mend, Swift, in order to avoid a mistake prejudicial to his fortunes, declined to write a further account of the

Unfortunately there was no one but St. John to manage the House of Commons. Bromley was wholly in the interest of the Church and the October Club. Even St. John sometimes joined in the demand that more of the old set be turned out and punished. Yielding to this clamor would be a resignation of power to the hot churchmen and would make it easier to represent the Queen's ministers as favoring Jacobites. Jacobite votes might be useful in a pinch, but St. John ought not to have suffered such men as George Lockhart and William Shippen to be chosen to examine the public accounts. That whole affair had been mismanaged.

To accuse opponents in office of corruption was part of the game of those who were out, but only the hot-headed amateurs now on top in the House of Commons would have proceeded to cases after getting power. The other day Swift, no doubt reflecting St. John, had pronounced it a capital offense to have dismissed the late ministers unless they were guilty as charged. In case of a break with Marlborough, this dangerous weapon might be used—the greater reason not to court a break. Meantime, the absurd charge that thirty-five million pounds were unaccounted for chiefly revealed the ignorance of those who sponsored it and invited Walpole's devastating replies.

St. John's latest enthusiasm was for peace. If necessary, he would first agree with France and then by pressure bring the allies to accept the terms. A while ago it was an expedition to Quebec finally sent under Abigail's brother, John Hill.

affray for public circulation lest he offend one or the other of his patrons. Mrs. Manley, to whom he passed the chore (*A True Narrative of What Happened at the Examination of the Marquis of Guiscard at the Cockpit, the 8th of March, 1710–11*), contrived an ingenious narrative which left the reader uncertain whether the animus of Guiscard was against Harley or St. John (*cf.* Swift, *Journal to Stella,* Temple Scott's edition, pp. 137, 159; subsequent references are to this edition of that work). Boyer, no friend to St. John, had another explanation of the supposed animus against the Secretary of State. The latter, having previously shared Guiscard's pleasures, now not only assumed the rôle of chief examiner but denied a request for private conference as well, thus incurring the enmity of the accused. This scarcely supports the *Examiner's* explanation that Harley suffered as the next friend of St. John (*Political State,* I. 269ff.; *Annals of Anne,* IX. 331ff.). Peter Wentworth's story reported second hand from Argyll that St. John ran Guiscard "thro' the belly," the latter having intended an attack on St. John "who had used him very ill, as had the Duke of Marlborough" (Cartwright, *Wentworth Papers,* pp. 185f.).

Rochester had wanted to stop it after the Emperor's death, but St. John insisted, and it had gone. Chiefly it would mean a waste of funds. And peace was further off than St. John thought unless Marlborough could be won to help. The Duke was still supreme on the Continent.

The Queen had sent Raby, the heir of the Wentworths, to The Hague to replace Townshend, but the Dutch liked him not. He lacked a competent secretary. St. John had cumbered him with Harrison, a writer of piffling verse, a relative for whom something had to be done, since he was failing to hold the town's attention with the *Tatler*. John Drummond could deal with the Dutch—not so well with Raby—but his work was unofficial.

None of the appointments to the Continent had turned out well. Rivers had helped little in Hanover; less in Holland. Orrery in the Spanish Netherlands merely replaced Marlborough and Cadogan with a friend. The sending of Peterborough to Vienna ought at least to have brought relief from an unsettling influence at home, but that temperamental peer had scampered about Europe regardless of his instructions and was now back in London. All and sundry were the Queen's suitors. Raby and Orrery would be earls. Rivers wanted more money to squander. The Duke of Hamilton had fixed his heart on an English title, which would open another Pandora's box.

More recently St. John had organized a childish club. A dozen or more youths and hangers-on dined with him every week, planets for whom he played the sun. The discerning would laugh at an imitation of the Kit-Cat Club. There was none in England the match of Tonson's group. A lesser club —its members soon affected to call it a "society" to avoid the comparison—in the same pattern confessed envy, exposing a wounded vanity better hid. It looked almost like St. John was trying to make a party for himself. Ormond was of his club; also, Swift.

Something must be done for that proud parson. He had returned a bank note sent with great good will. He would not be chaplain to the Earl of Oxford's family or any other.

Journalists were too scarce to spare him yet. The ministers managed a majority of his dinners, but that would not suffice. A queer dog. No matter how lightly the cloth hung, there was that about a parson beyond a layman's ken. Swift was a master of words. But he had to be supplied with matter and could not control his feelings. Quick to attack, as easy to wound; he found no comfort in the give and take of weekly writing. His *Examiners* would not last. A collection of them might be published to excuse the subscription of a few hundred pounds for their author.

Defoe was more useful, though with different folk. Luckily, Godolphin had left him on the payroll of the Queen. Less skilled with words, he had ideas. He had helped with the South Sea Company, with Scotland, and with Dissenters. None knew better what was stirring in England. His attitudes were so right that a few hints enabled him to steer his own course. An odd thing that these two, so different in temper, should enlist under the same minister. More curious still, Defoe understood Swift's ability to help; Swift had only contempt for Defoe. The priest was personal in his thoughts; the other had a broader view. The irony of convention and circumstance sent the abler man up the back stairs to consult in the dark, while the parson sat before the family fire. In the hurry of his new greatness Oxford had lately overlooked Defoe's remittance; he must remedy that neglect.

He would soon need every influence that he could bring to bear. His opponents had drawn swords and would neither give nor take quarter. Lacking superior cunning, he must oppose blow with blow. To foresee their strategy was easier than to meet it. More than any other single man, he had helped to clear the way for the Hanoverian family to reach the throne. Now he was to be misrepresented as a friend of the Pretender. He had not invited the support of Jacobites; their own blindness closed their eyes to what he meant. He much preferred the help of moderate men, but he could not yet afford to alienate any who came with votes.

Hitherto he had steered a middle course. By subterfuge, he had postponed the Church's claims. Every formal statement by Queen and Parliament had referred to Hanover. The Church was still afraid of Rome; therefore the Pretender's religion barred his way. But hereditary right and non-resistance, the doctrines on which he depended to support his claim, were fetiches dear to churchmen's hearts. These doctrines were defended in the *Examiner,* though anathema to readers of Defoe. By keeping Marlborough in Flanders, the Queen kept the support of many proud of his achievements there. Assured of the coöperation of Marlborough and Hanover—perhaps of one or the other—the ministry was safe.

There was an opening for peace which could not be neglected without belying the noise made against the previous ministry. Nevertheless, a separate negotiation with France, if known, risked the loss of both Hanover and the Duke, a prospect Oxford feared. Ten years of successful war had made France the national enemy, and the French King had declared openly for the Pretender. Opposing leaders, if the Lord Treasurer knew them, would ring the changes on *Pretender, Popery, France.* The storm might not be easy to live through.

On his side was the Queen. More correctly, he was the channel through whom she chose to act. Even on that point there was uncertainty. He had won her confidence in part by inculcating jealousy of her prerogative. That feeling, once aroused, did not subside. She was critical of advice, reluctant to yield again freedom of will it had cost so much to get. This had to be concealed from his own followers. His strength with them and Parliament depended in part on their belief that Anne gave him her confidence. The Sacheverell debates had convinced her that her right was not "divine," but she was apt to balk at unimportant little things, necessary parts of any leader's daily grist. Her management required patience, and he must go to Windsor on the morrow.

Swift had only been to Windsor once. He was to go several times again that summer. When Oxford first took him in July it was so suddenly he had not time to get a change of linen and borrowed a shirt from St. John to go "to court." His delight was childlike. "Windsor," he wrote to Stella, "is a delicious place. I never saw it before except for an hour seventeen years ago." Meantime, in his little room in Chelsea near Dean Atterbury's, whence for "exercise" he walked to town daily, he wrote as Harley or more often St. John wished. He quit Chelsea "for good" early in July, moving to a modest place in Suffolk Street. With Harley and St. John both away, he "sent to an ale house" for dinner or picked up "a hedge acquaintance in the City." More often he went to Mrs. Vanhomrigh's, where dwelt Vanessa.

Sometimes he despaired, remembering wistfully his willows at Laracor. The reflected grandeur he enjoyed might prove to be his chief reward. He boasted pleasure in scorning coffeehouses and the society of Addison and Steele or other friends of humbler days and in his invitations to the tables of the great. At Windsor he was gleeful on dining at the Green Cloth. Later he affected snobbish privacy in smaller groups. In honester moments he knew that his influence was successful chiefly when seconding motions others made. On his solicitation, St. John had appointed Harrison, his own kinsman, to The Hague. As yet he could not bring himself to ask outright the thing he wished, though he confessed it openly to Peterborough. He envied Atterbury, about to be transferred from Carlisle to Christ Church, Oxford, which he mistakenly thought would be "a warm, quiet deanery." He aspired to such another in England for himself, not an exorbitant ambition for one whose patrons ruled the state.

Daniel Defoe had a family to support, enemies to avoid, a country to serve. He used his ability and resources in each day's work, vainly hoping that the next sun would rise on better things. The renewal of his remittances heartened him. He sent written suggestions, asking now and then a "personal conference" to receive "hints . . . in public matters" for his "direction." For the moment he dwelt on Scotland and tended to magnify a tempest in a teapot occasioned by a Jacobite medal which the Duchess of Gordon presented to the Edinburgh Faculty of Advocates. He meditated also upon the possibility of profit from South Sea commerce, not an easy attainment without the privilege of trade with Spanish colonies.

Henry St. John was in his element that year. Peace was to

be made, and he was Secretary of State. Dartmouth scarcely counted. A kindly veil obscured the defeat of future hopes in another generation that he had to live. None dreamed that thus early he approached the pinnacle of his career. Louis XIV was to be outwitted. Marlborough was to be ditched. A halting Lord Treasurer and a hesitant Queen were to be moved to act. Terms were to be imposed upon the Emperor and the Dutch. Rewards would come to friends; humiliation, to his enemies. There would be time withal for fleeting pleasures of the flesh.[8]

Early in July Prior went secretly to France to get an authentic statement of the terms on which Louis would make peace. Through the Earl of Jersey an opening had been made before. Responsible statesmen understood that the death of the Emperor had changed the outlook. But deaths in the family of Louis made it less easy to leave Philip on the Spanish throne. For his part, Louis guessed that the English ministers were almost as anxious for peace as himself and sent Mesnager back with Prior to negotiate.

Prior had scarcely reached Paris when Oxford, returning from Windsor to London, learned that Newcastle, "the man in the world" he "most entirely loved," had fallen from a horse. News of his death followed soon. Later came word of the will by which the dead hand had defeated Oxford's hope that his own son as husband of the heiress might attain to the title of her father. Something might be rescued from the wreck. Though a nephew, young Thomas Pelham, got most of the estate, the daughter was still a tempting match.

The private aspect of the incident had to wait. The Privy Seal was vacant, another office to make enemies of disappointed aspirants. The Church party had to be pleased. Nottingham's claims were canvassed again and passed by. The Earl of Jersey was fixed upon in spite of reputed assistance

---

[8] Ball, *Correspondence of Swift*, I. 244ff.; Swift, *Journal to Stella*, pp. 114, 132, 164ff., 184, 194ff., 271; [Robert Walpole], *The Debts of the Nation Stated and Considered; Thirty-five Millions Accounted for;* Hist. Mss. Com., *Portland*, IV. 675ff.; V. 4ff.; *Bath*, I. 199ff.; Parke, *Bolingbroke Correspondence*, I. 110, 125, 246ff.; Lee, *Defoe*, I. 178ff.; Defoe, *An Essay upon the South Sea Trade;* Boyer, *Political State*, II. 97ff.

with the warming pan when, as it was alleged, Anne acquired
a half-brother and Britain a claimant to the crown. The Earl
defended himself from the taint of Jacobitism charged against
him. His death (August 26) resolved the matter the day he
would have got the seal.

Three days later Oxford proposed the health of the unan-
nounced official, and Prior, home from France, made the pun
that it was "so privy he knew not who it was." Swift and
other ministerial hangers-on were surprised the following
morning to find the place bestowed on John Robinson, Bishop
of Bristol. The moderates, it was hoped, would like one of
their number. Churchmen would be glad to see a bishop have
the place. Dartmouth reported from Windsor that the Queen
was cheerful, talking of nothing but the new minister.

Intrigues both public and private made it ridiculous to try
to keep Prior's trip a secret either in London or The Hague.
Rumors were soon abroad and published in the press. St. John
began as soon a campaign to defend the ministers from the
charge of partiality to France. Abel Roper's triweekly *Postboy* printed cleverly phrased dispatches in the guise of news
from The Hague. Early in September Swift published *A New
Journey to Paris* in the same cause. Purporting to be a narrative by Prior's French valet, it no longer made a mystery of
the trip. Both the pamphlet and the paragraphs in the *Postboy* apprised the public that negotiations had begun and that
terms might be expected soon. Swift made also a sly attack
on Marlborough.

Care was taken to rebut the charge that England sought a
separate peace. A more revealing point, and one the ministers' opponents were quick to see, was the method of the
negotiation. With Anne and Louis agreeing in advance, England's allies would have little to soothe their disappointments
if the Queen should not approve all of their demands.

The records contained so much against Philip and the
Spanish throne that this remained a major issue. Oxford and
St. John had obtained a vote from Parliament suspending
previous resolutions, but they knew what to expect from their
allies abroad and enemies at home. They had to be sure of

themselves before making this retreat from England's earlier position, though it had been clearly foreseen and foreshadowed in the *Examiner* since the Emperor's death.

Early in September a new triweekly appeared against Roper, the *Protestant Postboy*, its name a proof of its animus. Boyer was soon in the field with a pamphlet tracing St. John's hand in the *Postboy* and imputing to Swift the account of Prior's trip. The last author he described by name as a man of "Ambiguous and Contradictory" character, in whom "Ambition" was "predominant," swaying "all his other Passions" and directing "all his Designs." "He is this Day a Whig," the writer said, "and the next a Tory; Haughty and Stiff with most Men, Cringing and Obsequious with those in Power." A victim with a tougher hide might have wished to "Swinge" one who attacked him thus. Count Gallas, representing the Emperor, having now for a year behaved more as a minister from his king to the opposition than to the Queen, protested to St. John concerning the paragraphs in the *Postboy*. Roper was taken up and examined, but nothing more.

As the negotiations with Louis went on the Dutch were informed, though by agreement with them Marlborough was at first left ignorant. Suspecting that England might privily intend advantages at the expense of her allies, the Dutch pretended no enthusiasm. In fact, when shown some of the preliminary papers, Shrewsbury confessed, "there is something in them looks so like bargaining for yourselves apart and leaving your friends to shift at a general treaty, that I am confirmed the exposing such a paper (as it will be in the power of France to do) may create secret jealousy and complaint from the allies." But the ministers kept on. St. John advised Harrison at The Hague, when talked to privately, to say that Anne was "Queen of Britain, and that the interests" of that "island" were not "any longer to be deemed the property of other people." By September 27 Mesnager was ready to sign an agreement, *ex parte* in form, leaving England free to represent it as merely the basis for treating at a general congress later to be held.

Having fought with his usual success in Flanders, Marlborough proposed in July a campaign for that summer and the following winter which he hoped might win the war. Oxford's prompt remittances and the steps taken to complete Blenheim gratified him. He could not "expect" or the Lord Treasurer give "greater assurances and proofs" of "friendship." Stair went to London to explain the new program. Another messenger announced (July 27) that Marlborough had passed the enemy's lines preliminary to the siege of Bouchain.

St. John ordered the Tower guns to be fired on the night of September 11, announcing the surrender of the place. He hoped the Duke's friends would not allege an attempt to "ridicule," as had been the case when the lines were passed. But the plan for a sustained offensive went slowly in spite of Oxford's help. Dutch reluctance made the Duke despair. St. John thought it of "some use to have my Lord Marlborough's confession" to that effect. Perhaps the Dutch had grounds to hesitate. Raby, now Earl of Strafford, interrupted his honeymoon and went to Holland (October 2), instructed to enlist the approval of the States-General for the preliminaries just signed.

The *Examiner* was suspended after July 26 in deference to Marlborough's sensitiveness to criticism. The *Medleys* were interrupted two weeks later. Oxford finally summarized for the Duke (September 5) the progress made in the negotiation. Acknowledging this courtesy from his camp before Bouchain twelve days later, Marlborough added that "nothing in the world" would please him more than to help in making "such a peace" as might be "to the satisfaction of her Majesty and the good of the country." Lord Jersey's death reminded him that life was short. He craved a "speedy end of the war" in order that he might "enjoy a little repose."

This communication from the Lord Treasurer he later acknowledged again as a "singular mark" of Oxford's courtesy. Friends might say otherwise, but they misunderstood his "sentiments." He wished "nothing upon earth . . . more than an end of the war." "Her Majesty has not a subject that desires it more heartily than I do," he went on. "I am perfectly convinced that, besides draining our nation both of men and money almost to the last extremity, our allies do by degrees so shift the burthen of the war upon us, that, at the rate they go on, the whole charge must at last fall on England."

Despite efforts to soothe Marlborough's wounded feelings, neither side neglected appeals to the public. The Duke's own Chaplain, though denying it to his patron, published two pamphlets. Mrs. Manley replied to both. She worked under the supervision of Swift, now a sort of liaison man between St. John and the printers and booksellers. For a man of his spirit, it was a thankless task. He resented time lost cooling his heels at the convenience of the Secretary of State or the Lord Treasurer to get information, as he put it, to do their "business." [4]

Agreement with France assured, Harley and St. John were active preparing the public mind. Early in October came Defoe's able *Reasons why the Nation ought to put a Speedy End to this Expensive War; with a brief Essay at the Probable Conditions on which the Peace now Negotiating may be founded; also an Enquiry into the Obligations Britain lies under to the Allies; and how far she is obliged not to make Peace without them.* His audience was not yet ready for this strong doctrine. Hindered by enemies, he complained in a fortnight of the uncertainty of his ground, Oxford meantime having been too busy for a conference. If it was desired, he might be "yet able to conquer the obstinacy of a hot deluded

---

[4] G. M. Trevelyan, *The Peace and the Protestant Succession,* pp. 176ff.; "The Jersey Period of the Negotiations Leading to the Peace of Utrecht," *English Historical Review,* XLIX. 100ff.; L. G. Wickham Legg, *Matthew Prior,* pp. 149ff.; Hist. Mss. Com., *Portland,* V. 34ff., 69ff., 84ff., 95f.; *Bath,* I. 204ff.; S. H. Nulle, *Thomas Pelham-Holles, Duke of Newcastle,* pp. 12ff.; Swift, *Journal to Stella,* pp. 233, 260, 270ff.; Boyer, *Political State,* II. 153ff., 203ff.; *An Account of the State and Progress of the Present Negotiations for Peace;* Parke, *Bolingbroke Correspondence,* I. 266ff., 337ff., 362ff; Coxe, *Marlborough,* III. 438ff.; [Francis Hare], *Bouchain; or, a Dialogue between the Medley and the Examiner; The Charge of God to Joshua; in a Sermon Preached before his Grace, the Duke of Marlborough, September 9, 1711, being the Day of Thanksgiving for Passing the Lines and Taking Bouchain;* [Mrs. Manley], *A New Vindication of the Duke of Marlborough; an Answer to a Pamphlet lately Published called Bouchain &c; A Learned Comment upon Dr. Hare's Excellent Sermon.* Temple Scott agrees with Sir Walter in attributing the last item to Swift, but see Hist. Mss. Com., *Portland,* V. 95f., where Mrs. Manley claims authorship in an appeal for help.

party and at least take off the edge of that venomous spirit that" had "infected them." Within two weeks, in a different temper, he offered *Armageddon; or, the Necessity of Carrying on the War, if such a Peace cannot be obtained as may render Europe safe and Trade secure.* Still in London, Mesnager sent him an hundred pistoles for the first piece, learning later that he wasted money, the author being "in the service of the state." Boyer recognized the second pamphlet as the work of a "Treasury Volunteer." Defoe himself said later that Oxford's honest judgment at this time was that the war would last another year.

Swift boasted to Stella (October 10) his resolution to "ply the rogues warm" and to "have an answer" whenever "anything of theirs" made a "noise." Opponents kept him busy. He "sent and caused to be sent three pamphlets out in a fortnight." In the *Postboy* Roper began gradually to lead up to particulars "GLORIOUS and AVANTAGEOUS to the Nation and ALL the ALLIES." But Count Gallas rudely interrupted his plan by publishing in the *Daily Courant* (October 13) the draft of the preliminaries given to him for the Emperor. Anne declined further business with the Count, and St. John summoned fourteen booksellers and printers before the Queen's Bench to answer the charge of libel.

To humor Swift, Boyer was one, which caused him, in his account of the trial, to vindicate himself from the "pitiful Reflections of a Shameless and most Contemptible Turncoat whose Tongue" was "as *Swift* to revile as his *Mind*" was "*Swift* to change." "After all," he complained, "the Paragraph that bore hardest upon the *Weathercocke Parson* was in a Manner forc'd upon the Author by a Reputed Favourite of the Great Minister," presumably Defoe.

Unless all signs failed, the proposed peace would need defenders when Parliament met. Marlborough's attitude was not yet clear. He did not, he assured the Earl of Albemarle, "envy those . . . in the secret of what" was "now doing," though "heartily" wishing that it might "be for the best." Abandoning his projected campaign, he was coming home to recuperate his health. Anne herself was laid up with gout.

Oxford had another attack of gravel and trouble with his joints. Mrs. Masham was away in the late summer and early autumn for a confinement, from which she did not recover in her normal time. St. John wrestled with the Dutch, who were in no hurry to accept the preliminaries as the basis for a congress to make peace. He waited hopefully for delayed packets in mid-November.

They came at last and brought the news desired. They brought also Marlborough, and Baron Bothmer from the Elector of Hanover as well. Anne, having "this business of the Peace soe much at hart," was wondering in early November what she should say "when the Duke of Marlborough com's." Oxford, foreseeing that the Duke might require severe measures, prepared the way. The Queen thought the news of alleged misapplication of funds "something prodigious." When his Grace arrived in a critical mood, both she and her ministers were ready for the event.

There was need for action. London coffee-houses roared against the ministry. St. John, complaining of "villainous endeavours" to spoil the negotiations, pinned his hope on country members. Marlborough reached Greenwich amid a hubbub at a proposed celebration of the anniversary of Elizabeth's accession said to be patronized by members of the Kit-Cat Club. There was to be a procession to a bonfire for burning wax effigies of the Devil, the Pope, the Pretender, and a few cardinals. Rumor gave Oxford's likeness to the Pope. The trained bands easily took the images from a vacant house. Swift set Mrs. Manley to propagate the view that "there was never a blacker design found, unless it were blowing up the Parliament House." Her pamphlet appeared the day the Queen returned (November 24) from Hampton Court to St. James's. Opposing journalists explained that they had "no other design" than for the figures to be "carried in procession and afterwards burnt with the like solemnity as was remarkably practised on the 17th of November, 1679, when the Nation was justly alarm'd with a *Popish* Plot and a Popish Successor."

November 27, came a pamphlet destined to greater fame,

The Conduct of the Allies, and the Late Ministry, in Beginning and Carrying on the Present War. It made the point that the Church party had opposed the war from the start. England ought never to have entered it as a "principal." Her exertions should have been on the sea with restricted activities on land. Louis XIV would have recognized the Protestant succession without a war; he had acknowledged the Pretender only as a king, not as King of England. For ten years the nation had impoverished itself to enrich Marlborough and the monied men and to obtain undeserved advantages for the Emperor and the Dutch. The rôle of England's allies was almost more unfriendly than that of the French. This was strong doctrine, but something like it was needed in order to save the day.

The piece was recognized as the climax of the policy announced in St. John's *Letter to the Examiner,* and some attributed it to the Secretary of State. Others thought it to be by the same author as *Reasons why the Nation ought to Put a Speedy End to this Expensive War* [Defoe]. The writer claimed a confidential opportunity to know; he had delayed publication to the last minute. In fact, he had worked feverishly since it appeared that Marlborough would take a hostile part. The composition was a blend, St. John's thoughts translated into Swift's words. Foreseeing the probable need of the work, the Secretary of State had labored with the author for weeks in the summer as they went to and from Windsor or walked in pleasant avenues together there. He, Oxford, and others had carefully scanned the copy before it came out.

Speaking with manifest authority and coming at a critical juncture, this notable pamphlet was widely sold and read. So was a less conventional piece which appeared a week later. Following an audience with the Queen (November 27), Baron Bothmer, the next day, presented a memorial to the Secretary of State, which was published in the *Daily Courant* (December 5). Printed separately, it was sold by the thousands, appearing in one edition as a single sheet in order that it might be framed. A blast against the ministers and the preliminaries, it aligned Sophia for a time with their opponents.

Few felt the blow more keenly than Oxford. "Whoever advised that memorial," he said, "have given the succession a terrible wound, and we must do our best to calm the spirits of the people upon this head." But even before the memorial was published, Defoe had asked an interview to lay before him the "Madness and Rage" of his "enemies, and something also of the fears" of his "friends." His opponents were confident of "breaking all her Majesty's measures abroad." [5]

To the last Oxford knew not what to expect in the House of Lords when Parliament met (December 7). Ill, he had done his best, though querulous friends, unaware of his troubles, complained that he did no more. He had sounded Nottingham in mid-October to find that disgruntled peer surprised at the "honour"; though no "competent judge," accounts "in the prints" must be "imperfect," or the preliminaries were unsatisfactory. Poulett tried his hand in the same quarter with like success. The Lord was "sour and fiercely wild" as though having "lived long in a desert." Somerset reappeared at a cabinet in the summer, but withdrew again when St. John refused to sit with him. That Duke and his Duchess were now more at Windsor than the Secretary of State, and the Duke was recalcitrant in spite of Oxford's efforts to persuade him.

Scot peers complained of lack of attention in the previous year. They might not come to London till after Christmas. Some might be unable to come at all without financial help. The Duke of Hamilton, with proxies of the absent had also the patent of his English peerage, which would certainly cause a stir. Bromley thought that the House of Commons would accept the peace, but members were impatient to see both the punishment of those accused of "corruption" and "power"

---

[5] Boyer, *Political State*, II. 291ff., 389ff., 400ff., 418ff., 433ff.; Lee, *Defoe*, I. 186ff.; [Defoe], *White Staff*, Pt. III. pp. 48ff.; Hist. Mss. Com., *Portland*, V. 101f., 118f.; Bath, I. 212ff.; Swift, *Journal to Stella*, pp. 257f., 268, 278ff., 283ff.; Sir George Murray, *Letters and Dispatches of . . . Duke of Marlborough*, V. 563ff.; [Mrs. Manley], *A True Relation of the Several Facts and Circumstances on the Intended Riot and Tumult on Queen Elizabeth's Birthday . . . Published for the Information of all True Lovers of the Constitution in Church and State*, reprinted in Walter Scott's edition of Swift's *Works*, V. 399ff.; Coxe, *Marlborough*, III. 462ff.; Parke, *Bolingbroke Correspondence*, I. 477ff.

in the "hands of . . . friends." Learning of Nottingham's defection the day before Parliament met, Halifax confronted Oxford with the certainty of defeat.

On that decisive day Anne doffed her robe and returned to the chamber to hear the debate on her speech. Having less stomach for unpleasant scenes, Swift went to the City "on purpose to be out of the way." The time and place, the Queen said, had been fixed to treat of a "general peace," the Dutch concurring. Her own chief concern was that the "Protestant religion and the laws and liberties of these nations" might be "secured . . . by securing the succession to the Crown as . . . limited by Parliament to the house of Hanover." The best way to a successful negotiation was "to make early provision for the campaign." She earnestly counseled unanimity.

Nottingham proposed an amendment to the address, saying that "no Peace could be Safe or Honourable to Great Britain or Europe if Spain and the West Indies were allotted to any Branch of the House of Bourbon." Oxford made a point of order, which Buckingham overruled, and the floodgates could not be closed. Sunderland and Wharton supported Nottingham, a curious alliance of which the mystery was soon revealed. Anglesey on the other side repeated the stale charge that peace might have been made after Ramillies but for Marlborough's interest in prolonging the war. The Duke called upon the Queen and his former colleagues to witness his denial, but opposed the preliminaries. Cowper, Halifax, and Burnet supported the Duke. Shrewsbury and Buckingham said little in behalf of the ministry. The previous question was carried by a bare majority; the amendment, by a vote of 64 to 52. Somerset's voice against the ministry was loudest of them all, and the Queen selected him to lead her from the house. A similar amendment in the Commons was overwhelmingly lost.

A week later Nottingham's bill against occasional conformity disclosed the terms he made. Its easy passage through both houses is evidence of widespread fears that the policies of the ministers tended to bring the Pretender to the throne. The union of leaders as far apart as Nottingham on one side and Wharton and Sunderland on the other in favor of the Church and against France and the Jacobites revived memories of a similar alliance at the Revolution.

The Duke of Hamilton's hopes were disappointed by a majority of five. The cleavage was not the same as on the peace, but Scot peers were angry at what they regarded as a breach of the union. At a time when votes were needed, some of them would not attend.

In behalf of the Commissioners for Examining and Stating the Public Accounts, Lockhart (December 21) brought charges against Marlborough and asked that they be a special order for January 17. The next day that House adjourned to January 14 for the holidays. The Lords considered a bill to give the Electoral Prince precedence over all peers and addressed the Queen to preserve the unity of the allies. After the recess of the lower house, they adjourned only to January 2, allowing twelve days for further mischief before the Commons met.

The gleeful opposition was overpowering out of doors. Oxford craved a ballad on Nottingham's defection. Swift's *Excellent New Song, Being the Intended Speech of a Famous Orator against Peace* had as its refrain a none too brilliant pun alleging unjustly that the peer in question behaved thus because he was "Not-in-game." Roper went on with his papers. Publishers of the *Protestant Postboy* were committed to Newgate. Marlborough published a letter in his own defense; Hare, *A Defence of the Allies and the Late Ministry.* The Emperor expressed a belated desire that Eugene visit England to concert a new campaign. The ministers feared that he and Marlborough might rather become centers of demonstrations in London such as had been avoided November 17, and thus delayed the visit.

Christmas cheer was scant in ministerial circles. Halifax sent to Oxford, with greetings of the season, an offer of assistance, but doubted whether it would be of any use. St. John blamed his chief, alleging treachery also in the Queen. Such hangers-on as Swift and Lewis were frightened and in despair. The former, anxious for "security," asked St. John for a place abroad before the "change." Even Oxford, taxed for an explanation, answered with the quotation that the "hearts of Kings are unsearchable," which tended to confirm suspicions of his followers. It was the sort of crisis he labored to avert. Brought to face it, his stature was revealed as the first politician of the time.

Saturday night, December 28, before posting his weekly letter to Stella, Swift got an inkling of what was afoot. "Give me joy, sirrahs," he exulted. "This is written in a Coffeehouse." On New Year's Eve he moralized: "These are strong remedies; pray God the patient is able to bear them." His comment the next day reveals how little he understood: "The Queen and the Lord Treasurer mortally hate the Duke of Marlborough, and to that he owes his fall more than to his other faults; unless he has been tampering too far with his party." Then an involuntary second thought: "The world abroad will blame us. I confess my belief, that he has not one good quality in the world besides that of a general, and even that I have heard denied by several great soldiers. But we have had constant successes in arms while he commanded. Opinion is a mighty matter in war, and I doubt the French think it impossible to conquer an army that he leads, and our soldiers think the same; and how far even this step may encourage the French to play tricks with us, no one knows. I do not love to see personal resentment mix with public affairs."

Few of the Queen's servants bore Marlborough less personal resentment than Oxford. But his own fate and the future of the country seemed to be at stake. The allies were openly against him, and the Duke had taken their part. Merely to dismiss the great captain from all of his places (December 31) was not enough. He had to be discredited and his reputation destroyed as far as possible.

Anne agreed at the same time to call two new peers to the House of Lords by writ and to create ten more by letters patent. Among the ten were Oxford's son-in-law and Mrs. Masham's husband. Somerset and his Duchess were more difficult. The Queen insisted upon the latter. The Duke stipulated that he and his wife should both be either in or out.

But he relented after several weeks, and thus Anne kept the Duchess.

There was still talk of refusing to adjourn as the Queen requested when the House of Lords met, January 2, but the ministers had their will. Eugene landed four days later and received an official welcome in which Marlborough had no share. Oxford had time for breathing. But other treacherous crossings were ahead before he would be out of danger.[6]

[6] Hist. Mss. Com., *Portland*, V. 101ff., 133f.; VI. 131f.; *Parliamentary History*, VI. 1035ff.; Coxe, *Marlborough*, III. 469ff.; Cartwright, *Wentworth Papers*, pp. 220ff.; Swift, *Journal to Stella*, pp. 294ff., 308ff.; Ball, *Correspondence of Swift*, I. 312ff.; Boyer, *Political State*, II. 480ff.; Parke, *Bolingbroke Correspondence*, II. 48ff.

Chapter VI

A DESPERATE ENCOUNTER, 1712–1713

> The Principle which leads States Men to get into Places by any
> Means they can, leads them to make use of all possible Measures to
> keep themselves in Possession of that Power they got. . . . And if
> all the several Springs and Wheels, Engines and Arts, by which both
> the Parties wrought in the violent Opposing one another in these
> Things were known, they would appear equally unjustifiable and dis-
> honest. . . . It is evident, that neither Side could be said to stick
> at anything to offend or to defend.
>
> DEFOE in *The Secret History of the White Staff*.

OXFORD's defeat and recovery left his position both stronger
and weaker. He was on a better foot with Anne, who had to
choose between his advice and the loss of her ministers. But
his dream of support by moderate men was proving hopeless,
and he had little strength left to resist extremists in the
Church party. Nottingham's defection and the act against
occasional conformity cut the ground from under him, helping his opponents to identify his cause with that of the Pretender and to make the issue Hanover versus the Jacobites.
The loss of Marlborough made peace necessary. But the
treaty had to be favorable, or it would bring weakness at
home instead of strength. The Minister had to depend now
upon the good faith of France, and this very fact made him
liable to the charge of deserting the country's friends for its
enemies.

The Queen, the Church, peace, were the essential foundations of his power. He had to take the risk that Anne would
survive until peace was made and quiet followed, trying
meantime to divide his foes. They had recruited Marlborough
as a martyr to their cause. More important, they had captured
Hanover for the time and were strong with monied classes in

the City. That meant as well a capacity to make a noise with the London populace, which counted heavily in politics. Oxford's strongest weapon was the Church, but this with him would be a last resort. Experience showed that an aroused Church scarcely promoted quiet. In fact, everything turned on the Queen. Having little hope in that quarter, his opponents could disregard her feelings, which made them free to choose their ground. Thus handicapped, he had to press for immediate victory, while they could stand a siege.

"I have seen many of these Court Revolutions," Defoe wrote four days before Parliament met, "but of all the outed Parties that ever were seen, at least in the last fifty Years, none ever pushed with so much Fury at the Government who have dismissed them as these have done; nothing but downright taking Arms can be like this, and I am persuaded that only Want of Power restrains from the worst sort of Violence." That the ministers held on, St. John felt, was owing to their "own unshaken firmness" and "the loyalty of the Church interest, which even ill usage could not alienate." "We have struggled this winter," he said, "through inconceivable difficulties in opposition to a powerful faction at home, to all our allies and even the successor himself abroad; and I may say, we have combated an habit of thinking falsely, which men have been used to for twenty years."

In prospect was a grueling year. After a vigorous start at home, the ministers steadily lost ground, partly because of the snail's pace of the negotiations. Spring revived for Swift the thoughts of Laracor. He would not postpone his return to the end of the session, expected by the last of April, if his patrons would excuse him before. But autumn found him still trying to make "a paragraph for the *Post-Boy* . . . malicious as possible, and very proper for Abel Roper, the printer of it." The impatient St. John chafed at delays which subdued his hopes. The imperturbable Oxford and the Queen furnished most of the ballast for the ministerial vessel in the storm.

The ministers were reluctant to accord to Marlborough the full crown of martyrdom, but his friends demanded vindication, and the Church party in the House of Commons was let loose. As a preliminary step, Walpole was expelled from the House and sent to the Tower. St. John wished a peerage, and Bromley was a poor substitute. As the current joke went, " 'twas necessary to kill his Bull Dog" before tackling the master. Swift commented on Walpole's fate that it would be "a leading card to maul the Duke of Marlborough for the same crime"; and so it proved.

Condemning as "unwarrantable and illegal" deductions from the Quartermaster's funds, the House wished an accounting also of those from the pay of foreign troops and requested the Queen to take steps for redress. Townshend and others who had negotiated the Barrier Treaty with the Dutch in 1709 were voted "enemies to the Queen and the Kingdom." Cardonnel, Marlborough's secretary, was expelled from the House for conduct described as "unwarrantable and corrupt." To strengthen Anne's hands for dealing with the Dutch, the House voted and made public a composition of Sir Thomas Hanmer, St. John, and Swift entitled *A Representation of the Commons to the Queen on the War with Spain, the Barrier Treaty, and the State of the Nation.*

The new Lord Privy Seal went to Utrecht as Strafford's colleague. Long residence in Sweden gave him knowledge of affairs in northern Europe. The situation at court made it as well to have a churchman in lay office at a distance from the Queen. Neither he nor Strafford was the ablest diplomat of the time, and they worked poorly as a team. To hasten action, Thomas Harley was dispatched in February to call at The Hague and Utrecht, but more especially to complain in Hanover of the behavior of Bothmer, to begin where "Rivers left off" and give assurances that the Queen and her ministers were favorable to that house and that its interest in the "succession" was "sacrificed to that of a party."

The Scot peers had to be humored. Defoe had warned Oxford in the previous summer that they were "an odd kind of people, to say no more of them." "Episcopal in judgment," they were not on good terms with the "generality," who adhered to the "kirk" and who were the bulwarks of the Queen's strength. The defeat of the Duke of Hamilton's peerage united his colleagues and some members of the Commons in a demand that the Anglican Church be tolerated in Scotland and that lay patronage be restored. Members of the Church party in England were anxious to help their brethren in the "northern part of Britain," and Oxford had to yield, exerting himself through Defoe and his old friend, William Carstares, to induce clergymen in the established Church of Scotland to accept the inevitable after sending a "Representation" against it.

Swift, Defoe, Roper, and others were busy all the while. Mrs. Manley was too ill to help much. Swift's *Advice Humbly Offer'd to the Members of the October Club from a Person of Honour* in January diplomatically blamed the Queen for Oxford's mishap, indulging in mild criticism of the Lord Treasurer in the tone of St. John. At least, the Church party had more to hope for from the ministers than from their opponents. Oxford would now "be in earnest, after the united and avowed endeavours of the whole party to strike directly at his head." He had hesitated in the past owing to a lack of "that power . . . thought due to his station"; wanting it, he desired the "reputation of it, without which he neither could preserve the dignity, nor hardly go through the common business of his place." In this "difficult case," he had sometimes to "preserve his credit by forbearing" what was "in his power, for fear of discovering what" was not.

These revelations were too true to be wholly pleasing to the Lord Treasurer, and the author took care in concealing his hand. Neither he nor Oxford relished St. John's malicious reading of the pamphlet in their hearing, though Swift boasted, "I carried the matter very well." He was disappointed that the piece did not sell. Apologetics seldom do.[1]

His patrons were served better by *Some Reasons to Prove that No Person is obliged by his Principles as a Whig to Oppose her Majesty or her Present Ministry*, which appeared in June. It made the point that the issue was between "peace"

---

[1] Hist. Mss. Com., *Portland*, V. 82ff., 137, 139, 147ff.; Parke *Bolingbroke Correspondence*, II. 89ff., 160; Swift, *Journal to Stella*, pp. 320ff., 359, 395; *Parliamentary History*, VI. 1067ff., 1126ff.; Cartwright, *Wentworth Papers*, pp. 253ff.; *Lockhart Papers*, I. 345ff.

and "war," the "last" and the "present ministry"; not between Hanover and the Pretender, as the opposition said. One not likely to get office under either faction was better off as things stood than he would be under the government of men who sought power by "stirring up the City," by "inciting the foreign ministers to direct the Queen in the choice of her servants," by "infusing jealousies into the next heir," by efforts to "blast the credit of the nation," and "by using weekly papers to revile persons in the highest employments." In the following month *A Letter from the Pretender to a Whig Lord* was an effort to attach the stigma of Jacobitism to the friends of the peer addressed by name (Wharton). Godolphin, Marlborough, and his Duchess were said to be as "devoted" to the Pretender as to the Whigs.[2]

The Conduct of Parties in England, more especially those Whigs who now Appear against the new Ministry and the Treaty of Peace supplemented Defoe's work in the *Review*. He took the part of the Kirk against the Scot peers without waiting for Oxford's approval. In May he published *The Present State of Parties in Great Britain; Particularly an Enquiry into the State of the Dissenters in England and the Presbyterians in Scotland*. About the same time came *The Miserable Case of Poor England fairly Stated . . . or the most powerful and convincing Reasons why the Elector, the Dutch, and the Rest of the Allies, the late Ministry, and the Lower Church are against Making a general Peace with France; and all the main Objections in Opposition to it fairly answered*. Some of the arguments in *The Conduct of the Allies* were translated into more concrete facts and figures. It was "written without doors," the author told Oxford, "for the use of those chiefly" who knew "nothing but without doors."

The volume of the *Review* for that year went on longer than usual in the expectation that the paper would cease when the tax on the press took effect. In what was intended to be the last number (July 29), Defoe considered in retrospect his efforts during the previous eight years to defend "truth and

---

[2] The identification of persons and situations in notes to this pamphlet by the editors of Swift's works are not always to be relied upon.

liberty." With encouragement from Oxford he gladly went on for another year. In his homely figure when he finally laid it down, the *Review* was his "Whore." He was grateful for freedom in writing it. "What I approve I defend," he said in the preface to the eighth volume; "what I dislike I censure without any Respect of Persons." When the Lord Treasurer, commenting on this preface, asked him to go on, the journalist was effusive:

Whatever you have done for me, you never yet so much as intimated (though ever so remotely) that you expected from me the least bias in what I should write, or that her Majesty's bounty to me was intended to guide my opinion. . . . This fills me with peace under all their Clamour, that I serve a master who scorns the service of a mercenary conscience, and who at the same time that he does me good, leaves me full liberty to obey the dictates of my own principles. . . . I make this acknowledgment with thankfulness to your Lordship, and as a testimony to your past goodness to me, that you never laid the least injunction on me of one kind or other to write this or that in any case whatever.

Roper's triweekly thrusts at his rivals, the *Flying Post* and the *Protestant Postboy,* were in the form of real or feigned news items designed to serve the will of St. John. The *Examiner* still spoke, though Swift insisted in a feebler tone since he seldom wrote for it. Charles Leslie offered *National Reflections upon the Present Debate about Peace and War.* Even Anne's physician, John Arbuthnot, caught the fever and published in turn *Law is a Bottomless Pit; John Bull in his Senses; An Appendix to John Bull in his Senses; Lewis Baboon turns Honest;* and *John Bull's Pollicies and the Proposal for Printing a very Curious Discourse in two Volumes,* . . . *a Treatise on the Art of Political Lying &c.* He was a member of St. John's club, now revived, but not so flourishing as before. An illustration of his humor was the disguise of the Bourbon family name as "Baboon." The Dutch were "Nic Frog." England was "John Bull," a happy characterization, lacking which the piece might not have outlived the puffs of Swift and other friends of the author in the court circle.

It entertained more than it influenced the readers that it won.

Perhaps it reflected a state of mind in St. John's group. John Bull "understood his business very well; but no man alive was more careless in looking into his accounts, or more cheated by partners, apprentices, and servants. . . . Nic Frog was a cunning, sly whoreson, quite the reverse of John in many particulars." Marlborough as "Hocus" was "an old cunning attorney who enticed Bull into a lawsuit"; namely, the war, much to the embarrassment of his purse. In fact, "a good swinging sum of John's readiest cash went towards the building of Hocus's country house." And so the story went, until Bull and Frog fell out and parted company. Said Bull in the end, "I am so busy in packing up my goods, that I have no time to talk with you longer."

That end came in early autumn, when the Duke of Ormond, who had succeeded Marlborough as British commander in Flanders, refused to help Eugene in an attack on the French. St. John dispatched (May 10) "the Queen's positive command" to "avoid engaging in any siege or hazarding a battle" until further notice. This order was known to the French command, but Ormond was to keep it from his allies. He complained to Oxford in a fortnight that he could "make no more excuses for delaying entering into action" and was "very impatient to hear what" he might "own" and "do." St. John solaced him (May 17) that "True glory results from obeying the Prince one serves punctually, and promoting the interest of one's country steadily, in preference to all other considerations of private honour or advantage." Ten days later final orders were again postponed. Meantime the embarrassed Duke might take part in the "siege of Quesnay" after first "sending a trumpet to the Marechal Villars" notifying that he would. Within another four or five days he would have word whether further "action" would be necessary.

A day before the last notice was sent the public learned through the *Flying Post* that Ormond, when requested to co-operate with his allies, showed an order from the Queen not to "fight or undertake a siege." Defoe informed Oxford that this news stirred a "mighty popular clamour" and did "much mischief." If true, he thought the order justified "by the con-

duct of the Dutch, the Imperialists, and other Confederates."
He undertook to say something "without doors" to "take off all
the edge of the popular surprise some people" thought they
had "raised in the nation and turn all the mischief against
themselves." He called his pamphlet *Reasons Against Fighting, Being an Enquiry into the Great Debate, whether it is Safe
for her Majesty or her Ministry to Venture an Engagement
with the French, Considering the Present Behaviour of the
Allies.*

Both houses of Parliament considered the subject. The
Commons by a large majority voted confidence in the Queen.
Halifax, who moved the question in the Lords (May 27), had
doubted since the first of the year Oxford's "power to save the
nation." The Lord Treasurer was confident that Ormond had
followed instructions, but declined to say what the instructions
were. The prospect of an early peace made a fight imprudent.
Nevertheless, while refraining from a general action, he felt
that the Commander would give assistance in a siege, "orders
having been sent to him for that purpose."

In fact, these orders were dated the day of the debate and
were sent after it took place. Marlborough could not help
wondering what a siege would be like that did not risk a battle.
In the course of the debate, Poulett accused that Duke of using troops recklessly in order to "fill his pockets" by selling the
commissions of slain officers. The prospect of an early peace
enabled the ministers to carry the question, but Marlborough
sent Lord Mohun with a challenge to his accuser. More reluctant to use his sword than he had been to use his tongue, Poulett
permitted his wife to suggest that Dartmouth intervene by the
Queen's authority to stop the duel.[3]

The death within a year of three dauphins of France, leaving
a single, sickly infant between Philip of Anjou and the French
crown, did not smooth the way to peace. If Philip was to keep
Spain, it was hard to be sure that he would not get France also.
Faced with a choice between the crown he wore and the pros-

---

[3] Lee, *Defoe*, I. 194ff.; *Somers Tracts*, XIII. 295ff.; Hist. Mss. Com., *Portland*, V. 176f., 180, 212ff.; *Dartmouth*, p. 309; George A. Aitken, *The Life and
Works of John Arbuthnot;* Parke, *Bolingbroke Correspondence*, II. 319ff.;
341ff.; *Parliamentary History*, VI. 1135ff.; Coxe, *Marlborough*, III. 506ff.

pect of the other, he preferred the one in hand, renouncing for its sake that of his grandfather. Anne was thus finally able (June 6) to tell her Parliament "upon what terms a general peace" might be made. She had omitted nothing in her efforts to "procure for all" her "allies" what was "due to them by treaties" and "necessary for their security." But the thing she had "nearest at heart," "the assuring of the Protestant succession as by law established in the House of Hanover," she had taken "particular care" not only to have "acknowledged in the strongest terms, but to have an additional security, by the removal of that person out of the domains of France who" had "pretended to disturb this settlement."

For these and other reasons recited in the speech, British armies in Flanders thenceforth refrained from the war, and Dunkirk was occupied as a hostage for French good faith. When Continental troops subsidized by the British remained with Eugene to fight, their pay was stopped. Thus ended England's active part in the war which William and Marlborough began. St. John warned Hill, who went from England to occupy Dunkirk, that Ormond "could not be in a very good humour." There was little reason for pride in the part he had had to play.

Though both houses of Parliament thanked the Queen, Marlborough said bluntly in the Lords, "that the measures pursued in England for a year past were directly contrary to her Majesty's engagements with her allies, sullied the triumphs and glories of her reign, and would render the English name odious to all other nations." Strafford, at home for the debate, alleged that by "secret correspondence" the Duke discouraged the Dutch from making peace. Godolphin objected to the proposed sacrifice of the Portuguese trade in the prospect of one with France. But the normal desire for peace after a long war moved a majority of the peers to approve. Parliament was adjourned (June 21) to await a further word from Utrecht. It was prorogued July 8, releasing Walpole from the Tower. The negotiations dragged, and there were eleven prorogations before the two houses met again for business.

To strengthen their position, the ministers obtained addresses in favor of the proposed peace, most of them containing a specific reference to "the Protestant Succession in the House of Hanover." These addresses were described at the time as "Compliments, owing to the Prevalency of Party . . . for the most Part, procured by the Friends and Arguments of the Ministry in order to justify any Counsel and Measures which the latter" had "resolved to pursue." But the labor of getting the documents framed, voted, and presented committed to the cause the men entrusted with these tasks, ministered to their vanity, and capitalized their prestige in the ministry's behalf. Any party in power could obtain addresses when it wished, but they were testimony of its strength and tonic for supporters.

The opposition labored through these months to convince the country that the purpose was to sacrifice the allies to France and bring in the Pretender. They conjured with the name of Marlborough and the pride in victories he had won. His Duchess, it was said, entertained lavishly at St. Albans under army tents erected on their lawn. Pamphlets were dispersed. Walpole wrote in his own defense and in favor of the Dutch. His constituents at Lynn had reëlected him. His *Short History of this Parliament*, printed in great secrecy, was a sharp attack on his opponents. The *Flying Post*, the *Protestant Postboy*, and the revived *Medley* made habitually the same appeals. Even the *Spectator* had its fling before the end of the year.

Steele and Addison had conducted this daily since March, 1711, in an effort to amuse themselves and entertain the town amid the noise of politics. Their friends in the Kit-Cat Club excused them from party services, enabling them to keep their places with a good conscience. When the Bishop of St. Asaph collected and republished four of his old sermons with a timely preface, the conductors of the *Spectator*, lacking matter for the day (May 21), inserted the preface and a paragraph from the *Postboy* on the reported death of the Pretender.

But the House of Commons (June 10) condemned this document to be "burnt by the Hands of the Common Hangman" as "malicious and factious, highly reflecting upon the present Administration of public Affairs under her Majesty, and tending to create Discord and Sedition amongst her Subjects." Swift added fuel to the fire in *A Letter of Thanks from my Lord W[harton] to the Lord Bishop of Asaph in the Name of the Kit-Cat Club* and also in a contribution to the *Examiner*.

On the day that it condemned the Bishop's preface, the House of Commons considered another paper from a more important source. Since the ministers took office, statesmen in the allied countries had now and then addressed communications to the English public as well as to the Queen and her advisers. The Dutch sent (May 25) *A Letter from the States General to the Queen of Great Britain.* Anne expressed her own feelings before she received the vote of displeasure from the House of Commons. She complained that the letter was "printed and published almost as soon as" it reached her, a procedure she thought "equally contrary to Good Politicks and Decency." She hoped the like would not be "done again." Previously, the Dutch had published in the *Daily Courant* (April 3) *A Memorial Showing that the States General of the United Provinces are wrongfully charged by the Resolution or Votes of the House of Commons of the Parliament of Great Britain.*[4]

The country was slipping away from the ministers. They depended for support chiefly upon the Queen, the Church, and satisfaction at the end of a burdensome war. But Anne was not immortal. An illness that very summer frightened her servants, while their opponents exaggerated the ailments that she had. Oxford carefully stayed away from Windsor until the regular time appointed for his going, lest he disturb the public mind. Swift was encouraged a little later that, having passed safely her climacteric, the Queen had a new lease on life, a mere whistling to keep off fright. The Church alone, for all its strength, was too narrow a bottom for a ministry, and fear of the Pretender, artfully spread in spite of frantic efforts to prevent it, might easily surpass the joy at peace.

Colonel Horace Walpole, who took pleasure in opposing his nephew, Robert, reported from Norfolk in late September that he never knew that county in "a greater ferment." Defoe, going northward about the same time by the Stourbridge Fair

---

[4] *Parliamentary History,* VI. 1141ff.; Parke, *Bolingbroke Correspondence,* II. 411.; Boyer, *Political State,* III. 343ff., 431ff., 452ff., 459ff.; IV. 40ff.

and Lynn, reported from Lincoln his discoveries. He seemed to be "out of her Majesty's dominions and in the territory of King Walpole." The partisan spirit amazed him. The people, "smothered with the smoke or mist of their delusions," were "made lunatic with the madness of their leaders."

Examples of "preposterous, ridiculous, incongruous things" believed were, "that the Queen is for the Pretender, the ministry under the protection of France; that Popery is to be tolerated; that as soon as a Peace is declared the war with the Dutch will be proclaimed; that the French are to keep their Trade to the South Seas; that the people will be brought to address the Queen not to interrupt the hereditary right of the Royal line since the heir is willing to abjure Popery; and the like." This in Norfolk. Elsewhere, he found the same "general distemper," though lacking "the same warmth." The "best men" were disposed to "moderation," but the "poison" was "unhappily spread from London," and Dissenters especially were "made everywhere to believe that the Ministry" was "for the Pretender and that French Government and Popery" were its "design."

Defoe was trying to combat this spirit, but he reported Newcastle to be worse than any place he visited save Lynn. If he suggested in a coffee-house that "the Queen was not a Jacobite or that the Ministry were Protestants, that the Pretender was not just coming ashore," he was heard "with a kind of amazement." To make matters worse, the "Jacobite Party" behaved with an "impudent assurance." These were reports of a journalist trying to make a point. But the Queen and her ministers clearly had an uphill fight if they were, as Defoe insisted, the "only security . . . left against the Jacobite faction." They betrayed their fears by trying to suppress hostile propaganda and by encouraging countermoves.

Defoe himself began openly in the *Review* to plead with friends of Hanover to support the ministers lest the latter be forced in self-defence to turn Jacobite. They would not do this unless "driven to some inextricable Labyrinth in their affairs . . . or forsaken of God and their understandings." Nevertheless, he was bold to say "very plainly that the Circumstances of the Nation and the Triumphs of Parties" seemed to "prepare everything for the Pretender, even in Spight of the Ministry." If things went on, he was convinced several days later, it would be "impossible to prevent the Pretender." The house of Hanover could no more "come in plain Force excepted as things" then stood than the moon could "shine when the Sun" was in the "Meridian." Within a fortnight he warned again that "one conversing with the country People and with the Mob in every Part of England" would discover a growing kindness toward the Pretender, chiefly an admission that opponents of the ministers were carrying their point.

The *Examiner* remarked that in the same month in London, on the night of the Princess Sophia's birthday, "all Engines were set to work. Money and Liquors were plentifully distributed among the Rabble attending on the Bonfires. Huzzas were raised at proper periods, and amicable Correspondents maintained between the Grand Personalities in the House and the People in the Street."

The same paper had complained in April that the *Postboy* was its only ally, while the other side had the *Medley,* the *Protestant Postboy,* the *Flying Post,* the *Postman,* the *Observator,* and the *Daily Courant.* The *Medley* replied with a more correct statement of the facts. The *Daily Courant* and the *Postman* were no more partial than *Gazettes,* being chiefly purveyors of the news. It counted as its allies the *Protestant Postboy,* the *Flying Post,* and the *Observator.* Opposing were the *Examiner,* the *Postboy,* and the *Review,* which last the *Examiner* would not own. Supplementing these were written newsletters by Dyer and Roper.

Calling the licentiousness of the press to Parliament's attention in January, the Queen recommended that it "find a remedy equal to the mischief." Rejecting proposals to register all printing presses and to require books, pamphlets, and papers to bear the names of their authors, printers, and publishers, the ministers finally decided to levy a tax of a halfpenny per copy on papers and a shilling on each advertisement. Defoe thought the effect might be to substitute the quill for type in the purveyance of news. The *Protestant Postboy* promised future quiet sleep, undisturbed by the "clamours of noisy and unsatisfied Hawkers."

Samuel Buckley, publisher of the *Daily Courant,* was haled before the House of Commons in April and committed to its Serjeant at Arms for printing the *Memorial from the States General.* The imposition of the tax caused the *Observator* and the *Protestant Postboy* to suspend; the *Medley* appeared a few weeks longer as a contribution to the *Flying Post.* Early in September Hurt, the printer, and Ridpath, formerly author of the *Observator,* later transferred to the *Flying Post,* were arrested on a warrant from the Secretary of State and confined in Newgate. Friends of Ridpath contributed funds for bail, and he wrote on in a chastened style.

The ministers betrayed their fears by magnifying trifles. In March was a flurry about "Mohocks" or "Hawkubites," who were condemned by proclamation, though even Swift was soon a little ashamed of the part he played. Another incident was the "bandbox plot." A toy infernal machine consisting of two inkhorns pointing in opposite directions, loaded with powder and bullets, tied in the box in which they were inclosed, were delivered, sealed, to Oxford. Swift was there and bravely intervened to open the package and protect his patron. This second narrow escape of that valuable life did not inspire horror. Enemies in telling the story turned the laugh on the rescuer.

A more serious incident for those concerned was a duel between Lord Mohun and the Duke of Hamilton, fatal to them both. Mohun had taken Marlborough's challenge to Poulett. McCartney, who had served under that Duke, was Mohun's second and was accused of stabbing Hamilton after his own principal fell. Hamilton was on the point of going as Ambassador to France. Friends who thought him to be a Jacobite concluded that his death was by design to thwart the service they expected to the cause. Marlborough was accused of giving encouragement to duels.[5]

---

[5] The quarrel between Hamilton and Mohun seems to have been private, but the incident is shrouded in a maze of conflicting evidence which it is not pertinent to traverse here. Swift, *Journal to Stella,* pp. 351ff., 373, 383, 386f., 391, 393ff.; Hist. Mss. Com., *Portland,* V. 228ff.; *Dartmouth,* pp. 300ff.; *Review,* Oct. 11, 14, 25, 1712; *Examiner,* April 17–24, Oct. 9–16, 1712; *Medley,*

Surviving notables from earlier days passed from the scene in these exciting times with little note. Richard Cromwell's death recalled a troubled generation that left an heritage behind. The Duke of Leeds left a grandson as husband for one of Oxford's daughters. Lord Rivers died soon enough for the Duke of Hamilton to enjoy for a brief space a sinecure he had obtained when Marlborough was dismissed. Perhaps Godolphin in September left a greater vacancy, though his body lay in the Jerusalem Chamber for days unburied, waiting for enough friendly Knights of the Garter to bear his pall. Even Oxford rebuked a writer in the *Postboy* for comment while his old colleague was at the point of death. Swift was honest, if he was less humane. "It is a good jest," he said, "to hear the ministers talk of him now with humanity and pity, because he is dead and can do them no more hurt. . . . I heard Lord Marlborough is growing ill of his diabetes; which, if it be true, may soon carry him off; and then the Ministry will be something more at ease."

That Duke, surviving, suffered attacks on both his public and private life. The *Examiner* urged the Attorney General to bring suit for the recovery of funds alleged to have been misapplied, using arguments that indicated the venom of its attack. It blamed him (April 13) for the incidental horrors of the war:

> What a deplorable Sight it was to see Men with their Limbs shot off lying upon the Field in such an abandoned, wretched Condition that Ravens and Crows have fallen upon them for Carrion. Wanting proper Persons to dress their Limbs, their Wounds putrified to such a degree that Dogs knawed their Flesh while they were yet alive. Amidst this Torture, thousands expired that might have been preserved if the General had not sunk the Money designed for Medicines and Surgeons. No Age, no Country, how barbarous so ever, hath ever given us such an Instance of Cruelty and Avarice.

After the prorogation the Duke decided to escape from a scene that brought so little pleasure and so much chagrin. Some of the ministers were reluctant to grant him passports, but Oxford intervened to speed his going. He and Anne agreed

May 5–9, 1712; *Parliamentary History*, VI. 1063, 1125ff.; Boyer, *Political State*, III. 235., 318.; IV. 214ff., 370ff.; Cartwright, *Wentworth Papers*, p. 310; *Lockhart Papers*, I. 400ff.

that it was a prudent move. "I did not think it worth while to trouble you with the obstructions one meets with," he apologized to Arthur Mainwaring the day after the passports were issued, "for when I undertook it, I was resolved not to be deterred from finishing it."

This was among the least of ministerial family jars. St. John was now Viscount Bolingbroke, but he wished to be an earl. Anne vetoed his ambition, as she had the year before condemned Harcourt to a barony when he aspired to be a viscount. "Since I asked too much," St. John wrote petulantly, "let the Queen be so good as to give me nothing." But he accepted the lesser rank, and, to humor him, was permitted to go to France in August to negotiate personally with Louis and Torcy.

Returning, he had friction with Dartmouth. Erasmus Lewis, Secretary in the office of the latter, wrote to Oxford from Windsor (October 13) that Bolingbroke treated his colleague "last night on two or three occasions in so rough a manner that he believes it will be impossible for you to find any expedient to keep them together." Since Bolingbroke was necessary "during the negotiations," Dartmouth was ready to retire. But Anne urged him to hold on, believing him to be an "honest man" and his loss "prejudicial" to her service; she hoped that Oxford would support her in the stand.

The Lord Treasurer was increasingly distrustful of his colleague; the latter, more impatient with his chief. The Church party continually pressed for changes, which Oxford and the Queen opposed. Anne was persistently her own mistress. "You cannot wonder," she explained to Oxford in November in refusing a request, "that I whom have been ill used soe many yeares should desire to keep myself from being againe enslaved; and if I must always comply, and not be complied with, [it] is I think very hard and what I cannot submit to, and what I believe you would not have me." Swift, Lewis, and others whose hopes depended upon good will among their patrons tried to keep the peace, but sometimes they despaired.[6]

For weeks Swift had worked on a history of the negotiations

[6] Swift, *Journal to Stella*, pp. 382, 383, 386f., 390; Boyer, *Political State*, IV. 59f., 62f., 151f., 420f.; Coxe, *Marlborough*, III. 528ff.; Cartwright, *Wentworth Papers*, p. 302; Hist. Mss. Com., *Portland*, V. 194ff., 231ff.; *Bath*, I. 213, 222ff.; Parke, *Bolingbroke Correspondence*, II. 484f.

to be let loose when peace was made. But he was discouraged and tired of waiting. "There is a devilish spirit among the people," he wrote in mid-November, "and the ministry must exert themselves or sink." He threatened before the end of the month not to print the work in hand until the "court" decided "to do something about" himself, a resolution he might have known he lacked the will to keep. He had proudly refused to publish his collected *Examiners* by subscription, preferring to offer them on their merits in a small volume. They moved slowly, and he admitted that the *Medleys* in the same format might be selling better. New Year's Day, 1713, he felt that the division among his friends had "now spread more than ever." "Burn politics," he exclaimed, "and send me from courts and ministers."

January 5, "a bloody cold day," he called in the morning at the Duke of Ormond's, who had lost a daughter, and "looked off" while the bereaved father wiped his tears. A few hours later in front of his own grate he overcame his pride and put his case to Oxford: "I must humbly take leave to inform your Lordship that the Dean of Wells died this morning at one o'clock. I entirely submit my poor fortunes to your Lordship."

The Lord Treasurer invited him to dinner more often; some weeks, every day. For amusement, he commissioned Swift to write an address to be proposed on the Queen's speech in the House of Lords when Parliament should meet, but would not see the draft until the day before the meeting. Owing to the delay of the peace, this was postponed from week to week like Swift's preferment. After two months, he was losing hope. "What will all this come to?" he asked. "Nothing. My grandmother used to say, more of your lining and less of your dining." The subject fretted him by March 1. "Talk not to me of deaneries; I know less of that than ever by much."

Three days later he canvassed the humiliation of an empty return. Tisdall, Stella's former admirer, was a pretty fellow, as she said, "and when I come back to Ireland with nothing, he will condole with me with abundance of secret pleasure." He complained that Lady Masham, who had miscarried that year, neglected the Queen to nurse a two-year-old son who was ill.

Opponents of the ministers were also giving thought to journalists. Mainwaring did not survive long after Marlborough got his passports. Ridpath was brought to trial in February and found guilty, though defended by some of the ablest anti-ministerial lawyers. His sureties forfeited the bail (£600) given on notice of appeal, enabling him to escape to Holland. Steele abandoned the rôle of *Spectator* in December, 1712, to undertake that of *Guardian* (March, 1713). He and his contributors retained the tone of the *Spectator* essays, desiring to keep their public. But the first number of the new paper announced that "Parties" had become "too violent to make it possible to pass them by without Observation." The conductor promised impartiality, but added: "I cannot be Neuter. I am with Relation to the Government of the Church, a Tory, with Regard to the State, a Whig," an artful dodge in the prevailing public mood.

While the court awaited peace for the meeting of Parliament; and Swift, his preferment, Addison was persuaded to complete and stage a play long kept in hand. The title suggested classical lines which the aroused factions easily appropriated to support the feelings of the hour. The author called on Swift to ask him to the rehearsal and was invited to dine with Bolingbroke. At dinner there was no escape from politics or from a toast to Somers by the guest. Gossipers misunderstood the incident, but it gave the play a longer run. Contending parties tried to use its popularity, as they seized every other means to draw the public in their strife.

The opposition had the easier task, in that the author was a member of the Kit-Cat Club, but Bolingbroke collected fifty guineas for Booth "for acting the part of Cato so well that opposed a perpetual Dictator." This was thought to be a "home strock" in Peter Wentworth's circle. When young "Sim" Harcourt reported to Prior at Paris the rescue of "Cato from Whigism," the latter spoke to Shrewsbury, the Lord Chamberlain, in the hope of getting further "encouragement" for the actor.

In these same weeks Swift and Steele began a feud. The

Guardian interrupted (April 28) his literary lucubrations and warnings to the Church against freethinking to condemn the *Examiner* for a reference to Nottingham's daughter, incidentally calling the writer of that paper a "fawning miscreant." Since the press throve on controversy, the *Examiner* replied with a *tu quoque,* recalling that the *Tatler* also had indulged in personalities. Steele banteringly apologized over his own name (May 12) for calling the *Examiner* a "miscreant," a word signifying "unbeliever." Familiar friends sometimes told him that he talked with the *Examiner;* others accused him of "laying with her." It was immaterial whether the journalist wrote against him in the "Character of an estranged Friend or an exasperated Mistress."

Amid his disappointments in those days Swift described Steele as insisting "with the utmost malice" that he was author of the *Examiner* and abusing him in "the grossest manner he could possibly invent." Pouring all of this out to Addison, he asked: "Now, sir, if I am not the author of the Examiner, how will Mr. Steele be able to defend himself from the imputation of the highest degree of baseness, ingratitude, and injustice?" He recalled his own intercession to save Steele's place. The *Examiner* (March 25) had expressly denied his authorship. He could prove by Harcourt and Bolingbroke that Oxford had reproached him for Steele's failure to requite the favors done.

A man of the world, though not always practical in business, Steele was surprised at so much heat where the fire was so small. He doubted frankly whether his obligations to Swift were as great as the latter thought. If the ministers told him so, it was to "laugh at him." He was naturally "glad" of words spoken in his behalf. As to the *Examiner,* he accepted the common report that Swift was its "accomplice," heeding a denial in the paper as little as he would expect others to regard a similar repudiation of himself by the *Guardian.*

This letter seemed to Swift to add "insult" to former injury. He forgot the adjectives in his letter to Addison, and assumed the rôle of a wronged and innocent friend. In a long letter, recapitulating his own merits and the blows he felt, he accused Steele of trying "to ruin his credit as a Christian and Clergyman." A mean man might have smiled at Swift pleading his cloth.

But in those weeks Swift saw the whole world in a conspiracy to do him wrong. Lewis showed him (April 13) "an order for the warrant for the vacant deaneries" with his name left out. He sent word by Lewis that he blamed Oxford only for failure to give timely notice when he found the "Queen would do nothing." He told the Lord Treasurer in person the same day that he must now return to Ireland; he could not stay in London "with any reputation" without "something honourable immediately." The two found Ormond, still Lord Lieutenant of Ireland, who seemed to consent that Sterne, the Dean of St. Patrick's, Dublin, become a bishop, and Swift succeed as dean. All ecclesiastical appointments were held up to await the announcement of this.

A fortnight passed. Abigail left her son to intercede with Anne and weep with Swift. Bolingbroke invited him to dine. When Ormond (April 16) consented to the Queen, Oxford decided it must be "Prebendary of Windsor." Word came on the morning of the eighteenth that Anne would decide by noon. At three in the afternoon she gave in for St. Patrick's. But the next day Ormond was unwilling for Sterne to be an Irish bishop. Swift might have any other deanery. Exasperated, he requested that Duke to "do as he pleased" and leave him out, whereupon Ormond gave in too. It was not what Swift wanted. For several years it would add little to his income. But it saved his pride. He boasted no "joy" at the thought of passing his "days in Ireland," confessing sadly: "I thought the ministry would not let me go; but perhaps they can't help it."

It was well that Swift was going home. London would not be the same place for him again. The scene had changed before he went in early June. While the *Guardian* and the *Examiner* buffeted each other, Steele wrote personally (May 26), admitting that the last turn of the affair between them convinced him "it was impossible for a man to judge his own case." He was grateful for any favors from Swift, but unable to understand the hard words in the letter to Addison. Replying the next day amid his preparations to go to Dublin, the new Dean dwelt on his friend's offense. "It was only calling a clergyman of some little distinction an infidel; a clergyman, who was your friend, who always loved you; who had endeavoured at least to serve you; and who whenever he did write anything, made it sacred to himself never to fling out the least hurt against you." He added in a postscript, "in the only thing I ever published under my name, I took care to celebrate you as much as I could and in as handsome a manner as I could." He had promised to return to London the next winter, but might never see Steele again.

Swift wished to frequent the market place, but did not like a jostling crowd. A journalist thus thin-skinned would scarcely serve in days ahead. After his preferment became an immediate point, his patrons used him no longer in the former way. The *Examiner*, as he said, had an editor whom he did not know. But he contributed an essay as late as February in defence of Erasmus Lewis, and it helped the paper and the ministers for the report to be abroad that he still wrote. His pamphlet was left unpublished, though carefully embedded in it were barbed shafts aimed at Marlborough, Wharton, Walpole, Sunderland, and their friends. The treaty was delayed so long that it was not opposed. New questions arose with which Swift was little qualified to deal.[7]

Even before Swift's quarrel with Steele began, George St. John, Bolingbroke's brother, arrived (April 3) with the treaties, and they were soon made public. The oft-prorogued Parliament met (April 9) to hear Anne recite in her speech pleasure in what she had done "for securing the Protestant succession" and her "perfect friendship" with the "House of Hanover." Lords and Commons thanked her forthwith, and Swift's cherished work was useless.

But trouble brewed. The year's money bills were hurried through to make way for an early dissolution. A malt tax was

----

[7] Hist. Mss. Com., *Bath*, I. 228; Swift, *Journal to Stella*, pp. 271f., 361f., 407ff., 413ff., 422ff., 450ff.; Coxe, *Marlborough*, III. 531; Boyer, *Political State*, V. 155ff., 377ff.; Cartwright, *Wentworth Papers*, p. 330; Parke, *Bolingbroke Correspondence*, IV. 112; Ball, *Correspondence of Swift*, II. 33ff.; George A. Aitken, *Life of Richard Steele*, I. 378ff.; *Examiner*, Feb. 2, 1713.

laid on the Scots equally with the English, the first levy of the sort, since it was postponed by the Act of Union to the end of the war. The war, it seemed, was over. Bolingbroke would have made concessions to the Scots. But he and Harcourt rallied an increasing number who were critical of Oxford. In early June they obtained from Anne the see of Rochester for Atterbury, and he was thenceforth of their coterie. Oxford yielded with a wry face, finding his chief joy in the readiness with which the canons of Christ Church parted with their Dean, now transferred to Westminster. These opponents scarcely wished as yet to supplant the Lord Treasurer. They hoped rather to prod him to steps that they thought overdue. He naturally began to think that they might wish to do more.

The Scots made trouble. Lockhart engineered a meeting of their lords and commons who agreed almost to a man to support a motion to dissolve the union. Oxford tried to persuade them to desist. Failing, he besought Halifax to help again, as he had promised to help with the peace if there had been need. The Lord Treasurer's correspondence with that friend aroused suspicion in his own circle that the two meditated a coalition, which was totally outside the range of possibilities. The day before the question was moved in the upper house, Halifax wrote to say that Oxford might "be assured of being effectively supported in the maintaining the Protestant Succession and the Union."

The Scots dickered with both sides. Most of the opposition peers were ready for any move to harass the ministry. The Earl of Findlater, maker of the motion, had helped to carry the union. So had most of the English lords who now voted that it be dissolved. Halifax favored delay. He might be willing to dissolve the union if it could be done without endangering the succession. Oxford rallied every peer he could, including members of the Church party who had opposed the act on its passage. "It was very comical," Erasmus Lewis wrote to Swift already on his way to Ireland, "to see the Tories who voted with Lord Treasurer against the dissolution of the union, under all the perplexities in the world lest they should be victorious, and the Scotch, who voted for the bill of dissolution, under agonies lest they themselves should carry the point they pretended to desire."

Bolingbroke was confirmed in discontent. "We act," he wrote to Shrewsbury, who had gone to France in Hamilton's place, "as if we had nothing to do, but get this session over anyhow. No principal of government established and avowed, nobody but my Lord Treasurer, and he cannot be in every place and speak to every man, able to hold out hopes and fears, or give a positive answer to any one question."

The opposition had better luck against the bill for implementing the eighth and ninth articles of the treaty of commerce with France. It touched influential groups and had ramifications not apparent on the surface. A lucrative trade had grown up with Portugal involving a large vent for woolens and a share of the carrying trade with Brazil. The silk industry depended in part upon raw material from the Levant, where cloth and fish were marketed. Frightened merchants in London and elsewhere obtained petitions to Parliament; others responded to propaganda by opponents of the ministry. Dropping his *Review* for other reasons, Defoe was engaged to write for *Mercator, or Commerce Retrieved,* a triweekly started in the latter part of May to combat noise made against the trade with France.

In spite of the petitions within and clamor out of doors, the Commons easily passed the bill through its earlier stages. But on the final question of engrossment (June 18) the opposition had reënforcements it did not expect. Sir Thomas Hanmer of the Church party, wont to rally around Bolingbroke at whose request he had forgone a trip to Italy to attend the session, made a long speech saying that he was convinced by arguments of the "traders and manufacturers," that he would not be "blindly led by any ministry," and that he would vote the "convictions of his judgment" against the bill. John Aislabie and Francis Annesley, younger men in the same group, echoed his view. The question was lost, 194 to 185.

Opponents rejoiced at this turn. The ministers stood charged by members of their own household and had to do something to retrieve the cause. Bolingbroke informed Oxford that the Dutch knew of the defeat before the official letter arrived. "Indeed, my Lord," he urged, "we make a despicable figure in the world. You have retrieved many a bad game in your time; for God's sake make one push for government." For once he could not blame the Lord Treasurer. Even in his account to Strafford he did not presume to do so, though a rumor was soon abroad that Oxford was at fault. Coming to town shortly after the division, Peter Wentworth was told, "Lord T[reasurer] did not labour in it heartily." Esther Vanhomrigh, reflecting gossip in another circle, wrote to Swift that Oxford had "been extremely to blame, for all his friends advised him to let it be dropped by consent till next session." A less suspicious man than the Lord Treasurer might have scented a conspiracy.

Bolingbroke thought that this report of Oxford giving up the question was intended to "hurt the court," but that it would have a contrary effect. A pamphlet with a plausible explanation was soon abroad to quiet provincial supporters of the ministers. The Lords Anglesey and Abingdon decided to dissent and persuaded Hanmer to the same view. The latter, with a self-appointed deputation, informed Oxford that the Church party felt the bill should be postponed until after the election. Bromley, the Speaker, was told that the ministers had no objection to this course. But other ministerial leaders in the House, not having authorized this move and having come through heat and labor almost to the end of their task, saw no occasion for delay. The matter came to a head at noon the day the final question was appointed on the floor. Weak leaders saw no alternative to going on. Hanmer's group felt this treatment to be unfair; others thought Hanmer too officious. Neither group desired what took place.

Five days afterward Hanmer himself proposed and became chairman of a committee to prepare an address to the Queen designed to repair the damage. She was thanked for what she had "done in the Treaty of Commerce with France, by laying so good a Foundation for the Interests of her People in Trade," and humbly desired to appoint "Commissioners" to treat further on the question. The House agreed to the address, resolving to present it in a body. Anne thanked the members. She had obtained "so great advantages in trade" with "no small difficulty," but she would do the best she could. So, within doors, the matter ended. Outside the fun went on, pamphlet following pamphlet. August 7 appeared the first number of a semi-weekly, the *British Merchant; or, Commerce Preserv'd*, in answer to *Mercator*. The conflict was to outlast the Queen. This matter in abeyance, Oxford made haste to obtain a grant of half a million pounds to pay the Civil List arrears contracted prior to 1710. Ever since he took office the Queen had had a straitened purse. A warrant for thirteen thousand pounds in his own favor had remained unpaid since December, 1711, for want of funds. Perhaps he foresaw storms ahead.

General James Stanhope, now a civilian leader of the opposition, to embarrass the ministry, proposed an address urging Anne to have the Pretender removed from Lorraine, where he had lived at Bar-le-Duc after he was forced out of France by the treaty. Wharton made a similar motion in the Lords. Both houses were unanimous, and the Queen promised her best efforts, but added to the Lords, "if we could cure our animosities and divisions at home, it would be the most effectual method to secure the Protestant Succession."

She appointed July 7 as a day of thanksgiving to celebrate the peace, but was too ill to go to St. Paul's on that date. She went to the House of Lords nine days later to make her last speech to the Sacheverell Parliament. She was glad that peace had followed a victorious war. The need now was, peace at home. "I hope," she concluded, "for the quiet of these nations, and the universal good, that I shall next winter meet my Parliament, resolved to act upon the same principles, with the same prudence, and with such vigor as may enable me to support the liberties of Europe abroad and reduce the spirit of faction at home." [8]

[8] *Parliamentary History*, VI. 1208ff.; *Commons Journal*, XVII. 354ff.; 435ff.; Ball, *Correspondence of Swift*, II. 41, 47; Hist. Mss. Com., *Portland*, V. 270ff., 299f.; VI. 123ff.; VII. 14ff.; *Lockhart Papers*, I. 412ff.; Boyer, *Political State*, V. 366ff.; 383ff.; VI. 1ff., 16ff., 118ff., 135ff., 170ff.; Parke, *Bolingbroke Correspondence*, IV. 139, 165f., 184; Cartwright, *Wentworth Papers*, pp. 337f.; *A Letter from a Member of the House of Commons to his Friend in the Country relating to the Bill of Commerce; with a true Copy of the Bill, and the exact List of those who voted for and against engrossing it;* A. K. Manchester, *British Preëminence in Brazil*, chs. i-ii.

CHAPTER VII

THE SETTING SUN, 1713–1714

They who affect to head an opposition or to make any considerable figure in it must be equal at least to those whom they oppose; I do not say in parts only, but in application and industry and the fruits of both, information, knowledge, and a certain consistent preparedness for all events that may arise. Every administration is a system of conduct; opposition, therefore, should be a system of conduct likewise; an opposite but not a dependent system.

BOLINGBROKE in *The Spirit of Patriotism.*

THE end of the session found Oxford suffering with gravel. Bolingbroke longed for Shrewsbury's return. It was necessary "for those who must in honour and good sense unite in the same measures to come to some peremptory resolution." He complained to Prior (July 4) that he was "unfortunate" in all his "negociations." Three weeks later he grumbled openly:

Our enemies are in themselves contemptible and our friends are well inclined. The former have no strength but what we might have taken form them, and the latter no dissatisfaction but what we might have prevented. Let the game which we have be wrested out of our hands; this I can bear; but to play like children with it, till it slips between our fingers to the ground, and sharpers have but to stoop and pick it up; this consideration distracts a man of spirit, and not to be vexed in this case is not to be sensible.

Bromley had written to Oxford the day before urging haste in the dissolution after making changes necessary.

The day that Bolingbroke complained to Prior, the convalescing Oxford wrote a letter to his colleague which he showed in advance to Lady Masham. She saw as well the answer in which Bolingbroke several days later opened his mind. The writer pledged anew loyalty to his chief. Perhaps he pledged too

131

much. He would "never engage in any other interest" as he "had an extraordinary occasion very lately of declaring." He expected, hoping always to deserve, opposition from "Whigs" and was not surprised at "ingratitude and impracticability . . . among Tories." That which broke the "hearts" of Oxford's friends was "unpreparedness to encounter such attacks," due to "want of encouragement to some" or of not "using authority over others." Too much "honey" was "consumed by drones," using the "Queen's favour against her service." The Lord Treasurer ought to delegate power, leaving himself time to "supervise"; he was "pulling at the beam," when he ought to be "at the box whipping and reining in." As to public affairs, the French balked at the destruction of Dunkirk; it should be "either demolished or kept." The writer would not mention Dartmouth; he thought Bromley ought to keep the chair; he disliked the proposal about Benson; the House of Hanover was playing "the Devil," but he was "too much in the dark to meddle in so nice a case."

Pausing at Hampton Court on her way to Windsor (August 8), the Queen dissolved Parliament. The shifting of men in places, on which Oxford and Bolingbroke disagreed, took longer. Neither the Lord Treasurer nor Anne thought it prudent to depend wholly on the Church party. Bolingbroke, owing partly to personal discontent, imputed to his chief decisive blame. Discounting Dartmouth, he thought an earldom better merited by himself. If the negotiation of the peace was worth a Garter, he felt that he deserved it more than Strafford, whose services had been mediocre at best. He would not believe that Anne herself withheld the favors he desired.

In this mood, he saw slights where none were meant when shifts were made. Dartmouth refused to serve longer with such a colleague. The Bishop of London's death opened a way to translate Robinson to that see, permitting Dartmouth to succeed as Privy Seal. To humor the Scots, Findlater was made Lord Chancellor for their country with a supervision of judicial business there, which Harcourt did not like. The Earl of Mar became Secretary of State for Scotland. But Bolingbroke thought that the revival of that office diminished the prestige of the northern department. To appease him, Dartmouth's successor, Bromley, was given that assignment and Bolingbroke transferred to Dartmouth's former duties, some of which he had freely usurped while the treaty was in progress. Benson became Lord Bingley; and Sir William Wyndham, son-in-law of Somerset, Chancellor of the Exchequer. Hanmer was promised the chair in Bromley's room. Portmore was to succeed Islay as a Scot peer in the Lords, which completed the alienation of the latter's brother, John Campbell, Duke of Argyll. Shrewsbury was to go to Ireland in lieu of Ormond, who kept the army as Captain General. He kept also an ill humor, because Oxford would not facilitate changes that he wished among his officers. The Lord Treasurer later said that his own power was nominal after that summer.

Meanwhile, his opponents were busy with the public. Though Ridpath was an exile and the printer of the *Flying Post* had stood in a pillory, Steele for an interval had better luck. The death of his mother-in-law brought a modest estate enabling him to support himself in Parliament. He resigned his place at the stamp office with a view to greater activity, in which he hoped that his privilege as a member of the House would be protection. The last number of the *Guardian* appeared October 1; on the sixth was published the first of a triweekly, the *Englishman; being the Sequel to the Guardian.*

In the *Guardian* he had criticized delay in destroying Dunkirk. Tugghe, a deputy of the magistrates of the town, by begging leniency from the Queen, opened the way for the topic. Having found a seat in Parliament, in September Steele addressed to his borough a pamphlet, *The Importance of Dunkirk Considered, in Defence of the Guardian of August 7th in a Letter to the Bailiff of Stockbridge.* Swift, who had returned to London in the summer, replied in *The Importance of the Guardian Considered, in a second Letter to the Bailiff of Stockbridge.* This performance might well have been justified in terms the author used to defend the *Examiner:* "We reckon here, that supposing the persons on both sides to be of equal intrinsic worth, it was more impudent, immoral, and criminal to reflect on a majority in power than a minority out of power." Another hand lent Swift help in *The Character of Richard Steele, Esq., with some Remarks by Toby, Abel's Kinsman.*

Perhaps as important as Steele's positive propaganda was the hindrance of Defoe, hitherto Oxford's most effective agent with the public. When creditors were incited to prosecute him for debts, the Lord Treasurer hastened the payment of his allowance. But the journalist made his old mistake of trying to use irony in defending the ministers against the charge of Jacobitism. Ridpath and others informed against him in April. Oxford sent William Borrett, a solicitor of the treasury, to get him off under pretense of making sure that sufficient bail was offered. Parker, the Chief Justice, unsympathetic with the ministry, asked Borrett privately whether the crown meant to prosecute. The Solicitor evaded by referring him to Bolingbroke, which made another complication. The intent of the opposition was to silence Defoe, to discredit him by making public his alliance with Oxford, or to reflect on the latter if he should protect one accused of writing against Hanover.

To avoid any of these results, Defoe suggested that the ministers undertake to prosecute and then delay doing it. The plan was too clever in so tense a time. Opponents of the ministry were relentless, and the Attorney General felt obliged to go on. By commenting on the case in the *Review,* the author made himself liable to citation for contempt and marked the end of his long labor in that medium. In its expiring number (June 11) he rejoiced that *Mercator* had taken up his work and seemed to have encouragement and "original papers," favors he never "pretended." About the middle of November, at the last moment it would serve the purpose, Oxford saved him by a pardon from the Queen.

Recovering from his illness, the Lord Treasurer went to Windsor (August 4) to be installed one of six Knights of the Garter. Three weeks later he was in Cambridgeshire with Anne's permission to attend the marriage of his son to the daughter of his late friend, John Holles, Duke of Newcastle. Though he went so quietly, Bolingbroke commented, it might have been "to get a mistress" for himself rather than a "wife" for his son, he did not escape intrigues at court. Abigail wished him to send only two "favours," one each for herself and the Queen, "none for the Groom of Stole." Anne cautioned through Bolingbroke that the bride be called "not Lady Harley, but Lady Herriot Harley" to save her rank as a duke's daughter. Bolingbroke congratulated his chief on the marriage of the last of his children, and that without charge to the crown. But the Secretary of State did not go to the wedding, and Oxford recalled that he had not been to the house of his colleague since February, 1711. Returning to Windsor, he solicited the title of his late friend in order to perpetuate it in his son, a "never enough to be lamented folly." Though he spoke only to Anne and Abigail, he felt that it was held against him as a "crime."

The death in three months in childbed of his daughter, Lady Carmarthen, witnessed the futility of human plans. At Windsor Bolingbroke interrupted a letter of complaint that the Queen was favoring Dartmouth and Lady Somerset. His condolence was general; anything specific would be impertinent to one "as well armed against these severe trials as strength of reason and fortitude of mind can arm a man." Dartmouth was troubled at the "loss," but knew the father "had resolution enough to support any misfortune." Defoe advised that "truly noble and sublime remedy . . . resignation." Canon Stratford saw a churchman's lesson in the "calamity," teaching "how entire our dependency is on God for everything that is dear to us." Swift, who knew the daughter, adopted with less excuse a parson's rôle. "To say the truth, my Lord, you began to be too happy for a mortal; much more happy than is usual with the dispensations of Providence long to continue. . . . God Almighty . . . thought fit to punish you with a domestic loss, where he knew your heart was most exposed; and at the same time has fulfilled his own wise purpose by rewarding in a better life that excellent creature he has taken from you." A truer note was struck by Arbuthnot, the Queen's physician and the court jester, who addressed himself to Swift as Oxford's friend. Remembering

the funerals of six of his own offspring and the bedsides of
many departed patients, he had a fellow-feeling for a "condition for which" he knew that "philosophy and religion" were
"both too weak," and advised attending to business as the
"best cure . . . by diverting the thoughts." [1]

There was business enough if he had a heart for it. He
heard within a week that Bolingbroke said on one of his rare
visits to his wife at Bucklebery: "I and *Lady Masham* have
bore him [Oxford] upon our shoulders and have made him
what he is, and now he leaves *us* where *we* were." The plausible grounds for his colleague's complaints probably made
Oxford readier to base suspicion on this report. The Secretary of State encouraged this tendency by a letter from
Windsor a week later.

He regretted so "little show of government" amid "difficulties" requiring "that all the powers of it should be exerted."
His failure to call on Oxford was due to an expectation of
seeing him at Windsor, not because he gave himself "airs" or
had "the least lukewarmness." Dartmouth, on the contrary,
"every night" did "the former with a witness. The pigmy
stretches and struts and fancies himself a giant." Abigail
wrote the same day that Anne was better and looked for the
Lord Treasurer. Orrery was plaguing Bolingbroke to send him
abroad to escape from "these squabbles," so apt to hurt the
reputations of those at court.

Defoe got ready a pamphlet in the hope of allaying the
fever of the Dissenters. Oxford spent December 7 at Windsor,
where the Queen remained for her own comfort, careless of
the convenience of her ministers, especially of one ill and
bereaved. The next day she wrote to him for three thousand
pounds for new coaches and liveries which she had forgot

[1] Hist. Mss. Com., *Portland*, V. 277ff., 308, 311f., 324ff., 359ff.; 466; VII.
162ff., 173; Parke, *Bolingbroke Correspondence*, IV. 180, 183, 201; Ball, *Correspondence of Swift*, II. 86ff., 92f.; Lee, *Defoe*, I. 207ff.; *Review*, June 6, 1713.
Defoe's three pamphlets that gave trouble were *Reasons against the Succession of the House of Hanover, with an Enquiry How far the Abdication of
King James, supposing it to be Legal, ought to Affect the Pretender; And What
if the Pretender should Come? or, Some Considerations of the Advantages and
Real Consequences of the Pretender's Possessing the Crown of Great Britain;
An Answer to a Question that Nobody thinks of, viz., But What if the Queen
should die?* All appeared in the early months of 1713.

to mention. Having pen in hand, she could "not help desireing you againe when you com next, to speake plainly, lay everything open and hide nothing from me, or els how is it possible I can judg of anything. I spoke very fully and sincerely to you yesterday, and I expect you should do the same to her that is sincerely your affectionate friend."

Bolingbroke invited him to ride to Windsor again a week before Christmas, seeing an "opportunity of giving new strength, new spirit to your administration and of cementing a firmer union between us and those who must support us." Wishing a little respite, Oxford did not go. Christmas Eve, Bolingbroke wrote to say that the Queen was ill. Lewis reported, Christmas Day, the general amazement that Oxford was not there. But he tarried in London, where Anne was reported dead, and his opponents openly rejoiced. Though she might recover from that attack, her days were numbered. The seat of government might be as appropriate a place for the Lord Treasurer as the bedside of a dying woman. Perhaps there was little left for him to do at either place. He had a premonition that his work was near an end.

If he had read the letters in which the Duke of Berwick now and then sent from Paris a whiff of the fresh air of common sense to the credulous coterie at Bar-le-Duc he might have taken heart. Whatever the English populace was taught to fear, Marlborough's nephew saw in saner moments the hopelessness of the Pretender's cause. Though trying to convince himself that Oxford's interest obliged him to support James, by the beginning of the new year he felt that a man "so dark and incomprehensible" must be a "knave at bottom." When Marlborough, in a panic to insure against a possible danger, applied to James for pardon, Berwick understood that his uncle intended merely to safeguard himself. In April he confessed to James that, though the Elector of Hanover ought not to get England without opposition, the fact was, little could be done without money, an army, and English officers. The "law" favored Hanover; the Dutch were pledged on the same side; France and Spain had promised to hold aloof.

With his own following divided and the tide of opposition

running strong, Oxford wondered in these months whether the Pretender would turn Protestant to get the crown. French advisers joined to urge the step. Fears of his success, systematically inculcated for two years by opponents of the ministry, had reached a stage tempting the Queen and her servants to turn Jacobite in self-defense. The insuperable obstacle, now as always, was the loyalty of James to his parents and their Church. When Charles Leslie undertook in 1713, as he was accused of doing the year before, to convert the Prince to Anglicanism, he chiefly lessened his own welcome at the forlorn court. Stubborn persistence on this point alienated help which for the moment the Pretender might have had at the expense of his integrity. Oxford gave up the thought. But he and Marlborough had actually served James II, William, and Anne. They would not be sure of the accession of the German house until its prince was on the throne, though apparently they had taken every precaution to bring that end to pass.

In the interval, opponents of the ministry emphasized the view that the Lord Treasurer and his friends were Jacobites. Steele got ready in the closing weeks of 1713 a piece sponsored by the Kit-Kat Club. According to Boyer, though "expectations" had been brought "to a pitch few Writers" could attain, *The Crisis*, when it appeared, "rather exceeded" than fell "short of it." Dedicated to the clergy of the Established Church, its method was to reprint the statutes providing for the Hanoverian succession with comments to intensify the fears that these laws might be frustrated by the designing men in power.

Swift's diagnosis of the success of this pamphlet had much of truth. For several months the *Englishman* had advertised the publication at the proper time of a "pamphlet called the *Crisis* . . . to open the eyes of the nation." "At the destined period" a "huge train of dukes, earls, viscounts, barons, knights, esquires, gentlemen, and others" went to "Sam Buckley's the publisher . . . to fetch home their cargoes in order to transmit them by dozens, scores, and hundreds into the several counties. . . . It was a pamphlet . . . against

the ministry, talks of slavery, France, and the Pretender.
. . . . It will settle the wavering, confirm the doubtful, instruct
the ignorant, inflame the clamourous, though it never be once
looked into."

But the bubble Steele inflated needed a puncture; not to be
explained. With his own wizardry with words and a little of
Defoe's understanding, Swift might have helped to rescue his
patrons from the charge of playing a part which, except for a
desperate moment, they did not intend. But Oxford and
Bolingbroke were too suspicious of each other to give him help.
Consequently, much of what he wrote was little above the
maliciously personal small talk with which a journalist might
compliment his rival of the day. "The author of *The Conduct
of the Allies* writes sense and English," he boasted, "neither
of which the author of *The Crisis* understands." Interrupting
this strain, he vented his own feelings on the Scots in words
that a little later he was sorry for.[2]

Anne received and knighted the Sheriffs of London and
Middlesex, when they went to Windsor (December 30) to
learn the true state of her health. She sent a letter to the
Lord Mayor, February 1, announcing her intention to open
Parliament in person by the middle of the month. Whoever
wrote the speech she made, when taken in a chair (March 2)
to fulfill that promise, expressed her real feelings. The peace
and public expressions on her recovery and return to the city
made her glad. But she was sorry more care had not been taken
"to suppress these seditious papers and factious rumours by
which designing men" had been "able to sink credit." Some
had "arrived to that height of malice as to insinuate that the
Protestant Succession in the House of Hanover" was in danger. They could only "mean to disturb the present tranquillity

---

[2] G. M. Trevelyan, *The Peace and the Protestant Succession,* pp. 266ff.;
English Historical Review, XXX. 501ff.; Hist. Mss. Com., *Portland,* V. 371ff.;
VII. 174; *Bath,* I. 243; *Stuart* I. 271ff.; *The Public Spirit of the Whigs set forth
in Generous Encouragement of the Author of the Crisis, with some Observations
on the Seasonableness, Candour, Erudition, and Style of that Treatise;* Boyer,
Political State, VII. 1ff.; Aitken, *Steele,* I. 416ff. Letters from the Duchess of
Marlborough to Mrs. Jennings (*Letters of the Duchess of Marlborough*) show
that the Marlboroughs were afraid that Anne would be succeeded by the
Pretender.

and bring real mischief." She exhorted Parliament to imitate her efforts to "unite . . . differences."

Wharton in the House of Lords called attention that same day to a "scandalous Libel entitled *The Public Spirit of the Whigs.*" When he went to read the offensive passage from a copy picked up in a stall, he was embarrassed not to find the words he sought. An earlier edition contained the evidence. Barber, the printer, and Morphew, the publisher, were taken up; the author was undiscovered, though his identity was known. The Secretary of State for Scotland four days later announced that procedure against the printer and publisher in the lower court estopped further action by the Lords. The Queen offered three hundred pounds for the discovery of the author. Her Lord Treasurer sent him furtively a hundred for expenses.

Steele made his debut in the House of Commons on the opening day, congratulating Hanmer, the Speaker, on his part against the ministry in the previous spring. Defoe suggested to Oxford the same day the necessity of suppressing the "unexampled fury of party." The Minister had the "fountain of honour, the strength, and the right" on his side, but opponents boasted that they had "thrown away the scabbard." The writer was sorry Swift had "laid himself so open," but the move against him invited similar tactics on the other side. The opposition planned to encourage Steele "to make speeches in the House and print them, that the malice of party" might be "gratified and the ministry be bullied in as public a manner as possible." If the "virulent writings of this man" might not be "voted seditious" none might, and "if thereupon he" might be "expelled, it would suppress and discourage the party and break all their new measures."

Oxford received from Defoe (March 10) excerpts from the *Guardian,* the *Englishman,* and *The Crisis,* described as "Heads of Scandal." The next day his brother complained against Steele on these points in the House of Commons. After a week for preparation, the accused member spoke three hours in his own defense in a House cleared of strangers, with Addison sitting by to prompt. After he went out, and candles were brought in, Walpole in his behalf recapitulated current charges of Jacobitism against the ministers. There was no need for oratory on the other side. A large majority adjudged Steele guilty of publishing "seditious libels" and expelled him from the House.

This act betrayed the fears of ministers and their insecurity with the public. As their leader, Oxford had to bear the blame. Men in opposition attacked him; men in office attributed their difficulties to the inadequacy of his leadership. The clamor of the crowd could be withstood if they could either win the confidence of Hanover or intrench themselves in power so securely that they could not be ignored. Should Anne's death leave them both suspected abroad and divided at home, they had little left to hope.

Oxford loved power and had the faith of a successful man that it belonged to him. Now that it was slipping, he cherished more the causes he had served. The peaceful accession of Hanover would be a notable achievement; thus far it was in large degree his handiwork. It would be worth a sacrifice if it could be brought to pass. The new King might be grateful to one who served him well.

Bolingbroke, Harcourt, and Atterbury, younger men, lacked this consolation for hopes unrealized and had less optimism for the future. Discredited with the English populace and at Hanover, their way ahead was dark. They had shown no mercy, and they had little to expect should their opponents come to power. What they had, they owed to Oxford and the Queen, who exercised her will through him. If he would not bestir himself, using her favor while it lasted to regain the ground already lost, it would be folly not to do the best they could without him. They knew his talent for leadership, how wise he was in counsel. But lately he had seemed to lose interest in the fight and to resign himself to drift. Feeling that their enemies should be attacked in order to avoid defeat themselves, they wanted him to sound a call, eliminate the hesitant, and close up ranks for the decisive struggle just ahead.

They voiced anxiety and offered help. Harcourt with "inexpressible concern" (March 17) discerned a "storm gathering for sometime." Bolingbroke, ten days later, was unaware of "having ever deserved ill" from Oxford and wished to see him "at the head of the Queen's affairs and the Church of England Party" as long as he lived. The Lord Treasurer's brother was induced to hint (March 29) the usefulness of a more punctual attendance on the Queen, an "often expressing of a resolution to do or hazard anything for her service," "frequent meetings with some of the Lords and Commons," and allotment of "more time for the despatch of business by getting out earlier and being freed from those who" were "only leeches of time." "The leak" that had sprung could not be "stopped without pumping."

Bolingbroke unburdened himself to Strafford about the same time. The disposition of the houses of Parliament was good, but "unimproved." Adherents of the ministers waited in vain for a lethargic court to "regulate their conduct and lead them on." Efforts were afoot to induce "My Lord Treasurer to alter his measures, to renew a confidence with the Tories and a spirit in them and to give a regular motion to all the wheels of government." The writer was "sanguine enough to hope for" success; it "would be a pity to lose by management what none" could "wrest by force."

Oxford suspected this strategy of his colleagues. He had yielded more than he thought prudent in the previous summer. They might be plotting to deprive him of his power if not of office. Though committed to the Protestant succession, he feared that they might be tempted to declare for the Pretender if they still found themselves suspected at Hanover after they had rallied the Church party and filled the offices with its partisans. The current doctrines of hereditary right and passive obedience made this change easy, now that few disputed the legitimacy of the son of James II. Jacobites in Parliament had supported the ministry with the express consent of the court to which they looked for guidance. To change openly to the narrower bottom of the Church party would make it difficult for Oxford to seek favor with Hanover without losing this Jacobite support.

Oxford's critics complained of his secretiveness. How could

he play openly the cards he held? The Queen was increasingly difficult. Encouraged by his opponents, Abigail reflected that her four years in Anne's favor had not brought a tithe of the rewards bestowed upon her predecessor. With even more anxiety than the rest she faced a change of fortune if the Queen should die. Critical of Godolphin's extravagance, Oxford was penurious to a fault with public funds, and thus was handicapped in making easier his way at court. Even the loyal Dartmouth now began to doubt, offering to quit if it would "relieve other people's uneasiness."

Instead, the Lord Treasurer tendered his own resignation in the hope, as he wrote Dartmouth, of making his colleagues "know themselves." Abigail refused to deliver a message "so disagreeable" to Anne. When the opposition moved in the Lords that, the Protestant succession being in danger, the Queen be requested to offer a reward for the Pretender, the ministers rallied their forces and amended the resolution to read, that the succession was in no danger in Anne's reign and that she might offer the reward when she thought it necessary. Her reply to the address was pointed: "It would be a real strength to the succession of the House of Hanover as well as a support" to her "government that an end" be "put to these groundless fears and jealousies . . . so industriously promoted."

Bolingbroke was encouraged. "The Whigs have affronted the Queen and teased her servants almost a month without control," he wrote to Prior (April 20); "at last a spirit has been exerted which should in my poor opinion have been sooner shown, and they have been defeated in all their attacks, though fortified by a considerable detachment from our party." "Had we done in the last session as we have done in this," he commented to Strafford, "the peace had been long ago sanctioned, commerce opened with France, and the cry about the Protestant succession silenced."

His optimism was short-lived. Baron Schutz had requested (April 12) from the Lord Chancellor a writ summoning the Duke of Cambridge (the Electoral Prince) to attend in the House of Lords. In order to consult the Queen, Harcourt made excuse. He told Schutz later that the writ issued with the others as a matter of course and was only held until requested. Oxford agreed to send Lord Paget to Hanover to lend dignity to the mission of his relative. Already on the scene, Thomas Harley was instructed to explain to George and his mother that Anne would be affronted if the Prince insisted on his rights. The Queen expressed her feelings in a letter to Sophia.

Denied access to the English court, Schutz went home. The public learned Anne's side from a pamphlet, *Hannibal not at our Gates, or an Enquiry into the Grounds of our Present Fears of Popery and the Pretender in a Dialogue between my Lord Panick and George Steady, Esq.* In *A View of the Real Danger of the Protestant Succession,* Defoe suggested that the ministers had taken every possible precaution in favor of Hanover and that the current panic was the greatest danger to that house. The excitement produced four new papers: the *Reader,* the *Monitor,* the *Patriot,* and the *Muscovite.* The *Lover,* which Steele started in another strain in February, also took up politics.

Bolingbroke thought that the dismissal of Nottingham's son from the Jewel Office would be "worth the removal of two Whigs, and more grateful to our friends." Oxford meditated rather another effort to conciliate the Elector by paying the balance due for troops that had refused to follow Ormond in 1711. He appealed also to Halifax and Cowper. The former thought the country headed for "inevitable destruction," though they all professed "to mean the same thing." Those seemed "most to blame" who had "power to make good their professions by their actions." Cowper suggested that the Lord Treasurer exert himself "speedily . . . to get those out of power" who would "not so much as profess themselves to be for the true interest of their country." Bolingbroke complained that Oxford's brother introduced the question of paying the Hanoverian forces surreptitiously in the committee on supply without the previous knowledge of himself or Anne. He advised his friends to oppose it until they knew the pleasure of the Queen. He would support Oxford if the latter would "be pleased to honour" him with "thoughts of what measures" were "fit to be pursued."

Paget postponed going to Hanover, wishing a peerage before he went. Rumor said that Bolingbroke opposed his setting out and got the better of his chief. The Earl of Clarendon finally went, with John Gay as his Secretary, a mission as important in literary as in diplomatic annals. Thomas Harley came back home, leaving Oxford only private friends at Herrenhausen to emphasize his merits as supporter of the Electoral house and to decry Marlborough, Wharton, and the rest. One of Strafford's correspondents at home, recalling that diplomat's experience with an episcopal colleague at Utrecht, reported (May 25) the activity of "another bishop," encouraging the "breach in the ministry" and wishing "it worse than at first." The word was, that Bolingbroke as a Jacobite would be turned out.

That lord expressed himself to Strafford as resolved to court "the successor in no manner . . . inconsistent" with his obligations to the Queen. After her, if he survived, he would be loyal to the new régime. Meanwhile, he resented "artifices" used to "insinuate" that he "leaned to another interest and that the disputes . . . at court were occasioned by the favour of some men to the Pretender's cause." In this mood, he supported a measure intended either to discredit Oxford with the Church and Queen or to force him to greater zeal in their behalf. On its face, the Schism Bill proposed to eradicate dissent by prohibiting Dissenters from training children in their faith. When moving the bill in the House of Lords, Bolingbroke showed "the advantages it would be of in uniting the nation and stifling for the future the divisions" that so often made it weak.

Defoe tried to persuade Dissenters that his patron, obliged by political exigencies to support the bill, would do his best to mitigate its terms. While it pended, opponents of the ministry brought a charge reflecting on Bolingbroke's official conduct. The Viscount wrote to Oxford (June 3), asking help. "I am ready," he said, "to take any method you prescribe. I have neither power nor capacity to act alone in a matter of this importance, and if I had both, I know too well the order and subordination which is essential to government to attempt any such thing." The point was the twenty per cent. of the Assiento Contract reserved for Anne, it was said for the private benefit of Lady Masham, Bolingbroke, and Arthur Moore. The last was Bolingbroke's adviser in negotiating the commercial treaties with France and Spain.

The South Sea Company, now in hands less friendly to the ministers, notified its expectation that those who hoped to profit from the trade should take some risk. As a solution for the matter, Anne suggested to the House of Commons (June 9) that the share assigned to her be appropriated for the nation's debts. It transpired that Robert Monckton, a henchman of Oxford's late friend, Newcastle, was the Commissioner of Trade who raised the question. Consequently talk of changes did not cease.

"Lord B[olingbroke] goes on still merryly, and in his cups and out of his cups brags what a mighty man he is," said Peter Wentworth (June 29), gossiping to his brother. Recent events tempted him to break with Oxford. He complained to Strafford in mid-July that the Queen's affairs were in a "deplorable state by that glorious management with which . . . no man must presume to find fault." He had begged the Lord Treasurer "as a friend" to "alter his conduct and to represent to the Queen . . . that her government was at the brink of ruin." Anne would have to "extricate herself from these difficulties." He would decline "no danger, no labour . . . except one, . . . that of trusting the same conduct a fifth year" which had failed in the previous four. He accused Oxford of treating secretly with the opposition.

Anne addressed to Parliament (July 9) the parting hope that it would meet her again "early in the winter . . . in such a temper" as would be "necessary for the real improvement of . . . commerce and of all other advantages of the peace." News of the enlistment of troops in Ireland for the Pretender had determined her to offer the reward authorized by the House of Commons. Thereupon, the Lords suggested that the sum be fixed, not at five, but at a hundred thousand pounds. In this atmosphere, tense from years of party strife, a flimsy rumor started fears that banished sanity from sober minds.

The summer's problem was to find a ministry to ride the storm.[3]

The mercurial Bolingbroke was the ablest of those now pushing for a break with Oxford. But the uncertain Harcourt and the imperious Atterbury stood higher with the Church and Queen. The Secretary of State might have to enlist under them, should he break with his chief. In his hands, perhaps they would be easier clay. He might in time live down the Queen's distaste for his own way of life. At the moment he teased his neglected lady at Bucklebery with the promise of a month with her when Parliament rose. Her friends suggested that his new allies might have advised that he pay more attention to his wife.

His reputation would not vanish in a day. A choice story was his boast, "That he had done the Business of those dam'd Dogs the Dissenters in the Morning, been Drunk with the best Champaign in the Afternoon, and at Night went to Bed to the finest Whore in England and had the Pleasure to be tuckt up by a Couple of Peers." Peter Wentworth, entertaining his brother with a variant of the anecdote, identified the "blackguard Girle" as "Bell Chuck," a discarded mistress of Orrery, and the young peers as the lords Jersey and Bathurst. He thought they made "no pretty figure in the world to be pimps for his Lordship."

The court's contending factions made the Queen's life miserable through the early summer. Oxford elaborated proof that Bolingbroke had tried to undermine him since Guiscard's attempt. The Lord Treasurer now suspected of Jacobitism the colleagues who criticized his leadership. Harcourt, Atterbury, and Lady Masham urged Anne to dismiss him. Abigail refused in early June to carry further messages. Swift, at the same time, disheartened at the wrangling of his friends, went off to rusticate in Berkshire.

With him he took his portmanteau full of papers on which

[3] *Parliamentary History*, VI. 1256ff.; Boyer, *Political State*, VII. 215ff., 322ff.; VIII. 145, 228ff.; Hist. Mss. Com. *Portland*, V. 380ff., 400ff., 437ff.; Ball, *Correspondence of Swift*, II. 129ff.; Cartwright, *Wentworth Papers*, pp. 358ff., 382ff.; Coxe, *Robert Walpole*, I. 72ff.; Aitken, *Steele*, II. 2ff.; Parke, *Bolingbroke Correspondence*, IV. 493ff., 508ff., 529ff.

to meditate. In a last effort to reconcile his patrons, he sent anonymously in a disguised hand the manuscript for a pamphlet, through Charles Ford, the Gazetteer, to John Barber, the printer. Aware of the uncertainty of his place, Barber showed the manuscript to the Secretary of State. Recognizing merits, Bolingbroke thought that a few changes would suit it better to his case. He was too busy to make the changes, and publication was delayed. Swift and Ford found fault with Barber and Bolingbroke, though with slight excuse, since Swift knew well the liberties taken by any supervisor of the party press.

This incident confirmed in Swift distrust of Bolingbroke, which had grown in passing weeks. He had aspired to succeed Thomas Rymer as historiographer in order to transmit to posterity the fame of Anne. The place paid but two hundred pounds. Swift did not know it, but Bolingbroke sent his request to Shrewsbury, the Lord Chamberlain. The latter appointed Thomas Madox, a more appropriate successor to the compiler of the *Foedera,* eagerly sought by gentlemen of that age to fill their shelves. None of Swift's many talents qualified him for this place.

A month of quiet in the country with his papers and his thoughts inclined him to the side of Oxford. Moved by a generous impulse, he wrote that the Lord Treasurer's public actions had often "angered" him "to the heart, but as a private man never once." "The memory of one great instance of your candour and justice," he added, "I will carry with me to my grave, that, having been in a manner domestic with you for almost four years, it was never in the power of any public or concealed enemy to make you think ill of me, though malice and envy were often employed to that end." Pondering in his solitude events of the past few months, the Dean concluded that the Queen herself and perhaps the Duchess of Somerset were chiefly responsible for the failure of his hopes.

Lewis informed him (July 17) that Abigail told the Lord Treasurer in her own house that he "never did the [Queen] any service" or was "capable of doing her any." Oxford suffered these reproaches silently and supped with her and

Bolingbroke that night, but went out openly vowing vengeance. Those "under his banner" called her "ten thousand bitches and kitchen wenches." Arbuthnot, the same day, thought that Lady Masham and her faction had defied Oxford without knowing "how to do without him" and "without any scheme or likeness of it in any form or shape." The Lord Treasurer still held "with a dead gripe the little machine," the symbol of his power.

Anne was soon to go to Windsor, and changes, if any, would be made before she went. So thought (July 22) both Ford and Lewis. Oxford and Bolingbroke still met "every day in the Cabinet." They ate and drank together "as if there was no sort of disagreement" and afterward gave "one another such names as nobody but ministers of state could bear without cutting throats." Great preparations were making to receive Marlborough, who was coming home. The sport in coffee-houses was filling offices in the new ministry.

A conversation between Swift and Lord Harley at Oxford the same day inspired questions Swift proposed to Arbuthnot: Oxford, he was told, would be out in a few days, but "What can be your new scheme? What are your new provocations? Are you sure of a majority? Will not the Dragon [Oxford], when he is out, be able to draw off your friends? Lord Bolingbroke's language to me was quite contrary to his proceedings. Therefore I do not approve the last." Arbuthnot answered two days later that he and Swift were accused of keeping Oxford in, when he offered to "lay down." "I was told to my face," he continued, "that what I said in the case went for nothing; that I did not care if the great person's [Anne's] affairs went to ruin, so I could support the interests of the Dragon." Oxford's discomfiture was said to proceed from the Queen, not Bolingbroke. The writer thought the Lord Treasurer so "ill used" that he could not serve her for the future upon tolerable terms.

Swift neither wished to break with any of his friends nor to breathe the troubled air at court. "I now hear," he complained to Arbuthnot (July 25), that the historiographer's place "has been disposed of these three weeks to one Madox. I wonder Lord Bolingbroke knew nothing of it. So there is an end of that, and of twenty reflections one might make upon it. If the Queen is indifferent in these matters, I may well be so too." Canon Stratford, at whose house Swift saw Lord Harley, thought that the Dean would "behave decently" to his old friend, but would "adhere" to Abigail, which was less than just. On the day he wrote to Arbuthnot, he wrote also to the Lord Treasurer. He meditated return to Ireland, but "if you resign in a few days, as I am told you design to do, you may possibly return to Herefordshire, where I shall readily attend you, if you soon withdraw."

The hard-pressed statesman had appreciated and shown proudly Swift's earlier letter. He was even more grateful for this offer of kindly company and wrote to accept it the day after he was dismissed. He believed that "in the mass of souls" theirs were "placed near each other." His closing verse was as pathetic in form as sentiment. He sent it also to his sister to break the news that he was out.

> To serve with love,
> And share your blood,
> Approved is above;
> But here below,
> The examples show
> 'Tis fatal to be good.

On the day Oxford wrote to Swift, Lewis reported that the "runners were already employed to go to all the coffee-houses." "They rail," he said, "to the pit of Hell." To justify her action, Anne alleged that the Lord Treasurer "neglected business; that he was seldom to be understood; that when he did explain himself, she could not depend upon the truth of what he said; that he never came to her at the time she appointed; that he often came drunk; that lastly, to crown all, he behaved himself toward her with ill manners, indecency, and disrespect."

According to Defoe's inspired account, the dismissed minister spoke plainly enough at parting. The "people who pretended to succeed him would embark her Majesty in impracticable schemes, which, if her Majesty's own wisdom did not prevent it, would be her ruin." They would embroil her with her subjects at home and with neighbors and allies abroad. "Fully convinced it was always her Majesty's settled Resolution to preserve the Succession as it was established in the House of Hanover," he felt that "the Safety of her Majesty's Person and Reign, as well as the Peace of her Dominions after her Decease, depended upon preserving that Succession unalterable, as her Majesty had always expressed herself in Publick and in Private resolved to do." But the men she was about to trust, he was "satisfy'd," aimed at things "which if they did not directly advance the Interest of the Pretender yet tended to the Prejudice of the Succession of Hanover, and at least to keeping open the Breeches among the People." "No honest Man could join with them" after his proof of their "dangerous Designs." When the Queen realized that he had "lost her Favour to preserve her Person and Government," he hoped that she would not "lay that Sin to his charge."

Turning then to Harcourt, Atterbury, and others present, he "exposed their new Schemes to themselves, ridiculed their impolitic measures, and foretold them to what Distresses they would reduce themselves in a little Time, putting them in Mind of a Debt which they would owe to the National Justice at last and how unwilling they would be to pay it." Whether he railed or prophesied was not yet clear, but reunion with his old friends was made difficult.

Those who unhorsed him were not ready for their chance. They lacked a plan and time to make one. Anne's health, recently better than usual, suddenly gave way. There was no one to take the lead. Harcourt might have been Lord Treasurer in time, but that depended upon the Queen, now at the point of death. Argyll and Somerset appeared at Council and took part in the deliberation. Hearing that the Queen revived, her assembled Councillors unanimously desired that she name Shrewsbury at their head. Harcourt himself guided her hand to place in that of the last of the Talbot Dukes the white staff of the last Lord Treasurer. Whatever may have been the case before, none now attending, with the possible exception of Atterbury, thought of any successor but the one prescribed by law.

Barber had written to Swift the previous day, postponing an intended visit, when he would have taken "letters from Lord Bolingbroke and Lady Masham" urging him not to go to Herefordshire. "Pray do not go," he said; and again concluding, "For God's sake, do not go." By the same post, Lewis wrote that Oxford was "in council; so are the Whigs." Lady Masham had not received him "kindly." "Poor woman," he pitied her. A day later, Barber still recounted Bolingbroke's schemes for reconciling Swift with Lady Somerset and setting him "right with the Queen." Bolingbroke himself sent the same day his well-known bitter laugh: "The Earl of Oxford was removed on Tuesday; the Queen died on Sunday. What a world is this, and how does Fortune banter us!" Even so, he took heart in his postscript: "I have lost all by the death of the Queen but my spirit; and I protest to you I feel that increase upon me. The Whigs are a pack of Jacobites; that shall be the cry in a month, if you please."

Swift had no wish to lose his place in the new reign and went to Dublin to take his oaths. Oxford wrote to George I, making the most of services rendered. He congratulated the King on coming to the throne of his "ancestors." "I had the honour in two previous reigns," he said, "to express my love to my country by promoting what is now come to pass, your Majesty's succession to the Crown of these Kingdoms. It remains now that I assure your Majesty I shall study to show the zeal and devotion wherewith I am, Sir, your Majesty's most dutiful, most humble, and most obedient servant."

Oxford with the rest awaited the coming of the monarch he had done more than most others to place upon the throne. Whether or not he would enjoy the fruits of the triumph depended upon the Elector, who, since the death of his mother in early June, had been statutory heir of the British crown. Proverbially it was hazardous to trust the gratitude of a prince, but Oxford could do nothing else. Those whom Anne had enabled him to dislodge from power in 1710 liked him even less than those who had persuaded her to supersede him in her last hours.[4]

[4] Hist. Mss. Com., *Portland*, V. 464ff.; VII. 190ff.; Ball, *Correspondence of Swift*, II. 139ff.; Cartwright, *Wentworth Papers*, pp. 391ff.; Parke, *Bolingbroke Correspondence*, IV. 561ff.; *Parliamentary History*, VI. 1337ff.; Boyer, *Political State*, VII. 491ff.; VIII. 14ff.; *Flying Post*, July 22–24, 1714; [Defoe], *White Staff*, Pts. I–III; [Francis Atterbury], *The History of the Mitre and the Purse;* Swift, *Some Free Thoughts upon the Present State of Affairs, an Enquiry into the Behaviour of the Queen's Last Ministry*. David Nichol Smith, *The Letters of Jonathan Swift to Charles Ford*, pp. 11ff.

CHAPTER VIII

ANOTHER DAY, 1714–1716

As for the late *Ministers*, . . . the great *Engines* they made use of for keeping up a spirit against all Truth and Right were those very *Mobbs, Riots,* and *Tumults* which alone could keep a Multitude in such Ferment as to make them admire and press for their own Ruin. They thought it their Interest to govern by the Passions of the Crowd and were peculiarly dext'rous in the Management of them. They were possess'd of the full cry and the Noise of the Nation and likely, in all Probability, so to continue. . . . Their Security consisted in keeping up that vile Spirit to the Height. It is the Security of the King and his Government to have a Stop put to it and to remove every Opportunity that may give Fuel and Encouragement to it as far as is consistent with the Constitution and Liberties of the Nation.

JOSEPH ADDISON in *Arguments About the Alteration of Triennial Election of Parliaments*, April, 1716.

I

THE KINGDOM WAITS

AUGUST, 1714, was a long month for English leaders, anxious to know the King's mind. The unanimity of his proclamation made it less easy to support the view that the Queen's servants were Jacobites. The personnel of the regency and the designation of Addison as its Secretary revealed little. Harcourt was *ex-officio* chairman. The unforeseen dismissal of Oxford a few days before Anne's death deprived him of a place in the group. Shrewsbury sat by express designation and also as Lord Treasurer. Nottingham had a seat, with Marlborough and Sunderland left out. After a fortnight, Bolingbroke's circle felt that the "list" revealed "no ill disposition" and thought the King "not apt to be hasty in removing the persons he found in employment." That Secretary of State wrote to George in French three days earlier than Oxford's letter—in fact, the very day he wrote to Swift—testifying his "joy" on "becoming the subject of so great a prince." He would serve him with the same loyalty given to the Queen, "whether at court, in parliament, or in" his "county." Peter Wentworth noted his Lordship's bonfire the night the King was proclaimed and the "finest illumination in town at his house in Golden Square." Ford reminded Swift that Bolingbroke had proposed the new Lord Treasurer both "in Council and to the Queen" and thought that the two might work together with Shrewsbury at the head.

Dartmouth wrote to George a day later than Bolingbroke. His relations with Anne made it his "duty in particular" to assure the King that "no subject in" his "dominions" did "more sincerely rejoice at the zeal and unanimity . . . expressed by all sorts of people for securing" the succession. Three days later, Peterborough brought the news from Paris that Louis XIV would abide by his treaties. On the same day Erasmus Lewis reported to Swift that the town was filling up. "We are gaping and staring," he said, "to see who is to rule us. The Whigs think they shall engross all; we think we shall have our share." Factions in Council and Parliament still vied in showing favors to the new house.

John Erskine, Earl of Mar, was not easy in his mind. On the last day of the Queen's life he had helped to make arrangements for the peaceful enforcement of the law, praying that "God direct the people . . . to behave themselves right and prevent making" the country "a field of blood and confusion." A week later, he noticed that Anne's ministers were still called Jacobites. The King's coming would precipitate the question, "who shall be most in his favour, and it must be time only that can show who will be togither." He would probably lose his place. If paid his arrears, he did not care; then he would "do the best" he could for himself. Remembering his inability to speak a language the King could understand, he was more pessimistic in another week, but still disposed to look out for himself, though the new house would find him a "faithful subject." He wrote before the end of the month to remind the King that an Erskine had been "honoured with the care" of his "Majesty's Grand Mother" and to offer himself "as faithful and dutiful a subject and servant as ever any" of his family had been.

Ten days after the Queen's death, Harcourt was troubled and sought Atterbury's advice, because he had not written to the new monarch. That prelate urged the Chancellor to open his mind "plainly and nakedly," writing as head of the party. "One way of addressing him," the Bishop added, would "risque more. This I could wish your Lordship would do, and would take the steps proper to enable you to do it; but I do not find your Lordship so disposed, and therefore am silent on that subject." Harcourt was not an intrenched churchman, and meditated a safer course.

Atterbury and Bolingbroke tried for a while to reunite with their old colleagues. But they had given wounds too deep. As one of Oxford's followers, Lewis preferred to "see his dead Carcase." Had not "Charteris, Brinsden, and all the runners been employed to call him dog, villain, sot, and worthless?" Should he "join them" after this? Atterbury himself denied any obligation to Oxford, loading "him with a thousand crimes." Lewis thought "his greatest in reality was preferring" the Bishop.

More practical in his thoughts, Oxford tried to concert with Dartmouth and Bromley what to do. He felt in doggerel his own case to be better than that of "those who did conspire for to bring in James, Esquire" and now hoped to be "saved by their own bonfire." Several things seemed clear. The King lacked information for forming a "competent government or administration." No faction could form one by itself. Opponents of the Queen's last ministry had not "amongst them credit enough or perhaps sufficient spirit to form such a settlement." This "settlement should be made by understanding among those wishing it." It was a plan he long had had at heart; he did not yet appreciate the ground that he had lost. Onlookers at the procession, when the new King was proclaimed, heard both hisses and cheers for Bolingbroke; but no cheers for the dismissed Lord Treasurer.

Peter Wentworth bubbled over as usual. He hoped that the new King would give him a better berth at court. He rejoiced at his Majesty's gracious replies to letters Strafford had written. Since the journey to England lay through Holland, the Ambassador at The Hague would have early access to his new master.

Absent from this feverish atmosphere of hope and vain desire, Swift had insight which he sometimes lacked. He wished Oxford (August 15) "good success in this new scene" and "credit enough with the King to set him right in his opinions of persons and things." He was "tempted to think" it a "peculiar favor of Providence" that his patron was out before the death of Anne, but warned him that he still had "as hard a game to play as any man . . . in England." In less danger perhaps, he would be censured as much as though he had held on to the end.

A week earlier, without fixing blame, the Dean had reproached Bolingbroke that he and Oxford had not held together. In consequence, he said: "Your machine of four years modelling is dashed in pieces in a moment; and, as well by the choice of Regents as by their proceedings, I do not find there is any intention of managing you in the least." The Council contained men in earnest either about the peace or the succession; it was impossible to think the King impressed with the good disposition of the Church party. As for the future, Bolingbroke was in the prime of life. To be head of the Church party was "no mean station." The question was, whether one "now a general who had lost a battle and confidence in himself and his troops" would "go on with the same vigour" as in "early youth." Leadership was needed, said the Dean. "We have certainly more heads and hands than our adversaries; but it must be confessed that they have stronger shoulders and better hearts." If employed to manage the elections, he would guarantee to the new government a majority in the new Parliament.

A week later (August 13), Bolingbroke was still hopeful that the "violent measures" which "would be advised" might not be "pursued." The country was never in a "better temper," and he could only trust his own "conduct to clear" him. If employed, he would serve the King on the same principles as he had the Queen "to the last gasp"; otherwise he would discharge his "duty honestly and contentedly in the House of Peers."

Watching the crowd, Defoe could not at first perceive its drift. A week afterward, he began to contribute to the *Flying Post and Medley,* which Hurt started in the Hanoverian interest, when Ridpath found another printer for his *Flying Post.* But the "surprising turn given by the immediate hand of Providence to the state of things" led him to hold up (August 3) a pamphlet "actually in the press and a part of it printed off" designed to vindicate Oxford's "person and conduct" and to expose his enemies.

In the latter part of August, the "juncture" was still "so nice" that he could "hardly tell which way to direct words so to suit the fluctuating tempers of the people as not to do harm instead of good." He thought it prudent for the moment to deal in "generals," though he still designed a publication to distinguish Oxford's ministry from that which would have followed had the Queen survived. In answer to a piece, probably by John Oldmixon, pointing out *The False Steps of the Ministry after the Revolution, Shewing that the Lenity and Moderation of that Government was the Occasion of all the Factions which have endangered the Constitution,* Defoe defended his earlier patron from too great clemency and by implication suggested that William's example would do to emulate.[1]

Oxford and Bolingbroke might well have mused that month upon the martyrs they had made. It was a formidable list: Sunderland, Townshend, Stanhope, Walpole, Marlborough, Steele. On the day the Queen became ill, papers carried the news that Thomas Pelham-Holles, Lord Pelham, heir also of much of the estate of his uncle, John Holles, Duke of Newcastle, celebrated by a sumptuous feast his coming of age. Townshend, who the previous year had taken for his second

---

[1]Both of these pamphlets are in *Somers Tracts,* XIII. 559ff. That of Defoe is there attributed to Walpole.

spouse Dorothy, sister of Robert Walpole, had Pelham's half-sister for his earlier wife. Stanhope married the same year Lucy, youngest daughter of the famous Governor Pitt. On the day in mid-August that Bothmer wrote to inform the new King's intention to command his services, she presented him with twins, the first offspring of the wedding. Pelham was already thinking of his marriage later made with Harriet Godolphin, whose two grandfathers were joint heads of the Queen's great ministry.

Marlborough, the surviving member of that partnership, had neither taste nor talent for domestic politics. His prestige and his wealth made him as necessary in a government as his Duchess made him undesirable. The younger members of the opposition had worked as equals in the Queen's last years and hopefully awaited their rewards. None had achieved unquestioned leadership; the King would have to choose.

Bothmer, who had helped against the peace, was sent over from The Hague again in June, 1714, to regain the ground lost by the false move of Schutz in asking for the writ. Clarendon, who reached Hanover only a few days before Anne's death, reported to Bromley that George would not speak to Schutz on his return; but he thought that "Bernsdorff," the Elector's minister, was governed by Robethon, his Secretary, who from the point of view of Bromley's party was "as bad as bad" could be.

Bothmer was shrewd. The plan was, for Marlborough to take immediate command of the army if the Pretender's friends should make a show of force. But Oxford, through Thomas Harley, raised doubts in Bothmer's mind concerning the Duke's own relations with the rival court. There was no need for troops, and Bothmer thought it better to delay bestowing the command. He heard his master's proclamation from the carriage of the Duke of Buckingham.

Events did not break well for Marlborough. After months of exile, he was hurrying home to help preserve his country from a Roman Catholic king imposed by France. Contrary winds delayed, and he learned before he landed that Anne was dead and George proclaimed. He hesitated how to make his entry to the city where his old mistress lay a corpse. Some friends suggested a procession, which others thought in questionable taste. He started with just two hundred, but the number grew. Some voices acclaimed him; many shouted on the other side. His carriage broke down at the Temple gate.

Though Bothmer greeted him, there were unasked questions concerning his omission from the list of regents. If his absence made it prudent to have one near at hand, Sunderland might have served. The Duke tarried in town only long enough to take the oaths and to entertain at dinner (August 6) Bothmer, Stanhope, Walpole, and the rest. Two days later he went to Windsor and thence to Bath to see his daughter, Lady Sunderland, already ill of the disease which in a few months was to cause her death.

His immediate task performed, Bothmer hurried back to Hanover to know his master's further will. When young James Craggs, who had gone thither to carry the official notice of Anne's death, returned about the middle of August, Ford observed to Swift that though nothing was given out, the "Whigs looked dejected"; their friends, "very much pleased." The King had sent permission for his predecessor's funeral, at first set for Sunday afternoon, August 22. On Saturday it was found that "the ladies could not get their clothes ready," and the ceremony was postponed to Tuesday. Even then the Duchess of Somerset pleaded ill and left her Grace of Ormond to be chief mourner. Atterbury officiated as Dean of Westminster and laid away the body of the last of the Stuart sovereigns beside her husband in the vault. On Thursday Defoe published a piece in the *Flying Post and Medley* designed to serve the King, but reflecting on Ormond and Anglesey. Anglesey was among the Regents, and Defoe was taken up.

Nevertheless, the day was just about to dawn. On the last Saturday in the month (August 28), Bothmer returned from Hanover bringing news that the King would further delay his coming to stop in Holland. The following Tuesday about noon Shrewsbury, Cowper, and Somerset went to the Cockpit, shut and sealed Bolingbroke's offices there, and told him that the King had no further need of his services. Bromley and Mar remained as Secretaries of State, but this step could scarcely be interpreted as favorable to the dead Queen's ministers. Hitherto, their opponents had chiefly gloated when they saw the Secretary of State waiting bag in hand in Addison's office. Notifying Robethon of the action the same day, Bothmer inclosed the letters of Bolingbroke and Mar to the King. The former had asked to speak with Bothmer.

After that interview, the deposed Secretary tried by tawdry humor to conceal from Atterbury his chagrin. He was neither surprised nor concerned at the fact of his removal, but the "manner" of it "shocked" him "for at least two minutes." He had "writ the King" and "spoken with" Bothmer. Sunday he was going home not to return until he had "advices from hence." To the "grief" of his "soul," his party was "gone" for "lack of men of business" who would "live and draw together." Still, nothing would "fright" him from doing "right for the Church and the Nation," though the method of doing it might now have to be "altered."

Word was soon abroad that Oxford had achieved his rival's fall. Bothmer was entertained that Bolingbroke himself repeated it. Addison informed Robethon (September 4) that the removal had "put a seasonable check to an interest that was making in many places for members in the next Parliament." The people "relished" it, ascribing to him "in a great measure the decay of trade and public credit." On the same day Bolingbroke held a farewell levee of clergy and friendly noblemen before he went to the country for his wait.

On the day that Bolingbroke was dismissed from his service, George Lewis, Elector of Hanover, already in his fifty-fifth year, bade farewell to his orangery at Herrenhausen and started for the scene of his new duties as George I, King of Great Britain. Had he understood fully the difficulties confronting him, he might have been even more reluctant to plunge from these familiar places into an undertaking so difficult and likely to bring so little pleasure in the uncertain case of his success. At that stage there was no drawing back, and many of his more serious problems, unforeseeable from past experience, did not trouble him as yet.

He had only been to England once before, a fleeting, youthful visit as a possible suitor for the hand of the princess who now bequeathed the crown. There had been many changes since that time, which if he had known of them, he would not have understood. The little knowledge he had of the people was by hearsay. He did not speak their language. He could not share their feelings, which was a more serious matter than inability to think their thoughts. Without ceasing to be Elector, he had become King, lacking imagination to separate the offices in his mind. He would always be George Lewis, a single character, incapable of a dual rôle.

A study of the experience of the other foreign King who in his time had worn the English crown would not have helped. William had never learned how to be on good terms with his island people and had always trusted Dutch advisers more. His heart was in his Continental task. George could scarcely realize the fixed determination among his new subjects, set forth frankly in the Act of Settlement, to deny him privileges experience with William had taught them to withhold. They demanded that a prince past the meridian of life, Protestantism his chief qualification for the crown, now of a sudden learn to feel and act an English patriot's part.

His handicaps were many. He succeeded a pious woman who left behind a swarm of ladies in the court circle and others out of it aspiring to shine there. Their applications, already pouring in, revealed them only less ambitious than the men in search of place. He had shut up his own wife. Such womenkind as he would take would be a hindrance rather than a help. His daughter-in-law would have to bear this burden, but if she magnified her circle enough to serve the purpose, the chances were, she would embroil herself with him.

He had also to be head of a Church with a dogma and ritual of which his knowledge was probably as slight as his taste for them. This Church was scarcely less powerful in the country than the government itself, and could not be defied. He had to learn how to work with its friends when necessary, to conform outwardly, and to dissemble emotions he might never learn to feel. Many churchmen still attributed to the King divine, hereditary right. To them he would always be a foreign usurper, to be tolerated, if at all, only because the native-born, legitimate Prince was loyal to his father's faith. Perhaps the hardest task was to select immediately from a multitude of eager candidates the ministers through whom to exercise his power. With little knowledge or experience to guide, he had personally to make this choice on which the fate of his entire reign might turn. If he took seriously those loudest in their loyalty to his house, it would be dangerous to retain the Queen's old servants until he learned to know the men he might command. Little wonder he made no haste to be in his new realm, postponing questions that were difficult. Perhaps in Holland he might glean some insight on his way.

Regardless of the Act of Settlement, he could not do without his German servants. They had to be his chief advisers until he learned whom else to trust. Thus far they had been engineers of his remarkable success. They had more enthusiasm for the venture and hoped to profit more from it than he. Their expectations might, indeed, at times inhibit good advice. They did not fully understand the envy and distrust that they would meet. They were tolerated, because they had to be endured while George had no one else on whom to lean.

Having worked in England, Bothmer had more insight than the rest. He suggested Townshend to the King as Bolingbroke's successor, though Sunderland also wished the place. Noting the warmth of members of the Regency at the thought, he cautioned Robethon that George must not change his plans and land at Harwich instead of Greenwich, where the anxious gentry were planning to assemble when he came. Earlier, he had warned the Hanoverian ministers that while Bernstorff might lodge in the Palace, "Görtz and others" should live in furnished houses in the neighborhood. He entreated Görtz "not to think of putting the expense of his tables or any other expense for the court" that he would bring "upon the civil list." To do so would not only be "contrary to the laws," it would be bad politics, in that it would "exasperate" people in England, making them less inclined to mitigate the terms embedded in the Act of Settlement. "We may depend upon it," he said bluntly, "that this pretension of maintaining our Hanoverian court in this country at the expence of England would not be admitted."

In his fortnight at The Hague, George found the Dutch solicitous to help and Strafford ever eager to attend. He and his son sailed on the *Peregrine* shortly after noon, Thursday, September 16, attended by the Dutch and English fleets. They arrived at Hope, near Gravesend, the next day, mid-afternoon, but anchored on account of fog. Not until Saturday afternoon did they reach Greenwich.

Waiting in town, the anxious Oxford guessed from the Tower guns that the landing was at six o'clock and sent that night "John the running footman" to inform his son at Wimpole. Townshend had been sworn in as Secretary of State on Friday, which "some" out of doors thought "a great disappointment to Lord Sunderland." But Cadogan's appointment to Flanders was announced at the same time.

Apparently the King had pondered the advice of Bothmer. When, with the help of Peter Wentworth, he and the Prince stepped from the barge that brought them from the *Peregrine* to the shore, he greeted the Duke of Northumberland, Captain of the Life Guard, and Harcourt, who as Lord Chancellor was acting for the Regency. Then, waving proffered chairs aside, they walked to the royal house in the park attended, according to Boyer, "by most of the Nobility and great Numbers of the Principal Gentry, through an infinite Crowd of people, who still repeated their joyful Acclamations." After a little while the new arrivals withdrew to sup in privacy, leaving the majority to bonfires and illuminations. Only those in favor were summoned to attend within. Harcourt, Ormond, and Trevor were among the notables left without.

Townshend informed Ormond the next day that the King would welcome him at court, but required no longer his services as Captain General. Marlborough had to be restored to his old place. At ten o'clock on Sunday morning his Majesty came forth to greet important men. By eleven crowds thronged "all the Upper Rooms, Galleries, and the Hall below." Some "pressed so rudely about" him that George returned again to his bedchamber, where "only a few of the prime Nobility were admitted." In the surging crowd outside was Oxford, eager and early to pay his court. Surviving hopes were dashed by the formality with which his Majesty waved him by to greet the next man in the crush. He was not invited to the inner room with Marlborough, Shrewsbury, Somerset, Nottingham, Argyll, Townshend, Pelham, Halifax, Somers, Stanhope, and the rest.

Monday he rode "sledge way in his coach" in the procession from Greenwich to St. James's. The office of arms was puzzled about the arrangement, and it was noon before it left. Even then the two hundred coaches with six horses each were not in the prescribed array. At St. Margaret's Hill, Southwark, they met the Lord Mayor and heard an address by the City Recorder, Sir Peter King. The Tower guns were fired when the King took coach and also when he crossed the London Bridge. It was "a very fair day," brightened by bonfires into the night. Effigies of Sacheverell here and there were fuel in the flames. Oxford's daughter, Lady Dupplin, found some comfort that it was dark when the procession reached the Strand, and from there to St. James's the King could not be seen.

Harcourt learned from Townshend the next day that Cowper would get his seal. That Lord's wife had for some time corresponded with the Princess of Wales in the hope of finding favor in the new court. Cowper himself, as one of the Regents, had prepared an essay on English politics to guide the King, which his Lady turned into French to be given to his Majesty when occasion came. When he kissed hands, George greeted the new Lord Chancellor in French. The latter's reply in English was not defiant patriotism, merely evidence of inability to speak a language familiar to a foreign king.

His Majesty moved slowly. How could he know which of the pressing suitors for his favor would serve him best? Townshend, as the only Secretary of State of his appointment, was thus far mouthpiece of his will. Whether he would be prime minister was not yet clear. Such an official was wanted neither by the King nor by his German court. By placing the Treasury in commission and withholding the "white staff" after taking it from Shrewsbury they imagined that they would be rid of the prestige which in Anne's reign attached to the Lord Treasurer. None explained to them that the King's favor was only one important factor in making a minister first among his colleagues. A secretary of state, if he achieved the place, might be prime minister.

Their first thought was to fill the offices without regard to the existing factions, omitting only those suspected of sympathizing with the Jacobites. Nottingham and others of the Finch family came in, but Hanmer would not be Chancellor or Bromley Teller of the Exchequer. The tender of these places was contrary to the advice that Cowper gave. Perhaps this disregard of political realities was the occasion for his counsel.

Professing impartiality, he warned the King that it would be impossible to distribute favors without advantage to one group or another. It was for George to "determine" which should have the "chief share" of his "confidence." Having chosen, it was "wholly" in his "power by showing favours in due time" to procure a majority in Parliament for those he might elect. A party out of power ought to be used with "tenderness," but under the circumstances it seemed prudent to prefer men who had supported with zeal the Hanoverian cause.

Whether the King and the Germans wished it to be so or not, the recognition of Townshend and Marlborough and the refusal of leaders of the Church party to take the proffered places made Cowper's program inevitable in the end. August 20, Peter Wentworth thought "the Striff . . . who shall show themselves the most zealous for the present King George." But a month later, he found, "The Whigs reckon they carry all before them, and the Tories in a manner gave it up." Lord Berkeley of Stratton, after the bustle of going to Greenwich and the procession back to town, was afraid that the King would not remember a single face that greeted him. He hoped his friend, Strafford, had taken advantage of opportunities in Holland, for in England George was "soe beset by some people" that he heard only one side. Oxford concluded sadly that his old friends would all soon be out, since "zeal for the succession and loyalty" would not be "extraordinary advocates for any to keep their places who" had "no other characteristics."

But all obeyed the summons and pushed into the most favored places to see the final ceremonies inaugurating the new reign. Even Bolingbroke returned from Bucklebery for the coronation, appointed for October 20. Before that time Stanhope gave up a cherished military career to become Secretary of State in Bromley's place. For Scotland, Montrose succeeded Mar. William Pulteney, a young orator in the Commons soon to marry the rich and beautiful Miss Gumley, became Secretary at War; Robert Walpole, Paymaster of the Forces. October 11 Halifax was finally sworn in as the First Lord of the Treasury. That evening at Marlborough House he "hardly spoke a word the whole dinner time," looking "full of rage and as if he could have killed everybody at the table," because the white staff was denied.

Fortunately, that same day the Princess of Wales reached Rochester on her way to London. Her arrival was the excuse for other bonfires and illuminations. The first ladies of the land attended her to know their fate. Lady Cowper obtained her place. Women in the Marlborough set were favored too. Even the Duchess of Shrewsbury bedeviled the King until she was thought to rival his German mistresses, and he humored her with appointment as an extra in the list. The sarcastic remembered that she too was a foreigner and on becoming a Duchess had salved her reputation.

On the fated day a scafford fell outside Westminister Abbey, killing a score of the King's subjects who had come to see the show. Within, Lady Nottingham somewhat rudely elbowed Lady Cowper from her seat and up the pulpit stairs, where she had a better view and was moved to tears at seeing her "holy Religion thus preserved as well as . . . Liberties and Properties." She saw also Bolingbroke doing homage. He and the King there met for the first time, and the latter asked his name of an attendant. Hearing the inquiry, the Viscount "turned round and bowed three times down to the very ground." Oxford's family found no pleasure in the festivities of the court. Lady Dupplin did not attend the coronation, dining that night in company with her father.[2]

II

UNEASY STEPS

It was not Oxford's nature to give up a fight. Toward the end of September Defoe advised that it was the artifice of "the present politicians . . . to have it believed that all who acted under the late administration were enemies to the succession of the present king." In the "stream" then running "such absurdities" might "go down." "Honest men" could only "reserve themselves," hoping a better time to come. Within the next week appeared the first installment of *The Secret History of the White Staff,* an effort to explain how Oxford had made use of Jacobites and thwarted opponents in his own ministry to serve the Hanoverian cause. The sudden death of Anne prevented all the world from knowing the wide gulf between his views and the intentions of his colleagues, who conspired to turn him out.

Defoe offered also in the same month *Advice to the People of Great Britain,* showing what they "ought to expect from the

[2] For these events from the death of Anne to the coronation of George I see: Basil Williams, *Stanhope, A Study in Eighteenth Century Diplomacy,* chs. v–vi; Boyer, *Political State,* VIII. 88ff.; W. M. Torrens, *History of Cabinets,* I. 50ff.; James Macpherson, *Original Papers,* II. 535ff.; *Somers Tracts,* XIII. 631ff.; *Diary of Mary, Countess Cowper,* pp. 1ff.; Nulle, *Newcastle,* pp. 54ff.; Lee, *Defoe,* I. 221ff.; Coxe, *Robert Walpole,* I. 64ff.; II. 44ff.; *Marlborough,* III, 557ff.; Parke, *Bolingbroke Correspondence,* IV. 578ff.; W. H. Wilkins, *Caroline the Illustrious,* I. 163ff.; Ball, *Correspondence of Swift,* II. 211ff.; Cartwright, *Wentworth Papers,* pp. 409ff.; *Parliamentary History,* VI. Appendix, pp. ccxliiiff.; VII. 1ff.; Folkestone Williams, *Memoirs and Correspondence of Francis Atterbury,* I. 277ff.; Hearne, *Collections,* IV. 401ff.; John, Lord Campbell, *Lives of the Chancellors* (Phila., 1848), IV. 287, 344ff.; Hardwicke, *State Papers,* II. 522ff.; William King, *Memoirs of Sarah, Duchess of Marlborough,* p. 265; Philip Henry Stanhope, fifth Earl Stanhope, *History of England* (third edition), I. Appendix, pp. ixff.; Hist. Mss. Com., *Portland,* V. 476ff.; VII. 197ff.; *Mar and Kellie,* pp. 505ff.; *Cowper,* III. 109ff.; *Dartmouth,* pp. 320ff.; *Stuart,* I. 333ff.

King" and how "behave to him." Less than a fortnight after the coronation came the second part of *The Secret History of the White Staff*, elaborating Oxford's method of using Jacobites in order to thwart them in the end. The author enlarged also on the alleged conspiracy against the Earl in the last days of the Queen, imputing the chief blame to Atterbury, Harcourt, and Lady Masham. Bolingbroke had not entirely "adopted their Game"; "he neither had Folly enough to engage in so preposterous an Attempt as that of the Pretender, nor had he Ignorance enough" to follow such leaders. He cooperated with them in order to rule them at a later time. In the crisis before the death of Anne, when Atterbury gave "a Loose to his Passion, which boiling up to Despair caused him to go off the Stage *raving,* having neither Grace to repent of what was pass'd or Patience to consider what was to come," and Harcourt "stood wavering between every Opinion," Bolingbroke "by a few Words dissolv'd all the Conspiracy." His alleged speech was quoted at length, the pamphleteer admitting frankly that the speaker "was never in the Interest of the Pretender."

Defoe knew that neither the King's ministers nor some of Oxford's former friends would like this frankness. The latter soon replied in *The History of the Mitre and the Purse, in which the First and Second Parts of the Secret History of the White Staff are fully considered, and the Hypocricy and Villainies of the Staff himself are laid Open and Detected.* The author, Atterbury, it was said, called Defoe a "Mercenary that has been hired to raise a Dust." The pamphlet was a defense of the Bishop and Harcourt with a malicious attack on Oxford. Bolingbroke was represented in an uncertain rôle.

Canon Stratford reported Harcourt's son to be the sponsor of another pamphlet in reply. Confined for some weeks by a stroke, Defoe himself had to delay the third part of his work. Not all of Oxford's friends were sure that this activity would do him good. Arbuthnot thought the first part "either contrived by an enemy or by himself to bring down vengeance." All that Oxford could ever say would "not give him a single friend amongst the whole party."

These and other pamphlets were but symptoms of the emotions with which the country seethed, revealing the divided leadership of factions out of office. Those in place were having troubles too. Some said, Marlborough was seeking to "engross all power." Halifax remained disgruntled. Bernstorff admitted to Lady Cowper in late November that too much had been conceded to Nottingham and the Church party. Oxford heard about the same time that the Germans and their English allies were not congenial. Only "fear of the Tories" kept them "from outraging each other." It was no more possible to "guess" the outcome of the "confusion" than to "judge of the event of madmen's contrivances."

Then the Pretender intervened. November 13 the chief men of England received by post a declaration issued August 29 at Plombieres asserting his claim to the crown and Anne's sympathy with it in her last hours. As a brochure, it soon made one of the scores of pamphlets that were piled up in the stalls and hawked about the streets. Ballads were sung on city corners where the people passed. The frightened ministers were moved to act.

Townshend wrote to the Lord Mayor asking help. The King in Council ordered the Justices of Peace to "put into Execution with the utmost Rigour the Laws in force against Printing, Publishing, and Spreading of false and scandalous Libels." Within a few days, according to the current prints, London was "almost entirely rid of the Pestilent Vermin of Libel-Cryers and Ballad-Singers."

Their spirit was not quenched. Even on the night of the coronation, especially in provincial towns, some members of the Church party resented by force indignities to the image of Sacheverell. Atterbury's faction now labored to make Ormond the hero of their cause. The *Examiner* was revived. An expression of an Oxford student's wit appeared above a college gate: "A King a Cuckold, a Prince a Bastard." All factions labored to magnify their interests in the new Parliament. Those in the King's favor tried by compromise to avoid contests. Oxford hoped to save a little from the wreck. Atterbury's faction harped on *Church* and *Ormond*. That prelate sent forth an anonymous pamphlet, *English Advice to the Freeholders of England,* the most provocative piece in the campaign.

People were well disposed, he said, but enemies to the Church were busier than its friends. "Bank-bills, places, lies, threats, promises, entertainments" were "everywhere employed to corrupt men's affections and mislead their judgments." If the ministers won the next election, their opponents would not have another chance. "Clubs, coffee-houses, addresses" were full of accusations that the Queen's ministry had favored the Pretender. It was an ill omen that the "King's first compliment to his people after touching English ground" was the "removal of the Duke of Ormond." He was "brave, loyal to the Queen, held money in contempt, but he was a churchman and a churchman not to be perverted."

He was but one case. "All who lay under the imputation of having been esteemed by the late Queen were treated as enemies to the King." Churchmen could not "be too ill used" owing either to "the effect of a westerly wind some months ago and of Dutch air; of the Earl of Oxford's ordinary witchcraft, or the Duke of Marlborough's money." But if the Church party was Jacobite, why was "none of the traitors seized and examined; no papers nor evidence produced?" Had the ministerialists "another Oxford among them, of too merciful a disposition to bring offenders to condign punishment?" Perhaps not. He, "good man," had "not his equal upon earth." Evidence had been sought diligently; could it be that none was found? And so on to lists in paralleled columns of the things that would result from the choice of a Parliament favorable to the Church and one favorable to the men in office.

There were other writers on both sides. In January, 1715, from his bed, Defoe sent *A Reply to a Traitorous Libel intitled English Advice to the Freeholders of England.* The world had been unkind to the author since his royal mistress died, and he had offered earlier in the month *An Appeal to Honour and Justice* in apology for his own actions. He was at work on it when stricken ill. A little later in the month appeared the third part of *The Secret History of the White Staff.*

Bolingbroke came to town in the first days of the new year

to confer with Atterbury, Ormond, Strafford, and Arthur Moore. These were now the active leaders in the Church party; nevertheless, it was too strong to press to the wall. Divided among themselves, the ministers could not afford to leave to those they had unhorsed credit that could be taken away. Already they were preparing for any charges that there was evidence to make. Bolingbroke, they complained, destroyed his papers. Stair, who went to Paris in Prior's place, was ordered to obtain such information as he could. Strafford's papers were seized as soon as he returned. But Bernstorff complained to Cowper that Halifax would not coöperate against the old ministers and was too intimate with Oxford. Under the guise of a caution against Arians, the King directed the clergy not to sermonize in favor of hereditary right or to "meddle in affairs of state or government."

The Pretender helped again by publicly professing loyalty to his Church. January 8, Townshend introduced to the King the Lord Mayor and other citizens of London to urge action against those responsible for the peace. Three days later a proclamation issued against the author and publisher of Atterbury's pamphlet. The call for the new Parliament asked the constituencies to choose "the fittest persons to reduce the present Disorders" and to "have a particular Regard to such as shew'd Firmness to the Protestant Succession when it was most in Danger." In the light of this request, freeholders in Buckinghamshire and citizens of London instructed their members-elect to make inquiry into the conduct of the late war and the lost fruits of the victory. In the latter part of February appeared the first number of the *Observator; being a Sequel to the Englishman,* which appealed for the impeachment of the late ministers on the ground that nothing less could clear some men.[3]

Oxford and Bolingbroke went to the country after a stay in London in the early weeks of 1715. The former was ill and

[3] Boyer, *Political State,* VIII. 362ff.; IX. 15ff.; *A Complete and Impartial History of the Impeachments,* pp. iiiff.; Lady Cowper, *Diary,* pp. 12ff.; Cartwright, *Wentworth Papers,* pp. 434ff.; Hearne, *Collections,* IV. 418; Hist. Mss. Com., *Portland,* V. 501ff.; VII. 208ff.; Lee, *Defoe,* I. 239ff.; *Somers Tracts,* XIII. 522ff.; Hardwicke, *State Papers,* II. 528.

troubled about moving his books and manuscripts. His zeal as a collector helped to occupy his mind. At Brampton for the election, only in Herefordshire could he report success. Bolingbroke was beginning to be worried. He returned to town for the meeting of the new Parliament, but John Drummond reported to Oxford his "great concern" that some of Anne's old servants might testify against the others. Hearing that Stanhope, just back from a mission to Vienna, was going through the state papers, Bolingbroke offered to wait on him if he could help.

When Parliament met (March 17), the House of Commons was "weeded" with greater speed and fewer scruples than usual. At once the leaders showed their hand. The King's speech, which Cowper read, expressed obligations to those who had brought him to the throne of his "ancestors" and regret that "unparalleled success" in war had not resulted in "a good peace." The "Pretender" was still a danger in Lorraine. The "eyes of Europe" watched the first session of his first Parliament.

The address of the Lords (March 22) expressed their "wonder" and "resentment" that the Pretender was suffered to remain so "near" and pledged themselves to help his Majesty "secure what" was "due . . . by treaties; ease . . . debts; preserve the public credit; restore . . . trade; extinguish the very hopes of the Pretender; and recover the reputation of the kingdom in foreign parts" lost by the faults of particular men, not by "the nation in general." Trevor, Bolingbroke, Shrewsbury, Buckingham, and others thought the reputation of the kingdom ought to be maintained, denying that it needed recovery. Oxford was ill, and abode at home. Cowper, speaking for the ministry, censured no person in particular, but the "peace in general," imputing blame to the advisers of the Queen.

Walpole and Stanhope took the lead in the House of Commons the next day. When Wyndham, Bromley, Shippen, and others of the Church party objected to the address as a reflection on the Queen, Walpole said, the design was "to vindicate her memory by exposing and punishing those evil counsellors who deluded her into pernicious measures." Stanhope alleged again that papers were destroyed, but there survived enough to prove "the late Ministers the most corrupt that ever sat at the Helm." Ormond in particular, he named. Rumor said that a paper from Oxford found among the Queen's effects accused Harcourt and Bolingbroke as Jacobites.

The divisions on the addresses were, 244 to 138 in the Commons and 66 to 33 in the Lords. The King's ministers were in control, but they had pledged themselves to a perilous undertaking likely to unite most of the Queen's old servants in defense of her memory. With only circumstantial evidence, they had accused their predecessors of heinous crimes. Could they make it treason to have negotiated the peace, admitting all they charged? The answer to that question was never known. They found an ally they did not expect.

Prior was coming back from Paris. The ministers hoped that evidence might be got from him. He landed at Dover Friday, March 25. In London he saw the King and dined with the Secretaries of State. Saturday he was before a committee of the Privy Council. Bolingbroke went Friday to the theater in Drury Lane, bespeaking a stall for the next night. Disregarding Trevor's advice, he slipped out of town on Saturday and crossed the Channel, disguised as a valet to one of the messengers of Louis XIV. The *Gazette* (March 31) carried the examination of the Captain of the boat in which he went. Leaders of the Church party were in dismay. Something had to be done at once to counteract disaster to their cause.

There were two possible explanations of the step. Enemies said, it proved his guilt; he was a Jacobite. Friends, knowing how groundless was this charge, as naturally took the other view. Atterbury prepared a letter and circulated it over his name confessing fright. It purported to come from Dover, March 27. The writer had learned from "Some . . . in the Secret of Affairs" of a "Resolution by those" with "Power to execute it" to pursue him "to the Scaffold." He was "Prejudged," though guilty of nothing but "Zeal" for the late Queen. It was a comfort to have served her in the thing "she had most at heart, relieving her People from a bloody and expensive War." He was "too much an Englishman" to sacrifice his country to "any

Foreign Ally whatsoever." By feverish exertions, the Bishop and his colleagues restored among their followers some of the shattered spirit. They urged Bolingbroke in exile "to be quiet for their sake." Oxford in the country thought his old colleague's going "like his other practices," and thanked God he was "never in his secret."

April 5 the House of Commons requested from the King papers concerning the negotiations for peace. Four days later Stanhope laid before the House twelve volumes and three other small books, asking for a secret committee to digest the information and decide on action. Edward Harley volunteered to say that his brother "would neither fly his country nor conceal himself, but be forthcoming whenever he should be called upon to justify his conduct." Two days afterward, though ill and wishing to remain at home, Oxford was in the House of Lords to take his seat. Walpole was chairman and Stanhope an active member of the committee which went forthwith to work. Even so, many thought the ministers would be content to have their fling at Bolingbroke.

May 15 Charles Montague, Earl of Halifax, went to dine with the Dutch Ambassador, but was taken ill before the meal. His death of pneumonia the next day made easier the plans of colleagues who survived. He was succeeded by Charles Howard, third Earl of Carlisle, peevish hitherto because he was the only designated Regent without reward. Bishop Burnet passed from the scene in March; Wharton, Lord Privy Seal, in April, making a place for Sunderland to escape from Ireland, which he never liked. Somers was ill and had not long to live. Old hands were giving way to new.

June 1, debating a military bill, Shippen accused the ministers of setting up a standing army, twitted them about the clamor against the late Queen's ministers, and prophesied that the activity of the Secret Committee would end in "smoke." The next day Walpole announced his readiness to report. Nine days later he impeached Bolingbroke of high treason. Thomas, Earl Conningsby urged the same charge against Oxford. Several days elapsed between the voting of the charge and its transmission to the Lords to tempt him to escape, but he refused the chance.

Sir Joseph Jekyll, brother-in-law of Somers and a legal member of the Committee, confessed his doubt whether the evidence against Oxford would convict. Sir Thomas Cave, a friendly country member, wagered a bottle of red port that the Earl "would not run away or be beheaded if he stayed," though he had confessed the week before that if no others than Oxford and Bolingbroke should be impeached, he was "not of opinion to stay to defend 'em."

Ormond's turn was next, unless he made submission to the King. But he was easy clay in Atterbury's hands and hesitantly stood his ground. His growing popularity made his not an easy case. Even Addison acknowledged obligations to the Duke and did not vote when Stanhope made the charge (June 21). Told of the act, the accused replied: "They have power and I have Innocence, and God's will be done." John Aislabie of Yorkshire impeached Strafford the next day, but only of "high crimes and misdemeanors."

The *Evening Post* on the last day of the month carried a fictitious letter from Walpole to Sunderland which was in spirit too near the truth to tolerate. "We have nothing for it but a bold push," he said, "and accordingly determin'd to allow no Time to the Enemy to examine or consider the Report. The Impeachments will be for High Treason and other Crimes; and I wish we have not in the Resolution strain'd the Matter too far. . . . If on any drunken Holiday the Government is over-run with Riotous and Seditious Assemblies, what Opposition may we not reasonably expect, when we are leading the Favourites of the Faction to the Scaffold? If we fail in our Attempt, we must be content to bear the Yoke we have been preparing for our Enemies." Walpole called the letter to the attention of the House (July 1), which voted it a "false, scandalous, and traitorous Libel" and appointed a committee to investigate. On the same day a bill was introduced for preventing tumultuous and riotous assemblies.

It had become increasingly clear since Parliament met that something must be done. March 27 the borough of Wigan sent an address in favor of the peace. April 7, at a large meeting in Middlesex to honor the Lord Lieutenant, Pelham (now Earl of

Clare as a reward for services to the new house), a counter-address, drawn up by Steele, was adopted and presented by Townshend to the King, who made its author a knight. April 23, the anniversary of Anne's coronation, a City mob threw stones at those who did not take the time to huzza for that Queen and the Church. Six days later Ormond's birthday was celebrated at the Devil's Tavern, Temple Bar, after which were bonfires, illuminations, and a riotous mob. After the ball on the King's birthday (May 8) were bonfires and illuminations, but the next day was commemorated as the anniversary of the Restoration by the largest mob since the Sacheverell trial, yelling for "High Church and Ormond." Some said that the effigies burned looked like Cromwell; others likened them to Benjamin Hoadly, a churchman active for the new régime.

On the last day of the month Defoe, in the guise of a Quaker, published *A Seasonable Expostulation with and Friendly Reproof unto James Butler, who by the Men of the World is Stil'd Duke of O[rmond] Relating to the Tumults of the People.* A little later he offered in the same strain *A Sharp Rebuke . . . to Henry Sacheverell, the High Priest of Andrews, Holborn,* alleging that the preacher had been seen drinking to the Pretender. "For these Things," he said, "hath the Lord made thee a Hissing and a By Word among the People of the Lord."

July 7 Walpole brought in the articles against Oxford. Within two days they were engrossed and ready for the Lords. Denied all of the delay he asked on account of ill health, on Saturday, the sixteenth, the accused peer was ordered to the Tower. Seeing him at large in the interval and thinking he had been discharged, the mob shouted gleefully: "High Church, Ormond, and Oxford forever." Hearing the noise, partisans of the ministry in coffee-houses were in dismay until they learned of the crowd's mistake. Swift wrote at once to comfort his old friend (July 19): "You suffer for a good cause, for having been the great instrument of his present Majesty's peaceable accession to the throne. This I know, and this your enemies know; and this I will take care that all the world shall know and future ages be convinced of." This was a promise easier to make than keep. Future ages might refuse to be convinced.

The other articles of impeachment followed by the end of August. Meanwhile (July 20), the King approved the Riot Act, making it a felony when an assembly of twelve or more failed to disperse if ordered to do so by an officer of the law after a reading of the statute. That formality over, through the Lord Chancellor his Majesty expressed sorrow to find that "such a Spirit of Rebellion" had "discovered itself" as left "no Reason to doubt but these Disorders" were "set on foot and encouraged by Persons disaffected" to his "Government in Expectation of being supported from abroad." He hoped that Parliament would not leave the nation defenseless with "Rebellion actually begun at Home" and invasion threatened from without. A supply was voted the next day. The Habeas Corpus Act was suspended. The King was empowered to detain suspicious persons and to offer a hundred thousand pounds for the Pretender's capture.

This panic was not wholly without excuse. Ormond awaited at his house at Richmond earlier in the summer the outcome of the motion in the House of Commons. When Stanhope sent Robert Pitt, his brother-in-law, to give a timely warning and opportunity for flight, the message was too late. To the imprisoned Earl before leaving he said: "Farewell, Oxford without a head"; the alleged retort was, "Farewell, Duke without a duchy." There was no way to know which chose the better part. Stanhope snapped his fingers when told that the flight was toward the east of England, knowing it was expected that the Duke be active in the west.

Bolingbroke found France less pleasing as an exile than when he went as Secretary of State. Stair would not receive him. The Pretender began at once to plague him through Berwick as a "person esteemed and in vogue." That Prince's followers were encouraged for the moment, thinking that Oxford must soon follow Bolingbroke, and Ormond do something "to protect himself." Timid as usual, Marlborough sent a precautionary gift, which Torcy encouraged Berwick to take. If the Duke "had any Power" at home, it was in December "still a secret" to his Duchess.

Bolingbroke was pessimistic, warning James through Berwick (April 20) that among the English leaders only North and

Grey and a "very few others" were Jacobites "by principles"; as for the rest, "interest" was "what . . . now made them rightly inclined." Ormond was "honest, brave, popular, willing," but required "wise guidance." He agreed himself to write to Rochester, Wyndham, and Lansdowne. For the present he would do no more. He could not call on James without Stair finding it out.

By the end of June James solicited an interview as urgent. If he could only get to England with some money, he had faith that "Providence" would "do the rest." Bolingbroke was less sure of Providence, and wished a plan more practicable. Charles Kinnaird brought one from London early in July approved by Ormond and Mar; though the former was still at Richmond awaiting action by the House of Commons. The impeachments were depended upon to help arouse the people. Then, if risings could be managed in both England and Scotland simultaneously with the arrival of James bringing arms, munitions, and an army from France, the German usurper might be sent the way of the Pretender's father. Little wonder Stair was worried and obeyed instructions to keep informed.

Reports from England and conversations with Torcy and others in the *entourage* of Louis XIV encouraged Bolingbroke to think possible an undertaking which in the previous year he had dismissed. If the French could be induced to help—and it was plausible to think they would—why might not he and his friends play the same part as the faction then in power? The Pretender was at least native-born and spoke the language of the people he aspired to rule. The exile wrote (July 12), cautioning James to be careful of his confidants until the English situation should be "ripe."

Prudent in his old age, Louis XIV was fearful of "wrong measures." Only success would justify the steps that he was urged to take. James was in no mood to wait, and his mother complained that Torcy, Berwick, and Bolingbroke monopolized her son. At just this juncture, Ormond, thought to be busy posing at home as the hero of the party, took fright and came to Paris. Swift in Ireland could not make it out. He was "struck at the Duke of Ormond's flight." The report that he had joined the Pretender was "laughed at" and was "indeed wholly unlike him."

The time had come to act. Bolingbroke, Ormond, Torcy, and Louis took counsel together. Ormond, they thought, should not see James and give a new handle "to the Whigs to make a Noise." Louis had no money, but might get some from Spain. Arms also might be had from the same source to supplement those obtainable in France. The difficulty was troops. A more serious matter was the French King's health. Bolingbroke, Ormond, Berwick, and Torcy dined together after this conference and were mutually shocked. "You may, sir, assure yourself," Bolingbroke reported to James, "that his colour is changed to a livid paleness; that his voice is gone to a degree; and that it is hardly possible to conceive more alterations for the worse in four or five days' time." Whatever its effect upon the cause of James, until after the death of Louis little could now be done.

In England the dance went on. Steele revived his *Englishman* in July and August to trace the "footsteps of those who had lately betrayed their Queen and country into the hands of the French King." The day after the first number appeared (July 12), Defoe was convicted for his piece in Hurt's paper. Two days later he published *A Hymn to the Mob*, thinking to serve the King's cause. Impressed by "libels . . . successfully dispersed under the notion of public news," Steele meditated a *Hanoverian Post,* which did not see the light. When Walpole reported the articles against Ormond, one member, hitherto the Duke's follower, said that the flight convinced him that the "heads of the Tory party were a set of Knaves and Villains who designed to have ruined their Country and made it a Province of France." The articles against Bolingbroke had been engrossed the previous day.

Learning of these events, this accused Lord tried to convince himself that "measures taken to extinguish the flame" would "make it burn higher." Either James must save the "Church and Constitution of England or both must be irretrievably lost forever." When neither he nor Ormond responded to the charges against them the next week, they were attainted as guilty, an additional reason why they could not now draw back.

Having less to lose, James urged them to come to see him. Marlborough sent another remittance to his nephew, but Bolingbroke doubted his inclination to give real help. In his own saner moments, the prospect seemed dark. "The contretemps is terrible," he complained to James (August 15). Jacobites in England expected French troops and money. To go and fail without them would be fatal to the cause. So would action in Scotland, lacking English "push and strength." He and Ormond were now powerless in England until the rebellion began. He noted with regret that the English ministers, whether by design or not, seemed to have turned out the very men that James depended upon most. Later in the day, he transmitted Torcy's advice that James apply to the Duke of Orleans, the death of Louis being near.

The next day the Earl of Mar announced to a company of trusted friends in Scotland, invited to a hunt, that there would be a rebellion in England and Louis XIV would help. James sent him a commission, dated August 26, as Commander in Chief for Scotland. But on August 20 the French King died, and Orleans attended more to Stair than to James. On the same day in London, a ballad-singer, making sport of "Vagabond Tories," suggested that Wyndham, a knight of "fire" from Somersetshire, though still in England, was "equipping for Paris to prevent any schism in the party." Three days later, James thought everything ripe in England and delay dangerous. If there were still reasons why Bolingbroke and Ormond would not declare for him, would not the former see him secretly?

To the sympathetic Shippen in England as well as to Bolingbroke, the death of Louis XIV seemed to make a difference. He suggested, when Oxford replied to the articles against him (September 7), that the ministers be satisfied with their success against Bolingbroke and Ormond and drop the other impeachments. Aislabie answered that Oxford's reply was chiefly a repetition of *The Secret History of the White Staff,* and the replication was ordered to go on. A week later (September 14), the House of Lords instructed the Earl Marshal to "cause the names of James Duke of Ormond and Henry Viscount Bolingbroke to be razed out of the Roll of Peers." Earlier in the week

Mar had issued in Scotland a public declaration in favor of the Pretender. On the same day Bolingbroke wrote to announce his own open support as that Prince's Secretary of State.

But the death of Louis and the precautions of the English ministers were obstacles to his success. The new Secretary of State confessed to his sovereign that the more he thought about it, the more "impracticable" the business seemed. Within less than a fortnight Stanhope notified the House of Commons of the King's command to arrest several members as Jacobites, including Wyndham and Thomas Forster. The Lords Dupplin and Lansdowne were taken the same day. The Archbishop of Canterbury and all of his episcopal colleagues except Atterbury and Smalridge published a declaration of loyalty to Hanover and abhorrence of the rebellion started in Scotland by Mar. Another pamphlet offered ironical reasons for the absence of the missing names. Rumors said that James had landed or was on his way.

Wyndham at first made his escape, but later thought it wiser to submit. He was sent to the Tower, although his father-in-law, the Duke of Somerset, was ready to give bail. Forster, a relative of Lady Cowper, escaped to the north of England. Argyll, as head of one of the stronger loyal clans, was sent to Scotland to command.

Bolingbroke agreed that the premature activity of Mar made it necessary for James and Ormond to do anything they could. News of the capture of Wyndham and Lansdowne caused him to lose heart; they were men most likely to "take lead." Word came that Cadogan with Dutch troops was on the way. In the last days of September Bolingbroke warned James that his best hope of success in England was "to speak to the present passions of men." Ten days later he repeated this advice. Wanting much else, Ormond should take papers to disperse. In late years those had succeeded best in politics who had "by plausible appeals to the people gained the nation to their side." It was necessary to fight the faction in power with its own weapons.

By that method the peace had been carried and the current discontent with Hanover aroused. Without such appeals, James would lose "popularity," the "only expedient" that could bring his "restoration" to pass. "If the present ferment" was not "kept up," the writer felt, and "the present hopes and fears . . . cultivated by an industrious application of the same honest art by which they were created," James would "find general zeal grow cool, and a new set of compounders arise." The capture of Wyndham made it imperative, he urged again (October 13), that James link to his "cause that of the Church of England, of the Tory Party, and of" his "Sister's Memory." For this purpose he had himself got ready papers for James to sign and send abroad.

But that Prince was honest, loyal to his Church, unwilling to commit himself beyond his intent to perform. Resentful of this blunting of the only weapon that remained, Bolingbroke refused to subscribe to his own paper as revised by James. Ormond was unable to perform his part. The French Regent forbade Berwick to go. On his way to Scotland to help Mar, the Pretender himself found things at St. Malo (November 4), where he tarried eight days, "in a strange confused chaos."

In England, ministerial factions purged their ranks of those they thought to be lukewarm to the cause and drew together for defense. When most members of the Council hesitated to lay hands on the "proud Duke's" son-in-law, Townshend stood up boldly, winning the applause both of his colleagues and the King. In spite of opposition by Cowper and the Prince of Wales, Bernstorff, Sunderland, and Marlborough joined Townshend and Walpole to force Somerset out, making way for the Duke of Newcastle, the former Thomas Pelham, Earl of Clare. Walpole himself became First Lord of the Treasury and Chancellor of the Exchequer and was soon regarded as the most influential man in the House of Commons.

November 24, Mar notified James of his defeat at Preston. He wished for better luck another time. He hoped to see the King before he died. That hapless Prince was on his way to a reception free from warmth. On the day after Mar wrote, a frost began destined to be ten weeks long. The Thames froze over; booths were built upon the ice; members of the House of Commons called on Justices of the Peace to keep the way clear to its doors. Arriving in his "native country" in the last days of the year, James found that he could only preserve a little longer the fitful fire of a rebellion nearly quenched.

Fearing the kindness of Argyll to his fellow Scots, the ministers placed Cadogan in charge. Occasional processions were organized in London; appropriate effigies were burnt. Friday, December 9, prominent prisoners taken at Preston were paraded from Highgate through the city, their hands tied, on horseback, in order to impress the mob. Scaffolds were erected in Westminster Hall to make a spectacle of the trials of the peers. Cowper's Countess had persuaded him to hold on in October, when Somerset was forced out. Now, as Lord Steward, he had to preside with her own kinsman one of the accused.

Steele began to publish *Town Talk* (December 17), chiefly to discuss his current interest in the stage, but he did not neglect political affairs. His first number was reprinted as *A British Subject's Answer to the Pretender's Declaration*. Addison became a member of the Board of Trade, and Hoadly in the see of Bangor found a seat on the episcopal bench. Two days before Christmas, Addison began his *Freeholder*, which issued twice a week for the next few months. But his heart was never in the work. Perhaps he was already more interested in his approaching career as Lady Warwick's husband. The need was for a trumpet, as Steele said, and the *Freeholder* was a "lute."

Political journalism was not for Addison. In that very year a contemporary remarked "the great and still increasing number of newspapers . . . published every day . . . cram'd with the Hopes and Fears, or Surmises of Parties or Factions." This atmosphere was uncongenial for one advising readers to leave to the Prince and legislature "Speculations" about the "Constitution," "so far beyond their Reach." The rebellion, after the Pretender went back to France, proved to him that there was "Nothing more contemptible and insignificant than the Scum of a People when . . . instigated against a King who is supported by the two Branches of the Legislature." The government of King, Lords and Commons was "not to be controul'd by a tumultuary Rabble."

Going to the theater in mid-April, he complained that the audience was eager to make partisan applications of the author's lines, and listened "after nothing else." Polite assemblies resembled "boistrous Clubs." Those meeting over a glass of wine, before adjourning, threw "Bottles at one another's Heads." Authors wrote "with an Eye to the predominant Humour of the Town." "In Short" the "Relish for Faction" destroyed that "of Wit." A strange sermon for a preacher set to kindle fires of loyalty in a multitude whose affections a few months before had seemed to lean to the other side.

Defoe was not idle. Fugitive, anonymous pieces were sent forth as the occasions came. But while the rebellion was at its height the time approached for beginning his sentence. As a desperate measure, an inner voice inspired him to address the judge. Chief Justice Parker read his letter and verified his interpretation of the pamphlets published in the Queen's time. Convinced of the author's loyalty, Parker introduced him to Townshend.

The current journal on the other side appeared variously as *Robin's Last Shift* or the *Shift Shifted*. The first thought was for Defoe to take up that controversy on the Hanoverian side. On reflection, he seemed likely to help more the cause he had at heart by capitalizing the reputation he had made as a partisan of Oxford and Anne. The writer of Dyer's News-letter lay dead. Defoe obtained a share in the property and the management of the enterprise. Thenceforth its subscribers received items not wholly wanting the old flavor, but lacking "sting." Thus he cooperated with Buckley, publisher of the *Daily Courant,* to serve the ministerial cause. In a sixpenny *Account of the Great and Generous Actions of James Butler* he blamed the late Duke of Ormond for ambition, vanity, and wasting his estate.

Though public attacks went on, proceedings against the Queen's late ministers were interrupted in order to try the captured Jacobites. The Earl of Derwentwater and four others, having been impeached, confessed and were adjudged guilty. The King announced to Parliament the presence of his rival in the north and asked supplies. Amid the trepidation of the German court, Townshend and Walpole intrenched themselves in power. Those who sought mercy for the condemned lords were replaced by others readier to punish treason as a crime. Sunderland obtained Anglesey's place as Vice-Treasurer of Ireland. Nottingham and the whole family of Finches were put out.

But Cadogan complained that Argyll was "enraged" at his "success" in suppressing the rebellion and laid the foundation for a rival court that sought its favor through the Prince of Wales.

The cue of partisans of the Church was to allege cruelty by the ministry against the captives. Atterbury published *An Argument to Prove the Affections of the People of England the best Security for the Government*. Steele's sentimentality moved him to join in asking mercy for the condemned. But he discovered that favor did not lie that way. *Town Talk* ceased, and a pamphlet appeared in *Vindication of Sir Richard Steele*. Walpole moved a recess of the House of Commons until the sentences could be executed. Derwentwater and several others met their fate. Whether by connivance or careless neglect, several got away.

Meanwhile word came from Scotland that Mar and the Pretender had left for France. There were "still Hopes," the Earl thought, as long as "the King" was left. But he, James, and Ormond needed a scapegoat for their failure. They had scarcely reached Paris when they discovered a "general cry" against Bolingbroke for neglecting to obtain and send supplies. That Lord congratulated James on his escape: "You are well and the cause cannot dye, but will, in God's good time revive again."

But not with him to help. Ormond was sent to demand his seals in order that they might be given to Mar. Atterbury agreed, though in England the change required no little explanation to adherents of the cause. Some said it was the fault of the Queen Mother. Others were told that Bolingbroke and Ormond could not agree; others, that the former was a traitor. Stair was jubilant to Horace Walpole (March 3): "So poor Harry is turned out from being secretary of state, and the seals are given to Mar; and they use poor Harry most unmercifully, and call him knave and traytor and God knows what not. I believe all poor Harry's fault was, that he could not play his part with a grave enough face; he could not help laughing now and then at such kings and queens."

Those to whom Stair wrote in London scarcely shared this

mood. Robert Walpole informed his brother the same week that though the "Dismals" (the Finches) were out for making trouble in domestic affairs, there were still "storms in the air." They were trying through Robethon and Cowper's wife to persuade the latter to give up his seals. Even the Prince of Wales had been asked to help. The addition of Nottingham, Somerset, and the rest to those in opposition made it necessary for men in power to walk with greater care. Walpole himself was stricken when he was needed most and for weeks was at the point of death.

His loss was thought by Jacobite agents to be "irreparable," since he was "the greatest Parliament man and statesman on the Court side." They redoubled their efforts to take advantage of this opportunity and to regain ground lost in Bolingbroke. Atterbury undertook to reanimate the London crowds. As usual, wishful workers were optimistic. Argyll was reported to be disgruntled with Marlborough and apt to help. Mar wrote to the Jacobite agent in Madrid that the ministry stood upon "so rotten a foundation," were "so jumbled and divided among themselves, the people so exasperated, and the governing party . . . reduced to so narrow a bottom by people's leaving them daily, and their being forced to turn out others upon suspicion," that only a standing army kept the King upon his throne. A few troops and a little money would be enough to send the German whence he came. Six to ten thousand men would do the work.

The ministers lent plausibility to these hopes, declining to risk a general election with its attending noise. A bill was introduced extending the duration of Parliament to seven years. Defoe, Steele, and Addison were busy out of doors, while oratorical talent on both sides buffeted within. This "free Nation," said Atterbury in the Lords, "was now to be governed by a standing Parliament and a standing army." A correspondent informed Horace Walpole that nothing since his brother's illness had attracted so much attention. At the Grecian, where John Trenchard held forth, and at neighboring coffee-houses, people "bellowed loud against it," but it would be carried "in spite of all the drunken mercenary boroughs' letters, petitions, and remonstrances" that would be stirred up on the other side. And so it proved.

In the midst of this hubbub, Bolingbroke sent over letters by Brinsden to be circulated among the Jacobites answering charges made against himself. Somers had a stroke and died. Pleurisy hastened the end of Sunderland's wife. Edward Harley learned that the ministers did not mean to try his brother, but would keep him in the Tower as long as possible. Oxford sent through Dartmouth a message to Townshend, pleading his support of moderation in the past. Some, earlier held in prison, were discharged.

Bolingbroke was finding consolation in retreat with the woman who became his second wife. Learning in early autumn that Wyndham was about to be involved again in what he thought to be a desperate cause, he wrote through Stair to warn against the step. Already he was formulating in his mind the brilliant, longer letter to the same friend as his apology to posterity for lack of courage and sound judgment. His Jacobite career was at an end; his reputation, tainted through his life; never would he regain the ground that he had lost.

Even as early as the spring of 1716, some Jacobites in England thought that it would be difficult, after the divisions in France, to weld the party together again. One, listening to the debate on the Septennial Bill, noted that "the Tories talked like Old Whigs and Republicans against monarchy and ministries &c, and the Whigs magnified the advantages of unlimited, absolute power and prerogative, vilified the mob, ridiculed the people, and exalted the crown." Those dividing against the court were a "new strange jumble." But more confusion was in store, unless the King would take advice.

The Septennial Act was scarcely passed, before Townshend, Cowper, Marlborough, Sunderland, and Devonshire met to consider a regency if George should persist in his determination to visit Hanover. Townshend warned Bernstorff (May 19) that the "rage and spirit" of the Jacobites were only "smothered," not "subdued." The King's absence would be used to "alienate the minds" of many now filled with zeal. In case he went, the Prince would have to be left in charge, and ancient practices should govern the restrictions on his power. Grieving at his daughter's death, Marlborough had a stroke in that same month. Thenceforth his usefulness was chiefly in his name. The King persisted in his will. The German court suspected Townshend and Sunderland for the homely truths they told. Their master demanded that his son get rid of Argyll for advising that he claim as regent the full royal power. In part, it was a rivalry of leaders ambitious for military command. Argyll challenged Cadogan, who had received a Green Ribbon for his work in Scotland; apology soothed, but did not heal this wound. The Prince was disposed to stand by his friends and was suspicious of those who urged his father's view. A truce was made in time. Argyll and his brother were dismissed from the Prince's court. That Duke paid his respects to the King between eight and nine on the morning of July 7. The Prince rode in the coach in which his father left. That afternoon at two his Majesty sailed from Gravesend for his German home.

Behind were smouldering jealousies and doubts and Bothmer. With him went Bernstorff, Robethon, and Lady Schulenburg, now Duchess of Munster in the Irish list, but sour because denied the English rank. Townshend's wife was pregnant, and Stanhope went in order that the King might have a British minister. Under the circumstances, he seemed to be the fittest choice. Thus far the two Secretaries of State had seen with the same eyes while working with a common will.[4]

---

[4] For events from the meeting of Parliament to the departure of the King see in addition to items in the text: Hist. Mss. Com., *Portland,* V. 508ff.; *Stuart,* I. 357ff.; II. 3ff.; *Mar and Kellie,* pp. 511ff.; *Dartmouth,* pp. 322ff.; Lady Cowper, *Diary,* pp. 50ff.; Williams, *Stanhope,* pp. 171ff.; Boyer, *Political State,* IX. 198ff.; X. 56ff.; XI. 1ff.; XII. 34ff.; *Impeachments,* pp. xlivff.; *Parliamentary History,* VII. 42ff.; Margaret Maria, Lady Verney, *Verney Letters of the Eighteenth Century,* I. 330ff.; Wilkins, *Caroline,* I. 192ff.; *Letters of . . . Duchess of Marlborough,* pp. 118ff.; *Somers Tracts,* XIII. 676ff.; Ball, *Correspondence of Swift,* II. 277ff.; Lee, *Defoe,* I. xff., 248ff.; Torrens, *Cabinets,* I. 101ff.; Aitken, *Steele,* II. 63ff.; Hardwicke, *State Papers,* II. 532ff.; Stanhope, *History,* I. Appendix, pp. ixff.; Hearne, *Collections,* V. 88ff.; Edward Calamy, *Historical Account of my own Life,* II. 320ff.; Thomas Wright, *Caricature History of the Georges,* ch. i.; Coxe, *Marlborough,* III. 605ff.; *Robert Walpole,* I. 95; II. 50ff.; Lucy Aiken, *Life of Joseph Addison,* II. 173ff.; *Historical Register,* I. i.

Chapter IX

A LEADER APPEARS, 1716–1721

> The only Way therefore of dealing with Mankind is to deal with their Passions; and the Founders of all States and of all Religions have ever done so. The first Elements or Knowledge of Politicks is the Knowledge of the Passions; and the Art of Government is chiefly the Art of Applying to the Passions. . . . And because Passion and Opinion are so nearly related, and have such Force upon each other; arbitrary Courts and crafty Knaves have ever endeavoured to force or frighten or deceive the People into a Uniformity of Thoughts, especially of Religious Thoughts.
>
> Cato in the *London Journal*, July 29, 1721

I

A Split in the Ministry

THE political events in England in the last six months of 1716 were neither foreseen nor intended by any one concerned. Amid a diversity of circumstances, each tried to do as best he could the day's work as it came to hand.

The Prince and Princess of Wales thought it high time for the royal family to exert itself to win some of the popular favor it had thus far sadly lacked. The King's want of an English tongue and of a conventional domestic circle kept him reserved, aloof from those he needed most to gain. His absence afforded an opportunity for the son to try that which was beyond the father's power. Success would profit both, strengthening their hold upon the family estate.

The King was scarcely on his way, when word went round that the Guardian of the Realm and Lieutenant—the clumsy title of the Prince in lieu of *Regent,* which he wished—would make occasions for becoming better acquainted with his subjects. Less than a week after hearing that his father was in Hanover, he reviewed the guard in Hyde Park. Wednesday, July 25, he and the Princess went to Hampton Court. Men and women of all factions were welcomed there. Townshend and Walpole before long began to entertain at private tables lest the notion spread that the King's ministers were out of favor with his son. At first they were suspicious of these widespread kindnesses. Later, they found his Royal Highness ready to coöperate to do the nation's business. When enthusiastic subjects brought addresses approving his administration, he would not receive them unless directed to the King.

In late September he made a short progress and was entertained by the Earl of Dorset at Knowle, by the Duke of Newcastle at Halland, by the Earl of Scarborough at Stanfield. At Portsmouth he was greeted by the corporation while the trained bands lined the streets. At Tunbridge Wells he visited the chapel, took a turn in the walks, tasted the water, and gave his hand to several to kiss. He bestowed five guineas on the dipper at the well, gave three to women strewing flowers on the walks, and left six at the chapel for the poor.

These gracious acts, these gayeties, the first touches of color imparted by the new house to a society long drab and gray, were seen quite otherwise by the suspicious Bothmer and his agents in reports they sent abroad. In England that favorite plagued the ministers for colonial land or other favors for the profit of the German court. Habitual opposition to his will, even though he represented it as a proposal of the King, inclined him to see ill where otherwise he might have found no harm. And he was not the least important channel through which the absent King was kept informed.

The experiments of these months helped little with the constitutional problem of the relations between the court that went and that the King had left behind. The Elector of Hanover in October, 1715, had declared war against Sweden, a country with which the King of England was at peace. The King sent a fleet under Admiral Norris to the Baltic to protect his British trade. The Elector's ally, the King of Prussia, wondered of how much assistance this force would be in the war. George thought that it might help, but was unable to give a "written engagement," since "providing" the squadron pertained to him as "King," while documents of that war had to come through his "German ministers."

Unquestionably, the conduct of foreign relations was a prerogative of the King. On that account perhaps he was accompanied to Hanover by an English Secretary of State. But he left secretaries behind as well. Paul Methuen qualified as *locum tenens* for Stanhope. But would it be necessary to refer all matters for the advice of secretaries at home? For example, both the King and the Elector had ministers at Copenhagen, an important court that summer. Robethon was soon voluble to Polwarth, who represented the King there, sometimes even without the knowledge of Stanhope.

Recognizing the convenience of an avenue of communication other than the formal dispatches regularly sent between Stanhope and the King in Hanover and ministers at home, Stephen Poyntz, an employee in the office, was commissioned by Townshend and Methuen in the last days of July to carry on a secret correspondence by special messengers, with instructions that Stanhope show these letters to no one else except the King. By the same conveyance, Walpole and Townshend hoped to receive information which the whole Council need not see. Within a few weeks, Townshend was communicating to Stanhope formal opinions of the Prince and ministers at home different from the views of those abroad.

Stanhope had no thought when he left England in July of making common cause with the King and the German ministers against his colleagues. Indeed, he went chiefly because he had been loyal to Townshend's group. Nor was he ever conscious of any dereliction in his acts. He drifted away from Townshend because in differing circumstances they saw with different perspectives the questions they both had to face. In the end, they became suspicious of each other, and neither understood why, instead of drawing as a team, they pulled apart. The explanation was their common earnest will to serve the King.

In Hanover Stanhope was the responsible English minister

amid scores of court followers and hangers-on, the fountain of the King's advice, the avenue of his will. At his old home again, George tended to think and feel as Elector, though he had no mind to lay aside his functions as the King. The diplomatic crisis of the summer chanced to be with northern courts, and foreign relations were the sphere in which the English kings had hitherto retained their greatest power. Other northern countries—Denmark, Prussia, Hanover, Russia—had common hopes in the disintegrating Swedish empire built up by Gustavus Adolphus and later kings. With the consent of the others, the Elector had obtaned Bremen and Verden after he became King, thereby increasing the expectations of the rest. But the King had obligations to help Sweden, contracted some fourteen years before he reached the throne.

Since the King had a Baltic fleet, which the Elector wished to use, it was not easy to keep his functions separate. Robethon was a convenient subordinate, it being not always clear whether he spoke for the Elector or the King. A naval officer would scarcely disobey an order from the man who wore the crown. A minister might resign, as Stanhope threatened he would do before the year was over, but as long as he held office he had to be amenable to the decisions of the King. Without being aware of it, he tended to adopt the views held by his Majesty. He breathed the Hanoverian air, shared the anxieties of that court, its hopes and fears.

At just this juncture, the confederates who had hoped to share the spoil of Sweden began to disagree. The Czar of Russia, as a convenient way to Sweden, proposed to land troops in Germany, choosing a point in Mecklenburg on the Hanoverian border. It happened that Count Bernstorff controlled some villages at this very spot. The King of Prussia, respectful of the power of the Czar, was in no haste to make objection. The burden of defending the Empire was thus left with George. To Stanhope, with the King, this seemed clearly a situation about which something should be done. "I do verily believe," he wrote to Townshend (September 14), "things will come to an *eclat* perhaps before I can have an answer from you." Fortunately for the King's plans, Townshend discovered that the Swedes were listening to the Jacobites, who were about to be wholly deserted by the French.

Circumstances made it almost inevitable that the Duke of Orleans, as Regent for his nephew and himself next heir, would turn to England for support against the claims of Philip of Spain. The chief point was the *quid pro quo* that the English King would ask. The negotiation hung fire when George left London. It had begun both at Paris and through Horace Walpole at The Hague. The plan was a triple agreement by the English, French, and Dutch. The Regent thought it good diplomacy for the negotiation to follow the King.

Early in July the Abbé Dubois, Minister of the French Regent, went to The Hague and established himself incognito as a bibliophile. When Stanhope passed through on his way to Hanover, a meeting was arranged at Horace Walpole's house. After a visit to Paris, Dubois betook himself to Hanover, where a tentative agreement was reached (August 24) on all points except Dunkirk. The next month was spent ironing out that question to the satisfaction of English ministers, who insisted that the Mardyke sluices be destroyed. This agreement was reached in the last days of September, when George and Stanhope urged that the treaty be signed forthwith. The Regent might not be so anxious if England should become involved with Russia as well as with the Swedes. A draft was dispatched to The Hague with instructions that Walpole and Cadogan, who had gone thither as Ambassador, sign it, with the participation of the Dutch if they agreed, but without it if they declined.

Townshend was less impressed by all this urgency. Walpole at The Hague had promised the Dutch to sign no treaty unless they should come in. As always, they were readier to deliberate than sign. Walpole was resolved to keep his word, but offered, when the King insisted, to go home ill, leaving Cadogan to act. Mistakes in formalities at home caused more delay, much to the vexation of Stanhope and the King. Their own anxieties made them less inclined to understand the difficulties of ministers they left behind.

Townshend and Walpole had the thankless task of trying

to serve two courts, keeping the mood of England ever in their mind. Immediately after the King left, the Princess poured into the sympathetic ears of Lady Cowper her feeling that Townshend was "the sneeringist, fawningist knave that ever was." She even liked Sunderland better, since he did not try to conceal his enmity. She blamed both for the troubles of the Prince. The Countess thought Robethon's a sounder view. The King himself had decided to turn Argyll out, and his ministers acquiesced because the alternative was to resign. By the end of the month Walpole thought the Duchess of Munster more to blame. She would have remade the ministry before leaving, but for her hurry to get away. Townshend blamed Bernstorff; Walpole, Robethon more.

Even before the King left, Sunderland had thought to assuage his grief and improve his health at a German spa. The Duchess of Marlborough took charge of his children at her late daughter's request. His lucrative Irish sinecure and his office of Privy Seal gave him more ease than his restless nature had usually allowed. He liked as little as Townshend and Stanhope the intermeddling of the German court and remarked (July 24), when asking a commission for the Privy Seal to enable him to go, that unless the King returned in early winter "certain ruin and confusion" in England was in store. It was a changing world for him. The wife who had bound him to Marlborough was now dead. The Duke himself was ill, perhaps forever out of the political game.

In the last days of July Walpole found that Sunderland wished to be reconciled with Townshend and himself. He thought "common interest" tended so much to that end that there was no reason "to fear the contrary." His own chief worry, like Sunderland's, was the King's return. Sunderland thought his Majesty would come back for Parliament to sit; the Prince held the other view. Walpole informed Stanhope that it was "very materiall" to know which was right, else "nobody" could "answer for the success of anything." Ten days later, Walpole repeated his anxiety; otherwise, with the Prince showing equal favor to all groups, the credit of their party would decline.

When Cadogan left for The Hague in late August, and Sunderland started on his trip, Walpole found the latter inclined to use "his best endeavours to set things right." The Earl parted from the ministers at home "with all the professions and assurances of mutual friendship and union." Even the Prince was "easy and in good humor" and his ministers inclined to raise no issues that would endanger keeping him so. Stanhope reassured colleagues at home that they need not fear Sunderland's disservice with the King, since his Majesty had to be "pressed" to let him come to Hanover at all. As to the King's return, he was much less sure. Hitherto he had avoided mentioning the subject for fear of giving "uneasiness." Though not yet authorized to speak, he "verily" believed that he would come.

Townshend and Walpole made haste to say through Poyntz that the return was no light matter. Things needed to be done that were impossible "without the presence of the King to compose the differences and to animate the zeal of his friends." At any rate, they earnestly begged to know the royal will. The "time of year" required that they get ready to meet Parliament. Several days later (September 11), they rejoiced at the agreement with the French which enabled the King to "make a figure on the Continent" and secured "to him the balance and arbitration of the affairs of Europe." Might it not incline the King of Sweden "to submit to accommodation upon his Majesty's own terms?" Little wonder George was anxious to get the treaty signed.

Less wonder, Townshend and Walpole were vexed on learning in late September that the probability of an enlarged northern war was a chief reason why they should make haste with France. The business had been "so stupidly managed" as to promise "ruin," wrote Townshend as a damper to Stanhope's enthusiasm. Officially the same day the Secretary of State at home informed his colleague abroad that, in view of the relations of the Pretender with Sweden, the Prince and his advisers hoped for a consummation of the treaty with France, thought a breach with Russia unwise, and were opposed to the King's plan that Norris or any of his ships spend the winter in the Baltic Sea.

Dated two days later, but in the same dispatch, Townshend asked again the King's pleasure on the meeting of Parliament. Walpole wrote that he had the Prince's permission to recuperate in the country for a month. The session could be postponed no longer than the first of the year at most. If the Prince was to hold it, that was too much delay. He was perfecting a scheme to retire the national debt. Bothmer was still seeking favors which, if he did not desist, would likely cause trouble when Parliament met.

After a stay at Aix, Sunderland at length came to the court of his Majesty. Consorting with Stanhope, he soon breathed northern air. Though he had earlier opposed the treaty with France, he now heartily approved that Secretary's part. The affair with Russia seemed to be on a better foot, he informed Townshend (October 15), which would facilitate the King's return, a matter of "vast importance to the being of the . . . government," and thus a thing desired.

At home, the ministers had suppressed the papers that supported Jacobites. Their own journalists had fomented a dispute between Non-Jurors and the High Church clergy concerning the legitimacy of bishops of the national Church. They hoped to increase this cleavage by legislation in Parliament. Adherents to the Pretender were almost in despair. The active hostility of Bolingbroke was hindering their cause. Atterbury was designated responsible agent for James in England, and men were sent to collect money against the possibility of Sweden's help. But contributions were slow, and Atterbury made no haste to act. The French treaty would be well nigh fatal to the cause.

These threads came together unexpectedly in the next few weeks to make a curious pattern of events. George and Stanhope, wanting ready cash, remembered an agreement in the previous year for the employment of German troops. His brother-in-law away, Townshend decided (October 16) that the claim would have to wait. The German ministers made the agreement with Walpole at the point of death. Parliament had not voted funds. In "Walpole's case," he would expect the King's "commands for laying the matter at least before the Cabinet Council."

This letter reached Hanover while the French treaty was at The Hague, and Horace Walpole would not sign, while the Admiralty was asking that the Baltic fleet return. Stanhope had sent a favorable answer to Townshend's of the middle of the month. His Majesty was about to decide whether to return and open Parliament in person or not. Stanhope thought that the decision would be favorable. He had not told George that Townshend talked of "laying down." If that minister knew how "thoroughly well the King" thought of him and "how often he upon all occasions" expressed it, he would not have "said it" himself. Perhaps Bothmer had done Walpole disservice with the King. But George himself said that Walpole promised to find money for the German troops. It were prudent to "make the matter easy," since it would not do that "the King . . . say Mr. Walpole hath promised a thing, and that Mr. Walpole . . . say otherwise."

Another fortnight ended George's patience. In his own hand (October 31) he wrote to his minister at home, a thing unprecedented in his reign. He instructed Stanhope to write also, desiring that the answer be in French. That minister shared the King's anxiety at the delay and was inclined to blame the men at home. Denied permission to resign, he was readier in asking for the explanations that his Majesty desired.

Sunderland wrote to second this request. He never saw the King "resent anything so much." George thought himself and Stanhope "not well used" and was hurt at the reluctance in England to be concerned about the north. Sunderland himself believed an explanation to be due. He knew his letter to be imprudent, but the "King's service" and the union of those in it required that "these things" be cleared up, causing him to take the risk.

When these missives were two days on their way, Townshend himself sat down to write after a Council at Hampton Court. Robert Walpole had not come back. Horace attended Council by invitation in order that he might explain the message he was to take. The Prince and his advisers wished instructions on what they were to do. Steps ought to be taken both in England and Hanover against the Swedes and Jacobites. "Considering the obstinacy and inveteracy of the King of Sweden, the poverty and weakness of the Court of Denmark, the treachery and corruption of Prussia, and the little probability of any cordiall and effectuall assistance from the Emperor," George had "scarce any prospect . . . of extricating himself out of these difficulties into which northern affairs" had "plunged him without coming to a better understanding with the Czar." Under the circumstances, it was wiser to use "indulgence" with that Prince than "force." As to a naval detachment remaining in the Baltic for the winter, the Admiralty thought it would do no good and "ruin the ships."

There was need to keep the whole existing force in England both on sea and land. Unfortunately, this would call for taxes people were not inclined to pay. Lacking the King in "person," it was "absolutely necessary for his service . . . to give a discretionary power" to the Prince and ministers at home. It was as impossible to foresee what would "arise in either house" as it was to await "particular instructions from Hanover upon every sudden incident." Walpole had a plan for paying the public debt. The Archbishop of Canterbury and the Lord Chancellor had a scheme for strengthening the power of the crown in the Church. The trial of Oxford for treason should be dropped, there being no evidence to convict; that for misdemeanors should be pushed. An act of indemnity should be passed. The meeting of Parliament could not conveniently be deferred beyond the Christmas holidays. In conclusion, they repeated that without the King in person the Prince and those at home needed power to act. They sought to know the wishes of his Majesty.

With this formidable document, Horace Walpole left for Hanover on the morning of November 2. The letters to Townshend from Sunderland, Stanhope, and the King were already on the way. The recipient was scarcely in a mood for understanding what they wrote. He made no effort to conceal resentment that he felt. He addressed the King directly. A copy went to Stanhope. Thoughts of "usage" from one to whom he had "always been so faithful a friend" prevented him from saying more. Sunderland, he was "persuaded," would "excuse" the lack of any answer to what he wrote.

Robert Walpole shared this hurt. There could be "no greater misfortune than to incur blame and displeasure for those very things which a man thinks he has deserved well in." Perhaps it came of serving "at a distance." As to requests by Bothmer and payment for the troops, he would await an interview that Bothmer had desired. He had no recollection of it, but if the King said that he had promised to find money, his "own memory must fail." Since his Majesty had announced the postponement of Parliament to January 8, there were fiscal problems that called for care, and the things necessary would be done "with the greatest difficulty if at all."

Horace, blithely on his way, paused at The Hague, Tuesday, November 6, and left that night in company with a messenger from Cadogan, who was still trying to iron out difficulties Dubois made in signing the French treaty. At Göhre the following Sunday he learned of Townshend's letter from the King. He waited for his kinsman's answer and the return of his Majesty from the spa, expected in a week. In the interim he tried to explain to Stanhope and Sunderland the circumstances of the case. November 26 he was at The Hague again, returning home, hopeful that he would be able "to put the King's friends and servants" upon their old "foot of harmony and union."

He reckoned without the King surrounded by his German court. Weary of Townshend's rule, the current spat among the English ministers tempted them to act. Traveling in an "open wagon" part of the way from Hanover owing to a mishap to his chaise, Walpole was exposed to "violent storms of wind, hail, and rain" and thus reached The Hague with "extream paynes" in all his "joynts." Delay for treatment and later by contrary winds hindered his arrival in London until December 11. On that same day came Thomas Brereton with a message to his friend, Robert Walpole, to be delivered in advance of another to Townshend already on the road.

The latter was removed as Secretary of State, but might be Lord Lieutenant of Ireland. Walpole was to persuade his brother-in-law to accept. Should he fail and feel obliged to quit himself, Stanhope had agreed reluctantly to take for a while Walpole's place with Sunderland as Secretary of State. This alternative, Stanhope very much desired to avoid. He and Sunderland had done their best to keep the ministry intact. The King made up his mind upon information not obtained through them. He would simply not "bear" Townshend in the office that he held, "be the consequence what it" would. Admitting this, could Townshend afford to say that he would serve "upon no other terms than being viceroy over father, son, and their three kingdoms?" Was the "Whigg interest to be staked in defence of such a pretension?"

This rationalization seemed plausible to the two ministers laboring with the King in Germany. Conscious of their own good will in feverish endeavors, they little understood that they would be blamed themselves for that which they were trying to avert. The ministers in London, astounded at the act, appreciated as little the trials of their colleagues with the King. Loyal to Stanhope and his Majesty, they could not think of circumstances that would justify the blow. Unable to confer, angry leaders began recriminations that made more difficult an honest understanding of the case.

Townshend would not take the proffered place. His note to Stanhope crackled with emotion that he took no care to hide. He accepted his colleague's letter in the sense that it was meant. Not "vain enough" to think his services deserved the "fine things" said, he was "weak enough" to think that good opinion due to a "partiality" felt, an "idle notion" confirmed by the message "Horace" brought. His wounded feelings would take time to heal.

Robert Walpole did not need irony to make his point. He had not "let one mortal" see Stanhope's letter and never read parts of it himself without being so astonished that he knew not "what to say or think." Townshend had never thought that Stanhope would enter a combination of their enemies. Things could not be managed in England as Stanhope seemed to think. The explanation of the change in Stanhope in the twelve days between the departure from Hanover of Horace and of Brereton, he found it "vain to guesse and impossible to determine." Any one accusing him and Townshend of making common cause with Argyll, Islay, and the Prince against the King would "be found, pardon the expression, confounded liars from beginning to end." Stanhope should stay his hand until he got home. "Old friends were to be valued like old gold."

The English public was scarcely less surprised than ministers in London. Jacobites, almost in despair, began to pluck up hope. Opposition leaders decided that all might not be lost. The Duke of Somerset thought Townshend "very rightly kicked out from being . . . first minister and governor in Great Britain into a second governor in Ireland." Sunderland had been "false even to his best friends" and would fall "unpitied." Stanhope had no interest in the nation. He would become a peer and no longer "expose himself to the contempt" of the lower house. Should Walpole quit or be silent, there was a "great deal more still to be done," else they "had better not have done so much."

Brereton sent a more rational view to Stanhope through a kinsman. He had made it a point in "Court and City" to observe the effect of his message. The removal of Townshend was not accepted as the end. Unless Stanhope preserved his friendship with Townshend and Walpole, the King's loyal adherents would resent the move. City leaders had entreated Walpole to keep his place. But the "disaffected," silent ten days before, were "now as loud as ever in the coffee houses." Without a union of Townshend, Walpole, and Stanhope there would be a "long continuance of the present disorder and discontent."

Obsessed by the current notion that the trouble was due to rivalry between two factions led respectively by Townshend and Marlborough, the popular view, reflected by Jacobite observers, was that the Duke had won, and that Sunderland would be "Chief Minister." New Year's Day found Townshend convinced that the "Duchess of Munster, Mr. Bernstorff, and Mr. Robethon could give a much more exact and authentic account" of what took place. It found Stanhope and

Walpole with sober second thoughts advising each other to "grow cooler."

Stanhope was alarmed at the prospect opened by Walpole's letter. The King had a right to change secretaries. Walpole would be "responsible to the country" if he did not persuade his brother-in-law to accept Ireland. Reflecting on the subject the same day, Walpole found it difficult to explain to Stanhope the damage done in England. Townshend was hurt by the "manner" of the doing as much as by the deed itself. Stair in Paris, three days later, was puzzled to know "what the devil . . . Lord Sunderland and Stanhope" meant. "What," he asked again, "do Lord Townshend and Walpole mean?" Argyll's "part" was "mad," but could be understood; that of the others, merely "mad." Robethon reminded Stair of his obligations to Stanhope and warned him that the King would have no "cabals." His reply was that he too disliked cabals and wished to be recalled.

George left Hanover January 8. After a journey by coach from Canterbury, Saturday, the nineteenth, he reached St. James's at six in the afternoon. The city populace that night enriched the bonfires with effigies of Mar, the Pope, and the Pretender. The next day his Majesty went to church. Monday the City sent a deputation to congratulate him on his return and his son's administration in his absence.

For Stanhope it had been an anxious trip. On the way he wrote to urge Methuen to retain his place. Townshend and Walpole might "unking their master or . . . make him abdicate," but would "certainly not force him to make" Townshend "Secretary" again. To Walpole he was more emphatic (January 16), thinking it not "possible for all the men in England to prevail upon the King to readmit my Lord Townshend upon any other terms than of complying with the offer made of Ireland." That done, George now promised that in six months he might come back in any other place he liked. Stanhope paused at The Hague to celebrate the signing eleven days before of the Triple Alliance and to ask that the Dutch join in urging Townshend to give in, lest divisions in England endanger the fruits of that agreement.

The King in London helped to heal the wound by admitting haste in thinking that the deposed Minister was trying to obstruct. Townshend took the Irish place. The German court was jubilant again. Early in February Robethon had the "pleasure" to write Polwarth that "Lord Townshend and Mr. Walpole" had "received the King's command to visit Lord Sunderland after dining with him." He thought the dinner would be in a day or two at the Duke of Devonshire's, "and then all" would "go merrily and the friends of those lords in Parliament . . . concur unanimously to carry matters along all right." Which suggests chiefly that the Germans had not yet begun to learn how to play the English political game.

They and their King meant to have no foolishness. An order went forth that representatives at foreign courts should send duplicates of their dispatches in French for George to read. A substantial pamphlet had appeared (January 21), attributed to John Toland, entitled *State Anatomy of Great Britain,* elaborating the evils of parties and factions and suggesting among other things the wisdom of making English peers of certain foreign noblemen. At two in the morning of January 30 the Swedish Minister was arrested and his papers seized in order to find conclusive proof that he intrigued with Jacobites.

Things had not gone well for members of the latter faction in spite of divisions among their adversaries. The defection of Bolingbroke and the Anglo-French alliance were bad enough. But Oxford, who, despairing of justice from the King, began to listen cautiously to approaches from his rival, had little faith in Atterbury, the authorized agent of James in England. Not all the money sought for Sweden could be found, and the Swedes refused to accept a smaller sum. Fortunately for the faction, the seized papers did not name "any British man," but its sanest agents could only philosophize that the government's stroke would "have strong effects . . . one way or another."

Perhaps it did. Townshend was critical of his successor. Defoe sent forth anonymously *An Argument Proving that the*

Design of Employing and Ennobling Foreigners is a Treasonable Conspiracy against the Constitution, dangerous to the Kingdom, an Affront to the Nobility of Scotland in particular and dishonourable to the Peerage of Britain in general. Toland, he said, was merely the editor of *State Anatomy,* which had been "long hatching" and had been "talked of many days before it came abroad." Parts of it had been "handed about and rehearsed among the People" it was "calculated to serve." He blamed not the King, but "a set of selfish and designing Men, who, to engross Power, amass Wealth, and gratify the unbounded Avarice and Ambition of a few" cared not "what Dishonour they" brought "upon their Country, what Bondage they" entailed "upon Posterity." Boyer, ignorant of Defoe's relations with Townshend, thought the author purposed to disrupt the ministry.

His labors were not intended or needed for that end. The post that took to Polwarth Robethon's optimistic letter carried another from a private friend testifying of the habitual scene in English politics. The King locked himself in, appearing only at nights in the drawing room. The Prince and Robethon were at odds. There was the "same contriving, undermining, and caballing at the back stairs, the great ones hurrying back and forward and the little ones cringing after." Thus, when the King and his reorganized ministry met Parliament (February 20) to announce the breach with Sweden, they were unsure both of themselves and of their support.[1]

II

THE KING AND HIS GERMANS

The King's speech suggested action against Sweden, reduction of the national debt, and relief of the Dissenters. A

[1] Lady Cowper, *Diary,* pp. 109ff., 193ff.; Boyer, *Political State,* XII. 85ff.; XIII. 88ff.; Williams, *Stanhope,* pp. 193ff., 246ff.; Coxe, *Robert Walpole,* II. 54ff., 153ff.; Hist. Mss. Com., *Stuart,* II. 303ff.; III. 24ff., 429ff.; *Polwarth,* I. 97ff., 169ff.; Ball, *Correspondence of Swift,* II. 334ff., 360ff.; Torrens, *Cabinets,* I. 150; *Parliamentary History,* VII. 395ff.; J. F. Chance, *George I and the Northern War;* Wolfgang Michael, *Englische Geschichte im 18. Jahrhundert,* II. 27ff.

proclamation (March 2) prohibited trade with the Swedes. Two days later Stanhope introduced Edward Calamy to the King as a representative of the Dissenters to testify of their loyalty and to ask relief. Afterward Calamy published a pamphlet advocating the repeal of the acts passed in the reign of Anne. Proponents of the measure sent petitions. Some two hundred members of Parliament met at the Rose Tavern near Temple Bar (March 26) with Stanhope's approval to further the campaign. Steele and Lord Molesworth were on hand to help. Benjamin Hoadly, Bishop of Bangor, who had already published his *Preservative against the Principles of the Non Jurors,* preached (March 31) a sermon on *The Nature of the Kingdom of Christ* in St. James's Chapel in the presence of the King for the purpose of opening the way to action. But not all of the bishops were in his mood. Nicholson of Carlisle informed his Majesty that eighteen or nineteen of the twenty-five would be against the proposed step.

To the ninth edition of *State Anatomy,* issued the day after Hoadly's sermon, Toland affixed an answer to Defoe. The current cry against foreigners, he said, was aimed at the King, who being "his own High Treasurer" and "First Minister" would never "be frightened or forc'd out of his Measures nor . . . imposed upon in the Choice of his Servants." The author was favorable to the Dissenters, to Stanhope, Cadogan, and Marlborough, but critical of those who had at first opposed the Triple Alliance. The next day this same party cemented its union with a new recruit. Newcastle was married to Harriet Godolphin, whose grandmother furnished a dowry of twenty thousand pounds. The bridegroom dreamed, vainly as it transpired, of offspring that would mingle his blood with that of Marlborough.

The day after the wedding Stanhope took to the House of Commons a message from the King asking for money "to make good such engagements" as might "ease his people of all future charges and apprehensions upon this account." Shippen thought it a misfortune that "so excellent a prince" was so "little acquainted with the usage and forms of parliamentary proceedings." The speech, he said, sounded as if it might have been "penned by some foreign minister" and then translated into English. In the debates of the ensuing week others besides churchmen and Jacobites opposed the government. Walpole gave a silent vote for the measure, but some friends of him and Townshend were on the other side. Robethon sent a pessimistic report to Polwarth when the ministers carried their proposal (April 8) by a majority of only four.

The next day, by direction of the King, Stanhope wrote to dismiss Townshend. Walpole thereupon returned his seals and would not take them back, though George pressed him repeatedly. He moved the reduction of the debt (April 10) as a "country gentleman," not as a minister of the crown. Pulteney, the Secretary at War, and Methuen followed Walpole out. The former could not persuade himself "that any Englishman advised . . . such a message." He hoped that "an Englishman's speaking his mind freely" in the House would "make a German minister quake."

Stanhope as First Lord of the Treasury and Chancellor of the Exchequer undertook a rôle for which he had little talent or taste. Sunderland succeeded as Secretary of State with Addison as his colleague to lend dignity rather than give help. James Craggs, the younger, as Secretary at War was a lieutenant Stanhope would soon need desperately in the House of Commons. Newcastle became Lord Chamberlain and went with Marlborough to the Prince's house to flaunt his staff. Whether he formulated the principle or not, Walpole soon adopted the theory that an opposition should oppose. The new ministry was vulnerable, if he and other hostile factions could act in concert.

Churchmen and Jacobites knew in saner moments that with Walpole as leader the team would be incongruous; nevertheless they went on merrily. While Parliament was in recess awaiting ministerial changes, a hawker was arrested for vending a supposed letter from Bothmer to Schutz. Friends of the Prince were said to oppose his father's measures. Further, the German ministers could have no peace until Walpole's party was destroyed. If that leader should join forces with the Church, a storm would break making it necessary for his Majesty to remain in England instead of returning to Hanover where he longed to be. Sunderland had papers preliminary to a divorce from the imprisoned wife in order that the Duchess of Munster as Queen might provide an heir more tractable. The remedy was "dangerous, but the disease" admitted of no other cure. The ministers then in office were more complaisant than those replaced.

When Parliament reassembled, the King announced a wish to have his power "founded in [the] affections" of his people. Therefore he had given orders for reducing the army by ten thousand men. That nothing might be "wanting" to "quiet the minds of his subjects," he would propose an "act of Grace" for those "artfully misled into treasonable practices." If the Parliament would make haste to conclude its business, he would "meet it early the next winter" to enable it to sit in the "more usual and convenient season."

A week later Wyndham moved that Dr. Andrew Snape, Headmaster of Eton, who had replied to Hoadly's sermon, be invited to preach in St. Margaret's Westminster, the twenty-ninth. Robert and Horace Walpole joined the move. Surely one to whom the nobility trusted the education of their sons might also "be trusted with preaching a sermon before" the House of Commons. The invitation carried by a majority of ten.

The public mind was tender to the concerns of the Church. With Walpole on its side, the danger was too great to risk. Skilled in controversy, Hoadly knew that at times it was discreet to dodge. Snape's pamphlet was "industriously cry'd up by the Multitude," and the lower house of Convocation drafted (May 10) a representation to the bishops that Hoadly had "given great and grievous offence" tending to "subvert all Government and Discipline in the Church of Christ and reduce his Kingdom to the State of Anarchy and Confusion." The King prorogued the Convocation to prevent a further move.

A pamphlet war ensued, lasting for months. By the end of June Hoadly had transferred the controversy to the news-

papers with a chief point in it the veracity of himself and the
Bishop of Carlisle, and that depending upon the accuracy of
statements reported in clubs and otherwhere. After he and
his colleague had entertained readers of the *Daily Courant,*
the *Postboy,* and the *St. James's Evening Post* for a week or
more, Nicholson published *A Collection of Papers Scattered
lately about Town.* Addressing Hoadly, he confessed: "I am
weary of following your Lordship through all the Kennels of
the Town; and therefore have resolved to sit down a while
and reflect . . . on the several Dirty Tours we have made."
But it was to no purpose. In later stages the controversy
seemed to turn on Hoadly's kindness to a French refugee alleged to be a Roman Catholic.

Meanwhile, Oxford colleges were refusing to celebrate
Hanoverian birthdays with due joy. The Earl of that name in
the Tower wondered whether strife among his former opponents might not bring to him release. Shrewsbury, near
the end of his life, was too timid to bear a petition, but another friend got the question raised. The ministers welcomed
it as a chance to put Walpole in the wrong as the Chairman
of the Secret Committee that had preferred the charges. "If
I bluster," that leader told Bromley in concerting plans, "you
must take no notice of it, for I shall mean nothing." A dispute was maneuvered between the two houses concerning the
date of the trial. There was no prosecution at the time appointed by the Lords, and the prisoner went free. Stanhope
in the House of Commons seconded a motion to attaint. Marlborough, whose wife was trying vainly to nurse him back to
health, was led from the Lords' chamber in tears. A by-
stander thought that the "claps and huzzas" in the crowd outside "carry'd it" by a "great majority."

While this question pended, and the Commons discussed
a proposal from the Bank and the South Sea Company for
reducing the public debt, Stanhope indulged his natural feeling against his old colleague. Replying to Walpole and Pulteney, he confessed incapacity for the place he held and a
preference for that he had before. But he hoped to make up
by "Application, Honesty, and Disinterestedness, what he

wanted in Abilities and Experience." At any rate, he had no brothers or other relatives supported from the public funds. Walpole was ready with a counterthrust where his opponent's armor left him exposed. Bothmer and Bernstorff, he said, were men of honor, but there was about the court "a mean Fellow, of what Nation he could not tell, who took upon himself to dispose of Employments." Finding that this man [Robethon] had obtained the grant of a reversion, he thought it undeserved and kept it for his own son. Thereafter Robethon demanded £2500 in compensation. One reason why the speaker had resigned, was his unwillingness to "connive at some things that were carrying on." Other warm remarks ensued, but a fellow member counseled self-control. The rival leaders had "discovered nakedness"; their colleagues ought to turn their backs. By resolution the House commanded them to take no further steps in the dispute.[2]

In July, while Hoadly was leading his opponents into bypaths, Stanhope went to the House of Lords. His wife's father had just sold his famous diamond for £125,000. Robethon was sure that Stanhope's rise in rank did not involve a change at court.

The King with the Prince and his family went that summer to Hampton Court. His Majesty agreed to dine "every day in company," though not "in state," in an effort to carry on—perhaps in part to counteract—the good work that his son began the previous year. He limited to two weeks his stay at Pyrmont, drinking the waters for his health, and returned before the end of August to go shooting in Bushy Park, where he brought down a brace of partridges. He went to Windsor for the first time and hunted deer. Back at Hampton Court, he went early in October to Newmarket and saw Mr. Pelham's mare win the King's Plate. He visited Cambridge; heard scholars along the street shout *Vivat Rex;* was greeted

²Boyer, *Political State,* XIII. 241ff.; XIV. 1ff.; Calamy, *Life,* II. 366ff.; Torrens, *Cabinets,* I. 153ff.; Sykes, *Gibson,* pp. 72f.; Aitken, *Steele,* II. 123ff.; Hist. Mss. Com., *Portland,* V. 526ff.; VII. 430ff.; *Stuart,* IV. 222ff.; *Polwarth,* I. 211ff.; *Various,* VIII. 99; *Beaufort,* p. 97; Lee, *Defoe,* I. 269ff.; Nulle, *Newcastle,* p. 87; *Parliamentary History,* VII. 435ff.; Coxe, *Robert Walpole,* II. 168; *Letters of Duchess Marlborough,* p. 127; Ball, *Correspondence of Swift,* II. 388ff.; *Weekly Journal or Saturday's Post,* June 1, 8, July 6, 1717.

by the Chancellor, the Duke of Somerset; heard a speech by the Regius Professor of Divinity; and saw degrees conferred. Orford entertained him at Chippenham. When he got back to Hampton Court (October 7), the Prince and Princess returned to St. James's for Caroline's approaching labor. His Majesty took time to go to Claremont, the Duke of Newcastle's new estate.

A visitor at Hampton Court that summer reported that the King spent ten days with more "ease and tranquility" than he had ever had before in England. He watched bowlers playing on the green and requested that the game be finished by lantern light. But relations with his son had not improved, and Sunderland tendered to the Earl of Carlisle the task of undertaking as Lord President to make them better. Negotiations were under way for the marriage of Sunderland's daughter to Carlisle's son. A peacemaker would soon be wanted more than any yet foresaw.

Walpole was thought to be determined on the ministry's overthrow, and pamphlets designed to that end were thrown about the streets. Defoe, now a colaborer with Sunderland, did his best to temper the tone of Nathaniel Mist's *Weekly Journal*. But the King at Newmarket forbade that Walpole and Townshend be invited to dine. Stair in early October warned the ministers, with their strength thus weakened, of the danger of undertaking legislation likely to arouse feeling. "If heat and impatience," he said, "will make you go out of the entrenchments and attack a formidable enemy with feeble forces and troops that follow you unwillingly, you will run a risk to be beat, and you won't get people to go along with you . . . by reproaching them that they are afraid."

The Princess was delivered of a boy, November 2, after an easy labor. The populace rejoiced, but the father wasted little ceremony when the grandfather came to call.

A few days later, when Snape and Sherlock, who had supported him against Hoadly, were removed as royal chaplains, Newcastle instructed Buckley to make it clear in the *Gazette* that the command was from the King. Sunderland and Stanhope were at pains to let it be known that they had no part in the further prorogation of Convocation that ensued. Nevertheless, when the King met Parliament (November 21), the Lord Chancellor represented him as hoping that "friends to" the "present happy establishment" would "unanimously concur in some proper method for the greater strengthening the Protestant Interest," which he felt would result from "the union and mutual charity of all Protestants." Robethon wrote the next day that the session had "begun very well and with great unanimity." But a Jacobite observer saw a ray of hope. "The church in this kingdom," he said, "is a tender point. The danger of it will inflame the people, and as soon as the motion is made, that may be forwarded by divers measures."

The time for this good work had not yet come. The infant Prince was christened in a week. The parents, without the grandfather's knowledge, had asked the Duke of York and the King of Prussia to stand as godfathers to their first-born in Great Britain. But the King recognized the prudence of humoring his new subjects, and the honor was claimed as attaching to Newcastle's office. The father, as an unwilling host, resented his unwelcome guest. The excited tone and the German accent with which he spoke caused a misinterpretation of what he said. The frightened sponsor went hastily to the King, who poured out pent-up feelings on his son. The incident became the topic of the year and was the subject of solemn communications to foreign courts. Again Dissenters had to wait.

At first the Prince was ordered to keep to his quarters, but, on sending a letter of submission, was released, though banished from the court. After swooning several times, his wife went with him, leaving their children with the King. Jacobites hoped that the excitement would cement relations between followers of Walpole and the Church. They undertook to coöperate in diminishing a proposed supply for troops, which did not seem to be a harmful move. But Shippen repeated his regret that the King was unacquainted with the English "language and constitution," commenting that parts of the speech proposed by his ministers seemed "rather calculated for the meridian of Germany than Great Britain." Walpole made an opening for retreat, but Shippen claimed the crown of martyrdom, going to the Tower for "reflecting upon the King's Person and Government." Walpole voted with the majority to let him go, not wishing to incur royal displeasure to help a Jacobite.

Sunderland was absent taking his third wife. He had applied for the hand of the eldest of the three Misses Tichborne, but had to take the youngest, just fifteen. The financial advantage in the match was on her side. When word went round that the lonely widower wished some one to supervise his house, the bride expressed a lack of training in and taste for such pursuits. Ten months from the wedding she bore a son. The Duchess of Marlborough hoped now that all the world would see she "did not guide him." But those accustomed to associate his Lordship with the Duke found it hard to attribute his present power to his own political skill and to the wit with which he used the King.

He needed all the art he had. Addison was desperately ill before the end of the year. A pamphlet was widely circulated in its last days (*The Defection Considered, and the Designs of those who divided the Friends of the Government in a true Light*) blaming Walpole for most of what had happened. Moved by "Luciferian Pride, and fall'n from his high Station," he had "since acted the Part of an Angel of Darkness" amounting almost to "criminal Conspiracy." Nevertheless, when Parliament met, the deposed leader demonstrated greater influence in his House than the mediocre speakers for the King.

Cowper, whose wife was still in the household of Princess Caroline, learning of a project to ask for a hundred thousand pounds for the King to give his son, composed as best he could a letter in Latin to advise against it, as tending to encourage further dissensions. Members would "raise disagreeable questions," such as why the Prince's eldest son was educated in Germany? Mobs would be collected; the King would lose friends. In the House of Lords, North and Grey ventured (January 16) to take "Notice of the great Ferment that was in the Nation."

Newspapers and other periodicals copied from the *Amsterdam Gazette* accounts of the dispute between father and son that were sent abroad. One remarked that this narrative might satisfy "those for whom it was designed," but at home, there was a "restless spirit." This despite the explanation of ministerial writers, such as Thomas Brereton in his *Critick*, that the King had "through the whole affair behav'd himself with the highest heroism and self-denial in asserting the cause of the British Peerage, which was insulted in one of its noblest Members, against his own son." The act "must sure endear him to the nation forever." No punishment would be too severe for "sycophant Incendiaries" insinuating the contrary, hoping to "aggrandize themselves by the Division of the Royal Family."

About the middle of January Philip, Earl of Wharton, a secret Jacobite though still behaving in the traditions of his father, was made a Duke in order to still at least one voice. The spirit out of doors did not improve. Shrewsbury died February 1, and five days later the infant son of the Prince of Wales passed from a world which in a few weeks of life it had helped no little to set by the ears. When Convocation reassembled on St. Valentine's Day, the Prolocutor interrupted a protest against the Bishop of Bangor to announce its further prorogation. Hoadly himself thought that the controversy had ceased to turn on "Differences in Doctrine" and that it now exemplified a "cruel Behaviour of Christians and Divines" likely to "make the Ears not only of Christians but of every honest Heathen . . . tingle." Stanhope informed Stair from the Cockpit (February 17) that the ministry anticipated trouble with the Mutiny Bill even in the Lords, but would carry it by a slender margin.

In early March came changes long past due if the ministry was to go on. As Secretary of State, Sunderland had been no match for the King and his German advisers. Stanhope had military ambitions and a real talent for foreign affairs, but was unqualified for either a political or a financial rôle. To remedy these misfits, as Lord President and First Lord of the Treasury Sunderland undertook to manage the King and domestic politics. Stanhope as Secretary of State, with the younger Craggs as a colleague to succeed Addison, had work more suited to his taste. John Aislabie, a pedestrian Yorkshire squire, as Chancellor of the Exchequer became the responsible minister of finance. Cowper resigned in April and went to the country on a plea of ill health. A month later Parker, with more amenable legal advice, got the Great Seal; later he became the Earl of Macclesfield.

Sunderland's task would test his skill, and he needed the utmost effort of his renewed youth. In one quarter he was making headway. Robethon congratulated Polwarth on his discretion in obeying the King's English rather than his German ministers. "Our German Ministers," he said after the change, "have no voice in the government here except Bernstorff, who can do nothing at all." Four days later he was regretful that Sunderland had not even "consulted M. de Bernstorff. It would have done no harm."

The new chief minister had scarcely taken charge when he sent Craggs a "very vile paper" distributed that day at the Cocoa Tree. It contained speeches in Parliament by Shippen and others and was sent to all the larger towns by wagons and packhorses. Most of them might be seized if officers in the country had orders. But his task was lightened by the inability of Jacobites to work together. Many in England thought Atterbury "bizarre and unaccountable." Mar, still Secretary of State, was at the "Villa Pamphilia" in early April, "walking and drinking syllabubs," with "nothing to say before the post" went. In Paris Bolingbroke constantly courted Stair in the hope of returning home.

Stanhope had work to do which led him to sup that summer with Bolingbroke in Paris. A project, on foot for some months, was a quadruple alliance with the French, the Emperor, and the Dutch for the purpose of enforcing the peace that was necessary if the English ministry was to stand. But Cardinal Alberoni, the Minister of Elizabeth Farnese and her weak husband, had other plans. Both he and the Emperor had designs in Italy. The latter finally came to an agreement in the spring on condition that the English send a fleet to the Mediterranean. The French Regent hesitated to risk trouble with Spain, and Dubois, sent to London to concert the alliance, was slow to act. The plan was to allot Parma and Tuscany to the Spanish Infant. But Alberoni dispatched a fleet to Sicily as well.

Stanhope went to France about the middle of June to hearten the Regent and to counteract French ministers who were seeking to thwart Dubois. That done, he hazarded a trip to Madrid in a foolhardy effort to win Alberoni. Meantime, the English fleet in the Mediterranean under Byng, finding that the Spanish would not hearken to words, used action. Luckily for Stanhope, he was out of the country before word reached Spain of this mishap. As a countermove, Alberoni was treating with Russia and Sweden, while listening, as every English enemy did, to overtures from Jacobites. But the Emperor signed the treaty while Stanhope was in Spain, and Alberoni encouraged a conspiracy against the Regent which stimulated France to act. Some of the danger from Sweden was removed in December by the death of Charles XII. But by the next spring the Pretender himself had followed the futile Ormond to Madrid.

Luckily for Sunderland and Stanhope, these affairs were British, and the German ministers had a secondary part. But they were only scotched and had not quit the fight. Moreover, a Spanish war might not be easy to defend. A Jacobite observer assured Mar in late August that Byng's victory was the current talk and that if Spain interrupted British trade, the South Sea Company would be undone and the kingdom ruined. Mar and his advisers meditated a journal to help on this good work.

Defoe began in September the *Whitehall Evening Post*, addressing at the same time some humorously frank advice to Mist, with whom, under the circumstances, he found it difficult to work. "Speak of the King decently," he said, "of the Ministry respectfully, of Ladies modestly, of your Enemies warily, of guilty great ones ironically, of the Crimes of Rulers emblematically, and in all cases relate matters of Fact warily. Above most things speak cautiously of Judges and Courts of Justice, but above all things have a care of Parliaments. Tell your Tales of them as of Things done without Doors and heard at second hand. In a Word, write a *noli me tangere* upon their Proceedings, and even think of them with Fear and Trembling."

Preferring stronger weapons, Sunderland wished (November 1) the officers of the crown to "lay hold of friend and foe, and plague all alike who took the liberty of publishing false news." He hoped Buckley, soon to become Gazetteer for life, and Delafaye would "lay every one by the heels as often as they caught them trifling. He would give £200 a year to some wrangling, teasing attorney that knew how to tear and rend these wretches." Defoe had learned how to adapt the policy of his journal to the circumstances of the hour. A writer for newspapers, he said, ought to aim "not only to give Intelligence, but that all his Intelligence be calculated for the public Good."

Persistent rumors, after Stanhope's return to England, said that he and Sunderland were at odds. Perhaps they sometimes disagreed, but that was not their greatest trouble. To counteract the effect of these rumors, Robethon assured Polwarth that the two dined together at Hampton Court. They were dining thus on the evening of October 8 with the Spanish Ambassador, when Sunderland was called to London to the bedside of his wife. The son arrived before its father did.

The ministers had reasons for concerting action before the time for Parliament to meet. Opposing them were the Prince and his following, Walpole, the Jacobites, the remnant of the old Church party, the King's German ministers; an odd assortment, but formidable if they could be brought to act together. The ministers themselves depended upon their ability to manage the King and their success in using his favor to win the support of Parliament and the populace. Their plan of campaign was complicated but clever. It would not be easy to do all that they had in mind even though, as now seemed unlikely, they could avoid a war with Spain.

When the King met Parliament (November 11), he dwelt on his success in concluding "such terms and conditions of peace and alliance between the greatest princes of Europe" as would inspire others to follow the "example" and thus "make any attempts to disturb the public tranquility not only dangerous but impracticable." But he admitted that Spain, instead of listening to "reasonable terms," had given orders to fit out privateers in West India ports. He hoped that his navy in concert with his allies would procure redress. He asked supplies, urging "vigour," "dispatch," and "unanimity." He had done his part; it remained for Parliament to complete the work.

Dissenters, still an influential group in towns, were restless at delay in their relief. Knowing how hazardous the move, Stanhope finally introduced in the Lords (December 13) a bill for "Strengthening the Protestant Interest," and it was seconded by his chief. Against them, besides Nottingham and North and Grey, were Devonshire, Townshend, Oxford, Islay, and Cowper. The intention was to repeal parts of the Test Act in addition to the measures passed in Anne's reign. But, in order to obtain action at all, it was found necessary to limit the bill to a repeal of the Schism Act and that against occasional conformity. Even then the ministers depended upon the Scot lords for their majority. A bill for the regulation of the universities was drawn by the Lord Chancellor, but was not introduced.

While this action pended, the King announced (December 17) a declaration of war with Spain. With Walpole and Pulteney joining Shippen in attacks at every turn, the ministers needed new allies. Before the end of December Robethon assured Polwarth that a projected agreement with Argyll and Islay, a rival Scottish interest, would not interfere with his own hopes. In the midst of these events the Countess of Warwick bore Addison a daughter, and Steele was left a widower by the nagging Prue. Perhaps her nagging was not wholly undeserved.

The ministers next strove to put their journalistic house in order. J. Roberts, a bookseller in Warwick Lane, took over the *Whitehall Evening Post*. Defoe resumed his work with Mist. His method is apparent from a passage addressed to that editor (April, 1719): "I find thou art fond of being made popular, and of doing things to be talked of, whether good or evil." Defoe's usefulness as a journalist had diminished, though long experience had increased his skill. His *Robinson Crusoe* appeared in the same month as the letter to Mist. But newer writers were appearing, better fitted to cope with problems of the day than those who bore the scars of previous reigns.

Thomas Gordon, a Scot from Kircudbright, had just come to town. His education fitted him for work he was to do. Perhaps the type of journalism he helped to shape was due in part to training he had had. Widely read in the historians of Greece and Rome, he was familiar also with Locke and the myriads of other British writers who had published in the generations just behind. Therefore, he was seldom at a loss for an analogy to make a point while seeming to recall a previous incident. Having grown up in an atmosphere of controversy, he took seriously the time's disputes. But a sense of humor gave him sanity and made him tolerant, enabling him to sense a momentary mood. His distaste for ritualism, natural in a Scot, was tempered by respect for actuality.

Ambitious to make his fortune or a name by marketing his talents, he came to London to seek the patronage of booksellers and the publicity of the coffee-houses. Each of the "great Coffee Houses" in that time, according to Lord Molesworth, had "one or more Men of Authority" who "held the Chair in Disputes" and fixed the "Value of Opinions just as Stock Jobbers" did that of "Stocks in Exchange Alley." "Inferiour Auditors" submitted with "great Alacrity" to the "Force of these Gentlemen's Reason and Eloquence." At the Grecian, John Trenchard usually held forth; his pamphlet had helped to prepare the climate leading to the reduction of William's army in his later years. Gordon's humor appealed to Trenchard. They soon discovered that on the Church their views were similar. Therefore Trenchard was just the man to acquaint the newcomer with the political realities of the day.

Gordon's early pieces, inviting public notice, were prepared with greater pains than he was able to bestow on many that he later offered to a larger audience. Among the first was *A Dedication to a Great Man concerning Dedications: Discovering amongst other Wonderful Secrets, what will be the present Position of Affairs a Thousand Years hence.* In the guise of an historian of the year 2718, he recorded achievements of such contemporaries as Sunderland, Stanhope, Cadogan, Marlborough, Addison, and Hoadly. The Duke of Newcastle, he foresaw as one "who from his early Infancy to the End of a most distinguished and honorable Life gave infinite Proofs of a large Soul and a disinterested Love to Mankind, Liberty, and the more elegant Arts."

In another apology he tried to capitalize prevailing currents of contemporary feeling: *A Modest Apology for Parson Alberoni, Governor of King Philip, a Minor, and universal Curate of the Spanish Monarchy; the whole being a short but unanswerable Defence of Priestcraft and a new Confutation of the Bishop of Bangor.* He touched his subject with a lightness unusual in the journalists of the day. A stationer having entrusted to him an "Inkhorn," he found "upon a Tryal" of his "Genius," that he "could make as good a Figure in Print" as some other "famous Writers whose Merit" was "best known to themselves." Not one of the answers to his piece "would be worth reading," but, at the "earnest Request" of his bookseller, he would "write and publish a Reply" for which he hoped the market would be large.

In the second edition he insisted that this pamphlet was aimed only at those who "felt themselves hit" by it. Speculations concerning the author led him to declare that his name had not appeared in print. Among others, Defoe got credit for the work. Utilizing this success, Gordon offered next *An Apology for the Danger to the Church, Proving that the Church is and ought to be always in Danger; and that it would be dangerous for her to be out of Danger. Being a second Part of the Apology for Parson Alberoni,* in which he admitted that the former work had "been laid at the Door of a Gentleman or two" whose names did him "Honour." Thus launched, his hand would soon find work to do.

The older journalists had a final fling. The King's relations with his son made both his British and his German ministers fearful for the future. Perhaps they might contrive a remedy. Since the contemplated danger would involve the Duchess of Munster as well as Sunderland and Stanhope, George was made to feel a personal interest in the success of the proposal brought forward in the latter part of February after most of the session's business was done. It was part of their agreement with the Scot recruits.

Having laid the train as best they could, the Duke of Somerset proposed the measure (February 28) with Argyll for a second, supported by Sunderland and Carlisle. The scheme was to limit the increase in the English peerage forever to five lords in addition to those already in the House; in lieu of the sixteen elective Scots provided for in the Act of Union, the King was to designate twenty-five to be succeeded by lineal heirs.

Sunderland found it difficult to get support. Middleton, the Lord Chancellor of Ireland, and his brother, Thomas Brodrick, stubbornly refused to do more than stay away, though told that the bill was "the King's desire, not the act of his ministry." Another problem was to select twenty-five Scot lords who would be docile in the future and not arouse the opposition of the men left out.

Oxford wondered, when the bill was introduced, why the King's ministers took no better care of the prerogative of the crown. Thereupon, the King sent a message (March 2) saying that he had "so much at heart the settling the Peerage" that he was willing to consent. Nottingham objected that the measure was contrary to precedent; and Cowper, that it violated the Act of Union. Townshend joined the opposition, and the fight was on.

Steele interrupted his grief and his foolish project of a ship with a pool for transporting fish to start the *Plebeian* and the *Moderator*. Commoners should keep their right to become peers. Not interested in being a lord himself, before he finished he affected to be "very apprehensive of being a Vassal." Though in poor health, Addison, amid belated joys of fatherhood, replied, patronizing his former friend in the *Old Whig*. Richard Molesworth, a peer in the Irish list, still hopeful that the ministers might help to provide for a large family of ambitious sons, defended their measure in the *Patrician*, which was announced in a preliminary pamphlet, *A Letter from a Member of the House of Commons to a Gentleman without Doors*.

These small quarto, sixpenny, periodical essays were supplemented by pamphlets. Trenchard's was most notable, *The Thoughts of a Member of the Lower House in Relation to the Project for Restraining and Limiting the Power of the Crown in the future Creation of Peers*. The bill, he said, was the result of "court Intrigues" supported by "Sollicitations" and kept "Secret till the latter End of the Sessions, when country Members" were "at their Seats and Lawyers in their Circuits."[8]

The controversy was interrupted after a few weeks. Seeing the opposition to be strong, the ministers dropped the bill. The Duchess of Munster was consoled by an English title as Duchess of Kendal. Argyll became Duke of Greenwich in the same list. Thomas Pitt, brother-in-law of Stanhope, became Baron of Londonderry in Ireland. The "prodigious Number of Coffee-House Papers," that had "of late appeared like Comets," vanished from the scene. Steele waited in vain for Addison's third number; his old friend died before the end of June. Showing his disappointment, the King prorogued Parliament (April 18) with a parting hope that "animosities" would be laid aside. Early in May he was *en route* to his German home.[4]

[8] Remembering vaguely hearing his father say that he published a pamphlet on this question, Horace Walpole in his *Catalogue of the Royal and Noble Authors of England* attributed this work to Sir Robert. Subsequent writers have accepted this guess, though a collection of the works of Trenchard and Gordon published before the *Catalogue* was compiled listed Trenchard as the author. Aitken in his *Steele* (II. 217) identifies Walpole's pamphlet as *Some Reflections upon a Pamphlet called the Old Whig*. But this item also is accredited to Trenchard in the collected edition of his pamphlets and seems to have been written by the author of the preceding work. See *A Collection of Tracts by the late John Trenchard, Esq.; and Thomas Gordon, Esq.*, 2 vols., 1751, published just after Gordon's death.

[4] Hist. Mss. Com., *Polwarth*, I. 299ff.; II. 16ff.; *Various*, VIII. 100ff.; *Stuart*, IV. 548ff.; V. 158ff.; VI. 291ff.; VII. 48ff.; *Carlisle*, pp. 21ff.; *Portland*,

Stanhope went again, leaving Charles Delafaye as Secretary of the Lords Justices, of whom this time Argyll was one. Accompanying the King also was Bernstorff and the Duchess of Kendal. The English ministers were trying to widen the breach between the Duchess and Robethon on one side and Bothmer and Bernstorff on the other. But Bernstorff had not given up the fight. June 30 Craggs urged Luke Schaub, Stanhope's trusted subordinate, to consult his chief and the Duchess in an effort to set matters right. The "sales of offices and other underhanded dealings" caused "incredible" trouble. There was no "distinction of persons or circumstances: Jacobites, Tories, Papists, on the Exchange or in the Church, by Land or Sea, during the Session or in Recess," provided there was "Money." The diplomatic situation in the north was favorable, if the English ministers were free to act, but not "as long as that mischievous old man [Bernstorff]" retained his "influence." Under the circumstances, Stanhope was "on the point of resigning every day." He favored the suggestion of the Duchess that "every one speak" who had "the least degree of influence."

Robethon the same day had to admit that his recommendation to Bernstorff might now hurt instead of help. Stanhope reported to Craggs a momentary victory "over the old man." The King had overruled him "twice in Council before all his German Ministers . . . with an air of authority." But before long the Duchess requested Sunderland's presence in Hanover to help. "I think we may weather the danger," Stanhope wrote his chief. It might then "deserve consideration" whether the King on returning to England could be induced to leave Bernstorff behind. The Duchess was "bitterly incensed against him" and would act with them.

In England, Sunderland was harping on an earlier chord.

V. 533ff.; Boyer, *Political State*, XIV. 83ff.; XV. 1ff.; XVI. 197ff.; XVII. 98ff.; Lee, *Defoe*, I. 273ff.; II. 71ff.; Hardwicke, *State Papers*, II. 559ff.; *Letters of Lady Suffolk*, I. 16ff.; *Parliamentary History*, VII. 500ff.; Campbell, *Chancellors*, IV. 318ff.; Stanhope, *History*, II. Appendix, pp. lxiiff.; Torrens, *Cabinets*, I. 182ff.; D. H. Stevens, *Party Politics in English Journalism, 1702-1742*, p. 107; Sykes, *Gibson*, p. 73; Williams, *Stanhope*, pp. 273ff.; Coxe, *Robert Walpole*, II. 171ff.; Calamy, *Life*, II. 371ff.; *Original Weekly Journal* (Applebee's), April 4, 1719.

Unless the King returned before the middle of November, Parliament would be difficult to manage. Nevertheless, about eleven on the morning of August 20 he "took water" at Whitehall to board the *William and Mary* at Greenwich for the requested voyage. A few days later a pamphlet entitled *Truth is but Truth as it is Timed* suggested that the House of Commons could learn of affairs in the north by calling "a certain Exotic Baron." "To see any Length in the Interests" of the state was "a Talent now given only to Foreigners."

Sunderland informed Newcastle from Hanover (October 11) that the King was determined "to push the Peerage Bill, the University Bill, and the Repeal of the Septennial Bill," measures which the Duke and his friends were assumed to wish. Moreover, the "world" would be "convinced" by what his Majesty would "both say and do" that "neither Bernstorff nor Cadogan" longer had "credit," nor would any "foreigners" be suffered "to meddle in British affairs."

Newcastle was already a sounder politician than his colleagues and had little enthusiasm for their program. The "Peerage Bill" he approved and the "University Bill," as a help to its passage through Parliament. He thought that measure would pass if represented as his Majesty's personal desire. As to the repeal of the "Septennial Bill," he feared that it would hurt more than it would help. Besides, he apprehended no danger of losing a general election if Parliament should last "out its time." The "great point" was to see to it meanwhile that Walpole and his friends should be "so incorporated with the Jacobites" as to make them helpless with the public.

Stanhope thought the repeal of the Septennial Act to be a good measure in itself, but was willing to give way if the Peerage Bill could be passed without it. Newcastle might be sure that the King would return early in order to put Parliament in a good humor, but his Majesty had it much at "heart not to be baffled a second time." As to Bernstorff, he could not "promise that the old man" would be left behind, but could send assurance that the King would "doe whatever shall be proposed to him to make everybody sensible that he is not to meddle in English business." Bernstorff was "exceedingly piqued and mortified" thereat and had vented "his spleen" against Robethon, "his immediate subordinate." With the help of the Duchess, they were trying to except the latter from the list of German ministers.

Leaving Hanover, November 11, the King reached London by coach from Gravesend at seven in the evening a week later. Sunderland was soon busy with the task in hand. Learning that Carlisle could not come to town, he wrote (November 18) requesting a proxy. He congratulated that Lord upon a matter, "which I know you have long had at heart and which will contribute more to the King's and the public service than any other thing; that is, the resolution the King has taken, not to suffer his Germans to meddle in English affairs, he having forbid them to presume so much as to speak to him about them; and this he has ordered all his servants to declare to everybody to be his resolution, and tells it himself to as many as come to him." The Peerage Bill would be recommended in the speech and brought in the first week of the session; the University Bill would be pushed also.

Ministerial journalists prepared the public mind. Pamphlets explained the reasons for previous defeat and offered arguments for present victory. Those of the year before were hawked about again. A meeting of opposition leaders at the Duke of Devonshire's found the noble members ready to give up the fight. But the undaunted Walpole announced his resolution to oppose singly if need be. Steele came forward with *A Letter to the Earl of Oxford* the day the bill was sent down to the Commons, a peace offering to followers of that Lord who had opposed the measure in his House. The Brodricks persisted in their view. Even Molesworth began to wonder whether the ministers would ever reward his hopes unless, instead of helping them, he showed ability to "hurt." Walpole in the Commons made one of the most studied and effective speeches of his life. Again the ministers had to yield. Bystanders marveled that they "should bring in" the bill without "a probability of carrying it."

They deprived Steele of his share in the patent of Drury Lane, whereat he started the *Theater* (January 20, 1720) to air injustice he alleged. He had just been penalized five hundred pounds for absence from the Commission on Confiscated Scot Lands. Newcastle, the Lord Chamberlain, forbade the journalist to write to him, see him, or visit him more. A pamphlet soon appeared depreciating what Steele had done both as manager and journalist. This seemed unjust to the "poor Plebeian" who "at the entrance into old age" had just "lifted" his "head out of obscurity into noise, clamour, and envy."

Defoe made profit from his pen without the patronage of men in power. Fearing that his countrymen might catch contagion from the spectacular rise of Law in France, he had published in July *The Anatomy of Exchange Alley; or, a System of Stock-Jobbing; Proving that Scandalous Trade as it is now carried on to be Knavish in its Private Practices and Treason in its Public*. British speculators were winning tidy sums. Stair warned Craggs that the bubble would soon burst, but Stanhope, a little to Stair's disgust, when he went to France in January after the fall of Alberoni, dealt with John Law in making ready to negotiate a peace at the Congress of Cambray.

Defoe returned to the subject early in the new year in *The Chimera; or, the French Way of Paying National Debts laid open*. He had begun to take a hand in the *Daily Post* in the previous autumn in addition to his other ventures. " 'Tis the Misfortune of the Town," he said, introducing the project, "to have much News, but little Intelligence; Truth ill told, Lies ill covered, Parties ill serv'd." He promised impartiality with "clear and unbias'd Reasons to explain doubtful Cases" in an effort to "give an Account of the News Foreign and Domestic in the best and clearest Manner."

The *Daily Journal,* the third paper to seek a place on each morning's breakfast table, appeared January 23, 1720. It admitted that it might surprise "a vast Number of People to see a Newspaper come thrusting itself into the Coffee Houses . . . already so overstocked with them that" there was "never a Politician, not even of those who smoke you three or four Pipes of the best Virginia at a Sitting in one of those Intelli-

gence Shops who" had "Time or Patience to read them all."
The publisher boasted correspondents on the Continent and
at Edinburgh and Dublin, but based his chief hope of success
on the difficulty of getting advertisements inserted immediately in the existing journals. He would not charge a double
fee to those in haste to advertise.

John Trenchard published about the same time *Some Considerations upon the State of our Public Debts in General and
of the Civil List in Particular.* Gordon, his protégé, still looked
for a suitable sea on which to launch his journalistic ship.
Concerning the Church he sympathized with Hoadly's views.
Trenchard had opposed the Peerage Bill and was suspicious
of Stanhope's offer of Gibraltar if necessary to get peace with
Spain. Dissenters were at the moment dividing into factions.
Might not an essay periodical help to win some of them to
conformity with a liberal national Church? A carefully written pamphlet with a sly attack on Sunderland felt out the
way. *The Character of an Independent Whig* was published
while the Peerage Bill was pending. Boyer pronounced it "a
remarkable Pamphlet" treating "High and Important Matters
of State and Political Government with a firm bold Spirit
answerable to its Title." The reference to Sunderland was incidental to comment on gambling as a "dreadful Vice." One
who committed his all to the "Chance of a Dye" might "prove
but a faithless Guardian of the Publick." Who would "trust
their Property with one who" could not "keep his own?"

That this passage "nettled to the Quick some great Men"
was clear on the appearance of *The Character of Two Independent Whigs, viz. T. G[ordon] of the North and Squire
T[renchard] of the West.* But Gordon would not be diverted
by a personal attack. The "second part" of his pamphlet,
*Considerations Offered upon the Approaching Peace and upon
the Importance of Gibraltar,* appearing New Year's Day,
announced the early beginning of a periodical he had in mind,
directed against the "Malignity" of "aspiring Ecclesiasticks."
In the "Teeth of the Act of Settlement," he took it for granted
that ministers would not embark upon a northern war. He
hoped that peace with Spain was now in prospect, but to yield

Gibraltar would be an act of treason. In his new venture he did not hope to rival Hoadly but to support him by starting "new Topicks" and throwing "the same Subject into new Light."

The *Independent Whig* lasted fifty-three weeks. The author admitted in setting out that "Whoever goes about to reform the World undertakes an Office obnoxious to Malice and beset with Difficulties." In a dedication to the lower house of Convocation, he announced that there could be "no Medium between Popery and the Reformation," between Hoadly's views and a "Popish Revolution." He advocated the "Spiritual Supremacy of the Crown; the Rights of the Laity to judge for themselves; the forming of all ecclesiastical Polity by the Legislature; and consequently . . . creating Clergymen by the Civil Power." But he could scarcely have chosen a more unpromising year to launch his work. That what he wrote had merit and was apposite to circumstances in the time is clear from its repeated publication.[5]

III

WALPOLE AT THE HELM

In addition to the Peerage Bill, the King had recommended to Parliament (November 23, 1719) the lessening of the public debt. Law's spectacular success in France tempted British ministers. The war with Spain curtailed the little profitable trade the South Sea Company had previously had. A group of its directors, John Blunt, Sir George Caswell, and Robert Knight the more active, began to wonder whether trade was, after all, the easiest road to wealth. Perhaps Aislabie and his fellow ministers joined the directors in their scheme more because of inability to understand its implica-

[5] Lee, *Defoe*, I. 303ff.; II. 106ff.; Aiken, *Addison*, II. 22f.; Boyer, *Political State*, XVII. 494ff.; XVIII. 105ff.; XIX. 2ff.; Hist. Mss. Com., *Polwarth*, II. 192ff.; *Various*, VIII. 281ff.; *Carlisle*, p. 23; *Onslow*, pp. 458ff.; Torrens, *Cabinets*, I. 230ff.; Stanhope, *History*, II. Appendix, pp. 1xxixff.; Hardwicke, *State Papers*, II. 585ff.; Williams, *Stanhope*, pp. 314ff.; *Parliamentary History*, VII. 606ff.; Calamy, *Life*, II. 425ff.; Aitken, *Steele*, II. 219ff.; Cartwright, *Wentworth Papers*, p. 447; Coxe, *Robert Walpole*, II. 173ff.

tions than as reward for profits promised to themselves. The elder Craggs, Postmaster General, joined with his son to push the measure through.

An obvious opposition move was to enlist the Bank, which had a natural interest in the debt. When it was clear that the South Sea Company with ministerial support would out-bid the Bank, the next step was to make sure that the offer made, especially for the long term annuities, should specify a definite quantum of stock sufficient both to encourage hold-ers to accept the offer and later to protect them in case the price of stock should not hold up. On this point came the chief fight in the House of Commons.

Craggs wrote to Stanhope from the Cockpit (December 27) that he thought the project would succeed. Though not so sanguine as Sunderland, he did not even despair of doing something about the Civil List. The first scheme was offered to Parliament January 21. Walpole and Thomas Brodrick called it in question. Steele published *The Crisis of Property,* followed by *The Nation a Family* and discussed the subject so pointedly in his *Theater* that ministers were said to think of expelling him from the House again. The Company's chief trade, he said, would probably be "stockjobbing." Openly he charged that members of Parliament had been permitted to subscribe at a profit in advance. Trenchard lent a hand in *A Comparison between the Proposals of the Bank and the South Sea Company, wherein it is shown that the Proposals of the First are much more advantageous to the Publick than those of the Latter, if they do not offer such Terms to the Annuitants as they will accept of.* It was not a plan for paying debts, he said, but "a Job to get Plumbs for a few Prospectors, ruin Thousands, and disappoint the Publick." In Mist's *Journal,* Defoe compared the specula-tion already begun to gambling with dice and asked whom it would profit to have things sell for more than they were worth.

Supporters of the bill alleged that to make the definite offer desired would defeat its purpose. While the point hung fire, "Stock-Jobbers in Exchange Alley were in perpetual Hurry, being toss'd about between Hopes and Fears upon the different Accounts they received." The Company got its way in committee, March 23, by the narrow margin of 144 to 140. When the news was known, the stock rose from three to four hundred. Thenceforth, said Boyer, "Artificial Engines and secret Springs were set to work both at Home and abroad by those who had no small Concern in the Success of the Affair." Defoe in Mist's *Journal* warned "country Gentlemen and rich Farmers" said to be on the roads from all parts of the kingdom, each "expecting no less than to ride down again in his Coach and six" that though there would be some "prizes" there would be "many more Blanks."

The South Sea directors were more at ease than the ministers who made them so. The mounting debt on the Civil List was not yet paid. More distressing, Sunderland and Stanhope learned in these weeks of a scheme of the Germans to make common cause with Walpole and the Church party for a new ministry. The fears were real, whether the report was true or not. The easiest remedy seemed to be to win Walpole themselves. With his help, they might perform more easily their financial task as well as make political defense.

Walpole warily insisted upon a reconciliation between the Prince and King. Else, in a short time another rival faction would embarrass those in power. The negotiation was so secret it was said that scarcely ten men knew it was on foot at all. Walpole and Townshend had to take subordinate rôles. The Princess did not even get her children. The disgruntled Cowper finally refused the proffered Privy Seal. Pulteney was hurt, thinking he ought to have been consulted in advance. Lord Lumley took a letter from the Prince to his father St. George's Day, April 23. Later the son went to the Palace in a chair. Neither side showed friendship, but the crowd without rejoiced.

Seeing Bothmer and Bernstorff in another room, Stanhope twitted them in French: "La Paix est faite." Thinking that he spoke of foreign matters, they asked whether the dispatches had come. Told that the reconciliation was between the Prince and King, they said: "Monsieur, vous avez été bien secret dans vos Affaires"; to which the gloating Stanhope answered: "Oui, oui, nous l'avons été . . . le Secret est toujours nécessaire pour faire les bonnes Choses." Bothmer was moved to tears.

There were other wounds that needed to be healed. Craggs, trying to make his peace, admitted to Caroline that he had been among those criticizing her party for opposing measures of the King. "Yes," she replied blandly, "I was told that you had condescended so low as to call me a Bitch." Bernstorff warned her at first not to "forget who turned Townshend and Walpole out." Later, ignorant of what was going on, he affected not to care.

Before the end of the month he confided to Lady Cowper that the error in the beginning was to let "the Secretary of State be minister instead of servant." She answered that her husband thought most of their troubles would have been avoided had there been a "Treasurer." "But your Treasurer," said Bernstorff, "has such unlimited Power here in England, that one can't think of it as endurable." "What do you think of the Power of the Earl of Sunderland?" she asked. "I have seen several Treasurers, but none with the Authority and the unlimited Power of the Earl of Sunderland. The Earl of Oxford never had a Quarter of the Power, nor the Insolence, that Lord Sunderland has." Bernstorff left England with the King that summer never to return. Robethon and his son were naturalized by Parliament in a year. Kendal retained her power to work with English instead of German ministers.

Walpole had to find the money for the debt upon the Civil list. The fever of speculation in the City showed a way. May 4 Aislabie took to Parliament a message from the King asking approval for the patents of two insurance societies, the London and the Royal Exchange, whose promoters had "offered to advance and pay a considerable sum of money for his Majesty's use." Each promised three hundred thousand pounds.

Thomas Gordon interrupted his work on the *Independent Whig* to publish *A Learned Dissertation upon Old Women,*

Male and Female, Spiritual and Temporal, in all Ages; whether in Church, State, or Exchange Alley, very seasonable to be read at all Times, but especially at particular Times, which years later was remembered against him in another controversy. After pages of fooling he commented on the "late Union of the Whig Chiefs" and the existing "Concord between St. James's and Leicester Fields." He hoped the ministers would now do some of the things neglected hitherto, such as making peace with Spain. Atterbury wrote to the Pretender (May 6) that things looked discouraging for their cause. New tactics were necessary, now that the Church party no longer held the balance of power.

Money flowed freely in London that summer. Lady Cowper commented sourly that the country's new "Lords and Masters" had more court made to them than the minister or "Kendal and Kilmanseg." The topic of conversation when members of substantial classes met was how much each had made. From the Prince of Wales to the humblest merchant whose name had prestige to persuade his friends, all were utilized by the promoters, who left few tricks untried in selling stocks. Most of the devices familiar in later times were used. Rumors poured through coffee-houses and the press. Great ladies gave their orders from tea tables adjacent to the Exchange.

Carrying on for Mist while he was in prison, Defoe began that summer to write also for Applebee's *Original Weekly Journal.* He or another of its news writers commented (July 9) that since the "late hurlyburly of Stockjobbing" there had "appeared in London 200 new Coaches and Chariots, besides as many more now on the Stocks in the Coach-Makers' Yards; about 4000 embroidered Coats; about 3000 gold Watches at the Sides of Whores and Wives; some few private Acts of Charity; and about 2000 broken Tradesmen."

But South Sea stock went on rising, and holders of the kingdom's promises to pay pressed eagerly to exchange these securities for shares in the new venture at prices that no sober man could justify. The "Madness of Stock-Jobbing is inconceivable," wrote Edward Harley to his brother, who remained at home. The impending "fate" was "too easy to be guessed." But Blunt was made a Baronet for "raising the Public Credit to a Height not known before." So widespread was the speculation that directors of the South Sea Company were alarmed at the success. The King published a proclamation, June 11, prohibiting corporations not chartered for the purpose from offering their stocks.

On that same day George prorogued Parliament with hopes for the success of the scheme and a parting wish that his subjects would "lay aside those partialities and animosities" which had hindered them from "living quietly and enjoying the happiness of a mild, legal government." South Sea stock then sold at the rate of a thousand pounds for a hundred-pound share.

After Walpole was made Paymaster and Townshend Lord President, the King set sail again for Germany. Bernstorff and Stanhope went with him, but Robethon this time remained behind and planned to go to Bath in August for his health. "It is impossible to tell you," the exulting Craggs wrote to Stanhope (July 15), "what a rage prevails here for South Sea subscriptions at any price." The Bank had to place tables in the street for those crowding to exchange the redeemable annuities. There had been a gay dinner at Sunderland's with Devonshire, Newcastle, Carlisle, Townshend, the Speaker, Walpole, and himself on hand. They "got some very drunk, and others very merry."

Other Cassandras croaked besides Defoe. The Duchess of Marlborough thought it "a strange paradox that South Sea Men" should give £134,000 for £45,000 in land, while the public subscribed for "their stock and give a thousand pounds." She persuaded her husband to sell his holdings at a profit of a hundred thousand pounds; she decided not to part with their government securities unless compelled to do so.

By the middle of August clouds appeared which sent Sunderland to Hanover. Before the end of the month Defoe wondered in Applebee's whether those who got out in time would be permitted to keep what they had won. Pamphleteers were speaking frankly. There was *A Letter to a Conscientious Man Concerning the Use and Abuse of Riches . . . shewing that Stock-Jobbing is an unfair Way of Dealing and particularly Demonstrating the Fallaciousness of the South Sea Scheme,* alleging specifically that the promoters knew in advance the impracticability of paying dividends without the means of earning them and had "no Intention" of doing so.

The directors had found it easier to persuade holders of public obligations to give up their claims than it was to dispose of their own stock at the inordinate profit they now coveted after the saturation of the market. Having floated one issue at a thousand, they could not permit the price to fall below that point without injustice to subscribers at that figure. To prevent this, the Company began to make loans through its banking subsidiaries for the balance after a small initial payment on subscriptions, accepting the stock at its inflated value as security for the notes. In order not to lose business, other bankers had to follow suit.

By the first week in September even these frantic measures needed reënforcement. When the stock began to fall, many holders of government securities for which stock had not actually been issued demanded their return, only to learn that in the formality of offering the exchange the owners had delegated to agents of the Company power of attorney to fix terms. A complaint was aired in *A State of the Case Between the South Sea Company and the Proprietors of the Redeemable Debts.* A meeting of proprietors and annuitants was called for September 8 at Merchant Taylors' Hall.

By nine in the morning the room was full, with many clamoring at the doors. The senior Craggs was there to speak. Hungerford, a well-known wit and lawyer, was put up to win the crowd. The directors, he said, deserved confidence. They "had done more than the Crown, the Pulpit, and the Magistrates could do." They had "laid asleep, if not wholly extinguished . . . Domestick Jars and Animosities." Monied men had "increased their Fortunes"; country gentlemen had seen the value of their lands "doubled and trebled"; not a few even of the clergy had "got great Gains." The Duke of

Portland, who was heavily involved, lent his voice. A dividend of thirty per cent. was announced to be paid at Christmas, with fifty per cent. to be paid semi-annually after that. Nevertheless it was necessary to defeat a resolution permitting the withdrawal of public securities offered in exchange for stock. The stock continued to go down.

Perhaps heroic action might avert disaster. Craggs brought together the directors of the Company and the Bank. Walpole came up from the country where he went to spend the summer and was enlisted to help persuade the Bank. After a session, September 19, at the house of Craggs, lasting from nine in the evening to three in the morning, a tentative agreement was minuted by Walpole as the basis for a contract. A meeting of the proprietors of the South Sea Company was called for the next day to authorize the directors. Pulteney made a speech to help. He had not sold his stock in the "panic," and if "the nation was ruined" would "think it a scandal to be rich." This time the motion passed authorizing relief to dissatisfied annuitants. But proprietors alleged in open meeting that the trouble was due to rumors that directors had "betrayed their trust."

The authorized negotiation took place, but directors of the Bank, in view of the alarm, ultimately refused to endanger the credit of their institution in a palliative, which by that time it was clear would not restore the desired confidence. Even before the negotiation began (September 13), the hardheaded Thomas Brodrick wrote to his brother in Ireland that "the Consternation" was "inexpressible, the rage beyond expression, and the case so desperate" it was impossible to foresee what might be done. While the negotiation hung fire (September 21), the Lords Justices sent an urgent request that the King return and call his Parliament, lest the panic encourage the Pretender to make a fresh attempt.

At a meeting of its directors, September 22, the Bank declared the usual dividends for the year. The next day it invited subscriptions to a proposed issue for supporting public credit, and long lines of subscribers took the three millions offered. The Prince of Wales subscribed thirty thousand pounds; the Lords of the Treasury, a hundred thousand for the King. But a run on the banks and goldsmiths had begun. The Sword Blade Company, a banking subsidiary of the South Sea, closed September 24. By the end of the month South Sea stock was back to one hundred-fifty, where it was on February 2, before the rise began.

Boyer commented at the time:

Thus in the Compass of eight Months we have seen the Rise and Progress of that mighty Fabric, which being wound up by mysterious Springs and artificial Machines to a stupendous Height, had fixed the Eyes and Expectations of all Europe; but whose main Foundations being Fraud, Illusion, Credulity, and Intoxication, tumbled down to the Ground as soon as this ambidextrous and selfish Management of the principal Projectors was discovered. With its Fall Multitudes of unwary but covetous Persons were unfortunately crush'd and not a few ancient and honourable Families almost entirely ruined.

A writer in the *Freethinker* confessed he found it "a Pain to converse in Public Places . . . a Torment to visit private Families," since "every House" was one of "Mourning." A social upheaval was taking place. "The Wealth, the Inheritances of the Island," he said, "are transferred to the Meanest of the People. Those chiefly have gained who had nothing to lose. The Nobility, the Gentry, the Merchants have become a Prey to the Idle, the Licentious, the Spendthrifts: Men whose Habitations were not known."

Some foundation in fact for this exaggerated picture is seen in the habit in a later decade of attaching optimistic estimates of estates possessed in hundreds or thousands of pounds as a justification of press notices of births, marriages, and deaths. The crude measurement of wealth rivaled for a time family, land, political place, and similar evidences that a name deserved insertion in the news. In this social atmosphere journalists and politicians had to work.

Thomas Brodrick did not think all lost September 27. Sunderland was caught, misinformed by the directors, and many of his friends were ruined. Only those bent on "revenge" would favor "extremes." Brodrick thought that he might himself be called "a South Sea Man" before the end. Wyndham, his own fingers badly burnt, had less hope. There was "not a penny stirring" and, since Walpole had left town again, little prospect of "better things in a few days." Sunderland in Hanover, as the man having "the principal direction of affairs," had few illusions about what he faced. Those in power would have to bear the blame. He would not have gone to Germany that summer, he wrote to Carlisle, but for the opinion of friends that it might be "of use to the public service." He comforted himself that without his help it would not have been possible to persuade the King to "an early return and an early session."

In this same week in October, Jacombe, Under Secretary at War, suggested to Walpole a scheme for marshaling the Bank, the East India Company, and the South Sea Company in one great bulwark of the national credit. He notified that minister a few days later that every one "wished him in town," though confessing that little could be done until "people's fears and distrusts of one another" had time to cool. A fortnight later he was less sure: "They all cry out for you to help them, so that when you come, you will have more difficultys on you than ever you had. For though you are perfectly clear of this sad Scheme, yet you will be prodigiously importuned by all sufferers to doe more than any one can doe; and more than you in your judgment would think ought to be done, if it could be done."

The King sent word that he was on his way. October 12, a proclamation appointed November 25 for Parliament to meet. In the intervening weeks the ferment raged. The very day the King left Helvoetsluys, Trenchard and Gordon published the first of their *Cato's Letters* in the *London Journal,* a weekly which had as yet made little noise in the coffee-houses. The subject was Gibraltar. There was less talk now of yielding it, but ministers ought to purge their minds of having entertained the thought.

The next letter touched the subject of the hour. "Jealousy and Revenge in a whole People, when they are abus'd," said the authors, "are laudable and Politick Virtues. . . . You may at present load every Gallows in England with Directors and Stock-Jobbers without the Assistance of a Sheriff's Guard or so much as a Sigh from an old Woman, tho' accustom'd perhaps to shed Tears at the untimely Demise of a common Felon." The "Resurrection of Honesty and Industry" was hopeless with that "sort of Vermin . . . suffered to crawl about, tainting" the "Air and putting everything out of Course." The next week saw the work go on. Answering the question, "Well, but Monstrous as they are, what would you do with them?" the authors said in brief, "Hang them." "If the ordinary Channels of Justice could be stopp'd by Bags of Money, or by Partnership in the original Guilt, the enrag'd, the abus'd People might be prompted by their uppermost Passion . . . to have Recourse to extraordinary Ways . . . often successful, tho' never justifiable."

Lord Molesworth was thought to have a hand in this paper. Defoe's son assisted with its routine work. It resembled Applebee's and Mist's in being a combination of weekly essay, news paragraphs, and advertisements. For its printer, it was part of the day's work, paid for much like any other. For the publisher, it was merchandise which sold the better when coffee-houses roared with comment. For the coffee-men, it was a bait attracting customers. It was the chance that Gordon long had sought. Those wishing to quiet England and start business on its way again found it to be an obstacle. Boyer noted that it contained the "loudest Cries for Justice" heard when Parliament met.

At that time Thomas Harley thought the ministers "bent on restoring credit" and that they would "beat down the Bank, or Walpole, or anything else" hindering "so good a work." William Pulteney, disappointed that the King's return made the stock fall instead of rise, brooded on the "ridiculous sum" he might have made by selling out in time. He had heard that Walpole held to his old grudge against the South Sea Company and had prevented the Bank from giving it relief. Lady Lechmere wrote discouragingly to her father (Carlisle) that the stock was still falling; "when or whether ever it is to rise" she had "not heard."

Having no program to offer, as the time approached for Parliament to meet, the ministers put it off until December 8. Thomas Harley in the meanwhile found money "damnable scarce." Defoe advised in Applebee's (November 26) waiting for the official plans to be discovered. Cato, the same day, ridiculed the current talk of giving to the South Sea Company St. Christopher's, an island worth only three hundred thousand pounds, "a Sum almost sufficient to make the Fortune of an under South Sea Clerk." There could be no "Attending to any new Scheme till Publick Robbers" had been punished. "Such mighty Mischiefs as these Men" had done would be "but meanly atoned for by such infamous Lives, unless their Estates" were "confiscated" as well.

Sir Humphry Mackworth in *The South Sea Scheme Considered in a Letter to the Right Honourable Robert Walpole, Esq.*, advised the Minister addressed that the nation looked to him for relief and would applaud it at his hands. Gordon supplemented his contributions to the *London Journal* with *A Letter to a Leading Great Man Concerning the Rights of the People to Petition and the Reasonableness of Complying with such Petitions*. He advised Walpole that people looked to him "at this Time when the National Distress is as much Greater as your Power is now Greater to remedy it." They thought him to be both "able" and "willing" to "relieve the general Calamity; and ready to punish with strictest Justice the Authors and Abettors of that Calamity" as a first step toward restoring "public Credit." He was "preferred to some of the chiefest Trusts," was a considerable "Figure in the House of Commons" and "at Court," was now "courted and caressed more than formerly." "Perhaps," said the writer, "you are the only Instance that can be produced in this or any other Age in whom so many Things have concurred to make you necessary for the Publick." But "Discontents" rose "high," and the "Generality" feared "some extraordinary Step by the Promotion" of Walpole's "Genius" to protect "great and mighty Criminals from the Indignation of their injured Fellow-Subjects." "Sir," he concluded, "the People of Great Britain will not be disregarded." If the "late Conspiracy" was thought to be so "formidable" that it was "wiser to connive and not to prosecute," that it was "dangerous to inquire further into it," it might prove to be "more dangerous to let it alone."

To the King, who also wished his help, the troubled leader answered, that "with great reluctance and in obedience . . . to command" he was "prevailed upon to undertake anything relating to the South Sea affairs." He was "too sensible of the many difficulties" attending "any scheme . . . to hope that satisfaction" could be "given to the infinite number of sufferers." Individuals would have to take their losses. There was a measure of conflict between their interests and that of the government itself, which it would not be easy to resolve. Bystanders thought that he might watch his chance "to destroy the ministry," in which case the latter might "justly demolish him."

His decision was not easy. The choice was between ready victory of an hour and a difficult defense of ground already held in the hope of intrenching himself for the future. His behavior would test his measure as a statesman, but the battle would leave scars whichever way he went. Walpole had been a manager in Sacheverell's trial. Old men could still recall the Popish Plot. Property and lives would be involved. The King and his family were under fire. If the political structure in the hands of Sunderland, Newcastle, Stanhope, and their like should be destroyed, it might not be available as an instrument of power or any other in its place. But courage was required to face the rising storm.

Wednesday night, December 7, only a hundred members gathered in the Cockpit to hear the speech. There was talk of adjourning to await a better "temper." Walpole was ready the next day to try to save the wreckage. The ministers had to accept an amendment to the address from Shippen and Bromley limiting their efforts to restore "public credit" to measures "consistent with the honour of Parliament, the interest of the nation, and the principles of justice." Cato's letter for the week, asserting that the "British Lions crouch'd to a Nest of Owls," asked "can we survive the Remembrance without Revenge?"

The House of Commons was scarcely a deliberative body. A majority of its members were a mob on a man hunt. Defoe, trying in Applebee's to support the government, could only suggest that "to fill People's Heads with Notions of Plots and Conspiracies" was scarcely a way to cure the "National kind of Madness" existing at the time.

Parliament accepted Walpole's suggestion that the contracts of the Company with annuitants be allowed to stand in spite of the subscribers' plea that they were made by fraud. That point should be left to courts of law. It accepted also the scheme adapted from Jacombe of engrafting a part of the South Sea stock on the Bank and the East India Company. But this was merely an expedient for inspiring confidence, in the hope that sanity would return. Ministers did not oppose a motion for prohibiting the "infamous practice of stock jobbing." Horace Walpole himself said that the "South Sea scheme was begun with a cheat, carried on by fraud and villainy, and ended in misery."

The Christmas recess added little to hope of quiet. The Duchess of Marlborough, hearing that the Duke was again represented as a Jacobite, was indignant at Sunderland, Craggs, and the rest of her former allies and sought through the Duchess of Kendal permission to make denial to George himself. The King's equivocal reply stated a disposition to judge the reports "by the behaviour of each of you in regard to my service." The young John Carteret, second baron of that name, at home from his mission to Sweden, informed Polwarth (December 20) that though the ministers thought they would be able to prevent absolute confusion, it was a good time to be abroad.

Thomas Brodrick wrote to his brother in Ireland that Walpole had made the most of his case; if his postulates were sound, his conclusions were right. Atterbury felt again that Jacobites need not give up hope. Carlisle's daughter even heard a rumor Christmas Eve that the books would be opened again for South Sea subscriptions at a thousand pounds. But Cato, by the end of the year, despaired of Walpole as the country's savior. "When certain Cliques were at odds . . .

it was thought convenient for both Sides to come to Terms; for one Party wanted to fill their Coffers, and the other to save their Bacon." Reports the first of the new year were that Aislabie would be given up and perhaps Craggs.

Parliament reassembled (January 4) disposed to restrain South Sea directors from leaving the kingdom. Shippen congratulated the Commons on their "vigour and spirit" and suggested restraint of no less guilty great men as well. Craggs took this charge personally and offered to give satisfaction either in or out of doors. Molesworth, "past sixty," would answer on the floor, but hoped that younger members would look the Minister "in the face" outside. January 10 Walpole defended his bill for "engraftment," speaking "several times for above two hours, and by the torrent of his masterly eloquence carried the votes of many members who had been staggered by the arguments of the opposite side." But a secret committee for investigating the Company was authorized, and in the ballot for members the ministers carried only two of their friends. Thomas Brodrick was its chairman with Molesworth as a colleague to urge him on.

That Lord's son, in straits for money in a foreign post, got cold comfort. His brother advised that he retrench; his father, that his own activity in Parliament was not calculated to help stocks "rise again." "We are all in a lamentable condition," he concluded, "and to complete our misery, knavery is triumphant everywhere." Trenchard and Gordon agreed in *The Sense of the People Concerning the Present State of Affairs . . . in a Letter to a Member of Parliament.* "When a Nation is exasperated and a Minister is become heartily disagreeable," they said, "the only Way for an honest Servant to express his Love to his Master is to yield up all, and the most popular thing a Prince can do is to give up those that are disgustful to the People." Edward Harley, who had just returned to town for the first time after the previous summer, compared the difference to that between day and night. "Boundless insolence in . . . supposed wealth" had given place to "dejection, lamentations, and confusion."

Stanhope and Sunderland parried attacks from Cowper in

the Lords. The "estates of criminals whether directors or not directors," Stanhope said, "ought to be confiscated to make good the public losses." Sunderland admitted supporting the measure in the hope of relieving the country of the burden of the long annuitants, but "no man would imagine that so good a design could have been so perverted in the execution as to produce quite contrary effects." One who found it as "easy to raise the dead as £200" said that both Sunderland and his father-in-law's family lost, "having borrowed money and sold out nothing."

Both the Lords and the Secret Committee of the Commons began inquiries. Blunt, Knight, and others were called to testify. Knight appeared before the Secret Committee, January 21. He had acted with the approval of directors that he named. Pressed for papers, he begged permission to attend the summons of the House of Lords. He left town that evening. Urged privately by a City merchant to tell what he knew, he replied that to do so "would open such a scene as the world would be surprised at." He left a letter explaining his wish "to avoid the weight of an infamy" he thought "too heavy"; it was impossible to escape "the appearance and charge of prevarication and perjury."

Walpole made terms. February 2, Sir John Vanbrugh went to congratulate on the "King's promising him to be first Commissioner of the Treasury and Chancellor of the Exchequer at the end of the session." Sunderland was again to become Secretary of State. Stanhope was to overreach Cadogan and realize his ambition to succeed Marlborough as Captain General. The King had written to the Duke with great expressions of kindness, asking him to resign. The letter was the talk of the town, and the Duchess resented it. But this sound arrangement was never made. Fate staged a melodrama few authors would have dared to write.

Questioned by the Lords Friday, February 4, Blunt pled a previous examination by the Secret Committee. Wharton suggested in the comment after the witness withdrew that the "best of princes" might be made "odious" by men who, like "Sejanus" of old, divided his councils to serve their private ends. Stanhope also drew an analogy from ancient lore. The patriot Brutus, to save his country, had sacrificed his own "degenerate son." Perhaps neither the excitement of this incident nor previous indulgence with Newcastle, Craggs, and the rest was chiefly responsible for his stroke that night. Newcastle and Carteret became ill also. But Carteret and Dr. Mead saw Stanhope the next day and found him doing well. Sunday at 8 P.M. he died.

Craggs was stricken Saturday, with smallpox it was feared. Before Stanhope was buried, Townshend had his seals. After a nine days' illness, the younger Craggs died at three in the afternoon, February 16, while Stanhope's funeral cortege was on its way to Kent and Brodrick, for the Secret Committee, was making the first installment of his report. Cato the previous Saturday thought parties chiefly useful in helping leaders to "get good Jobs." "Let us not therefore," he said, "hereafter suffer ourselves to be set together by the Ears and make Crowds, which are the Harvests of Pickpockets." Defoe lamented that the writers for the *London Journal* stooped to "Partialities and Inhumanities" for "Ends too base to mention."

Estimating the effects of the report the day it was made, Edward Harley wondered whether Sunderland would be able to "keep his ground." Aislabie and the directors would probably be "given up" and put "upon the same foot"; Caswell would be expelled. Bromley, he reported, came to the House but did not speak. Wyndham was "pickled in South Sea." Harcourt was trying to "heal his South Sea wounds." It was uncertain how far Walpole, who led the House, would "permit his followers there to sink under their corruption." Thomas Harley thought the next day that Walpole had undertaken to "screen Sunderland and the German ladies," leaving Aislabie and the rest to "take their chance." Cadogan was ill. Marlborough was in the House of Lords and looking well, but could not keep his tear ducts in control.

Two days after Brodrick's report Walpole moved in Committee that the property of the directors be confiscated and applied to the losses of their company. He had already begun to manage the Treasury, though he would not take complete control until the session ended. He accepted Carteret as Sunderland's nominee to succeed Craggs. On the last day of the month he set his teeth for an unpleasant task. Charles Stanhope, Secretary of the Treasury and a relative of the deceased Lord, asked that the Commons deal immediately with his case. Brodrick's report left a cloud on his name. Managers of the Sword Blade Company confessed that in the documents quoted it was used without his consent. By crude erasures they had tried to conceal the fact that it was used at all. The transactions in question were known to be not for his profit, though he admitted entrusting to Knight for investment whatever money he had to spare. No appeal to the emotions was neglected, including references to his relative just dead. The acquittal was by the narrow majority of three. To accomplish that which Walpole had undertaken would require all the art he had.

Brodrick wrote his brother a week later (March 7) that it had "put the town in a flame." Aislabie's case was due the next day. Steele spoke for him in general terms. Walpole's corner sat "mute as fishes." The accused was expelled from the House and sent to the Tower. Two days later Caswell suffered the same fate. Walpole procured the postponement of Sunderland's case after the narrow escape of Stanhope. March 15 it had to be faced. He and Henry Pelham contradicted Blunt's evidence on Sunderland's express word. Perhaps a more convincing argument was, as Brodrick said, if you "vote against Lord Sunderland the ministry are blown up." The majority over the 172 who voted against him was 61.

Friday, March 17, was appointed for the appearance of the elder Craggs. Thursday at 10 P.M. he died, leaving his daughters a fortune estimated at a million pounds. There were whispers of suicide. The Secret Committee, feeling a sense of defeat, agitated the return of Knight. Walpole had performed the promised task. It was part of the game to picture him as a screen. Perhaps he had a few consoling thoughts. He had got Sunderland off, but, as Edward Harley said, 172 was "a great number against a Prime Minister."

Cato the next Saturday offered a platform for a party, stating views curiously like Walpole's own. The people of England wished to keep Gibraltar, to have no war with Russia, to forget squabbles about Italy between the Emperor and Spain, to use the navy for the defense of trade, to have the heir of the crown bred in England and thus "reconciled by Habit" with its "Customs and Laws," to have Knight brought back. As far as Walpole had coöperated with others for the public good, he should "share the grateful Applause of good Men and the Reproach of the Bad." But let him beware. No "Degree of Virtue" would put him beyond envy, and "the barefaced Protection of innocent and offended Virtue" might be "misunderstood by popular Clamour, which misapplies often established and well known Facts." Replying the next Saturday to all the talk of a "Skreen," Defoe could only say that it was "one Thing to believe a Man guilty and another to have Evidence." A man might suffer in "Reputation" and still be cleared of a charge. On that same day (April 1), Sunderland resigned and Walpole got his place.

Cato and the Secret Committee kept on agitating the return of Knight, hoping still that Sunderland might be reached. Defoe consoled them that you angled differently for "little Fish" and large. Having fixed a dart in a "Whale," you got him in the end, though he appeared to get away. Daniel Pulteney, Sunderland's brother-in-law, tried to persuade Molesworth that credit would "not revive nor money circulate" again until the people were quiet. He had heard that Walpole was making an interest in constituencies where Sunderland had been supreme.

When friends of the Secret Committee wished to deal with Aislabie's estate as with those of the directors, Walpole urged (April 21) that to treat thus a person of "eminence" might be a "Precedent of dangerous Consequence." "The main bent of his speech," said Brodrick, "was to move the passions by mentioning over and over again wife, children, family." But the members sat "like so many stones."

Vanbrugh heard that writers for the *London Journal* were to blame, among whom Molesworth was named as one. Lechmere warned Walpole that more was expected of a man in "a higher Post." Shippen observed in the House, that the engraftment was a failure, and nothing else was done. Walpole replied that he "did not pretend to work miracles" and had "always opposed the South Sea scheme." Acknowledging the congratulations of Carlisle (April 29), he wished "it were possible to do the good" that was "expected and the necessities of mankind" demanded. Only of his "inclinations" was he sure.

A pamphlet appeared, *The Conspirators; or, the Case of Catiline.* It was "obvious to everybody," said Boyer, that the South Sea scheme was meant; it was easy to identify Sunderland, Walpole, and Craggs. Cato published (May 3) a more direct attack. His pieces, he said, were "read and approved by every intelligent Man in England except the Guilty, the Screens, the Hirelings and Adherents." "Who is it," he asked, "that might have checked and yet did not check rampant Rogues last Summer? And from what Motives proceeded such Omission? Who is it that openly screens open Guilt? Who is it that browbeats Pursuers of Guilt? Who is it that throws Obstacles in Parliament's Way? Who is it that lengthens out the Process? Who is it that strives to defeat the Enquiry? Who is it that makes Malcontents and then reproaches them for being so?" A "whipping paragraph," an enemy of Walpole thought.

Supporters of the ministry felt that something should be done. A writer in the *Daily Journal* (May 5) observed that of all "Virtues" there were "none more dangerous, or more narrowly bordering on the Confines of Vice than Zeal and Public Spirit which are apt to degenerate into Faction and Rebellion." A certain "Hebdominal Writer," a "crafty Changeling," had been "insinuating himself with many by pretending that theirs, his Country's, and Religion's Interest" moved him. Defoe in Applebee's (May 6) used a convenient proclamation of the King (April 28) against vice, profaneness, and "Hell Fire Clubs" to enforce the point. It would be no breach of the peace to take such an offender "by the Throat and swinge him in the next Horse Pond or cool his Brains at the next Pump;

no, tho' he were the Amanuensis to an Independent Whig or an Agent to those scurrilous Complainers who insult the King under the Notion of obtaining Justice against South Sea Directors. . . . Let but the World know that a Set of Hell Fire Men are concerned in any public Paper, and soon no Christian would read such a Paper without Disdain and Abhorrence."

The South Sea projectors offended first, Cato replied (May 13). The youths in the Hell Fire Clubs chiefly harmed themselves. "While we pursue Wolves and Tygers and the mightier Beasts of Prey, who if they are not destroyed will continue to destroy, we are not to be diverted by the Scent of a Fox or a Badger, tho' they may annoy a private Neighbourhood and dispeople Henroosts. . . . Here is a Test of Virtue and Innocence! Let us hang up public Rogues as well as punish private Blasphemers." The late directors, who "all pretended to be good Christians," might better have spent their time at a "Hell Fire Club."

Journalistic comment on the anniversary of the Restoration gave Parliament an opening to act. Charles Molloy in Mist's *Journal* hesitated to "return Thanks for a Deliverance from Rogues with Swords in their Hands, when we are ruin'd by Footmen, Pimps, Pathicks, Parasites, Bawds, Whores, nay, what is more vexatious, old ugly Whores! such as could not find Entertainment in the most hospitable Hundreds of old Drury." In a letter apparently not written by Gordon or Trenchard, Cato attacked Charles II for his reign in general and in particular for his treatment of the Scots. Gordon himself, the next Saturday (June 10) in a letter on "Libellers" commenting on the piece in Mist's *Journal,* admitted that at times it might be a libel to tell the truth.

Mist was already in prison. Wilkins, the printer, and Peele, the publisher of the *London Journal,* with Gordon and Molloy were summoned before the House of Commons. The printer and publisher went; Gordon pleaded illness and did not go. On the winning side for once, Defoe escaped arrest. The function of a "Journal," he said (June 10), was "to collect daily the best Intelligence of Publick Affaires." The term was "Nonsense" referring to a weekly, "but for exhibiting the Gross of their daily Collections in one general Paper to come out every Week." How these weekly "Collectors" came to be also "weekly Declamators, or rather Exclamators" was accounted for in different ways. Some thought it the fruit of "former wicked Papers" such as "Observators, Reviews, Rehearsals, Flying Posts, and other Libels," to which the previous age owed its "ill Nature" and "this Age the evil Precedent of insulting one another." One indulging only in "just Comments upon" news would find employment enough.

Perhaps so. Another journalist estimated the same month that five thousand people subsisted in London "by writing, printing, publishing, and vending newspapers." They were long since part of the atmosphere of the metropolis. "If there was no News, who would go to a Coffee House? If there was no Coffee House, where would Parliaments be directed? Diets advised? The Conduct of Princes examined? The Management of able and honest Ministers applauded and evil, corrupt ones censured?"

By midsummer the strife began to cool. The South Sea Company had to be released from payments due on sums it owed the government. The balance owed by the two favored insurance companies was made up by a levy of sixpence per pound on the Civil List itself. Aislabie was finally permitted to keep his estate as of October 20, 1718. Payments due by subscribers to the South Sea Company were canceled, and annuitants received compensation in stock. The debt of the nation was reduced by the gullibility of those it owed, but at a fearful cost.

For his loyalty, Steele made haste to claim reward. At the behest of Walpole and Henry Pelham, Newcastle ordered the managers of Drury Lane to account for his share of the profits, past and future. By the beginning of August Defoe congratulated the country on the prospect of "a new Scene of Affaires." People began "to take Heart again." Brodrick had been ill since spring and sorely missed. Molesworth, who disavowed the journalistic pieces of which he was accused, was disheartened, not knowing how he would live after the session ended. Latterly he had paid only sixteen shillings a week for quarters to a landlord without a maid. But he had had seventeen children, and nine were alive and well, so he moralized: " 'Tis enough."

Wilkins and Peele were let out on bail. Their paper had another tussle with the law, this time involving Benjamin Norton Defoe, who wrote an introduction to the proceedings against the South Sea Company, which it was proposed to publish. The press was broken and the issue seized even from hawkers in the streets. The son had learned some of the father's art. His introduction began: "Here appears the Cause of Widows' Sighs, the Orphans' Tears, the Ruin of Families, the Distress of Millions, the Sinking of Credit, the Discouragement of Trade, the Lowering of Stocks. . . ."

Defoe himself was angry that more important writers for the paper were permitted to escape, owing to "great Dignity and Quality, pretending that they are too great to be named"; his son had to give bond for a thousand pounds. It was both a good and hard year for journalists. Nicholas Amhurst had come to town in January from Oxford, where he found it uncongenial to reside as a supporter of the ruling house. He started *Terrae Filius* to exploit twice a month his grievances against his ungracious alma mater, meaning not to become engaged with "Defoe and Mist." But no London journalist that summer could leave the South Sea out.

None knew yet whether the controversy was done. Saturday, August 19, Stanhope's wife gave birth to twins. A week later Newcastle assured Sunderland that he had but "one thought," the "interest of the King, the Whigg cause," and Sunderland himself. "For God's sake, my dear Lord," he went on, "give me leave for to hope for the sake of the King and all your faithful servants, that you will continue at the head of the King's affairs, that the source and direction shall come from you, and that all others should act in the manner the King intends they should." As for their new allies, "You know I neither like their persons nor credit their interest." Whether he could learn to work with them, time would have to tell.[6]

[6] C. B. Realey, *The Early Opposition to Sir Robert Walpole, 1720–1727*, chs. i–ii, gives an account of some of these events with a different emphasis. See also Stanhope, *History*, II. Appendix, pp. xcff.; Hist. Mss. Com., *Portland*, V. 592ff.; VII. 267ff.; *Polwarth*, I. 632ff.; II. 576ff.; III. 23ff.; *Townshend*, p. 104f.; *Dropmore*, I. 64ff.; *Mar and Kellie*, p. 522.; *Various*, VIII. 287ff.; *Kelton* (12 Rept., Appendix, Pt. 9), pp. 200ff.; *Carlisle*, pp. 24ff.; *Dartmouth*, p. 326; Boyer, *Political State*, XIX. 1ff.; XX. 1ff.; XXI. 2ff.; XXII. 132ff.; Lee, *Defoe*, I. 318ff.; II. 203ff.; Knight Hunt, *Fourth Estate*, I. 197; *Parliamentary History*, VII. 628ff.; Coxe, *Robert Walpole*, II. 181ff.; *Marlborough*, III. 625ff.; Aitken, *Steele*, II. 238ff.; Hardwicke, *State Papers*, II. 604ff.; Lady Cowper, *Diary*, pp. 128ff.; *Suffolk Papers*, I. 51ff.; Williams, *Stanhope*, pp. 419ff.; Thomson, *The Duchess of Marlborough*, II. 320ff.; Nulle, *Newcastle*, pp. 135ff.; *Weekly Journal or British Gazetteer*, April 9, 1720; *Calendar of Treasury Books and Papers, 1720–1728*, pp. 21, 22, 26. There are collected reprints in various editions of the *Independent Whig, Cato's Letters*, and *Terrae Filius*.

Chapter X

A FIGHT BEGINS, 1721–1727

Is it possible that one of your age and profession should be ignorant,
that this monstrous beast [the rabble] has passions to be moved, but
no reason to be appealed to, and that plain truth will influence half a
score of men at most in a nation or an age, while mystery will lead
millions by the nose?

BOLINGBROKE to SWIFT, July 10, 1721.

I

WALPOLE GAINS

THE anxious Walpole found that summer tedious and trying. More than twenty years before, interrupting his university career, he had succeeded his father as a Norfolk
squire. Experience in two disillusioning decades had taught
him the realities of English politics. Conscious of power he
had won, genuinely disposed to do his country good, he was
not elated at his triumph. He knew better than most men
what his success had cost and the arts that would be necessary to keep the place he had.

His imprisonment in the Tower was evidence that he counted
both in Norfolk and the House of Commons. The power of a
Queen had humbled him. No less was the power of the King,
and it was not yet clear whether this power was to be Sunderland's or his own. The problem was, to win a man with whom he
could not speak. The Duchess of Kendal was the only way, but
she would always have her price. Her age made it expedient to
get rewards while there was time.

George's death would end her reign. Then, and at no distant day, would be another gulf to bridge. The reconciliation
helped, but good will was impossible between the father and
his son. Caroline might serve perhaps, but Kendal was the

problem now. Through her had come the power of Sunderland.

The chains of gratitude by which Walpole held that Lord were fragile and would break. Public humiliation might have hurt a man less proud. In the persons of Newcastle and Sunderland were the prestige of political tradition, of family connection, of landed wealth, of the art of management that Walpole could not do without.

Another problem was the Church. Walpole little liked the thought. Hoadly, Gordon, and the rest were laboring to change its tone, to make it tolerant, a force for wholesome good. He approved of their work, but could not wait for it to have effect. Shouts of Sacheverell's mobs still lingered in his ears. Better avoid emotions so dangerous when aroused. While dulling the Church's claws, he needed its support.

The whole art of managing crowds was yet unsure. Therein were pitfalls he could not foresee. A dozen years before, he burnt his fingers on the Church. This year it had been the clamor, scarcely stilled, of men who lost where they had hoped to gain. The journals, the coffee-houses, the mobs, were hurdles he had to take, implements he had to use. To suppress them all would be the simpler way. But power still reposed in royal hands, and weapons that harassed a man in office were useful when he was out. It was not easy to know what to do.

In the House of Commons were forty-five Scots. Sunderland and Newcastle still talked of a peerage bill to manage the northern lords. Increasing their number and giving them permanent seats scarcely seemed a helpful step. Better the flighty Argyll and the powerful Campbell clan. The first to leave the King for the Prince, that Duke had deserted the Prince again for the King. His people would never be paid enough.

London was distraught; its leaders in factions were at each other's throats. Walpole's knack at figures, his ability to talk of money as a practical man gave him a way there most politicians lacked. But divisions among themselves made the citizens a source of weakness instead of strength. The previous year had shown the power of grasping wealth. Not soon would fears then stirred be wholly stilled. Thus he would have to win and keep the power of the City if he would use it.

The color of his hopes thus seen was gray, not sharp and clear. Even at home, for lordly company the squire had paid a price. There were four children by his wife, but Carr Hervey, Lord by courtesy, son of the Earl of Bristol by his first wife, was the reputed father of her youngest son. The legal father did not foresee the odd rôles of that boy and his natural half-uncle, purveyors of the gossip of their time. The Minister's consolations were in food and drink, in his country estates, in rural sports, in the arms of the woman who later for a few months was his wife, most of all perhaps in the political game.

George prorogued Parliament August 10 to meet October 19. Carteret and Newcastle comforted themselves that Sunderland retained the confidence of the King; his Majesty was resolved that Walpole should not rule. But when Sunderland suggested the demotion of that Minister to Postmaster General, George merely asked whether Walpole had agreed. The disgruntled Earl sought support wherever it might be found. Optimistic Jacobites began to regard him as their man, though Shippen and Lockhart at Newmarket agreed that hostility to Walpole, not friendship for the Pretender, was the thing the Earl had in mind. But Atterbury had taken heart again. At the reconciliation of the King and Prince he had lost hope. A year later he saw a juncture "so favourable," likely "to continue for so many months," that he could not think it would pass "without a proper use."

In the few weeks of autumnal recess the press was quiet. Even Cato, Boyer said, seemed to have "prorogued Politics." Defoe, diverting himself with writing *Moll Flanders,* recalled the fate of Tutchin, suggesting that Mist be warned by the example. It was possible to "act safely and yet act smartly." Why call names when the same purpose could be served by exposing "Avarice, Treachery, Betraying public Trusts?" Those "known by Character, the Satyr" would "bite as close as if they were known by Name." To quiet fears frequently expressed, the *Whitehall Evening Post* announced (October 14) that Parliament would be dissolved after the approaching session.

In his opening speech the King advised precautions against the plague, apparently a harmless topic. But the Quarantine Bill incited protest by the peers. In fact, there were protests in the Lords at almost every stage in the passage of almost every bill a divided ministry had to support in getting routine business done. There was one protest when the Lord Chancellor came to the House late, though Parker apologized, explaining that he was detained by business with the King. When, on Sunderland's motion, this protest was expunged, the expunging was protested as well. Sunderland's next device of a standing order to arrest the recording of protests at two o'clock the next sitting day merely brought dissentient peers earlier to the House with hastier statements for the press.

These protests were part of a program to arouse the nation for the election just ahead, the second since the death of Anne. Most of them were Atterbury's work, revised by Cowper to make sure that the desired warmth of statement was within the law. The French Minister reported to Paris that the former Lord Chancellor's name was on twenty-four of twenty-six protests of the session and that every day he made "eloquent" and "envenomed" speeches in the House. The activity of Cowper and Wharton gave the protests a weight they would have lacked had they been too exclusively Atterbury's work.

Rumors persisted that Walpole wished to prolong the life of Parliament again. Archibald Hutcheson, who had opposed the Septennial Act, had written against the South Sea Company, had been a member of the Secret Committee, and who managed the estates of the Duke of Ormond, now by letter and interview tried to pledge Sunderland that the dissolution would take place. January 23 he introduced a bill in the House of Commons to prevent "corruption" and to secure "greater freedom in elections." Eight days later appeared the first issue of the *Freeholder's Journal,* conducted by Atterbury's henchmen, but open to Hutcheson when he had a mind to write.

Cato had taken up his pen again. In a preface to the letters published in this month Gordon boasted for the *London Journal* "more friends and readers than any paper that" had "hitherto appeared in the world." Defoe, who wrote against them these weeks in Applebee's, accused Gordon and Trenchard of making "themselves popular by writing a Newspaper fill'd with Clamour at private Grievances . . . not sparing the King himself."

In the Christmas recess Walpole was ill. Sunderland was "never known to be so easy and gay." Persistent rumors said that Walpole, if he recovered, would leave the Treasury to Pulteney, or Carleton, or Spencer Compton and retire to the quiet of the Lords. With health restored, he kept his place. But if a new Parliament was to be chosen amenable to their will, the strife among the leaders would have to wait.

Some Seasonable Thoughts relating to the Ensuing Election appeared in January advising harmony and forgetfulness of the South Sea while the Protestant succession was at stake. Gordon in *Three Political Letters to a Noble Lord Concerning Liberty and the Constitution* urged the importance of Parliament as custodian of things held dear. But he remarked that formerly a "Prime Minister would think he had done and deserv'd sufficiently if he had brought three or four of his Relatives into Posts of the Administration." Trenchard decided to stand for Taunton and in the pamphlet that he wrote was more discreet. He admitted in *Seasonable Advice to the Electors of Great Britain with a Word or two Relating to the Influence of the Clergy in Elections* that protection of the Protestant succession and the Protestant interest was paramount, taking precedence over such temporary differences as that concerning the South Sea.

Gordon as Cato shrewdly observed that men ever talked in "Generalities," but acted from interest when moved by "Fear." "Men thus formed and qualified," he said, were "the Materials for Government. For the Sake of Men" it was "instituted, and by the Prudence of Men it must be conducted; and the Art of political Mechanism" was "to erect a firm Building with such crazy and corrupt Materials." Trenchard's candidacy inspired Defoe to send to Applebee's a piece, *On Pride.*

The *Freeholder's Journal* hammered away in Westminster. Both Molesworth and Hutcheson aspired to capitalize their service on the Secret Committee in that city in a popular interest. As the time for the contest approached it became clear that Atterbury's faction would claim a seat for its part in the fight. Hutcheson had substantial interests, and Molesworth thought it wiser to withdraw.

The Pretender had written to Atterbury the first week in the year hinting for him a "rank superior to all the rest." A contemporary noted that "the new ·gentry . . . raised by the late bubbles" were spending "out of their own pockets," not depending wholly upon "the court expense." Gordon in *A Compleat History of the late Septennial Parliament* recurred to the act of that name which Trenchard had opposed, adding as an appendix Hutcheson's projected bill for a reform. The important issue, said the *Freeholder's Journal* (March 7), was the question of septennial Parliaments. They might become "perpetual" in the end.

On that same day the King closed the session, warning members that "enemies" of his house were "reviving with the greatest industry the same wicked arts of calumny and defamation which had been the constant prelude to public troubles and disorders." March 10 the Parliament was dissolved. Opponents of the ministers indulged in bonfires, illuminations, and ringing bells. Some still wondered whether Walpole or Sunderland would prevail.

The ministers were successful, but results in places gave them food for thought. Argyll procured a majority in Scotland both of commons and peers. After a noisy poll, Westminster went for Hutcheson and Cotton, the latter in Atterbury's interest. A petition would be necessary to throw them out. More surprising, even at Hastings, one of the Cinque Ports, Hutcheson was able to win a seat in spite of all Newcastle could do. The Duke labored manfully, though confessing that the "diversions" of an election no longer appealed to him as in earlier years. At Taunton Trenchard was returned.

The *Freeholder's Journal* in disgust remarked (March 23): "When you know how well you deserved Curses and rotten Eggs, to push for a triumphant Chair is a Piece of Assurance." Boyer commented that the essays in that paper "were undoubtedly calculated to inflame the Minds of the People, and meeting with no small Stock of combustible Matter amongst them fail'd not producing the intended Effect." Sunderland agreed, and ordered the printer's arrest. The author announced that he would go on as best he could. He marveled that those formerly opposed to "Passive Obedience" now claimed the "unlimited Power of Parliament." He thought a free people had "legal Rights" superior to any "legislative Power."

In the excitement of the election Toland died, inspiring the elegiac comment, "Great Cato best supplies great Toland's place." The Duchess of Kendal's rival was finally naturalized and became Countess of Darlington in the English list. Kendal's daughter was made Countess of Walsingham. Bolingbroke meditated the study of history at La Source. In March he complained to Polwarth in Paris on his way to Cambray that reasons for putting off his case might be ever found. He had acted a "fair part" and helped the ministers when he could.

Again the dice fell Walpole's way. After taking the sacrament from Hoadly, Sunderland died of pneumonia April 19 at three in the afternoon. Two days later his infant son, inoculated for smallpox, followed its father to the grave. His second child by his third wife was but four months in the mother's womb.

"I don't find the loss of my Lord Sunderland is likely to be much felt in our home affairs," Vanbrugh wrote to Carlisle within a week. "On the contrary . . . his particular friends" showed plainly that they did not think of "listing under any new general on the foot they fought under him, but" declared for "peace and unanimity." The King was troubled a day or two, but every hour added to his good content. By May 5 Vanbrugh felt that Walpole would probably have got the better in any case. He doubted whether Carteret and Carleton would go on.

At the moment the ministers had "crossed" another "Fox" to chase, though Walpole confessed to his brother that he was yet uncertain whether there would be a catch. In the weeks of the election, word came through the French ministers of a Jacobite plot, confirming information already in hand. Letters were discovered that might pin it on Atterbury definitely enough to act. But Walpole meant to avoid Godolphin's mistake and was not in too great haste to show his hand.

Failing to take advantage of the confusion of the elections, the Pretender's friends were now said to await the King's Continental trip. To thwart them, his Majesty decided not to go that year. George Kelly, alias Johnson, was lodged in the Tower after his correspondence had been watched awhile. Troops encamped in Hyde Park. Horace Walpole went to Holland to get help. A proclamation issued against Papists, Non-Jurors, and Jacobites. Townshend sent a letter to the Lord Mayor (May 8) asking coöperation with the King. The Lord Mayor and Aldermen agreed to help. Similar addresses from other corporations and from counties were soon on the road.

Hutcheson's efforts to concert measures with Sunderland were interrupted by the latter's death. About the middle of May he published his letters to that Earl with comment concerning his own contests in Hastings and Westminster. The question was taken up in the *St. James's Journal,* established the week before, and in the *Englishman's Journal* in the first week of June. The controversy became involved with the determination of Walpole and Sir John Eyles to compromise the differences between the Bank and the South Sea Company. Sir John was now head of that corporation.

Their proposal was approved overwhelmingly at a riotous meeting of the proprietors of the latter company, June 22. The Bank was to purchase annuities in the hands of the South Sea Company to the amount of two hundred thousand pounds a year, for which it was to offer its securities. In a public letter on the same day Hutcheson denied any hostility to Walpole. There were other reasons than the Minister's "High Station" to "divert" him, had he been minded to oppose.

Cato found himself that month hesitantly willing to join "any Party" in "just Measures." He and his friends would not "look with eagle Eyes into past Faults provided" there was "proper Atonement . . . by future Services," nor would they "envy particular Men growing rich" if they would "let the Publick thrive with them." But Gordon was among those who thought the alleged plot to be a trick of the ministers to unite people in their support.

Defoe, as "an old, decay'd, feeble Gyant," was told that age made him forget, and found himself in an uncertain time. Party distinctions were so "strangely altered," it was hard to know "which are honest Men, or where they live." Politicians, like "City Ladies," put off a choice of religion to see who would "court them." Before the end of the summer he advised journalists that a good plan was to tell "News so as to make . . . Friends merry and not make" themselves "sad." He had learned the lesson too late, if he had learned it even now.

There was news to tell in June on which he tried a failing hand. At four in the morning of the sixteenth the Duke of Marlborough died at Windsor Lodge. The body was brought to Marlborough House to lie in state while the Duchess faced the problem of arranging funeral rites. Fault would be found, no matter what she did. She would be criticized for spending either too little or too much. When word came that Jacobites meant to take advantage of the crowd, the pageant was postponed to August 9.

Not so the issue that the death had raised. The question of a successor had to be faced at last. The answer was strangely unforeseen. The office of Captain General was no more. Appropriate for the servant of a Queen who had to conciliate the Continental powers while he commanded her armies in the field, the King restored the title as an empty honor and compensation for the loss of power. The disappointed Cadogan received a regiment, was Master General of the Ordnance, and joined the Cabinet Council in July. He was not a colleague that the ministers had wished, but Argyll also was a military man, and they thought that of two evils they chose the less. To carry out the project then in hand might call for all the friends they had.

"I go tomorrow to the deanery," wrote Atterbury to Pope, July 30. There he expected to remain till he had said "Dust to Dust and shut off that vast Scene of pompous Vanity." Ten days later, leaving a heavily hung room in Marlborough House, a coffin covered with crimson velvet with a black velvet pall was taken at half past twelve "along the Road through St. James's Park, and the Upper Park to Hyde Park Corner, thence through Piccadilly down St. James's Street, through Pall Mall and by Charing Cross through King Street to Westminster Abbey," where the Bishop waited. When the long procession arrived at the west door, the select company who went into the church to the accompaniment of music by the organ and choir proceeded through the south aisle till they came near the choir and then, crossing into the north aisle, went up to King Henry VII's chapel, where the coffin was rested on a stand. An anthem was performed by musicians on a platform specially erected for the day. While the choir sang "Man that is Born of Woman" the body was deposited in the vault. The "Lord Bishop of Rochester, Dean of Westminster, in his Cope" pronounced in the prescribed ritual the pleasure of "Almighty God." The choir sang "I Heard a Voice from Heaven," and in conclusion the Garter King of Arms proclaimed the style of the deceased and threw upon the coffin the pieces of garter given him in advance. Outside, during the procession and the funeral, once every minute guns were fired at the Tower.

When it was over, the Bishop did not return to Bromley as he had planned. August 24 at three in the afternoon a messenger appeared in the deanery, where he sat among his books, to take him to a committee of the Council in the Cockpit and to the Tower. That same day his old friend, Harcourt, was summoned to the Council with a pension of four thousand pounds, following the precedent of Somers at the beginning of the reign.

Four days afterward, accompanied by the Prince of Wales, the King began a short western progress. Many of the

"Quality" awaited them at Hackwood, the Duke of Bolton's seat, where they lay that night, arriving at Salisbury the evening of the second day. At the Bishop's Palace his Majesty supped in public with as many "Gentlemen of the County" as could sit about his table. The next day he reviewed the forces encamped two miles away and attended services in the Cathedral Church. Back at the Palace, Bishop Willis voiced "Amazement" and the "intensest Indignation" that members of the English Church, regardless of the "Justice," "Wisdom," and "Clemency" of the King, should "perjure themselves," should "hazard their . . . Lives," should risk the "Blood and Misery" of rebellion "to bring in a Popish Pretender to be Guardian and Protector of a Protestant Church." A very large number of men and women were allowed to kiss the royal hand. Debtors were released from prison at his Majesty's expense. Donations were made to the Cathedral and to the poor.

At Winchester the Bishop greeted the party with similar concern. On the way to Portsmouth it paused at the seat of the Warden of the Forest of Bere. Naval officials were at the dock and representatives of the borough. Appearing on the quarterdeck of the *Canterbury* man of war, the King heard shouts from that ship's crew, from the docks, and from other vessels in the yard. The masses thronged the streets through which the royal party passed to rooms filled with "Nobility, Gentry, and Ladies" eager to greet his Majesty. Others were at Stanstead, where the Earl of Scarborough was host that night. On the evening of Saturday, the first, coming by Guilford, the party reached Kensington again.

The ministers took one further step in getting ready for Parliament to meet. When, early in September, Cato sent his usual letter to the *London Journal,* the printer sent it back. Beginning the fifteenth of that month, "Britannicus" took Cato's place. It was a shrewd move. The journal was the popular medium of the day. A churchman was needed for the work ahead, and Hoadly had the talent for the task. On the Church in general, he and Gordon were agreed. The Post Office was to have a substantial number of each weekly issue for which the ministers were to pay.[1] Britannicus began by sensing in the writers who had lately "governed the Politicks and Passions of Men . . . a Conspiracy to destroy the right Notions of Things from off the Earth," substituting the "Resentment and Anger of themselves and others." "Patriotism," he thought, was noble, but apparently anything would "do for a Patriot" that was "hot and stiff equally in every Point proposed."

Atterbury's friends were on the move. A print of his visage looking through a grate with sympathetic verses underneath was hawked about for sale. Public prayers were offered in churches on Sunday for his gout, the day after Britannicus first appeared. The engraver and printseller were taken up, but their work went on. Gordon and Trenchard were not disposed to quit. The first number of the *British Journal* appeared the week after Hoadly began to write. The "Publick" was "left to judge whether there" could be "any other Objection against the Letters published" in the new medium "than against those publish'd heretofore in the *London Journal;* and whether Cato" had in "any Instance changed his Conduct or his Politicks."

Edmund Gibson, Bishop of Lincoln, devoted to the Church and learned in her lore, sent a public *Letter to the Clergy of the Church of England.* Could they ask more than they had? The King consulted bishops on the bestowal of preferments in his gift. They had the "ordering" of their "own Interests." As it was the "Interest and Duty" so, he verily believed, it was the "Inclination and Endeavour" of the ministers to support the Church.

Atterbury was accused of treason against the ruling family. In his arrest, Gibson said, he "met with all the Civility," even "Tenderness which could possibly be shown to any one under Circumstances resembling his." To have confined him in his

---

[1] At first the number was 650; later it was increased to 2200. The price paid was twopence per copy, but it was alleged that the bookseller who made the arrangement withheld a halfpenny from his partners. *Treasury Books and Papers,* p. 421. See also Charles B. Realey, "The London Journal and Its Authors, 1720–1723," *Bulletin of the University of Kansas,* XXXVI, No. 23, which has appeared since the above was sent to press.

own house would have been unsafe; to have committed him to a messenger, disparaging to him. There was no alternative to sending him to the Tower. The clergy, "Men appointed to promote the Peace of Mankind," lay "under the Scandal of being a restless and ungovernable Body." A foreign, Popish Pretender, if placed on the throne, would bring needy, disgruntled courtiers in his train. The Church was better as it was.

Atterbury envisioned sympathic crowds thronging to an impeachment trial in Westminster Hall. He too recalled Sacheverell. But Walpole's plan was different. When Parliament met (October 9), Trenchard sat for Taunton undisturbed and Hutcheson kept his seat for Hastings. The return for Westminster was annulled. Philip Dormer Stanhope, Lord of the Bedchamber of the Prince of Wales, moved the reëlection of Compton to the chair.

Cowper and a remnant of the old group protested the suspension of the Habeas Corpus Act, but the familiar name, "Fr. Rossen," was missing from the list of signatures. Wharton took the prudent other side. Walpole explained in the Commons that some arrests had been deferred lest the offenders get release before the suspension of the Act. His colleagues in the Lords granted the permission Carteret asked that Atterbury might be detained. "I think you may now go play," wrote Canon Stratford to Harley in the country within a week.

Trenchard, designing to exploit a latent fear, revived his youthful sentiments in *A Discourse of Standing Armies*. The *St. James's Journal* published a supplement in reply. Britannicus thought the "Love of Popularity" the greatest enemy "true Patriotism" had. It tempted the study of "What the Passions and Clamours of a Multitude demand." A seeker of popularity, he said, "watches and nurses those Passions, humours and flatters them; indulges them in what they cry for; and increases . . . the Loudness of the Cry." He thinks himself, "vain Man," able to direct the storm he helps to raise. Hutcheson in Westminster was a case in point. He was not disaffected to the King; he merely wished to be a "Popular Man at the Head of Popular Discontents." But "more and more Madness" lay that way. The time had come "to shew in the Face of all the Powers of Europe that" England would "try all Methods rather than suffer a Popish Bigot," that she had "still Unanimity of Spirit and Strength enough to search the present Evil to the Bottom." The Right Reverend journalist was warming to his task.

Recalling Catiline, Cato wondered at the plot. Britannicus replied that those who argued thus should "at least spare Cato's Memory; and not oppose and vilify his whole Conduct under the Cover of his own Name." In early November Defoe was more interested in the cutting up of calico garments to make curtains before Christmas in order to avoid the provisions of an act of Parliament which was then to take effect. Of all the many plots that he had known, the one of that year seemed the "most unlikely, inconsistent, and improbable Attempt." The Earl of Derwentwater was reported to have said that the conspirators of his day deserved to be taken to Bedlam rather than to the Tower. This plot was madder still. About the middle of the month the old journalist moralized upon a rural villager hearing news: "When you send us Word, the great News is come to Town, and good Things are done for the King and the Nation's Interest; we make Bonfires and ring Bells and throw Squibs and Crackers and are very Merry; and when we hear Nothing, we are easy and Merry still, and hope we shall have another Bonfire one time or other; and thus we mind every one our own Business."

The ministers were also minding theirs. As usual, the Pretender helped. A communication was discovered addressed to various great men in England, the Archbishop of Canterbury among the rest, in which James proposed to protect the Church and to recognize George as king in Hanover, whither he might retire. As a "false, insolent, and traitorous Libel," Parliament ordered the hangman to burn it at the Royal Exchange. Britannicus made it the subject of his weekly essay. November 28 a new paper, *Pasquin,* appeared in the ministerial interest, the work of Nicholas Amhurst among others. Steele, who had just staged successfully his *Con-*

scious Lovers, contributed several essays to the cause. Even skeptics began to say, unless we are "unanimous in supporting the present Government . . . we must all be undone."

The ministerial candidates were returned at the new election for Westminster. Commenting on a letter to the Pretender from the Pope, Defoe thought in mid-December that this connection had shut the "Door against" the former in England and opened the "eyes of the abus'd Rabble when they have Huzza'd in his favour." "We are Protestants," he said, and "have nothing to do with the Pope or with Popery." A week later Britannicus agreed. It was "as evident a Proposition that Papists as Papists" were "direct Enemies" to the "present Civil Establishment" as it was that "it is Light because the Sun shines."

Having Parliament and the populace, the ministers recalled divisions among themselves. In the Christmas recess, Carlisle, one of Sunderland's old friends, was removed as Constable of the Tower. George acted personally, it was said. A French observer reported Walpole to be a "unique man," whom the King was unable to do without as financial administrator and manager of the House of Commons. Pulteney would replace Carteret as Secretary of State, he thought. Other observers in the first days of the new year agreed. The election had left Newcastle's affairs in a precarious state. Unwilling to accept a gift, a thing he detested in others, he thought an increase in salary to be a better way.

Atterbury's cause had not gone well. Even a personal tussle with his warden in the Tower did not win the needed sympathy. That official professed not to know how to defend himself against a "madman" and a "bishop." In Dublin, Swift shook a sad head at Gay's invitation for a visit. There could be no pleasure in awaking old thoughts and memories with all his friends in "poverty, exile, distress, or imprisonment" and his "enemies with rods of iron."

Nevertheless, a fellow Scot and relative advised Polwarth (March 1) that the ministry was chiefly held together by the plot. Still Argyle had won two thirds of the members at the election; Roxburgh, very few. Carteret might stand better at court, but the others were strong in Parliament. The dismissal of Carlisle had hurt. Roxburgh and Carteret would also go in time.

That same day Pulteney for the committee reported to the House the evidence against the conspirators. Soon it was published to the world. The first tests were against the lesser men. Thomas Brodrick and Raymond were among those selected to take the lead. Philip Yorke, the Solicitor General, drew the bill proposed for inflicting pains and penalties on Atterbury. The Bishop knew not what to do. After asking the Commons for permission to appear by attorney, he suggested to the Lords that it would impair their dignity for him to appear at all.

Gibson and Hoadly were on the peers' committee. Willis spoke in favor of the bill. Walpole himself appeared to testify of statements made by one of the Bishop's henchmen who had since been drowned. May 11 the accused spoke in his own defense. What he said was clever, but lacked the art to move. The evidence was forged; the case, not proved. Even his denials were phrased carefully; nowhere was the indignation of one wronged and innocent.

Hoadly canvassed the evidence at length in the *London Journal*. To guide talkers in coffee-houses and on the streets, he selected pertinent passages from the mass and pieced together circumstances to support the case. He described the Bishop's defense as the fruit of "Cunning," a desperate effort to dodge the issues that were involved. He affected indignation himself that one so highly honored, enjoying the emoluments of the King and Church he was sworn to support, should secretly conspire to do them wrong.

Writers in *Pasquin* took up the charge. Even Cato now chimed in. Gordon greeted the published evidence with *A Short View of the Conspiracy, with some Reflections on the Present State of Affairs in a Letter to an Old Whig in the Country*. Admitting that he was among those who "fancied" themselves "the only wise Men in the Nation," who had "laughed at and ridicul'd all that was advanced," thinking it "a Plot to stifle . . . Resentments against the

South Sea Transactions," he now confessed "Folly" in the midst of "fancied Wisdom." It was the way of Jacobites to "poison the Minds of the People from the Press." So little had he seen the design, that he had written "many Things . . . which seemed calculated for the Service of the Faction." But the "Monkey" had "too long made use of Cato's Paw." Thenceforward he was on the other side. To prove it, he offered in his old style *A Seasonable Apology for Father Francis, Chaplain to Prince Prettyman, the Catholic, but now lying in Durance under Suspicion of Secret Iniquity.*

Pasquin greeted the recruit. Quoting at length from Cato's *Letters,* which he admitted had made the fame of the authors on the South Sea affair, he said that they were as pertinent now. Even Harcourt rejoiced openly at the prospect of his old friend's fate. Stratford, who liked neither, marveled at what he had "lived to see between these two."

After the bill imposing pains and penalties on Atterbury, came another levying a hundred thousand pounds on Catholics to pay expenses of the plot. On Trenchard's motion, Non-Jurors were included in the mulct as well. May 17 Christopher Layer was taken on a sledge to Tyburn from the Tower. After he was hung, his head was "fixt at Temple Bar"; his quarters, given to his friends. Ten days later Parliament was prorogued. June 3 the King embarked at Greenwich for the visit he deferred.

Before he went, the faithful got rewards in Church and State. Walpole declined a peerage, which was given to his son. Pulteney became Cofferer of the Household; Richard Temple, Viscount Cobham, Governor of Jersey; Philip Stanhope, a Captain of the Yeomen of the Guards. Convenient deaths and the elimination of Atterbury permitted shifts on the episcopal bench. Gibson was translated to London; Willis, to Winchester; Hoadly, to Salisbury. Townshend and Carteret accompanied the King, and Walpole qualified to act for both. As one of the Lords Justices, head of the Treasury, and as two effective Secretaries of State, there was some ground that summer to call him an "overgrown" minister. Those arrested but not tried were now turned loose. Even Bolingbroke got a pardon from the King and started home. Only Cadogan, who tried secretly through the Secretary at War to realize his hopes, was informed that he was not Captain General or Commander in Chief, but merely Commander of the Foot and Horse Guards. Tuesday, June 18, accompanied by his daughter and her husband, Atterbury was taken from the Tower in a closed chair and put on board the *Aldborough* man of war. Friday he landed at Calais, an exile for his life. A story was soon abroad that he met Bolingbroke in passing and greeted him: "We are exchanged." Apparently they did not meet, for Bolingbroke did not come that way. Though not a remark that Bolingbroke would have relished or Atterbury would have made, it suited well the purposes of those who wished both smeared as Jacobites. A zealot at last, Wharton established the *True Briton,* beginning (June 3) to publish twice a week for the cause he had earlier espoused in secret. Thomas Stackhouse, in *The Memoirs of Dr. Francis Atterbury,* addressed to Pulteney, put the ministerial view. There was a "Disease" in the "Vitals" of the kingdom they wished to "expel"; "the Government had been pester'd with Plots and Insurrections too long to have any Patience." Atterbury was an "Example" and a "Warning." [2]

[2] Folkstone Williams, *Memoirs and Correspondence of Francis Atterbury,* I. 376ff., alleges that Walpole offered to make Atterbury Bishop of Winchester before taking steps against him. It may be true, though Williams finds so many faults in Walpole and so few in Atterbury that his undocumented reading of the evidence needs support. If the offer was made, it was probably in 1721; Williams mistakes the date when Walpole became head of the Treasury. See also on events treated in this section: Torrens, *Cabinets,* I. 305ff.; Nulle, *Newcastle,* pp. 136ff.; Realey, *Early Opposition to Walpole,* pp. 81ff.; *Parliamentary History,* VII. 911ff.; VIII. 62ff.; Coxe, *Robert Walpole,* I. 165ff.; II. 220ff.; *Marlborough,* III. 650; Lee, *Defoe,* II. 434ff.; III. 19ff.; Boyer, *Political State,* XXII. 412ff.; XXIII. Lff.; XXIV. 96ff.; XXV. 320ff.; XXVI. 18ff.; Stanhope, *History,* II. Appendix. pp. xviiiff.; Hist. Mss. Com., *Various,* VIII. 326ff.; *Portland,* VII. 311ff.; *Polwarth,* III. 76ff.; *Dropmore,* I. 67; *Carlisle,* pp. 37ff.; (14 Rept. Appendix, Pt. 9), pp. 513ff.; Lockhart, *Papers,* II. 68ff.; Sykes, *Gibson,* pp. 80ff.; *Reports from Committees of House of Commons,* I. 99ff.; Aitken, *Steele,* II. 273ff.; Walter Sichel, *Bolingbroke,* II. 500; J. G. Nichols, *Letters of Pope and Atterbury* (Camden Society, first series, vol. 73); Ball, *Correspondence of Swift,* III. 148; John Hoadly, *Works of Benjamin Hoadly,* III. 3ff., reprints the Britannicus letters to the *London Journal.*

II

Carteret Aspires

Rival factions in the ministry were jockeying for power. George liked to converse with one who spoke his native tongue, but in governing England experience taught that a minister should know also the language of Parliament and the populace, which Carteret never learned. That Lord inherited Stanhope's confidence in his superior talent for foreign affairs. Schaub at Paris and Polwarth at Cambray, he thought to be his men. Roxburgh and Cadogan at home would pull his oar. The Brodricks in Ireland, he hoped to win. Once in Hanover and out of Walpole's way, his own ability and sympathy in northern affairs would please the King. Carteret was young and full of hope.

Townshend and Walpole were warier and held a stronger hand. By a firm alliance with the Duchess of Kendal they sought to keep the King. At home, Walpole was left in charge; Townshend was trusted to thread his way abroad. Before midsummer he was ready to confess, it was no easy road. "If there be a place in the world where faction and intrigue are natural and in fashion," he wrote to Walpole, "it is here."

Walpole and Newcastle worked together. The Duke's knowledge of English politics, ability in managing seats of power, taste for details in their localities, patient attentions to important men, sound judgment based on a willingness to take advice and an habitual second thought made him an indispensable lieutenant for one who wished to rule. With Townshend's help he had thwarted Cadogan, although they struck the blow through Carteret.

A relative of Polwarth reviewed the scene and sent advice to guide that absent Lord. Carteret, he said, had wished to leave one of his friends on guard at home, suggesting Roxburgh for the place. Failing that, he went to Walpole to make up. At Hanover he had begun a new attack. Roxburgh and Cadogan were Carteret's only friends of note. In short,

Polwarth should correspond with Walpole over Carteret's head. Walpole would "get the better and was upon an honest bottom." The alternative for Polwarth was to quit being a Scot and marry the Countess of Walsingham.

Bolingbroke's return was not an aid to ministers at home. He was effusive in the friendship offered and all too eager in his wish to help. His shrewdness made him choose the stronger side. He wrote to Townshend and, with his consent, to Kendal and the King. He was ready to go to Hanover to plead his cause. He conferred with Wyndham, Bathurst, and all that group, who wished to unite with Walpole if that Minister agreed. Walpole discouraged this negotiation as imprudent. August 9, at dinner in his house, he advised the suppliant that going to Hanover would do his plea no good. Townshend reminded him that Parliament's action did not "entirely depend upon the King." In an altercation with Walpole, Pulteney had earlier threatened that he would raise the case in Parliament in order to get it voted down. August 11 the exile left again for France. Only Harcourt gave him encouragement. Wharton in the *True Briton* (August 19) longed "to hear some Court Orators set forth this Gentleman's Merit."

In Hanover the fight was warm, though Townshend thought he won on several fronts. After the fiasco with Cadogan, the King agreed to sign no English paper except in Townshend's presence. July 16 the two Secretaries of State and the King agreed that to keep Sweden in line against a threatening Russian fleet would take two hundred thousand pounds. Three days later George and Townshend vetoed the proposal of Carteret and Bernstorff to pay ten thousand to the Swedish Minister. Townshend "never saw the King so right." Carteret courted Bernstorff and Kendal's other rivals in the German court.

Walpole promised the money, but hoped that it would not be spent. To get it, his Majesty would have to return before the intended time. In general, he was "mightily inclined to be cautious" on matters in the north. There was no use in talking of the next session yet with danger of a war ahead. He thought England would better stand "neuter" for a while. He had dis-

covered intrigues by Carteret against them in the previous
year and had told Bolingbroke that they could not by "rash"
measures "hazard the King's affairs." There were stories
that Carteret would soon come home to set up a new ministry as Stanhope and Sunderland had done. "These stories
. . . and the True Briton" were the "only things" causing the
"least disturbance" at home. Before the summer ended
Townshend was as reassuring and could tell of other triumphs.

In order to conciliate the Countess of Platen, Carteret exerted himself through Schaub to obtain the French title of
Duke for her daughter's prospective husband. The King consented to the request, but would not make it a state matter.
While it hung fire (August 2), Cardinal Dubois died. A friend
of Orleans, ill inclined to Schaub, returned to court. Prudence
suggested that a more congenial observer go to Paris. Townshend persuaded George that Horace Walpole was a proper
man. He could set out for Hanover, pausing at Paris on the
way. Better still, Townshend remembered that Portugal
would be a party to the treaty to be signed by England, France,
and Spain. The King through Carteret sent Horace credentials
empowering him to act. The case was clear to Carteret and
Schaub; perhaps also, to waverers at home.

The business with Portugal did not consume all of the special envoy's time. Nor did he at first oppose the title that
Schaub and Carteret were trying to obtain for the suitor of
Platen's daughter. But Schaub understood no doubt that
those "having credit enough to get so near a relative sent
over to superintend him" might, if they would, do other things
as well. Orleans had found in Dubois's papers a letter seeking to persuade the French that Townshend and Walpole had
little credit with the King and Prince.

On the morning of October 1 Horace Walpole left for
France. Robert wrote to Townshend later in the day. It was
very well for the Duchess to talk of quieting things at home.
It could not be done in the face of an open cabal, with opponents boasting every little triumph, while he and Newcastle
had to keep still. If that "contest" was "suffered to subsist,"

and the King could not to be "persuaded to make it very plain on one side or the other," when Parliament assembled, things would go awry. But in Hanover Townshend gained another point. With his assistance the Duchess of Kendal triumphed in the German court. The King appointed a minister dependent on them there.

From Ireland came less comforting reports. In order to supply some needed token, copper coins a patent had been granted to William Wood. The project was inherited from Sunderland. Kendal as usual had claimed a mulct. Sir Isaac Newton, Master of the Mint, was asked to give advice. Walpole thought that he had never handled a tender point with stricter care. But the Brodricks, after their South Sea fight, had little hope from him. Grafton, the Lord Lieutenant, handled them with an amazing lack of tact, which seemed to Walpole almost to invite the line they took. The Declaratory Act of 1719, asserting the supremacy of English courts, was still fresh in Irish minds. Fuel was made ready for a fire. In the Irish Parliament that year the flame burst forth. Lacking control, it soon began to spread.

In late August Walpole warned Grafton of the danger if he did not act in time, though he thought it to be rather a "popular run without consideration than any solid mischief." A fortnight later Grafton complained that in spite of Middleton's promise not to interfere, the Chancellor's son had made a speech suggesting the possibility of impeaching the "first minister" in England for Irish acts. He thought the outcome would be unpleasant for Walpole and himself. Ten days later, he thought that Middleton was still more to blame. Soon he asked that the Lord Chancellor be dismissed. The Irish Parliament had addressed the King demanding a remedy of the grievance as a condition of voting the year's supplies. Townshend warned Carteret that the project was begun by Sunderland.

Hoadly in the *London Journal* and Wharton in the *True Briton* went on with their canvassing of Atterbury's case. Defoe marveled to see "behind the coarse Skreens of a Three Halfpenny Scribbler" a bishop and a duke at odds. Bolingbroke advised Swift that he was a changed man, reserving for one woman love that in younger days he spread abroad. Arbuthnot wrote that Oxford was a "little deaf," but retained other "good and bad qualities" as of old. The Dean himself in May escaped from Dublin and the noise following Vanessa's death, leaving in unfriendly hands her papers, including an imprudent poem of their happier hours.

Early in September "Tom Brodrick and Mr. Trenchard" were at Bath with some of Walpole's friends, who hoped that "dangerous machinations" would not be imputed to their holidays. Walpole's daughter married the Earl of Cholmondeley's nephew the middle of the month. October 10 a rival passed when Cowper died. At Blenheim six days later the Duchess of Marlborough was surprised when Somerset came to court. In mid-November Carr, Lord Hervey passed away. Orrery told the Pretender a blunt and obvious truth. His opponents had a loyal army, control of funds, Parliament, and the fleet; his friends were in despair.

Exactly a week later, the English resident at Paris informed Polwarth of the death of Orleans. Schaub and Horace went to Versailles to see what they could do. The Duke of Bourbon was the new Regent. London was excited at the news. Walpole and Newcastle scarcely knew which way to turn. Law and Bolingbroke were asked to give advice. Though Horace kept a cooler head, December 15 found him "once more upon a precipice," due to the help that he was asked to seek. Bolingbroke called with a letter from Harcourt the very moment that his own from Robert came. He had to accept an invitation to dine. He would trust his undesired partner as little as he could, hoping once more for guidance from his "fortune" and his "stars." If he was ever an "itinerant minister again" the fault would not be his. In fact, he urged his own recall, or he would be as ridiculous as Schaub.

He managed better than he thought. Bourbon also had to feel his way, and Bolingbroke was helpful with that Duke. To the theory that in foreign relations Carteret was the man of chief account, Bolingbroke replied that he and Townshend were of equal weight. What was more, one as considerable as

Walpole in the British ministry "did not fail to have his weight in council upon foreign as well as domestic affairs." Privately, he suggested that Horace take a more aggressive part and offered help. The part was taken, but without the help. Finding that the Bishop Frejus opposed the granting of the mooted title, he confessed to Bourbon that the matter was of less concern to George I than it was to Carteret and Schaub.

In the midst of these negotiations, Trenchard died. His Majesty reached England December 28 for the Parliament that was soon to meet. Bolingbroke hoped that it would pass the act he wished. If that could not be done, at least he craved the right to get back his estates. Horace was asked to send this letter to Harcourt, keeping the matter from Carteret and Schaub.

Near to the end of his career, Cato meditated on the ways of politics. "In raising Parties and Factions, Inflaming" went "a thousand Times further than Reasoning or Teaching." The "Secret in Politicks" was "to drive the Nail that will go. . . . The lucky Adjusting of Times and Seasons, taking Advantage of prevailing Prejudices and Pannicks, and Knowing how to humour and lay hold of the predominant Enthusiasms of human Nature" had "given Birth to most of the Revolutions in Religion and Politicks that . . . ever happened in the World." Men were "easiest operated upon" by those who knew best "how to dally and play with their Foibles," either "naturally" or "by Design."

Whether the furor in Ireland, as the ministers felt, came by design or not, it taxed their skill to quiet it. Grafton was a broken reed. Middleton thought the ministers misled. The Lord Lieutenant had provoked his son. Wood's copper would not go, and Walpole should be told. It was odd he had "so poor generals," having "so many troops."

In England the Church began to quiet down. Gibson helped with episcopal changes. Walpole wrote to Newcastle the opinion that "he must be Pope" and would as willingly be theirs "as anybodies." He was "certainly the man among them with whom" the ministers "ought to manage and cultivate."

Walpole willingly would do his part. "We grow well acquainted," he went on. Newcastle agreed: "He has more sense and I think more party zeal than any of them. . . . I intend very soon to take an opportunity of writing very largely . . . upon pretence of the several vacancies that are amongst the King's Chaplains, and shall endeavour to do what I can."

The King congratulated Parliament (January 9) on peace in Europe, suggested a reduction in the public debt, and urged the use of this breathing spell for the "encouragement of trade and navigation, the employment of the poor, the exciting and encouraging a spirit of industry in the nation." A little progress was made on these questions, which were things Walpole had at heart. The book of customs was revised. An excise was substituted for the import duties on tea, coffee, and cocoa, tending to suppress smuggling, and increasing the annual yield of revenue by £120,000. The usual opposition to the army was the subject of the chief debate.

Without giving up what he had won in politics, the Minister hoped for compromise and quiet. The Brodricks tried to explain the Irish troubles and test their ground. They reported in January that Carteret and Roxburgh had defeated an effort to give to Cobham Cadogan's command. Argyll would have had the Ordnance had the scheme gone through. St. John Brodrick thought the blow to Walpole great at the "beginning of the session." True, the Minister was "a very considerable man," with influence in the House of Commons, but Carteret had "at least as much credit with the King." That Lord advised the Brodricks to insist upon something for themselves besides retaining Middleton as Chancellor and as one of the Lords Justices in the Irish list.

A talk with Walpole a few days later tended to change this view. That Minister claimed credit for defending Middleton against the Lord Lieutenant. He had tried to get a place for St. John Brodrick, but was opposed by Sunderland's old group. A conference with Carteret four days later found that Lord claiming that he deserved the credit. Through him Middleton had become a Lord Justice in the first place and remained one now. Grafton would probably be recalled. Dorset and Bolton were candidates to succeed. By early March Argyll was listed as a candidate too.

Walpole was slyly busy in these weeks. He asked St. John Brodrick to make a ministerial motion, assuring him of friendship for his clan. By late in March St. John had changed his mind. "I can't but think Walpole must prevail," he said, "and for that reason endeavour to be as well with him as I can." The Minister's interest in the House of Commons was "prodigious," and thus it would be "pretty hard" for him to be withstood.

Other straws pointed the way the current flowed. In January Horace Walpole pressed in vain for a decision between himself and Schaub. He was persuaded to swallow his pride and stay. March 22 he was allowed to ask for Schaub's recall. April 1, writing to Grafton, Townshend gently broke the news. To heal divisions among his servants, the King was moved to act. He hoped that Grafton would be pleased with Carteret as Lord Lieutenant in his room. Newcastle would have the place as Secretary of State. Grafton could be Lord Chamberlain if he wished. Middleton learned that he would keep his place. He was told that Carteret had not lost prestige with the King. Wood's patent was the chief bugbear that he had to face.

At last Swift saw a ray of hope. Here was a Lord Lieutenant he had met. The Brodricks, he thought, had won their fight. His part would be to add more fuel to the fire. Forthwith, he sent a letter to Carteret. Inclosed he sent another addressed to Irishmen at large. He took for granted the Lord Lieutenant's help. But the circumstances were far from what he thought. His letter to Carteret was ignored. To save his pride and justify his boasts, he wrote again, affecting humility to conceal his hurt: "I could have wished your Excellency had condescended so far as to let one of your under-clerks have signified to me that a letter was received." Carteret admitted being in the "wrong"; he had been out of town.

The ministers urged the King that year to stay in England. There was a contest in the City with which they needed him to help. There were plans for the universities and the Church. The Jacobites would give less trouble if he stayed. Parliament could meet in autumn, enabling him to get an early start next spring. His Majesty agreed.

At Gibson's suggestion fellows in Oxford and Cambridge colleges were to be designated preachers for the Royal Chapel in Whitehall with honoraria of thirty pounds a year. Prebends were to go to some ill qualified to preach. Regius professorships in modern history and languages were established at both the seats of learning. The underlying purpose was "to create a general dependence and raise a general expectation amongst the clergy." Oxford at first sent only a letter by a "Bedell" expressing thanks, but a better state of mind seemed on the way.

Older actors were passing from the stage. Mist was fined again a hundred pounds; the printer of the *True Briton*, four times as much. Exasperated, Mist attacked Defoe. Newspapers began to turn the latter's pieces down. His journalistic course was nearly run. Mrs. Manley had a fifth volume of *The New Atlantis* ready, and publication was designed. It was blackmail, but her printer found Walpole to be better pay. Before the end of summer she was dead. In early June Steele assigned his income for his debts, while he went off to Wales. Within that week Sacheverell died. Oxford had passed away a week before. A changing world had scarcely missed them when they went.

Journalists of the day were preaching peace. Wharton had dropped his paper in the spring. "Britain is at last reconciled to its own Happiness," said Hoadly in the *London Journal,* "and willing to be free and prosperous and safe upon the only Terms which can possibly make it so. . . . Its King, its Senate are at Leisure from intestine Tumults and intend the Care of its true Glory and cultivate the Arts of Humanity and Peace." The King, Walpole, Townshend, and Newcastle met with the Duchess of Kendal to consider questions of the day. Carteret, though he had not gone to Ireland, no longer went to court. Walpole was "absolutely the helm of the government," a French observer thought. It was fortunate for France that

Carteret was out, since he was inclined to favor the Emperor at her expense.

In Ireland the summer added heat. Writing anonymously as a "Drapier," Swift persisted in his work. Disappointed in his hope of becoming Primate when Boulter got the place, Archbishop King of Dublin supported Swift. Facts had little place in what was said. Copper was treated as the basic currency of the realm. Prices of all commodities would be upset; the economic structure, overturned. The constitutional relation of the countries was revived again.

Middleton learned in August that Walpole would give ground. It was too late to quiet Ireland thus. The patent would have to be withdrawn. The Minister wished to avoid the stigma of defeat. From Houghton, where his house was going up, he sent a scheme. It might suffice to quench a fire, which Walpole felt that Carteret had helped to start. Newcastle and Townshend in London were instructed what to do.

Popular frenzies, Newcastle was told (September 1), seldom came "by chance." "Small matters" could be "aggravated and carried to a very great height"; "secret management and industry" could "kindle a general flame." With the judges against the King, it was impossible to change the popular mind. No Irishman could "stem this torrent"; the Lord Lieutenant would better go himself. Whatever happened, Walpole explained to Townshend, good would come to them. Carteret would either quiet Ireland, probably "impossible" in view of the part that he had previously played, or would lose credit with the King by adopting the Irish view. His Majesty might see that persistence in the patent would not be worth the trouble it would cost.

When he arrived the reluctant governor was greeted by a "Drapier's Letter" more vigorous than the rest. Middleton advised that it was "highly seditious" and that the author and printer should suffer punishment. To his brother he called it a "hot-headed libel." A reward was offered of three hundred pounds. Swift braved the Lord Lieutenant in his court. Archbishop King advised that the Dean would confess his authorship and trust the country's will. If he did, Carteret was dis-

posed to arrest him and await the royal wish. Newcastle, he
said, could see how Swift and King estimated the "humour of
the people" with whom he had to deal. For months he and
Middleton were left to wrestle with the Dean and Ireland as
best they could.

"Peace" with all "powers abroad," "perfect tranquility" at
home with an "uninterrupted enjoyment of all civil and religious rights" was the news greeting Parliament when it met
(November 12). Hoadly in the *London Journal* confirmed the
thought. "The Nation is in good Humour," he said, "and therefore the Posture and Conduct of the whole is in a good Way."
The Society for the Reformation of Manners was active against
lewdness, gaming, profanations of the Lord's Day, drunkenness, and similar vices.

Thomas Gordon had reached a new stage in his career. To
four volumes of *Cato's Letters* he prefixed a memoir of his
deceased collaborator and friend. He married Trenchard's
widow, her first husband's third wife. He got ready for the
printer a second volume of his own essays as a companion for
the first, sent forth as *The Humourist* five years before (1720).
The second was a different book, because the years had made
of him a different man. His pen was now more practiced;
his mind was more mature. His years in London and with
Trenchard had taught him to discriminate and had brought
the disillusioning insight inevitable for those who observe at
close range the doings of the great and habitually set down
for sale the things they see and feel.

Life in the capital had grown sophisticated in the generation just behind. Gone was the bluff democracy of the public
rooms in earlier coffee-houses, when Dryden solemnly took
his place "every evening at Will's," the company waiting for
his word. The house was still remembered, but the scene was
changed. Men of note withdrew and did not court the common crowd. Select assemblies gathered in the private rooms.
"Conversation," if it had ever been the habit, was not now
the "Genius of the English Nation." "Conceiving" might be
as "pleasurable" as among "other People," but there was not
the "same Ease in bringing forth." "We cannot or we will

not," Gordon said, "tell all we know, nor do we care to hear those that will."

In such groups, contrary to the situation in a crowd, there was the "greatest Hatred of what the Ancients called Oratory." A popular speaker "must know a great deal without Ostentation, and must be very successful without Vanity." However, the magnet that still drew men to the coffee-houses was chiefly designed "to heat the Brain." Fortunately, "Newspapers and Coffee" were dispensed in a common shop; the "blue Apron Officer" who handed a customer the paper "applied" also the "composing Specifick, a Dish and a Pipe."

For the time there was a lull in "Libels," "most of the Malecontent Writers having made either their Peace or their Terms," and Gordon diverted himself by setting down "Rules for the use of Novices in the Way . . . lest the laudable Art of Defaming an Administration should be lost." With a "certain Delicacy and masterly Address," it was possible to "wrap up foul Meanings in clean Linnen and cloath the rankest Ideas in the most delicate Garb." The familiar methods, which he elaborated, were the "Allegorical Mode," the "Ironical or Mock Panegyrick," and a variety of uses of history by "drawing Parallels." With these arts, a man who could not "talk or write Treason without incurring the Penalty of the Laws" deserved to "lose his Ears."

There were enough men engaged in the art to constitute a society of their own. Gordon invented or frequented a club of such authors in the "City and Liberties of Westminster." He found them "Conversant with the Ways of the World," though living "above it," capable of the "deepest Humility" and of the "sublimest Flights." Agreed in hating society, they did not "love one another" and were held together neither by "Interest" nor by "Affection," but by "a kind of Spight," resembling that in the commerce of "midnight Cats." There was no "Thorough Fool" among them, nor was there a "Man of cool and perfect Sense." In their meetings might be seen "Ridicule grafted upon Fustian, Seneca crying Pippins, and Cleopatra in a Hackney Coach." But men who in weekly essays were at each other's throats there sat down "in a peaceable Confederacy" and "lit their Pipes at the same Candle."

Gordon himself was soberer than at first. Popular discontent began to seem to be a public danger; a "Tendency to Tumult, Sedition, and Rebellion," a "weak Part of the Constitution." It made little difference from "what poor smoke Spring the Torrents of Faction" took their rise, if "fed with Care and improved by Industry" under favorable conditions they did their work. "Whatever the Beginnings of Factions," the "Consequences" were the same. Thus it was "more seasonable to pity than to envy the Fortunes and Dignities of Princes or great Ministers of State; and to lessen or excuse their venial Faults."

In their case, he would think it prudent to avoid projects involving "Innovations in ancient and established forms of Laws, especially those concerning Liberty, Property, and Religion, which are the Possessions Men will ever have most at Heart." He would preserve the "true and common Interest of the Nation" at home, engaging with the stronger group if faction could not be stilled. Abroad, peace would be his pursuit. The chief end of government was the public safety; the consent of the public was essential to promote that end. A journalist in this mood was a godsend to a minister in power.

Lord Chancellor Macclesfield was impeached that year. The ministers had inherited him with the King. They were not sorry to see him go. His guilt was rather a weakness of the time than personal. His fall was evidence that times improved. A spirit of reform was in the air, though it did not prevent a wish to live at government expense. Walpole, an observer said, was "tired out of his life by the number of people" wishing places.

Whether the bill regulating the holding elections in the City of London, passed that session, was a reform or not depended upon the point of view. It accomplished a part of what proponents had in mind. The suffrage was restricted to freemen paying scot and lot with houses valued at at least ten pounds a year. Wealthier men were encouraged to become freemen by removing a restriction on the distribution of property by will. The Mayor and Aldermen, or a majority of them, were given a veto over the Common Council's acts. All popular objections could not be suppressed, but London henceforth was to be more amenable to men in power.

A debate in April on an appropriation for arrears on the Civil List took the break between Walpole and Pulteney to the floor of the House of Commons. The Cofferer of the Household had wanted to be Secretary of State. Opinionated and hot-tempered, he felt his disappointment. Without ability or influence to take the lead, he was not accepted at his own estimate of his worth. His unwillingness to endure longer a subordinate rôle made him henceforward an obstacle in Walpole's path. When he demanded an explanation of the extra expenditures, Walpole recalled a pension of five thousand pounds to Godolphin's family, enabling Pulteney to get the place he held.

Bolingbroke, whose own fate was at last pending, though admitting civilities from Pulteney, made haste to deny to Harcourt "private correspondence or even conversation with him." Sir Matthew Decker had stupidly withheld the proceeds of a considerable investment for the exile's wife the year before on the ground that the husband was attainted. Townshend would give help in this, and arranged for the lady to come and claim her money as Madame de Villette. While in England she reinvested eleven thousand pounds with the Duchess of Kendal in another cause. The King gave orders, and Walpole found it wise to yield. Political power was all he could withhold. Some of his own friends, as he foresaw, refused to go along. Jacobites would not support their erstwhile friend. It was not the victory Bolingbroke had hoped. Those who least wished to see him in England, he wrote to Swift, had "made it impossible" for him to live "anywhere else." He was "two-thirds restored."

By another bill the Highlanders of Scotland were to be disarmed. But the Duke of Wharton, the nearest to a leader the Jacobites now had left, assured his King that much could still be done. True, not all solicited had responded to the request that the restoration of Bolingbroke be opposed, and the ministers had shrewdly thwarted a scheme for agitating the Common Council against the City bill, but "all due care would be taken to work upon the different passions" of those "who seemed susceptible to appeals." Atterbury in April shook his head in doubt. True, in 1715 things "went far," and people were "much better affected both in England and Scotland now." But the army was "double to what it was then; . . . the spirits of men, . . . sunk by ill usage and frequent disappointments."

Newcastle's nephew, Lord Lincoln, succeeded Pulteney at the session's end. Argyll was Master General instead of Cadogan. The Order of Bath was revived, another "bauble" with which to reward the "boys," as Philip Stanhope said in verse. Before he took the Garter Walpole accepted a ribbon himself to convince others that it was not lightly bestowed. Thursday morning, June 3, the King embarked again for Germany. This time Townshend was the only Secretary of State to go.

Trouble in Scotland over the malt tax that summer enabled Roxburgh to be shelved. Islay, Argyll's brother, though not as Secretary of State, was left in charge. In Ireland, Middleton and Carteret did not agree. As matters were, the Chancellor knew that Wood's patent would have to be withdrawn. Carteret came round reluctantly; it meant that as Lord Lieutenant he had failed. He naturally felt that Middleton and Swift should share the blame. In September when the Irish Parliament met, Carteret announced the patent to be at "an utter end." Scotland and Ireland, Walpole thought, were "once more quiet"; he wished to "keep them so." With a view to "October hunting," he was trying to get his other business attended to.

Carteret felt that Middleton should go. Swift's publisher proposed to dedicate one of his letters to the Chancellor, saying "the Drapier himself would have been entirely silent . . . had he not had so glorious an example as your Lordship to follow." Middleton forbade. He would complain of the printer if he did. Again events had been unkind to Swift.

He aspired not to "divert," but "vex" the world, he wrote to Pope. To another friend he described himself as "sitting . . . in a corner" of his "great house" "like a toad." "Drown the world," he said, "I am not content with despising it."

Pope's "spleen" was rather "at the little rogues." Bolingbroke saw their petulance for what it was. "Pope and you are very great wits," he wrote to Swift, but "if you despised the world as much as you pretend, . . . you would not be so angry with it."

Carteret knew where victory lay. He asked a friend to go to Walpole and make terms. "If that friendship can be obtained," he said (September 29), "I shall think myself happy and be forever faithful to it; if not, you will bear witness that I endeavoured it." "We know him enough to watch him," Walpole wrote to Townshend, "and be upon our guard." The dismissal of Roxburgh had probably "frightened him." But with Pulteney, Roxburgh, and others in the opposition, it might be well to use him in the Lords. Middleton resigned, and Wood was recompensed, and thus this chapter reached its end.[3]

III

LINES ARE DRAWN

At Hanover in 1725 foreign affairs as usual engaged the King. Peter the Great had died in Russia, and his widow was placed in charge. Afraid to wait for an heir to the crown, the French ministers sent the Spanish Infanta home, and Louis XV took an older Polish wife. The Spanish refused to suffer the

[3] Ball, *Correspondence of Swift*, III. 111ff.; Lee, *Defoe*, III. 148ff.; Coxe, *Robert Walpole*, II, 253ff., 311ff.; *Horatio Walpole*, I. 111ff.; Hist. Mss. Com., *Portland*, V. 634ff.; VII. 361ff.; *Polwarth*, III. 282ff.; *Carlisle*, pp. 47ff.; *Various*, VIII. 378ff.; Boyer, *Political State*, XXV. 672ff.; XXVI. 43ff.; XXVII. 95ff.; XXVIII. 90ff.; XXIX. 175ff.; XXX. 70ff.; Sichel, *Bolingbroke*, II. 503; Realey, *Early Opposition to Walpole*, pp. 133ff.; Torrens, *Cabinets*, I. 323ff.; Nulle, *Newcastle*, pp. 157ff.; Aitken, *Steele*, II. 293ff.; Stanhope, *History*, II. Appendix, pp. xx, civ, cxxff.; Sykes, *Gibson*, pp. 83ff.; *Treasury Books and Papers*, p. 221; George Harris, *Life of Lord Chancellor Hardwicke*, I. 141; Archibald Ballantyne, *Lord Carteret*, pp. 105ff.; Wickham Legg, *Diplomatic Instructions*, p. xvii; *Parliamentary History*, VIII. 372ff.; Ralph Straus, *The Unspeakable Curll*, pp. 94ff.; Williams, *Atterbury*, II. 43ff.; N. A. Briscoe, *Economic Policy of Sir Robert Walpole*, pp. 56ff. 95ff.; William Maitland, *History and Survey of London* (1756 ed.), I. 534ff.; II. 1199ff.

French to mediate longer in their disputes, and the Congress of Cambray reached a futile end. In April Ripperda, the Spanish agent at Vienna, had negotiated an alliance between those crowns, and soon the news was known abroad. The Emperor got approval of an Ostend Company to trade with the East; the Spanish were to get Gibraltar when the chance should come. The Jacobites still buzzed in every hopeful court, and British fears began to be aroused.

Opposing allies were soon making terms. The King of Prussia came to Herrenhausen in July. England and France agreed to give each other mutual help. The Prussian King was moved somewhat by an attack on Protestants in Thorn. In September the Treaty of Hanover was signed by Prussia, France, and England. Money was needed to bid for Sweden's help. The Dutch might come in, frightened at the Emperor's threat to Eastern trade. Walpole was not so sure. If England had to go to war, he wrote (October 2), of which he did not like the thought: " 'Tis to be wished that this nation may think an invasion by a foreign power, or an evident design of such an invasion, the support of the Pretender, and the cause of the Protestant succession are the chief and principal motives that obliged us to part with that peace and tranquility and the happy consequences thereof which we now enjoy."

Back from Norfolk hunting in late November, he suggested that if Townshend's draft of the King's speech was to stand, the meeting of Parliament would better be delayed. Financial proposals would have to be changed; rumors of war had raised the interest rate. The Hanoverian Treaty would be opposed. He had learned by opening mail that Pulteney was intriguing on the Emperor's side. Townshend answered (December 7), that nothing "could prevent a war" but "vigorous" evidence of Parliament's will to act. The King and he were coming home.

Thomas Gordon volunteered *An Authentic Narrative of the late Proceedings and cruel Executions at Thorn.* The Pretender's wife went to a convent, weary of a sad estate. Bolingbroke vexed his first wife's friends by cutting a grove at Bucklebery, a "defence as well as ornament" to the place.

Elections for the Common Council in London found the ministers still unable to control. William Stanhope from Madrid reported Ripperda, now the Minister there, to be a "wild man," but hostile yet to France. Perhaps he could induce the King of Spain to give Gibraltar up. Then George I, embarking New Year's Day at Helvoetsluys, came through a storm of rain and hail as well as wind. Four days later a messenger arrived in London to say, the roads were blocked with snow. Not till January 9 did he with Lord and Lady Townshend reach St. James's.

The Middlesex authorities were busy with reform. A committee of justices were counting places where "Geneva and other strong Waters" could be had. Within the bills of mortality they found 6187 retail shops, whose customers were deprived of "Money, Time, Health, and Understanding"; women became the "Prey of vicious Men." Vintners and brewers, perhaps, were hurt as much. "Great and sudden" had been the "Decay of the Brewing Trade."

In his speech to Parliament (January 20), the King referred to Thorn. The diplomatic situation was reviewed and vigorous measures urged to secure the "blessings of peace and prosperity." Debate dispelled the rumors that Pulteney and Walpole had made up. Horace was at home to help. The wits had fun with the new Knights of Bath. One called Sir Robert the "member with a badge." The interest was so slight that Shippen did not divide against the Mutiny Bill. Walpole and Pulteney both lost their tempers as they sparred. When, in February, Pulteney asked for a committee on public accounts, opposition members helped to vote it down as "ill timed." Sir John Barnard, a City Alderman, upheld Walpole's side. Pulteney himself explained that he only meant to give the Minister a chance to show his "integrity" and "sublime character" to the world.

Erasmus Philips sent out in March the *Country Gentleman*. He later said that he had encouragement to begin and meant to be "entirely political." But the "Vices and Blunders" of the persons "at the Helm" did not fill up his space, and he included other things as well. Addison and Steele, he felt, had been beforehand there. When the parliamentary session closed, and the King hoped for a "safe and honourable peace," the journalist expressed another view. If Russia, Spain, and Austria conspired to oppose British trade, "let them consider" that "King George like mighty Neptune" claimed "Dominion of the Seas" and had a "gallant Fleet." One rousing the "Lyon from his Lethargy" should avoid his "Fury" or be lost. The "Beasts of the Forest" trembled when he roared. Should "Germany, an inland Country," insult an "invincible Island" by erecting an "Indian Company"? "No!" A "brave" people and a "valiant" King would "make the Emperor know . . . that the German Eagles, when their Wings are clipt, can mount no higher than a Dung Hill Cock."

Another journalist of greater fame returned to town that spring. *Cadenus and Vanessa,* Swift had learned, would soon come out in print. The health of Stella now for months had seemed to fail. In giving up Wood's patent the ministers had confessed defeat. When the Dean did not despair, he felt his strength again. Perhaps escape might still be found. Perchance he had a nuisance value to the court. The hope was faint, but there was hope. He steeled himself against familiar scenes and went to see what he could do. He took a treasured manuscript to use in case he failed.

Arbuthnot called twice on Tuesday, April 12, at his lodgings in Bury Street next door to the Royal Chair. The Princess of Wales would see him Thursday night. "Your people," he wrote two days later to Tickell, the Chief Secretary in Ireland, "are very civil to me." He "met a thousand times better usage from" those in England than from those he left behind. In the same week he explained to an inquiring Irish friend that the poem named was "written at Windsor fourteen years" before "on a frolic among some ladies." He had forgotten "what was in it," but thought it only a "Cavalier business," and those who would "not give allowances" must "choose." He could not help what people thought. He did not believe "the gravest character . . . answerable for a private humoursome thing" made "public" by the "baseness of particular malice" and "an accident inevitable."

He went to one of Walpole's levees among the crowd. Through Peterborough he had a private interview. At eight, the morning of April 27, he went. The story was, he frankly asked to have his exile end. Denied, he did not quite admit it to his friends. Walpole looked through the window of his Chelsea house and saw a tree, transplanted to the grounds. It did not flourish there, he pointed out, as it had done when in its native swamp. Thus closed the door of hope.

To Peterborough Swift explained at too great length that he had gone to talk of Ireland without a thought of other things. But Walpole's mind was fixed, and he had failed. The Minister's views could not be reconciled with "notions . . . of liberty" the British always "understood" to be "the inheritance of human creatures." Swift's first point was that "all persons born in Ireland" were "called and treated as Irishmen, although their fathers and grandfathers" were of English birth. It was "too true" and to his "sorrow," he said (July 3), that "he had not many weeks to stay in England."

To Tickell he wrote to say that he would return and of the vexing poem to try to make the best he could. "It showed how indiscreet" it was to trust in other hands the "keys" to "cabinets" wherein reposed important "secrets" one wished kept. Poor Stella. Since she had not long to live, he wished he might avoid the parting wrench, the agony of seeing her in pain. He had not got his thousand pounds, as they had heard, he wrote a friend. He only spoke of it to the Princess when he saw her last and bade "her tell Walpole" that he scorned to "ask him for it." The ladies should be shown this passage, because he knew that "Mrs. Johnson would be pleased." A man must save his pride.

But hope was gone, and England tired him now as it had never done before. "You all live in a wretched, dirty, doghole, prison," he wrote to Ireland, and yet the "place" was "good enough to die." The next breath, he boasted the "fairest offers . . . of a settlement" they could "imagine," "ten miles of London and in the midst of . . . friends." If only he were "ten years younger," he would go. But now the light of life was going out. Since he had been in England his "heart" had "been so sunk" that he was not "the same man" he had been and thought he would not be "again." He wished Stella to be told that he had bought a "repeating gold watch for her ease in winter nights." Perhaps she might never see it. His presence would be "a trouble to her and the greatest torment" to himself. If she should die at once, he would delay for six months his return, since the "remainder" of his life would be a "very melancholy scene."

To a younger friend of the cloth who asked for help, he gave advice. He had no weight, having broken with Walpole and Carteret. The important thing was to settle in England rather than pass his "days" in an "odious country and among" an "odious people." "I have been long weary of the world," he wrote again, "and shall for the small remainder of years be weary of life, having forever lost that conversation which could only make it tolerable." But this grief was premature, since Stella lingered on another year. In early August, Swift packed up to go. One weapon more he had, but almost feared to use. With utmost secrecy he sent his book to press, then Monday, August 15, left for home.

The winter brought another blow to hurt his pride. The world found him diverting when he meant to vex. His bomb did not explode. Its shell, the distant young in later times would handle harmlessly in academic play. Pope, Arbuthnot, and Gay made haste to write. "Gulliver" was in "everybody's hands." Erasmus Lewis wished a "key." Perhaps "satire" on "general societies of men" was "too severe," but none of consequence was "angry at the book."

Boyer, when he knew the author, struck a sharp, discordant note. In borrowing from Plato, More, Bacon, and Rabelais, he could have wished the writer had not "followed Rabelais so close." Some passages were "filthy" and "obscene." "Allusions and Alegories" were "so strong, so glaring, and so obvious, that a Man must be a great Stranger in the World in general and to the Courtiers, Statesmen, corrupt Senators, Rakes of Quality, Lawyers, Physicians, Virtuosi, Soldiers, Sharpers, and Women in particular to have need of a Key."

Within that summer of Swift's hopelessness, the callous world went on its way. Stanhope reported that Ripperda in disgrace had taken refuge in his house. The Spanish Minister in London wrote home (August 30) that Pulteney was intimate with himself and the Emperor's resident Minister. Before the time for Parliament to sit, Walpole would be accused of "malversation" and "mismanagement" of public funds. Walpole had heard of an incendiary design on Pulteney's house and called to warn his next door neighbor as a kindly act. Pulteney replied that if a fire should come he would rely on Parliament and Walpole to repay the loss.

In June the King of France dismissed the Duke of Bourbon, appointing Bishop Frejus (Cardinal Fleury) in his place. The Duke of Wharton, in July, became a duke in the Pretender's court, accepted for a while the Roman faith, and took a Spanish lady for his wife. The *Country Gentleman* contained a story of Robin, Danvers' coachman, who got his master's power and wrecked his coach. Lady Townshend, when she died in March, left a vacancy as mediatress between her brother and her Lord. Cadogan also passed from a troubled world.

Walpole sent forth *An Essay on the Public Debts . . . a Letter to a Member of the House.* His journalists took up the points he made. Pulteney broke his ground upon the other side. The piece was called *A State of the National Debt.* Walpole, he said, "confused" or else "disguised" the facts. Some debts were paid, but more were made. The public did not know the truth. Therefore, he appealed to all to join him in support of "Liberty" against "Patrons of Tyranny and arbitrary Power, which would not change its Nature or become less grievous"; though those "who once joined . . . in opposing it" should now be on the other side. It was high time to admit "past Errors," put an end to "destructive Animosities," and "unite in pursuing the true Interest" of a country thus oppressed.

With action promised, the leader then fell ill. Recovering, Philips (August 15) spurred him to the task begun. "New Labours for his Country must he bear . . . the dark Designs of Traitors to disclose" and "guard the Nation's Treasure from rapacious Hands," while raising "Merit, Virtue's Cause to fight, and check Ambition in its boldest Flight." This grandiose task required an abler pen. The convalescent wrote to Swift. Should he return, they might not part again "so soon." But the Dean would not return till spring. The journalistic fight required haste.

At that time three London dailies at each morning's breakfast told the news. More numerous were papers put forth in afternoons three times a week before the posts went out. The space allotted to domestic items began to rival that consumed by foreign notes. The advertisements grew in number and in length. As yet, for one who had a cause to serve, the weekly suited best. Cato's shadow lingered, and others tried to follow in his path.

A week was needed for the piece to be got ready and sent forth. A week was not too long for heated groups to talk of what it meant and heat themselves the more. In coffee-houses first the ferment worked. From those indoctrinated there the word went forth. It came in time to "all the Tradesmen's Shops, Alehouses," and other places of "common working" people's "rendezvous." On Saturday they hung "with an insatiable Itch of Curiosity" upon every "Sentence of a Paper," that was their "weekly Oracle." Some who saw these scenes began to be afraid.

Others felt that talk and type would not accomplish much if left to work alone. Daniel Pulteney, William's cousin, brother-in-law of Sunderland's last wife, began to exercise himself. Wyndham, Shippen, and their friends might help to make a party. Bolingbroke would lend a hand. Nicholas Amhurst was engaged to write. He used an easy quill, and two essays a week were planned. The first appeared December 5. A labored repetition of an essay by Philips was used to launch the *Craftsman* on its way. "Caleb Danvers" was the pseudonym that Amhurst took.[4]

---

[4] There is little evidence to support Sichel's suggestion (*Bolingbroke,* II. 246ff.) that Bolingbroke wrote the piece in the *Country Gentleman* and thus inspired the idea in the first essay in the *Craftsman.* The earlier essay was reprinted by Philips in the collected edition of his *Miscellaneous Works, Consisting of Essays, Political and Moral,* 1751.

The piece was pointless and was not pursued. Amhurst next made the hackneyed prayer of journalists who know they walk in dangerous ways for liberty of the press to publish "Thoughts on any Subject and in any Manner" not forbidden by the laws. Liberty to "undermine the Fundamentals of Government and Religion," he did not desire, nor to "calumniate Persons in high Power." The third number (December 12) treated of the public debts.

But debts were not the subject of that year. Count Palm, the Emperor's Minister, wrote home the following day that the King and "nation" were inclined for peace. Townshend was a hostile force, with Walpole and Newcastle his chief aids. If the Emperor and Spain would stand their ground, Pulteney thought their friends would gain and the ministers be "hard put to it." Pulteney, he repeated within the week, was "chief and weightiest" of English subjects and "well inclined" toward the Emperor's side. The trouble was in the King through the Duchess of Kendal, whom the ministers had. The German ministers were of slight account. Bothmer was well disposed, but feared "Townshend and Walpole too much." Owing to Hosier's voyage, the Spanish Minister in London had been recalled.

The English ministers were not idle on their side. Should there be war, they were not sure that France would help. Hoadly undertook to state their case. His work appeared in the last days before the Christmas week, *An Enquiry into the Reasons of the Conduct of Great Britain with Relation to the Present State of Affairs in Europe*. It was an inspiration and a cue to other writers on that side. To the question of the Ostend Company and Gibraltar was added a definite charge of promised help in placing the Pretender on the British throne. "If we still retain the proper Life and Vigour of Britons," the author asked, "what can we think of an Alliance between two powerful Princes formed against the plain Stipulations of Treaties in order to deprive us of our Glory, our Riches, our Strength, which depend all upon our Trade?"

The *British Journal* (January 7) insisted that Gibraltar must be kept. The *Craftsman*, on the other side, complained that the privileged East India Company was rioting in wealth. Commoners thus affected the "Port and Grandeur of British Noblemen." But the King met his Parliament (January 17) with a vigorous speech. He had "information" on which he could "entirely depend that placing the Pretender" upon the British throne was one of the "secret engagements" between the Emperor and Spain. If time should "evince that giving up the trade of the nation to one power and Gibraltar and Port Mahon to another" was "made the price and reward of imposing upon the nation a Popish Pretender, what an indignation must this raise in the breast of every Protestant Briton!" Shippen and Pulteney, Wyndham and Hanmer, spoke against the address, but the majority was more than three to one.

Opponents of the ministers had not struck fire. The *Craftsman* was but another paper in the stalls. Coffee-houses had to take it twice a week, but Boyer had not found it worth a note. Amhurst was prosy on the subjects of the day. His voice was drowned in the patriotic fervor of these months. The ministerial weeklies said that Hoadly's pamphlet did the work. People resented "with the utmost Indignation the monstrous Ingratitude of the Emperor and the Insufferable Insolence of the Court of Spain." Over twenty thousand copies of the piece had been disposed of in three weeks. Bolingbroke decided it was time that Amhurst had help.

January 27 the *Craftsman* carried "The Vision of Camelick." For once there was no reference to "public affairs," but a "purely amusing" piece, "entirely void of Reflection upon any Person whatsoever." This denial barbed the points when Walpole's friends admitted he was clearly meant. The depiction was of the minister of an Oriental prince, "a Man dressed in a plain Habit, with a Purse of Gold in his Hand. He threw himself forward into the Room in a bluff, ruffianly Manner. A Smile or rather a Snear sat on his Countenance. His Face was bronz'd over with the Glare of Confidence. An arch Malignity leer'd in his Eye." When the people did obeisance, he "trod over their Backs without any Cosening and march'd directly up to the Throne. He opened his Purse of Gold; which he took out in Handfuls and scattered amongst the Assembly." To this attack there could be no reply. The printer and the publisher were taken up.

But Bolingbroke had just begun. The *Occasional Writer*, number one, appeared. Ambitious to be famous by his pen, his first essays had "made a good deal of Noise in the World." But "Ministers of State" paid no "Respects to the brightest Talents when" they were "misapplied." English ministers in particular "from the Days of Burleigh" to the current time rewarded those who served them best. "Like a Lawyer," he was ready to devote himself to Walpole's cause. If "Morality" clashed "with the Interest of the State," the former must be "laid aside." A minister, even in "Prosperity," could no more "subsist" without his "daily Praise" than an author without his "daily Bread." In adversity, the case was worse.

"Believe me, sir," he said, addressing the Minister, "whenever Fortune abandons you, and who knows how soon that may happen, you will find yourself in a very forlorn State. At the Name of your Successor, those Crowds that attend your Levee will vanish like Spirits at the Dawn of Day. None will remain about you but such as no other Administration will condescend to employ." Even in that sad case, the author would gladly help for a share of the fortune "Industry and Parsimony" had "raised," say fifteen or twenty thousand pounds, "a trifling Sum for so great a Service and so weighty a Prince."

Then, speaking "without a Figure": "I would not have you flatter yourself that the undisturbed Quiet you have so long enjoyed is merely owing to your own Integrity and political Merit, or to the uncommon Prosecution of Hawkers and Pamphleteers, which has been carried on by the Direction of one of your principal Instruments." This "Quiet" was due to "deep and inveterate Designs." Many were "shocked" at the "Manner" in which he had "seized" power and the "Use" he had "made of it." They thought that his "Conduct was foolish" even with "Regard to his own Interest." They were merely waiting till his "Maladministration should become so glaring as to justify their Opposition even in his Majesty's Sight." Knowing his "Presumption and Distrust," his "Boldness and Pusillanimity," his "Indiscretion and Cunning," they depended upon him to help destroy himself. Already he was attacked for the management of public funds and evaded an accounting. Could a "Minister keep his Ground long" with "no other Defence than an implied Confession of his Guilt?"

As for the country's "foreign Interests," Europe was "never . . . in greater Confusion," and Britain had undertaken such a part "as no Nation ever acted which was not betrayed, or whose Ministers were not infatuated." All of this was Walpole's fault. Commerce suffered; war was imminent; France could not be depended upon to help. Gibraltar and Minorca were in danger. As to the Pretender, the "Spirit" in the country was no "longer without Knowledge" and was turning against the Minister who raised it up. That Minister would need a writer in his behalf. "Shocking" as this account must be, it was a true report. He who made it expected an answer in the next eight days.

The answer came. Walpole himself took up the gauntlet thus thrown down. The *London Journal* (February 4) carried his reply. The "Tender" of "Service" was very "kind." Though the author "scrupled" at signing his "Name," his "masterly Strokes" revealed whose work "it was." The proffer was declined with thanks, since Walpole did not need the help. And were he "so near sinking as to catch at such a Reed," he feared he would find the boasted "Qualifications . . . as little Useful *to* a Minister" as the writer himself had found them "*in* one." Nor was this sentiment peculiar to himself. "For believe me, Dear Sir," he said, "(as hard a Task as it is) you have united the Opinions of Mankind with Regard to you, and the decent Contempt which the better sort of them express for you is as strong a Mark of Dislike as the grosser Railery of others."

For other things than the offer, thanks were due. "Your kind Information," he said, "of what is laid to my Charge in the Company you frequent (if it is not merely the Consequence of your natural Propensity for Telling) is a Mark of Favour that claims my warmest Acknowledgments. And when you next assemble that candid Body, you will oblige me in telling them, I am as far from fearing the Justice of any Parliamentary Scrutiny into my Conduct as I am of being hurt by the unjust Reflections thrown out by those whose private Envy is their only Motive for public censure; and whatever Contradictions these Gentlemen may have observed in my Character, there is one which I may venture to assure you they will never discover, which is my ever being allarmed at an Opposition from one in the Impotence of Disgrace who could never terrify me in the Zenith of his Prosperity."

Upon one other point the author owned his creed:

Power will always be fluctuating amongst the Princes of Europe; and wherever the present flow of it appears (especially in open and direct Violation of our Rights) there is our Enemy, there the proper Object of our Fears. . . . And therefore you will pardon me, sir, for still differing from you, as I have always done, in foreign Affairs; and for not thinking that when our most valuable Branches of Trade are usurped, our Possessions attacked, and our present happy Establishment in the Protestant Line threatened, without Provocation and in Defiance of the most solemn Treaties, we are in this Case to sit still and wait to see whether other Princes and States will quarrel and fight among themselves for our Interest.

In conclusion he bade defiance, turning again the ironical offer down, saying:

I know how natural it will be for a Gentleman of your restless Spirit upon this Repulse to turn the Point of your Zeal against the Breast of him in whose Defence you offered to draw it. But I shall have many fewer Apprehensions in making you my Enemy, than I should have in receiving you as a Friend; because 'tis well known, you are as harmless in one Capacity as you are dangerous in the other. . . . I must inform you too, that if you design to be very scurrilous and abusive in your Invectives; your changing your Name in Libels as often as you have done your Party Politicks will not prevent your being discovered.

The public read these papers for what they were: a challenge and an acceptance for a fight. The *London Journal* reprinted Walpole's piece the following week. As a brochure it was sold about the streets.

Bolingbroke began to fear that he had overplayed his hand. At first he described the reply as "a stiff pedantic Piece" of some "scurrilous Scribbler" meriting "decent Contempt." A week later he was less sure and set up an exaggerated man of straw at which to aim: "How great! how free! how bold! how generous!" he said. Nevertheless, three things he would agree to do: "Decency and good Manners," he would "constantly preserve" without descent to personal "abuse." "Intire Disinterestedness," he promised in the "Cause of Truth," though he knew the "Rewards" of a Right Reverend "State Writer" on Walpole's side. He would observe a "strict Impartiality." "Posterity" would depend upon the pens of such as he. False statements could "become the general Opinion of Mankind." Political papers might go "out of Date as fast as a Gazette," and still the "Mischief" last. Historians would "perpetuate" the "Slander which the Politician broached."

The ministerial writers ground their weekly grist. March 2 the Emperor gave them help. He was indignant at a charge he knew to be untrue, of conspiring to place the Pretender on the British throne, and ordered Count Palm to call with an elaborate paper saying so. The next day this statement with a supporting letter was dispersed in print. The royal speech, it said, was "made for no purpose but to excite the Nation to a Rupture and open War with the Emperor and Spain." With "unwarrantable Inferences and Pretences," manifest "Falsehood" had been told as "indisputable Facts."

The British ministers thought that what they said was true. Count Palm was told (March 4) that the memorial published was "highly injurious to his Majesty's Honour" and framed "without Regard to Truth." The accompanying letter was more "insolent" and "injurious" still. No longer tolerable as a "public Minister," he should depart the realm forthwith. Parliament was notified of what was done and voted an address. Even Pulteney joined in the applause. Other addresses were soon pouring in. The *Craftsman*, with a dig at Hoadly, said (March 13) that the Memorial was a German bishop's work.

The *British Journal* (March 11) matched in paralleled columns the *Occasional Writer's* challenge and the answer made. The purpose was that readers in a "fair and open Light" might judge themselves and thus perceive the "Superiority so evident in the Reply." Reprinted as a pamphlet, it sold for sixpence in the stalls. When Swift came over in the spring, Bolingbroke sought to have him write a piece complaining that Walpole learned by spies of what he did. The point of the "Dispute," one public writer said, was whether the "Chief Minister" was "worthy of the Trust his King and Country . . . placed in him." The *Craftsman* merely charged, he got by methods "venal and corrupt" the "Popularity" that no one denied he had.

His printer freed from court, the *Craftsman* promised in irony not to offend again. "Allusions to particular Persons," he would not use, but could he help the applications readers made? Not, said an opponent, as long as "very ingeniously" he took care to use the "archest Method to retail such Scandal" as he had a "Mind to propagate" in "Colours" that would "elude the Penalties of the Law."

Trusting to their journalists for defense, the ministers tried to do their work. A French resident noted that Gibraltar was defended by "prompt and vigorous measures," by "large and frequent armaments" that in "so short a time" could not have been supplied by "any other power in the world." Amid this work, Walpole fell ill. His enemies triumphed, but too soon. Recovering, he "thumbed his nose at them" again.

The King's imprisoned wife had died the year before. The Countess of Darlington had also passed away. Kendal alone remained. Bolingbroke tried again through her. Walpole consented that his rival have an interview. It came to naught. The King pronounced his charges "bagatelles."

The parliamentary session was drawing to a close, when the *Craftsman* announced (May 13) that henceforth it would combine its previous essays with reports of the news and issue as the *Country Journal* once a week. If reproached for becoming a "common News Paper," the reply would be, that the "unexpected Conduct of some Men" had "called up the Undertaking," and he thought himself "obliged to go through with it" even to the extent of wearing out the rest of his life to serve his country. "Besides, . . . however mean or contemptible the Business of a Journalist may have formerly been," latterly it had become a "Post of Credit and Honour." Might he not hold the "Property of a Journal *in Commendam?*"

Two days later Parliament was prorogued. The Saturday following, Amhurst began to attack. Walpole was but a "mechanical Tool" and lacked the "Affection" of the King. Money was the "great and only Rule and Sinew of his Government." "Avarice and Prodigality" were his only passions. All this in a letter from the Orient. The *British Journal* (May 23) thought perhaps a "Gloominess of Mind" due to the "Inconstancy of the Weather of the Island" with the "Inclination of Mankind" to favor "evil Report" helped in "spreading those pernicious Products of the Press that envious and disappointed Persons contrived to disturb the public Tranquility in order to bring about" their will.

Sunday, the next day, the city was lighted up. It was the King's birthday, and he was sixty-seven years old. The last of May it was announced that he would go to Germany again. At the same time in Paris, England, France, the Dutch, Spain, and the Emperor agreed on terms of peace. Ten o'clock at night, June 2, a boy was given a childish wish. Young Horace Walpole was taken to see the King. The next morning at seven his Majesty left for Greenwich, where he embarked for home.

June 10 Amhurst found a "short and faithful Abstract of the Proceedings" of Parliament the best that he could do. The *London Journal* that Saturday, as a satire on the *Craftsman*, contained the first chapter of the first book of *The Life and Actions of Mr. Dismall the true Patriot*. None ever saw the next installment of the piece.

The following Wednesday at 3 P.M., while Walpole sat in the Treasury at his desk, a messenger came to say, the King was dead. The Minister went to Chelsea to get his coach and six. To Richmond then with all the speed he could, arriving after the family was in bed. The Princess swooned, thinking that he announced her daughter's death. The Prince with undonned "breeches in his hand" scarcely believed the news.

They dressed and drove at once to Leicester House. A crowd was there to kiss the new King's hand. The Privy Council was sworn in and the proclamation signed. The ceremony was postponed till day. Beginning at ten A.M. at Leicester House, then in Leicester Square, at Charing Cross, the Temple Bar, in Wood Street, Cheapside, and at the Royal Exchange the new accession was proclaimed.

The Lord Chancellor and Newcastle were sworn the following day. The Lord Mayor and Aldermen waited on the King. Prayer was ordered made for Caroline, the first Queen after Anne's death that the clergy named. Parliament was called to meet June 27. Persons in office were asked to keep their places for a while. Fleury in France had also heard of George's death, and Horace Walpole, without awaiting word from home, was asked to go straightway to London to give assurances to George II.

When Robert Walpole asked the King's commands, he learned that Spencer Compton was the channel of the royal will. To the Speaker then he went. That inexperienced Minister wished help in drafting the documents of the day. Newcastle sent word to Townshend (June 15), just returned, that Compton would probably be the "chief man" of the reign. Walpole had conversation with the King "about the Civil List." The Minister noticed that his own levee was slim that day; the Speaker's, full. The bees were buzzing where the honey seemed to be. Perhaps he would be out a while, though he had other cards as yet to play. His wife at the first court in Leicester House had been ignored till Caroline herself gave pointed recognition as a friend.

The *Craftsman* (June 17) announced that Dr. Robert King would soon retire from practice to spend "in the Country" the "Remainder of his Days." He had acquired a "comfortable Subsistence" on which to live. The *London Journal* announced the interruption of its scheme and eulogized the King just dead. Bolingbroke wrote that day to Swift, about to start to France in search of health and surcease from his grief at Stella's pain. It was not "common sense" to go when an "opportunity for quitting Ireland for England" was so near at hand. The Viscount and his friends were busy, not idle as Swift supposed.

When Walpole went to see the King, he noticed Pulteney

at the door. But he and Caroline had come to terms, and she was working on her spouse. The Speaker of the House knew Walpole's power there and did not find it hard to turn the offered Treasury down. Exactly ten days after the news arrived of the King's death, not knowing how things stood, Swift wrote to Ireland to say, the world was "strange." His friends had made him go to court to pay respects. The ministry would "be changed"; the King must be "excessive gracious" if he forgave "the treatment of some" men.

When Parliament met, however (June 27), Walpole was still in charge. The King upon "his royal throne," wearing his "crown and regal ornaments," in broken English announced his father's death. All factions joined to vote the settlements proposed, including a hundred thousand annually for the Queen should she survive the King. July 17 the session was prorogued; August 7 the Parliament was dissolved.

The *London Journal* thought (July 1), since Walpole still held on, that all was well. The *Craftsman* had a proverb for the case. "The Race," it said, "is not to the Swift, nor the Battle to the Strong; nor yet Power to Men of Understanding, nor Favour to Men of Skill." Swift wished it told in Ireland that he never went to court. Stella lingered on, and he remained in England, being ill himself and to "avoid arrival . . . in the very midst of grief." At last he went before she died and never came to England more.

Monday, July 24, the ministers were reappointed to their places. The next day their Majesties went to Kensington for the summer. The *Craftsman's* work had just begun.[5]

[5] Coxe, *Robert Walpole*, I. 243ff.; II. 417ff.; *Horace Walpole*, I. 238ff.; Legg, *Diplomatic Instructions, France*, IV; Chance, *The Alliance of Hanover;* *Parliamentary History*, VIII. 466ff.; Boyer, *Political State*, XXIX, 499ff.; XXX. 70ff.; XXXI. 57ff.; XXXII. 1ff.; XXXIII. 27ff.; XXXIV. 175ff.; Lee, *Defoe*, III. 387ff.; Ball, *Correspondence of Swift*, III. 258ff.; *Marchmont Papers*, II. 141ff.; Torrens, *Cabinets*, I. 341ff.; Williams, *Atterbury*, II. 187ff.; Realey, *Early Opposition to Walpole*, pp. 177ff.; Cartwright, *Wentworth Papers*, pp. 457ff.; Sichel, *Bolingbroke*, II. 246ff.; Hist Mss. Com., *Portland*, VII. 409ff.; *Dropmore*, I. 84ff.; Peter Cunningham, *Letters of Horace Walpole*, I. xciiiff.; *Daily Courant*, Jan. 22, 1726; *Weekly Journal; or, British Gazetteer*, Aug. 27, 1726.

Chapter XI

BOLINGBROKE'S CAMPAIGN, 1727–1735

There is no Theme so large and so easy, no Discourse so common and so plausible as the Faults or Corruptions of Governments, the Miscarriages or Complaints of Magistrates; none so easily received and spread among good and well-meaning Men; none so mischievously raised and employed by ill, nor turned to worse and more disguised Ends.

Englishman's Journal, July, 1722.

I

TOWNSHEND RETIRES

BOLINGBROKE may have been, as Stratford said in midsummer, 1727, "the most obnoxious man in England to court and ministry," but he was scarcely the "most friendless." He went forward with his difficult campaign in the *Craftsman* to discredit his rival and drive him from office. He wrote with an anonymous pen, making suggestions from behind the scenes while longing for the time when he could speak openly again in the House of Lords. In Parliament he had to depend chiefly on the willing Wyndham and the blustering Pulteney.

Walpole felt his way with George II, whose management required a different technique from that which had succeeded with the father. The Prime Minister's superiority to his opponents arose chiefly from an ability to face facts, playing the best game he could with the cards in hand. He found the new King to be obstinate, slow-witted, tough-minded, with a talent for writing love letters. The jealousy of a small man for his prerogatives inspired habitual attendance to the duties of his office. He would not act until he understood. Fortunately, aberrations of tenderness did not interrupt a genuine fondness for his wife, who suggested to her husband with tedious repetition the implications of any question of the day. Her patient skill and devotion to him made her an indispensable ally to a Minister who lacked the time, if he had had the art, to persuade the integrity of the sovereign he tried to serve.

Walpole held a part of his following on the assumption of favor with the King. The King accepted the Minister because of his supposed strength in Parliament and ability in affairs. But Parliament was apt to distrust a leader who did not speak confidently for the King. Thus the indulgence of frequent royal whims against Walpole's advice, especially in making military appointments, tended to weaken the Minister's prestige and to lessen his ability to do the tasks in hand.

George still remembered against Newcastle the episode at the christening. His correspondence with Townshend revealed a growing interest in foreign affairs. Not that he had premeditated plans. A nobleman soon to be intimate in his court generalized from this single experience that princes "act oftener without design than other people and are insensibly drawn into both good and bad situations without knowing how." In June another nobleman consoled the Pretender that the monarch in possession was "passionate, proud, and peevish"; though he talked of "ruling by himself," he would doubtless be "governed as his father was." That government might require all the "abilities in business and dexterity in courts and parliaments" that John Hervey, Lord by courtesy, eldest son of the Earl of Bristol by his second wife, thought Walpole to have. No man, remarked the same observer, "was ever blessed with a clearer head, a quicker judgment, or a deeper insight into mankind." These superlative qualities would be put to test.

While the parliamentary elections were in progress, the *Craftsman* (August 5) urged freeholders to give "Party Distinctions" a "finishing Stroke" by electing members of "great Abilities and Estates," well disposed to the existing establishment. Mist's *Journal* suggested the next week that with his ability to create peers the King could be opposed successfully only in the House of Commons. Even there circumstances favored a minister with the King's support, blessed with the persuasive arts that accompanied political success, and able to enlist the large corporations that throve on the national credit.

Few understood better than Bolingbroke the difficulties in his campaign. But he knew as well as a writer in the *London Journal* (August 9) "that certain Terms in Religion and Politicks" exerted "upon the unthinking and passionate Part of Mankind . . . all the Force of Mechanism and Demonstration." Thus such words as "Orthodoxy, Zeal, the Church, the Court, Whig, Tory, and the like" had in time "had their Sum of Importance or Weight of Infamy and been a fruitful Source of Divisions and Hatred." This writer sought to identify the "Love of Liberty and Toleration" as native qualities in a "Whig, a Protestant, and an Englishman."

Bolingbroke had to dispute this appealing monopoly of good words. An unfortunate past made it easy to anathematize as Jacobite any identification of his present cause with "Church" or "Tory." The unsuccessful advertisement of the *Craftsman* as the *Country Journal* was an effort to reanimate Shaftesbury's term, an artful name for a group associated chiefly in opposition to the court. It was said again that the old names "Whig" and "Tory" did not signify, that the issue was between the "Patriots," who had the nation's interest at heart, and a Minister who corrupted Parliament and held the King in thrall.

This plausible campaign had several weaknesses not perhaps foreseen. Necessarily, it centered the attack upon the Minister, making his fall its chief end. But none of Walpole's opponents, Bolingbroke least of all, seemed suitable to take his place. An alternative was to deny the need for a "Prime Minister," to assert indeed the unconstitutionality of such an office. The evil designs impelling a minister to aspire to this exorbitant power were attributed to the man who had achieved the place, making the attack on him personal rather than opposition to his measures. The same logic of circumstances engendered the plea that Parliament and the electorate were corrupt and finally that the King exalted his prerogative beyond the allowed limits. A remedial appeal to the public involved Bolingbroke in doctrines scarcely consistent with the thoughts of a champion of Church and Queen, but plausible enough for a patriot seeking the welfare of the country. There was one further doubtful premise: while laboring to manufacture feeling against his rival, he had to assume that the machinery was at fault if the maker of the louder noise did not prevail.

George II and his Queen were crowned October 4 with the conventional ceremony. Two days later they were invited to share the honors of Lord Mayor's Day. Followers of Walpole were still trying to elect friendly members of Parliament from the City. The delegation was divided in the end, two members tending to be for and two against the Minister. The situation was too uncertain, the stake of wealth too great to risk in party strife. A writer in the *Craftsman* (October 7) estimated that London and Middlesex paid a seventh of all "the Land Tax of Great Britain and more than a proportionate share of all the other Duties and Taxes." "The vast Trade and Commerce of the Metropolis" largely enabled the provinces to pay their part.

The Parliament finally chosen differed little from that which it replaced. The considerable expense of the elections was not chiefly evidence that members or constituencies were corrupt. A "Seat in the House of Commons," said a writer in the *British Journal* (October 21), had became "Part of a Man's Character, and a sort of necessary Appurtenance to a great Fortune." Men did not go to Parliament to seek wealth, but spent money to obtain seats which they filled with "Integrity and Honour." Recalling Sacheverell's time, the same writer admitted that people "poisoned by an ill Education" might be "abused by crafty Writers" and moved by infatuation to fill the benches of the House with "Fox Hunters" who would "holloa" and not debate. Anything to prevent "this Mischief" seemed to him to be "wise and wholesome." The *Craftsman* (October 28) attributed the indecisive result in the City to the influence of the "Bank of England, the South Sea Company, the East India Company" and the government offices that had to do with revenue.

Before the Parliament met for its first short session Mist had paid his fine and given security for good behavior. Richard Francklin had been tried for printing the *Craftsman* of the previous March 24. Amhurst had explained (December 9) that the reference was to Russia, not England, enforcing his apology a week later with ironical insistence that it could not have been the latter, which knew no "such creature" as a "Prime Minister." A new writer in the *British Journal* began on the ministerial side a campaign that was not to end while Walpole was in office.

His antecedents are unknown; his personality, shadowy; his name, uncertain. He appears both as "Arnold" and "Arnall" in the controversies of the day. Pushing himself forward as a supporter of the ministry, he became one of the most active journalists in his time. He now began to write as "Roger Manly of Lincoln's Inn, Esq.," in the *British Journal; or, Censor,* which began a new series January 20, 1728. In "Religion" he was "an honest Man and a Christian . . . an Advocate of Moderation"; in politics, "a true Englishman and a good Subject."

Onslow was elected Speaker. The King, whom crowds acclaimed on his way to the House, announced pleasure at the prospect of peace. The debates were on hackneyed subjects: reduction of the army, the pay of Hessian troops, the state of the public debt. At the end of May the session closed with royal congratulation for "zeal and unanimity." The chief activities and successes of the opposition that year were out of doors. Early in the winter the exiled Atterbury heard from his son-in-law that Walpole seemed to be "better established every day." If Spain would come to terms he would be "certainly Prime Minister for life."

When Ephraim Chambers completed his *Encyclopedia* and dedicated it to the King, Walpole presented his Majesty with a set. Thomas Gordon began to publish his translation of Tacitus, dedicated to the Minister himself as "the first who promoted it." Since Tacitus was a "Man of Affairs, a great Minister," the honor was appropriate. Walpole's long experience with men in public life enabled him to see "far into their

Bent and Foibles" and made him "conversant with the Mysteries and primary Operations of Government." He could appreciate Tacitus, since men were to be known "not by Theories taken up in Closets, but by Commerce with Men."

In his long prefatory essays Gordon revealed insight concerning politics. Reflecting habits as a journalist, he used aphorism and paradox rather than sustained exposition. He dwelt on the routine of princes and ministers and the reactions of people with whom they dealt, paying little attention to doctrines or systems. He had read Hobbes, Locke, and their kind, but the getting and keeping of power and the behavior of the ruled he thought to be of greater interest. The "People," he said, "are the Materials of Government, their Protection its End." He thought the preservation of their loyalty to rulers to be the central problem of the day and recognized the activity of religious leaders as a source of discontent. Going to the heart of that question, while reserving freedom of worship as an individual right, he favored the dependence of the clergy upon the government. The evil of "Popery" was not its superstition, but its power.

Like most contemporary observers of English politics, Gordon was intrigued by the use of names and shibboleths in frequent appeals to the emotions of the populace. He described the "Court" as a "great Exchange, where one or a few" had "Favours to dispose of, where many" resorted "to procure them, and where all therefore" strove "to outdo in pleasing every one" with the "same Aim." Nothing, he thought, kept "the Passions more awake than the Pursuit of Power." The people formed "by Habit and Direction," were what they were "made": "cruel and merciful, constant and fickle, fond of their Benefactors, ungrateful to their Friends, very patient, very furious, ungovernable and easy to be governed, greatly given to Change and greatly afraid of it, apt to love extravagantly, apt to hate implacably."

Schemes depending upon "the continual Rest or Suppression of the Passions" seemed to him to be "foolish and fantastical." But once "popular Opinion" had "consecrated a Man or a Name," actions associated therewith, "however wicked or foolish," were consecrated too. The force of the resulting "Authority" was "irresistible and infatuating," causing "Reason and Truth" to give way to "Prejudice and Words." "It is incredible," he said, "what Stubbornness and Force there is in the established Names, Customs, and Forms, which are often harder to destroy than Realities and Substances; and Signs and Titles frequently remain when the Things signified and denominated by them are gone."

In these same months, though friends regretted it, Pope in *The Dunciad* vented his ill humor on writers of his time, wasting poetical talent in quotable lines designed to poison the stream of literary history and mar the reputations of men he did not like. His friend, Gay, after years of obsequious court, had disdained in October as beneath his dignity the modest sinecure of Gentleman Usher to the Princess Louise. Friends who persuaded him to forego this provision, amply commensurate with any merits he could plead, were under obligation to help avert the disaster they invited to his hopes.

An opportunity came in the last days of January, shortly after the new Parliament met. Rich produced at the theater in Lincoln's Inn Fields *The Beggar's Opera,* which, after some years of labor, the poet had completed in the previous autumn. Inspiration for the characters came from Newgate rather than from environs of the court. Gay supplied words for sixty-odd songs set to familiar native tunes. Their general appeal is seen in the frequent successes of the piece when produced in later generations and even in other lands. There were, of course, as in most contemporary plays, topical allusions addressed to controversies of the day. These helped to win support the playhouse and the author sought.

Leaders of the opposition were on hand the first night to help to a good start. Ministers were present and joined in the applause. Walpole bowed in recognition of a stroke the audience applied to him. A run of a fortnight tempted Gay's friends to use the *Opera's* popularity as a weapon against the ministry. Arbuthnot in the *Craftsman* (February 17) suggested ironically that it merited the attention of the government on which obviously it was by "innuendo" an attack. Interpretations of specific passages gave them a turn the author little meant, inviting opposition wits to use their ingenuity for transforming a successful entertainment into a vehicle of political abuse. It was, they said, a "patriotic," "British Opera" and thus attracted patronage from the "outlandish" rival offerings in Drury Lane. With a robber as its hero, none could doubt the application meant. Thenceforth none who could read had time to doubt. Effective repetition made the points. By spring an opposition versifier boasted that none could "cope" with "Danvers, Swift, and Pope," and if "they could . . . they'd yield to Polly Peachum." By summer a writer in Mist's (July 6) was repeating the fiction that Gay failed of "Reward from Court" because suspected of "having written a Lampoon on Walpole." The writer commended *The Beggar's Opera* as "encouraging Morality and Patriotism" and as "an Antidote to Italian Opera."

Supporters of the ministry began to doubt whether it was wholesome for a thief to get "drunk and die" as a stimulus to mirth. A court preacher suggested that the performances in playhouses encouraged knights of the road. When Gay, by a spurt of industry, got ready a second part, incorporating frankly the attack on Walpole which his friends had insinuated into the first, that Minister declined to be represented on the stage for another season as a robber, and the Lord Chamberlain forbade the performance.

The author's friends made up his loss by subscribing to a published edition. The Duchess of Queensbury, venturing to solicit subscriptions in the royal drawing room, was forbidden (February 27, 1729) to come to court. She retorted saucily her surprise and pleasure at "so agreeable a command." The poet was deprived of his quarters in Whitehall and became a protégé of the Duchess and her husband. The latter was succeeded as Admiral of Scotland by the Earl of Stair.[1]

Another topic out of doors was the debt. Friends of Wal-

----

[1] This interpretation of contemporary reaction to *The Beggar's Opera* is based in part on unpublished papers prepared in my seminar by Messrs. J. C. Adams and E. C. Coleman.

pole insisted that it was less than in 1715. Pulteney and the *Craftsman* alleged that there had been no reduction since 1720. Thereupon, Roger Manly in the *British Journal* began to emphasize the personal more in his attacks on Pulteney. A contributor to the *London Journal* (February 17) enforced the same point in general terms. A man changing sides in a dispute might dwell on the "Pleasure of Revenge" until this "Passion" became a "Fury," with "Nothing so outrageous that it" did "not presume to justify." An observer in the less partisan *Weekly Journal* thought (February 24) that a "Stranger" visiting the coffee-houses and observing the "self-confident Front, solemn Air, and magisterial Tone" of critics of the ministers would imagine every "Board . . . fill'd with Statesmen impatient to display their exquisite Talents in the Service of their Country." That same Saturday the *Craftsman* explained that "Fear" might hinder the resignation of a "first Minister, though glutted with Corruption."

Supporters of Walpole replied as best they could and hindered their opponents when they found a chance. Robert Raikes offended Parliament in March by printing its proceedings in his *Gloucester Journal.* Edward Cave had sent the item from the Post Office in London and was prosecuted as well. The next month he was reprimanded on his knees and released after he had paid a fine. A writer in the *London Journal* (March 30) charged that Pulteney, though not himself a Jacobite, by "a fallacious Account of the national Debt" had done the "dirty Work" of that faction, thus increasing "Animosities and reëstablishing that Interest, which was before ruin'd and dwindling to nothing." The *British Journal* complained the same day of "the ungenerous and unmanly Appeals to the common People of England" with which the *Craftsman* was habitually filled. The writer consoled himself that the circulation of Mist's *Journal* exceeded that of the *Craftsman.*

April 12 the King issued a proclamation against running races on Sunday. A few days afterward he made a short progress to Newmarket. Students and scholars at Cambridge shouted *Vivat Rex.* Richard Bentley made a speech in the Senate House. His Majesty donated two thousand pounds to the university. Bells rang in other towns and villages through which he passed.

On the day the King set out (April 23), Philip Stanhope, Lord Chesterfield, left for The Hague. The next day William Stanhope started to join Horace Walpole and Poyntz at the Congress of Soissons. The Queen went to see the collection of Sir Hans Sloane in Bloomsbury Square.

Behind the scenes ambitious supporters were blaming Walpole for the disappointment of their hopes. It was impolitic to explain that the King would not always accept the Minister's advice. Lieutenants tried to allay suspicion by round assertions, where explanations could not be made. The *British Journal* (May 25), reflecting that "Ministers, tho' they always prefer, yet seldom choose," admonished that "Governors must indulge the Humours and submit to the Necessities of the Time, or Government" would "soon be at an End."

This weekly kept up its work after Parliament rose. A "plausible and popular Clamour against Perquisites and Corruption," it recalled (June 1), had "removed the Duke of Marlborough and the Earl of Godolphin" and sent Walpole to the Tower. People were "prone to Suspicions," it observed a fortnight later. The public was in "iminent Peril when unreasonable Fears and violent Uneasinesses" arose. "Once Men . . . let loose their Passions, none" could "foretell what Extravagance" would "ensue or how the Rage" would be restrained. "Discord" was "worse than Tyranny."

In the same strain a week later it recalled the "wonderful Effect the *good old Cause* had formerly on the Minds of Multitudes." The word "Patriot" was now used for the same purpose. "The common People love to be thought important," it philosophized the next week, "the more an Incendiary expatiates on the darling Topicks of the Rabble, the more readily does he inflame their Passions."

Four days after the royal family went to Hampton Court for the summer, Canon Stratford thought (July 6) that the ministers might "very justly look upon themselves as absolute," since nothing at home seemed likely to "give them any disturbance." A writer in the *London Journal* (July 13) agreed, but admitted by implication that the opposition made the louder noise out of doors. Among the ancients, neither a "Statesman" nor a "Philosopher" deferred to the "Judgment of the Populace." The "Mob" was "like a great tractable Monster led about by a popular Scribbler where and how" he pleased.

In other places the scene that summer changed. Horace Walpole, on whose sturdy common sense and loyalty his brother more and more depended in foreign affairs, was beginning to distrust Fleury, whom he suspected of making overtures to Spain. John Armstrong in July was sent to Dunkirk to see whether the Treaty of Utrecht was obeyed. The Earl of Waldegrave, who succeeded Walpole at Paris, did not get on with Chauvelin, the new French Foreign Minister. The Congress that met at Soissons in June dawdled away, none raising the troublesome questions that brought it there. With a nose for danger in foreign matters, Bolingbroke thought he saw a chance.

July 20 the *Craftsman* wondered whether the Congress at Soissons would do anything about Dunkirk. In the same issue another writer just returned from Norfolk marveled at Walpole's "Palace" there. "A particular Description of the Magnificence of the House, Gardens, Stables; as well as the great Variety of fine Pictures, the vast Quantity of massy Plate, and other costly Furniture would fill a Volume folio." A king could not afford such opulence. A month later the writer thought that with an "ambitious, rapacious, and corrupt," also withal a "lying Minister," the "unhappy Prince" was in a state of "Darkness and Confusion."

Meanwhile two exiles longed for home. Atterbury assured his son-in-law (August 25) that he now "had nothing to do with the Pretender" nor would have any more. That Prince had "so managed his business" that it was impossible to do him service. The Bishop wished to be free from the "suspicion" of trying. Some weeks earlier Wharton told Atterbury that it was "as well" to think him a "Turk" as a "Catholic." But when his profession of "repentance" to Horace Walpole was not received as he had hoped, he went his curious way again. Mist's *Journal* carried a piece from him (August 24) alleging that Walpole had suppressed the will of George I which branded his son as illegitimate.

The printer fled the country to avoid arrest. The *Craftsman* denied (September 4) sympathy with Mist, alleging the "true and only Design" of his paper to be "to expose the Characters of wicked Ministers antient and modern." For penitence and services rendered (September 5), the King granted pardon to the Earl of Mar. Two days later the royal family went from Hampton Court to Windsor to reside and hunt.

Ministerial writers, now that Mist had quit, attacked the *Craftsman* with new hope. One in the *London Journal* (September 28) described the paper as written with "some Wit but greater Malice." For two years the author had libeled the "Government and Ministry," "wrapt in Fable and Allegory . . . intrenched in Parable and Mystery," using "Scraps of Plays, Farces, Beggar's Operas, and Songs," ransacking "ancient and modern History for Parallels." There were also "Insinuations, Innuendoes, little Satyrs upon Families, Marriages, Houses, Lanthorns, bodily Defects, want of Teeth, not Bowing gracefully, Dancing gentilely, or Dressing politely." All was done with "some Learning, Invention, Wit, and Language," but the writer "seldom reasoned and never proved." Though he made "Men of Sense laugh" and "Fools admire," he "never convinced the Understanding or satisfied the Judgment of an unprejudiced Man." But through all these "Labyrinths," the ministerial writer meant to follow where the *Craftsman* led.

On that very day Mist's reappeared as Fog's, the author writing from the "temperate Side of Elysium," having died of an "appoplectick Fit." A week later the *British Journal*, though emphasizing the freedom of the press, quoted passages from Steele, Gordon, and even the *Craftsman* to prove that this "Blessing" might "become a Curse" when "prostituted to the worst Purposes and made the Engine of mighty Mischief." One might "reason on public Affairs" without attacking "Persons" or firing the "Passions."

The *Craftsman* defended its methods (October 26) on the

ground that an "overgrown Criminal" beyond the reach of "ordinary Justice" might feel the "Lash of Satire." Lacking a "Conscience" to be aroused, his "Fear" might "sting him with a Dread of Punishment; cover him with Shame; and render his Actions odious to all honest Minds." This method of attack might "at least" make "more cautious and perhaps at last bring down the *great,* haughty, and *secure* Criminal within the Reach and Grasp of Justice; at least no other Method" was "more likely to effect it."

In November a country physician bequeathed to Thomas Gordon a substantial estate, enhancing his income as the husband of Trenchard's widow. The testator had admired his writings and had seen him once casually at the Grecian when in town. The second volume of his Tacitus was yet to come, but Gordon sometimes sent essays to the weeklies on his patron's side. Perhaps the *London Journal* was now again the medium that he favored most. Bolingbroke, in the same month (November 23), began as "Raleigh" in the *Craftsman* to attack the ministry's foreign policy. So sanguine was he of success, he prophesied the fall of Walpole in a year. Armies and taxes had increased, he said, while trade was interrupted and manufactures had declined. A timid policy abroad would promise no relief.

On one point the King was moved to yield to criticisms which the *Craftsman* did not make alone. At half past three in the afternoon, December 3, the Prince of Wales arrived at Harwich. The next evening at St. James's he gave assurance that as his father's first subject he would "set an example" for the rest. The public was relieved and glad to have him come, not knowing the example he would set. His father had postponed the event and faced it now because afraid that Parliament might force his hand.

Raleigh would not take note of writers on the other side, but as "John Trot" he soon confessed that the *London* and *British Journals* could not be ignored. He salved his vanity by the assumption that Walpole and Hoadly were writing on the other side. He recurred to the thought that Gibraltar might be given up. Thus when Horace Walpole and William

Stanhope returned for the Christmas holidays and the session of Parliament that would ensue, the press was full of questions uppermost in their minds.

Inspired by Walpole, Roger Manly wrote an essay (January 4, 1729) which John Percival, a peer in the Irish list, thought "a clear, succinct account of the grounds of the present disputes" in Europe and worthy "to be kept and read more than once." Hoadly (January 20), in *A Defence of the Enquiry . . . occasioned by the Paper published in the Country Journal or Craftsman, January 4, 1729*, denied that he had written since his former piece, which Bolingbroke had attacked. He disagreed with that writer and thought the "worst" that could be said of the ministers was an unwillingness to plunge Europe into a war if it could be avoided. His pamphlet came out the day that Parliament met.

The King and his ministers had to speak in a defensive tone. Dilatoriness at Vienna and Madrid, they said, was "greatly encouraged" by "hopes" of "Discontents and Divisions" in England inspired thence. To convince foreign courts of unanimity at home was not an easy task. A ministerial writer thought (January 25) that the authors of the *Craftsman* had "the peculiar Happiness of an Invention constantly fertile of fallacious Insinuations to abuse their fellow Subjects and to distress the Administration." The *London Journal* (February 1) could only suggest the wisdom of "political Faith" in the ministry, since "private Judgment" would do no good and might "hurt the Publick" in a case where the "hardest Thing in the World" was to be certain of "Facts."

The *Craftsman* (February 8) was pardonably confident. The fall of Walpole might not come "immediately," but was on its way. In Francis Osborne's history of the reign of Elizabeth, Raleigh discovered that Queen to have had no "Blunderers in Office" during her contest with Spain. But in the last years of Elizabeth and the first of James there was a Treasurer, called "King Robin" at the time, "personally insolent" to the sovereign, "weak and scandalous" in policy, who instigated a new order of knighthood and corrupted Parliament.

The ministers were less easy to defend because of lack of unity among themselves. Newcastle suggested to Stanhope at Soissons (April 15) that Townshend had for a month engaged in a negotiation with France, kept secret from the rest. That Secretary seemed almost to have forgotten that Stanhope was abroad. As proof of his own mindfulness, Newcastle suggested a correspondence with Robert Walpole and Horace, withheld from Poyntz, who was ignorant of Townshend's lack of harmony with his colleagues.

The session dragged its usual length with inevitable debates on the size of the army and the Hessian troops. Merchants complained of Spanish "Depredations." The opposition succeeded with a bill against corruption in elections. Walpole defended reluctantly an appropriation of £115,000 to pay arrears upon the Civil List. General James Oglethorpe reported on conditions in the gaols. At the prorogation (May 14), the King announced that he would go to Hanover, leaving the Queen in charge at home.

With the King and Townshend out of the country, Bolingbroke hammered at the ministers. Fleury was said (June 21) to have confided to Berwick a remark of the British Ambassador that unless the Cardinal would "patch up a Peace . . . before December" the English ministers would "be hanged before Christmas." Walpole, however, had not quit the fight. The *Craftsman's* printer was taken up. Chesterfield at The Hague, busy defending his extravagance as intended to reflect credit on his country and denied coveted permission to go to Hanover, was instructed to send duplicates to Newcastle of letters to Townshend and his Majesty. The latter Secretary of State was threatening to resign, though Bishop Gibson warned him that he might not enjoy imagined "ease and satisfaction . . . in private life." Walpole was finding it harder since his sister's death to work smoothly with her noble spouse.

At the suggestion of Horace Walpole, he sent Stanhope to Spain to bring matters to a point, promising the peerage that the King had hitherto withheld. Newcastle assured Stanhope that Sir Robert had read Horace's letter to the Queen. In the same week her Majesty dined with the Minister at his Chelsea house. Stanhope reached terms with Spain in the Treaty of Seville, leaving the Emperor to be dealt with apart. Chesterfield was then given permission to visit the King, but thought it not worth while (September 2), since his Majesty would soon be coming back. He confided to Townshend, however (September 26), that eighteen months in Holland inspired a wish to spend the winter at home. There were rumors that Townshend as Lord President would no longer have a hand in foreign affairs.

To capitalize success abroad and counteract divisions in their family, ministers got ready to make more effective appeals to the public. Congreve, Steele, and Boyer had died that year. The *Political State* went on, supported by an association of gentlemen chiefly interested in the colonies and trade. Roger Manly withheld his pen from the *British Journal,* which for a few months more the printer tried in vain to keep afloat. As "Francis Walsingham," a good Elizabethan name, he now sent weekly essays to the coffee-houses on Thursdays as the *Free Briton,* unsupported by news and advertisements. James Pitt, a schoolmaster from Norfolk, took charge of the *London Journal* in the same way that Amhurst had the *Craftsman.* He provided an essay himself unless one came from Gordon or some other hand. Appropriating the name of the Elizabethan historian as a pseudonym, writers in Cato's earlier medium began to publish as "Francis Osborne" some of the ablest journalistic essays of the time. Even "Orator" Henley was encouraged to harry the opposition in his *Hyp Doctor.* Francklin was tried again and this time found not guilty. Lamenting the death of Steele (March 15), the *Craftsman* was reminded of Dunkirk and Sir Richard's earlier fears.

Osborne was sure (November 29) the *Craftsman* would not like the Treaty of Seville, having been convinced that "it would not be made." The conductors of that paper, he said, though knowing the merits of Walpole, pursued him "in weekly Libels with . . . unprecedented Malice and unexampled Fury." The refurbished *Political State* countered with statistics (December) the allegations of decay in trade. The unusual storms in that month kept in the port of London 436 ships loaded with exports for all parts of the world. In an ensuing epidemic of "Colds and Fevers," in which it was estimated that 150,000 were ill and 900 died, pamphlets appeared for and against the Treaty of Seville, opponents prophesying a break with the Emperor. A brochure entitled *A Hue and Cry after a Coachman,* dropped in St. James's Park (January 5, 1730) and shown to the Queen when walking there, described Walpole as having "Consummate Impudence," a "brazen Face," "full bodied with a brown Complexion," lacking a "Tooth in the fore Part of his upper Jaw," with "dirty Hands, light fingered, a heavy, slouchy, clumsy, waddling Gait, an affected Toss of the Head, a supercilious, sneering, grinning Look, . . . a malicious, vindictive, sanguinary Nature." If found he was to be brought to the "Axe and Block upon Tower Hill or to the Gibbet and Halter in Tyburn Road" and "dealt with" as he deserved.

In the midst of this bluster some of Pope's hangers-on launched the *Grub Street Journal* (January 8), though the poet soon lost interest. In his speech to Parliament, five days later, the King announced that the Treaty of Seville defeated "hopes of enemies" both abroad and at home, and he proposed a reduction of the army by five thousand men. Though such time-servers as George Bubb Dodington wondered whether it was prudent to enlist against Walpole, Hervey, having returned from abroad in these weeks and facing the necessity of giving up either Pulteney or the Minister, against the advice of his father, threw in his lot with Walpole. In truth, the crude attacks on that Minister and scandals circulated against the Queen betrayed a disappointment of opposition hopes.

It was necessary to change to Dunkirk a campaign intended to turn on Gibraltar. Bolingbroke financed investigations in advance. With much secret preparation, Wyndham moved (February 10) an inquiry into the state of the nation. Walpole's lieutenants wished to vote the motion down. Thinking he knew a sounder way, the Minister obtained delay until further information could be had. When the subject was renewed, and Wyndham made the motion planned (February 27), expecting Sandys to second it, one of Walpole's lieutenants, with the connivance of the chair, interposed another motion of similar purport without the sharper criticisms of the King of France. Immediately another ministerial cohort seconded. Opposition leaders raved in vain. The investigation was in ministerial hands. Before the committee was ready to report, the King of France agreed to remedy the conditions of which complaint was made. Hervey wrote a pamphlet on the ministerial side. Horace Walpole informed Stanhope, now Lord Harrington, that the "formidable inquiry that was to have confounded the ministry" had "ended in noise and smoke."

Four days later Newcastle emphasized to the new Lord that "Dunkirk Day" had quite "demolished the opposition in the House of Commons." Otherwise things at home went on well, though every day Townshend was more resolved to quit. Harrington himself might get the place. Walpole had taken pains to make it clear to members of the House that Bolingbroke had concerted with Wyndham, Pulteney, and Sandys the motion it had cost him so much pains to thwart. Newcastle complained to Walpole (March 24) that, between threats of quitting, Townshend tried to do Harrington ill offices with the King and said that Hanover was given up. But with "some strong assurances" on the latter point, they need not be afraid.

The *Craftsman* was again reduced to the complaint that Walpole was a "Prime Minister," whom it was futile to attack in "full Power" with "Vollies of Paper only." He had corrupted Parliament and had the favor of the King. He dealt in the funds with "loaded Dice" and thus became rich without the necessity of filching public money. "Great Officers of the Crown used to act independently of other Ministers," each in his several department. The constitution was thus impaired.

Osborne in the *London Journal* was safely left to cope with questions such as these. His views on history and the constitution were more akin to facts. "Powers which are *distinct*," he said (April 11), "and have a Negative on each other should also have a mutual Dependence and mutual Expectations."

Buzzing busybodies, such as Dodington, were again saying (April 17) that when the session ended Townshend would resign and Walpole retire to the Lords. The King tolerated the Minister only as a man of business, liking better Wilmington. The *Craftsman* insisted (April 18) that Walpole's name must be left out of any "Act of Grace," and complained that "Cabinet Councils" were "a Device of foreign Extraction and unknown to the Laws of the Land." Horace Walpole, notifying Waldegrave (April 21) of his prospect of serving at Paris under Harrington as Secretary of State, added that the session was coming to a "glorious conclusion." Newcastle (April 23) found himself, Harrington, and Henry Pelham under "great obligations" to the "Friendship" of Walpole, "not forgetting Horace." Hanover had been Townshend's "great merit"; the rest were represented to the King "as wanting zeal." The Duke had "purged" himself to his Majesty, who now proposed to depend upon him and Harrington for the electorate. "God bless Sir Robert," he prayed at the end, " 'tis all his doing; and let us in return resolve to make him as happy as we can." This "union and concert" of the new minister with his older colleagues, said Horace the same day, had "surprised and struck their enemies more than anything that could happen."

By May Day there was "so great a clam" that Horace had never seen the like. Bolingbroke (May 6) was anxious about his wife, who had gone to Paris in search of health. If she could not live at Dawley, his new country estate, all his "measures" for a "settlement" there would be "of small advantage or pleasure" in his "future plans of life." The King closed the session (May 15) with a complaint of "incendiaries" who from a "spirit of envy and discontent" labored "by scandalous libels to alienate the affections" of his subjects, filling "their minds with groundless jealousies and unjust complaints." Townshend went immediately to Norfolk. Hervey took up residence at court as Vice Chamberlain in Harrington's room. Chesterfield became Lord Steward, a place which Carteret on quitting Ireland had refused. Newcastle was satisfied.

But Osborne found that (May 30) the town still swarmed "with State Mountebanks, political Quacks, and reforming Vermin; who without a Shilling in their pockets to buy a Dinner" wrote "Satyrs upon the Age," crying "aloud for Orthodoxy in the Church and against Corruption in the State." The *Craftsman* was the vehicle of these cries. Eight or ten thousand copies were circulated each week through the kingdom, "insinuating by various Ways into the Minds of the People that the Legislature of the Nation" was "bribed and corrupted . . . that the King's Ministers, sometimes as Blunderers, at other Times as crafty, designing Men, . . . by cunningly distributing Places and Pensions" were "betraying the Rights of Subjects." As for himself, he thought the people might have "too much" as well as "too little Power." As long as "Power" and "Property" were in the same hands there was no great "Reason to fear." [2]

II

WALPOLE HALTED

Though things were quieter at home, unless the Emperor would come to terms, the King would not easily agree to the new deal abroad. Bolingbroke, encamping for a siege, extracted from Rapin's history suitable incidents for Amhurst to purvey in the *Craftsman* as from "Humphrey Oldcastle" when there was nothing of immediate account. But Osborne had studied history too and countered Oldcastle that summer at every point. The business of the *Craftsman* was not history, he said (August 29), but "Defamation," and he did that "ill Thing very well."

[2] In addition to citations in the text: John, Lord Hervey (Croker's ed.), *Memoirs*, I. 8ff.; Stanhope, *History*, II. Appendix, pp. xxxiiiff.; Coxe, *Robert Walpole*, II, 517ff.; *Horatio Walpole*, I. 295ff.; Lord Ilchester, *Henry Fox, Lord Holland*, I. 28ff.; *Suffolk Papers*, I. 236ff.; Hist. Mss. Com., *Portland*, VII. 450ff.; *Various*, II. 411ff.; *Carlisle*, pp. 55ff.; *Egmont Diary*, I. 7ff.; III. 323; Boyer, *Political State*, XXXIV. 152ff.; XXXV. 286ff.; XXXVI. 79ff.; XXXVIII. 82ff.; XL. 496ff.; Sykes, *Gibson*, pp. 134ff.; Williams, *Atterbury*, II. 264ff.; *Parliamentary History*, VIII. 630ff.; Legg, *Diplomatic Instructions to France, 1727–1744*, Preface; Torrens, *Cabinets*, I. 378ff.; Bonamy Dobree, *Letters of Chesterfield*, II. 85ff.; Sichel, *Bolingbroke*, II. 526ff.; I. S. Leadam, *Political History of England, 1702–1760*, pp. 339ff.

The *Craftsman* interrupted the history now and then to advocate the repeal of the Riot Act, to lament the decay of trade, and to shudder at the prospect of substituting an excise on certain goods for the land tax. The *Political State* began to carry monthly lists of exports and imports through the port of London, exclaiming in September, "and yet NO TRADE!" Bolingbroke found comfort (September 5) that whereas when the *Craftsman* first appeared there was "universal Quiet. . . . Few People enquired; fewer grumbled; none clamoured; all acquiesced. Now the Humour of the Nation" had "altered." Every man inquired with "Eagerness," examined "with Freedom," and generally took a more vibrant interest in affairs.

When the noble journalist (October 16) described Richard II as a King in the hands of evil ministers, Francklin was arrested again, though the *Craftsman* announced the next week a determination to continue the essays, using "the Authority of the best Historians." The reigns of Henry VI and Edward IV were made to illustrate (November 14) a faction raised by a powerful minister and a Queen. A fortnight later, the journalist denied that the ministers were justified in assuming a present application of these essays. "I have used the utmost Precaution," he said, "(consistent with my *general Design*) to avoid such Imputation," which was true enough. He congratulated the young Henry VIII the next week for dismissing his father's ministers, "the *most hated,* and the *most justly* hated Men of the whole Kingdom." Unfortunately, they were succeeded by Wolsey, who knew how to "insinuate without the Air of *advising;* and how to receive all *his own Suggestions* back from his *Master* in the Style of *Orders,* with the utmost Demonstration of implicit Submission to his Judgment and absolute Resignation to his Will."

Walsingham published weekly essays on the ministerial side. Osborne had the sounder history, but the applications of Oldcastle were now too sharp to bear. The *Daily Courant* began (January 1, 1731) to open its columns to essays, one complaining that the *Craftsman* had "for a Course of Years exasperated the Populace against the Administration," taxing "Parliament with the utmost Degree of Corruption," and thus a "Thousand different Clamours" were "set on Foot at once." The next day the *Craftsman* addressed the patron of the "shameless Crew" who wrote on the other side:

> Are you not *one* whose Measure of Folly and Iniquity is full; who can neither hold nor quit his Power with Impunity: and over whose Head the long-gathering Cloud of national Vengeance is ready to burst? . . . When next you meditate Revenge on your *Adversaries,* remember this Truth. The Laws must be destroy'd before they can suffer or you escape.

In the same issue was a fictitious letter purporting to announce from The Hague a pending treaty with the Emperor, recognizing the Pragmatic Sanction. This premature publication endangered the success of the negotiation that was under way.

Francklin and the publisher of the *Craftsman* were placed under arrest. Even the "hawkers" who sold the paper were taken up. Sir William Yonge got ready an anonymous pamphlet, *Sedition and Defamation Displayed,* with a dedication, addressed to the patrons of the *Craftsman,* in which Hervey identified Bolingbroke and Pulteney as "united in the strictest Friendship, Confidence, and Intimacy, . . . Associates in the great Work of demolishing (not Dunkirk) but the present Ministry." Yonge objected to personal scurrilities on the other side and could not help "pitying a Man of Sense . . . reduced so low as to be capable of so much Meanness as to mention on any Occasion the loss of a Tooth or the ungenteel Cock of a Hat as an Objection to a Minister."

All the conversation in London, wrote a correspondent of the *Eccho, or Edinburgh Weekly Journal* (January 14), was on the "great Crisis" in affairs. If the rumored accommodation with the Emperor or a general pacification had a basis of truth, it might redound to Walpole's credit. India stock went down six per cent. the previous Saturday on a report that the Minister and Newcastle were out.

In this troubled atmosphere Edward Cave perceived an unexploited market for goods which could be had on every hand.

The proprietors of the *Political State* since Boyer's death seemed unaware of the art with which he kept that compendium alive so long. At the end of January, 1731, appeared the first number of the *Gentleman's Magazine; or, Monthly Intelligencer,* in which was collected a "View" of "all the Pieces of Wit, Humour, or Intelligence daily offer'd to the Public in the Newspapers . . . of late so multiply'd as to render it impossible, unless a Man makes it a Business, to consult them all" and also "other Matters of Use or Amusement" that might be sent in. On the cover, identifying the arsenal from which it drew, were the titles of forty-five papers, five of them appearing every day. The attractive contents were the weekly essays reprinted in abstract or in full.

The Society for the Reformation of Manners had prosecuted in the previous year 251 persons for "lewd and disorderly Practices," 30 for keeping "baudy Houses," and 424 for "exercising their Trade and Callings on the Lord's Day." But the manners of journalists toward each other were apparently not reformed at all. When the *Craftsman* called Walpole a "Mock Minister," Osborne replied (January 16), that a "Mock Patriot" was just as bad or worse. Continuing, he reflected: "Such a Liberty was never taken with any Government, nor is it possible that a Government can long subsist which is made the *constant* and *standing* Jest of every Buffoon-Writer, and weekly represented to the People as the *weakest* and *worst* Administration in the World." Let the Craftsman thank God he did not live in the reign of Elizabeth, of whom he was so fond; she would have hung him "as he wrote."

Under the *Craftsman's* pseudonym appeared, January 20, *A Proper Reply to a late Scurrilous Libel, intitled Sedition and Defamation Displayed.* Hervey was taken to be the author of the previous piece. The reply was a personal attack, meant to humiliate and sting, inspiring from Pope some of his bitterest and least worthy lines. Because he used paint to restore the color which ill health took from his slender face, Hervey was dubbed "Miss Fainlove," a "delicate Hermaphrodite," and described as ready to "betray private Confidences," a "Circu-

lator of Tittle-Tattle, a Bearer of Tales, a Teller of Fibs."
Walpole was called "an Adventurer," with "Talents scarce
equal to the Truth, and Morals unworthy of the Lowest." He
was vain of his parts and boasted his pleasures, but "never
gained either Man or Woman but as he paid for them." He
corrupted and was "supported by the Corrupt"; he plundered
and protected "Plunderers." His brother Horace was a "Buffoon . . . turned out of Company for being saucy, ill bred,
noisy, scurrilous, obscene; the Jest and Scorn of Mankind."
Hervey was only a "pretty little Scribbler," a "dapper little
Author," whom even his "present Patron" would not have
"purchased" but for the "additional Satisfaction of having
purloin'd" him from "his next Door Neighbour."

Such words invited blows, or else they had to be ignored.
A challenge was borne by Henry Fox. Whether its author or
not, Pulteney was willing to defend the pamphlet "at what
time and wherever Lord Hervey pleased." Both men were
slightly wounded between three and four in the afternoon of
Monday, January 25, the snowiest day of the winter, in upper
St. James's Park. Pulteney promised not to attack his adversary again with mouth or pen, and Hervey bowed.

Parliament had met four days before. The King still feared
the war he labored to avert. Carteret in the Lords moved a
resolution against fighting the Emperor in Flanders or on the
Rhine. Pulteney and Wyndham repeated the motion in the
lower house. Pulteney made a "long and incoherent" speech.
Saving a few with Indians, he would be willing to burn all
"treaties" in the Palace Yard. That week the *Craftsman*
called Walpole a "Liar," a "political Mendicant" who flew
from "Treaty to Treaty," committing "Blunders upon Blunders" until at last he found "himself as well as his Master involved in Contradictions and impracticall Engagements with
all the Powers of Europe." Francklin, out on bail, was taken
up again.

A week later the *Craftsman* announced a resolution to proceed in spite of harsh treatment. Soon it retailed again the
history it had in store, complaining (February 6), "when we
formerly confined ourselves to general Topicks," opponents

"defy'd us to mention Particulars"; "when we come to Particulars, they roar out aloud that such Usage is not to be borne and call upon the civil Power to knock us down." Horace Walpole published a pamphlet, *Considerations on the present State of Affairs*. The duel inspired other pieces, more personal in tone. It became known in the month that commanders in the West Indies had orders to "repel by force" Spanish coast guards attacking British merchant ships.

The *Craftsman's* description of an orator as the "Mouth of the People" inspired Osborne to muse (February 27): on the contrary "he is a Mouth (and Soul too) to the People; he does not speak what they before felt, but gives the Ideas and Passions which they would never have felt had he not spoke. The Incendiary . . . will make the Matter combustible, and then actually set it on Fire . . . by the Magick of Words and Power of Sounds artfully convey'd, stamp Images where there were none, and induce a Belief of Grievances against the very Evidence of Sense." The talent of Pulteney, he remarked several weeks later, was "Mob Satyr"; therefore, he "should speak only," not write.

The ministers had to defeat a motion in the House of Commons for addressing the King to dissolve Parliament. Fortunately, the negotiations at Vienna were coming to a point; the treaty was signed in early March. Contrary to the advice of Horace and Chesterfield, Walpole and Newcastle had not confided in Fleury, lest Chauvelin should interfere. When the news reached England, it gave "a new turn to the countenances of the courtiers," and Walpole was "full of good humour." Oldcastle interrupted his history to hope (April 3) that this "Protestant Treaty" would "defeat all the bad Designs" of the "Popish Treaty" previously negotiated by Ripperda.

An observer saw "frequenters of coffee-houses" now divided between the *Craftsman* and the *London Journal*. The sponsors of the former needed a new subject to hold the interest of their following. A comment on "Patriotism" by Walsingham inspired in the *Craftsman* (April 24) a good reason to believe that another writer would soon publish a history of that subject. Daniel Defoe, long since inactive, died that month.

May 7 the Parliament was prorogued. On reaching home, the King hoped that the members would find "all attempts to raise a spirit of discontent by unjust clamours and misrepresentations vain and ineffectual." Coincident with the publication of the treaty (May 15), Oldcastle closed his historical essays with the blunt remark: "The King (and he alone could have done it) forced the Affairs of the Nation, as he had put his own long before, in the Hands of a Faction. The true Friends of the Constitution were divided, and divided, were too weak to prevail on either side."

Bolingbroke was tempted the next Saturday to defend himself and Pulteney more directly than hitherto against the "Clamour raised" by the "whole Posse of ministerial Scribblers." Walpole, who inspired them, was the "Object of just Clamour and of national Hatred." He "would confess," if he turned his eyes on himself, that he was "the principal Cause of the Grievances of his Country." Pulteney had not left his party because of "disappointed Ambition," but because he could not support the "dangerous Ambition, insatiable Avarice, and insolent Behaviour" of the man with whom he was formerly associated. Pulteney's ambition was that of "doing good" and "receiving the Rewards of Fame." As to the writer, Walpole took a "mean Advantage" of a helpless adversary. He had been a "Friend" but not a "Creature" of Marlborough. To Walpole he owed no "Gratitude." George I had extended mercy "unasked and unearned." He had engaged momentarily with the Pretender but not until attacked at home. Fate and Walpole together had made the world unkind.

Here was a chance the smarting Hervey craved. "The Mask is taken off indeed," he began his *Remarks on the Craftsman's Vindication of his two Honourable Patrons.* That journal now "openly avowed the Conduct of the late Lord Bolingbroke," who "insolently" challenged "all Mankind to prove that Guilt against his Character for which he fled the Kingdom and forfeited his Honour." None but the "most ignorantly stupid" could "think him honest." Those defending him had no "Sense of his Worth," but vindicated themselves "for employing such a Tool." They would never make him the "Partner of their Success." Sophistry was abundant in the arguments with which both authors enforced their sharp remarks. Bolingbroke's writing was more compact. Hervey's diatribe was keener and to the point. In the light of information then at hand, it seemed to readers better based on facts.

But Pulteney was a subject that Hervey relished more. Did he not seek a "great Employment"? Did "not his Patriotism take its Rise" when he had asked and been refused? Granted what he wished, "would he have fear'd any Wickedness or have found any Weakness in the Administration?" "If his Lust of Power, if his Appetite for Wealth, if his overbearing Spirit were Secrets with Mankind," they could be supported by "innumerable Passages with irrefragable Proofs." The career of "that Christian and lamb-like Patriot . . . so complaisant to the Queen and so religiously decent to the royal Family," an "original Pattern of Humility and Moderation," a "Man of Peace and Patience," afforded "no Instances of a vindictive Temper, no personal Spite and Resentment." He was "not used to be out of Humour whenever any one" taxed "him with the Truth." Hervey boasted that he confined himself to "public Behaviour," scorning "to enter into private Life."

Pulteney could not be silent in the face of this attack. But his *Answer to One Part of a late Infamous Libel,* in which his character was "fully vindicated," need not have merited the epithet "mad Book." His violent anger poured forth unrestrained. "Most noble Sir," he began, addressing Walpole, "your private Insolence is grown as insupportable as your public Corruption. . . . You may go on misapplying the publick Treasure and prostituting your royal Master's Name in your own dirty Service. But you shall know, Sir, that you have Men to deal with, and . . . your infamous Scurrility shall not go unanswered." It might be of use to "let the World into some further Particulars," since Walpole had revealed items that only himself could know. The insinuation that Pulteney was a Jacobite would not "find Credit" unless in "a certain Closet," where Walpole had "frequent Opportunity of working upon the Passions by false Representations and instilling the Sentiments" of his "own bad Heart without Contradiction." Perhaps "this Closet" was the only place in the kingdom where Walpole's "Assertions" could "gain any Belief." "Good God," the writer exclaimed, "what a Multitude of Falsehoods must you have told in this Closet." He had not liked Walpole when working with him, but was moved by "Party Prejudices." Furthermore, even "Sejanus, Wolsey, and Buckingham" might have been "very honest Men for Aught" Pulteney knew "before their Heads were turned giddy with exorbitant Power."

The author gave details of his own personal estate, admitting it to be large. But "what a Scene of Iniquity would be disclosed" by an inquiry into Walpole's. Pulteney had not seen in advance Bolingbroke's compliments and might not have approved of them if he had. But those opposed to Walpole were pledged not to treat with him without a change of "Measures" and the "exemplary Punishment" of that Minister. This pledge was due to no "Fit of personal Resentment" but had the "nobler Motives" of preventing terms that offered "Retreat and Security." "Consider now," the writer urged, "the desperate Situation into which you have brought yourself. The Gentlemen who openly oppose you are determined to put you upon your Tryal for all the fatal Blunders and Iniquities of a long Administration. Those who are obliged unwillingly to support you wait out of Patience for an Opportunity to give you up; which they have already discovered an Eagerness of doing as soon as they shall see that Protection withdrawn which you receive at present from the Influence of Power and Corruption."

Specifically, Pulteney denied that he had ever asked to be made Secretary of State. But details were dangerous for an angry author. He described a scene at the reconciliation of George I and his son, attributing words to Walpole it was easy for ministerial journalists to show had not been used. He went on to allege that the Prince was then "sold to his Father's Ministers by Persons who considered Nothing but themselves

and their own Interests and were in haste to make their Fortunes." On this premise was based an apostrophic conclusion: "This is the Man (behold him well) who reproaches
others with a Want of Duty to the King and Decency to the
royal Family, this base Wretch who is now deceiving and
flattering that very Person, whom he used so ill, to serve his
own selfish Ends."

Some weeks later Bolingbroke thought it prudent to defend
himself in *A Final Answer to the Remarks on the Craftsman's
Vindication and to all other Libels which have come or may
come from the same Quarter against the Person last mentioned in the Craftsman of May 22*. He kept his temper
studiously. He was not interested in personalities, but in national affairs. Pulteney's defense was none of his concern,
having been undertaken "by an abler Pen." Hervey's pamphlet was "Invective . . . the Railing and Raving and Throwing of Filth by a Madman." He confessed weakness in joining the Pretender and parried skilfully other charges he could
not refute. He had no defence against those resolved to retain
the charge of "Jacobitism" as a weapon to combat his rise.

To shield Walpole, Walsingham admitted writing Hervey's
pamphlet. Francklin was taken up again for printing that
which Pulteney wrote, but his trial was put off for want of a
suitable jury. Philip Yorke advised Newcastle that it might
be difficult to convict. But the grand jury of Middlesex presented the libels against the King, including Pulteney's. James
Pitt, conductor of the *London Journal,* was given a place.
Cave in June regaled his readers with the controversy arranged
in parallel columns. Lord Perceval recalled while watching
Devonshire kiss hands in June as Lord Privy Seal that Calig-
ula made his horse a consul.

Thursday, July 1, the King called for the Council book and
struck the name of Pulteney from the list. Osborne addressed
the ex-councillor that week (July 3) in a tone of high reproof:
"You had a good Character, and deserv'd it too; but your
publick Actions for some Years past have sullied the Glory
of it. . . . You have departed from the Gentleman, the Man
of Sense, the Man of Honour; you have broke through all

the Laws that were ever held sacred among Mankind." Because of hopes not gratified, he had "turned publick Writer; entered into *private Life;* betray'd the Confidence of . . . Friends; and published most scandalous and infamous Libels against all Persons in Power and Trust." "A high Concern for the Felicity of his *Majesty's Government* and the Prosperity of the People" impelled the writer to show the one he addressed "to the World in a true Light, that" he might "be less able to do Mischief."

There were rumors that the *Craftsman* would give up. Seven volumes of its essays were collected and printed off. But even in this hurly-burly other subjects pushed upon the scene. A writer in the *Edinburgh Eccho* reported people to be talking in London in the middle of May of British ships taken by Spanish coast guards in the Bay of Honduras. Friday, June 11, Captain Robert Jenkins of the *Rebecca* landed at the port, having sailed from Jamaica March 25, and reported mistreatment on his voyage. His story grew as the days passed, and ready listeners were found. Not all who heard it made the same report. All agreed that an ear was damaged. In Tuesday's *Daily Advertiser* one of the attacking party, seeing it "only hanging by a Bit . . . immediately wrung it off and flung it into the Sea." By Saturday the teller of the tale gave it a more artistic touch. The Captain was not scalped only because his head was shorn. An officer seized his "left Ear, and with his Cutlass slit it down; and then another of the Spaniards took hold of it and tore it off, but gave him the Piece of his Ear again, bidding him carry it to his Majesty, King George." The *Edinburgh Eccho's* version added that the Captain brought his ear to show the King.

Hearing earlier in the week how the story grew, Walpole sent for Jenkins to come to Chelsea and see him. June 17 the Minister despatched the Captain to Hampton Court to tell the incident to Newcastle and Delafaye. Benjamin Keene, British minister in Spain now that Harrington was Secretary of State, soon had the matter on his list of grievances to take up with that court. Before many weeks had passed Jenkins himself, on Walpole's recommendation, as master of an East

Indiaman, was sailing seas where Spanish *guarda costas* were not met.

The *Craftsman* wondered whether the story would not do. A "Merchant of Bristol" lamented (July 10) the fate of sailors in the Spanish main. "What a dismal Train of Ideas" the "plain Story of Captain Jenkins" raised in the "Minds of every thinking Person." "The barbarous Circumstances which attended this honest Man's Sufferings and their insolent Defiance of his Majesty, when they bid him carry his Ear, after they had cut it off, to King George must fill the Breast of every Briton with most lively Resentment." Should the "Legion of Writers . . . hired to extol the Conduct and to cry up the Vigour and Prudence of an Administration" prevail, when a "few despicable, ruffian Mulattoes and renegado Negroes" were suffered "not only to seize the Property, but to maim and mangle the Persons of his Majesty's Subjects and haughtily order them to carry their bloody, torn Members to their Prince?" Surely the day was "not far off" when a "deluded and insulted Country" would receive "full Satisfaction for all its Losses and Disgraces."

Osborne replied promptly (July 17) that to make the negotiation with Spain a party question would hinder settlement. The single ship, a legacy of the Treaty of Utrecht, would always cause trouble because of its excessive value. The Spanish disavowed many attacks by pirates and renegadoes in their seas. Trade with Spain would not be helped by pushing things too far. A difficulty in the conduct of the kingdom's foreign affairs, the same writer observed the next week, was the attending comment by men who, because themselves not employed, "would ruin their Country rather than not ruin the Ministry."

As the summer passed the *Craftsman* claimed the right to criticize the private as well as the public life of public men, boasting that its collected essays, though unsuccessful in their time, might damage Walpole's fame as handed to posterity. The *Daily Courant* noted (August 18) that Spain had disavowed the assailants of Captain Jenkins and would punish them if found. Several British vessels had been "justly forfeited" under the treaties. Perhaps there was a reason if the Spanish watched the British more closely than others. An examination of the "secret Trading carried on by the English" would reveal "Advantages" accruing to their country at the expense of Spain. The writer would man British ships sufficiently to beat pirates when attacked.

Ignoring Pulteney's vow not to accept a place, Walsingham in early autumn (September 30) dwelt on the embarrassing lack of an alternative ministry should Walpole and his associates go out. Would Aislabie have the Treasury to stop corruption or Bolingbroke be Secretary of State? Would Pulteney's leadership produce success? He had "no Talents for conciliating Men, no Abilities to form a Party." He was "cursed with a native Aversion to Business and addicted from Youth . . . to all Kinds of Idleness, Supineness, and Laziness." He consulted none, saw few, and was "distrusted by all." Even those who voted and acted with him were "hateful to" and "despised by" him.

Should the next Parliament be chosen as the fruit of his "inflammatory Writings," the House of Commons would be "filled with *veteran* Jacobites, High Church Fox-hunters, and Prerogative Men," whom Pulteney would be unable to control. But Osborne consoled himself that as a consequence of the success in foreign affairs and the recent furor of pamphlets the opposition had materially declined. A visitor at Hampton Court was reported (October 15) to have asked Walpole "what he had done to God Almighty to make him so much his Friend?" The *Craftsman* pled (October 30) the difficulties of one weekly against so great a "Swarm of Writers."

Francklin was found guilty (December 3) of printing his paper of January 2. The prosecution demanded a jury of substantial men. Notables on both sides were present at the trial. The *Craftsman* (December 4) reviewed and defended its previous work. A pamphlet, *The Case of the Opposition between the Craftsman and the People, occasioned by his Paper of December 4*, gave the ministerial view. The purpose had been to divide the ministry. In foreign matters, unscrupulous criticism had thwarted its efforts for the country. But Sir Thomas

Robinson, at home from Vienna and at Houghton the next week, found as "much cheerfulness and good nature" as he ever saw where there were a score or more of men together. Orrery, at Bath for Christmas, thought the censure of Pope for his attack on Hervey "universal and severe," with "none to take his part."

A timorous ministerial pamphleteer reviewed *The D'Anverian History of Affairs for the Memorable Year 1731* on the assumption that the "Narrative of a fictitious Fact" was a "real Fact to the Person perfectly deceived," producing the "same Passions, Emotions, and other Effects." He estimated that the *Craftsman* sold twelve thousand copies a week, obtained half of the cost of publication from advertisers, and made from sixteen to nineteen hundred pounds a year profit. Compilers of its news, with a "Countenance like an Undertaker's hired Mourners at a Funeral," eliminated the "agreeable," admitting only "dismal Things to excite melancholick Imagination," with a "Design to raise Discontents in People's Minds and Clamours against the Government." The use of the attack on Jenkins was a case in point. The conviction of Francklin had not helped. The writer thought a better way to reach his public might be to advertise in the *Craftsman.* Another journalist complained (January 19) that Bolingbroke's agents frequented "every Coffee House, Tavern, and Club to report the Conversation of the Company."

Walpole met Parliament January 13, 1732, anticipating an easier session. The King announced that Parma and Placentia were in possession of Don Carlos and that sixteen thousand Spanish troops were in Tuscany. Provision for the army occasioned the usual debate. Another pension bill was introduced. The opposition blamed the ministry for the bankruptcy of the Charitable Corporation. After much discussion in and out of Parliament, a bill was passed to protect British sugar colonies from competition with the French. Walpole diplomatically proposed to restore the tax on salt, removed the previous year, to enable a reduction in the land tax. This was an experiment, a forerunner in a shifting of burdens in order to reserve the land tax for emergencies and to enable it to be revived upon a fairer basis. June 1 the Parliament was prorogued, and the King announced a visit to Germany.

Chesterfield returned from The Hague that winter and resumed his residence at court. When granting leave of absence from the household to Henrietta Vane to visit her grandfather, the Queen sent word that the Maid of Honor might remain away for good. The pious Perceval thought her a "fat and ill shaped dwarf . . . with neither sense nor wit." Harrington boasted that it was unnecessary to marry her. He and Hervey disputed with the Prince paternity of her unborn child. Frederick provided a house after his mother dismissed her from the court.

Edward Vernon was violent in Parliament against the tax on salt. If he voted for it, he would expect "to be treated like a polecat and knocked in the head." Pulteney was still jumpy. He and Henry Pelham had to be admonished by the House not to proceed to blows. In February Francklin was fined a hundred pounds, and sentenced to prison for a year; he had to give a thousand pounds security for good behavior in the next seven years to come. Fog's printer was taken up again in March. But Osborne thought (March 4) the "Anti-Ministerial Writers" now to be "harmless enough to play with." By dint of much persuasion, Walpole finally induced George II to sign the charter for a Carolina colony sponsored by Oglethorpe and others. There "were times," he confessed to Percival, when "things could be done, other times when they could not."

When the *Craftsman* returned to the charge (April 29) that ministers usurped the power of the crown, the *Daily Courant* replied (May 5), that ministers did it more in the last four years of Anne. After Parliament was up, Osborne treated the subject at greater length (June 3). There was no "carrying on Business without a principal Guide or Director." There must be some one whom the Prince could "trust." A "Minister" must have friends to "support his Measures, cover his Errors . . . and recover him from a false Step." If "wise," he would not "take into his Administration Persons who" would not pay him "first Regard." Measures should originate in a council composed of "hearty Friends" and not in Parliament at large.

Pulteney thought he saw another issue coming forth. In *The Case of the Removal of the Salt Duty,* published the day that Parliament was prorogued, he alleged this to be the preface to a larger scheme, a "general Excise." He hoped it would be "opposed at every Step with the utmost Contumacy and Vigour as the last sure Blow to . . . Liberties and the Constitution." Osborne gave statistics in reply (June 24). The value of the total annual goods consumed, he estimated at eighty million pounds; the produce of land, one-fourth that sum. The rest was made by trade. The current high value of land was chiefly due to trade. Was it not "just that all pay Taxes in Proportion to their Expence?" An excise on "Luxuries" might be a fairer tax, "less burthensome to the People" than that on land.

For months booksellers had wondered why they suffered an interloper such as Cave to have the profits of his magazine. In May they launched a rival venture, *The London Magazine; or, Gentleman's Monthly Intelligencer.* Cave heard complaints that he was partisan in his "View of the weekly Essays and Disputes." His magazine was thrown out of many stalls. But both periodicals began to perform more adequately another service largely left to Boyer in the past. The rule against publishing the proceedings of Parliament was assumed to lapse when the houses were prorogued. The two magazines thus vied in carrying accounts of the "Proceedings and Debates."

Hoping for quiet times, Walpole himself meditated foundations on which to build the country's future greatness. His experiment with tea and coffee seemed to show that to warehouse such staples as they came in, collecting an excise in lieu of an import duty when they were sold, and permitting reexport without a drawback was a method more productive of revenue, leaving less room for fraud, than that which then prevailed. Colonial planters were complaining that they were at the mercy of English factors, from whose report on the quantity and condition of tobacco shipped to England they had no appeal. The substitution of an excise for imposts on such commodities as tobacco and wine would answer these complaints; frauds would be diminished, and the revenues increased. The success of the plan would tend to make London a free port, a center of the trade of all the world. The land tax could be removed. Only smugglers and dishonest merchants would suffer loss. The Minister thought the measure would be sound statesmanship, for which contemporaries would thank him and posterity bless his name. It seemed also to be good politics. Once the excitement of the change had passed, its merits would appear. Perhaps that was one reason for the frantic protests on the other side.

Protestant Dissenters in that summer's quiet began to seek fulfillment of their hopes. Osborne supported them, as was his wont. Another year would see the Parliament end. Might not the Test Act be repealed? Meetings were held. At least a promise of future action might be got. But churchmen soon were up in arms. Gibson opposed. The first number of the *Weekly Miscellany* appeared (December 16), conducted by William Webster, alias "Richard Hooker of the Temple, Esq.," to be devoted to the support of "Religion and Morality"; chiefly for the moment it opposed repeal.

The *Craftsman* scented the excise and gave hot pursuit. Such a tax would require an "Army" to support it and would open the way to "arbitrary Government." Beginning October 28, its writer would endeavor to explain the subject "in a Manner and Style adapted to the Capacity of all" his "Readers." The "very Word Excise," said a sarcastic journalist on the other side, "alarms the righteous Patriot, ever watchful of his Country's Good!" He had become an "Enthusiast" of the type of those who discerned the "Danger of the Church" in the "Time of Dr. Sacheverell." The *Craftsman* meant to see whether a gullible public would swallow the bait again. "Excise is a different Sort of Tax from Customs," it said (November 4), disfranchising in a measure "every freeborn Englishman." Officials would increase in number and "swarm like Locusts over the Land."

Seeing this campaign boiling up, Dissenters assembled in

Dr. Williams's Library (November 9) and were persuaded that their appeal would not succeed. Facts were stifled in a flood of eagerness to believe. A writer in the *Daily Courant* (November 18) saw a "nice and difficult Task" in trying to "counter prevailing Prejudices and popular Opinions, especially among a People so fond and so tenacious of their antient Customs"; "long use alone" gave a "Thing the Sanction of Law." Three days later another writer in that paper thought defending the "Ministry against the Opposition" like fighting with a "Hydra"; two or three more heads sprouted where one was "lopt off."

Walpole never showed more tact or kept his temper better. He felt it to be the most constructive program of his life. More than in most of his struggles, he had a reasoned hope of doing good; therefore the opposition seemed the more unjust. When he returned from Norfolk in December there was a consultation at his house to put Dissenters off. The Lord Chancellor thought the Test Act ought to be repealed. The Speaker did not think five members of his House would vote for it. As a man, Walpole was on their side; as a minister, he took the other view. He could not risk division in the rising storm. The day that Webster's weekly first appeared, Osborne announced that though the ministers thought the Test Act ought to be repealed, they found it inexpedient to do it then.

As the year closed a ministerial writer found the "Excise" becoming as "formidable as Popery and Slavery," and recalled that words could "influence as much as Reality." With "Prejudice annexed to Sounds," "artful Men" would "make them Tools" at "Pleasure." The *Craftsman* reported the same day (December 30), its words becoming acts. "Merchants Traders, and Citizens of London" met to oppose a measure not then introduced in a session yet to meet. This was a cue to other places where opposition members had the art to stir. The noise was loud enough when Parliament met (January 16) to drown the *Daily Courant's* wit (January 17), that Old Sarum and other denominated boroughs in its class opposed "Excises" laid upon the "Goods and Merchandise" in which they chiefly dealt.

As usual, the King regretted "heats and animosities," but would "not be diverted . . . from steadfastly pursuing the true interest" of the country. The Charitable Corporation, the pension bill, the land forces, the Spanish depredations, the Sugar Act, were taken up in turn. Walpole proposed (February 23) to use half a million from the sinking fund that year for a further reduction of the land tax against prospective improvements in the revenue. Pulteney was disappointed that the Minister had not opened instead "that Monster, the Excise, that Plan of arbitrary Power" so long awaited by the House. Henry Pelham was not surprised at Pulteney's ire. The opposition had pronounced the reduction of the land tax in the previous year a "most damnable Project," in that it blessed the country gentlemen "too much." Finally, to appease suspense, Walpole asked leave (March 7) to open up his subject the next week.

Oglethorpe went to Georgia early in the year. An epidemic of influenza raged. The Chancellor and the Speaker were both ill, and for a week in January Parliament adjourned. The bills of mortality showed the highest death rate since the plague. Did that contagion infect the public mind? "Is it Wisdom," Osborne asked (January 20), "to set the People in a Roar . . . to make them meet in Bodies all over the Kingdom and resolve strenuously to oppose an imaginary Monster in any Form or Shape?" Would it not have been wiser to await the scheme? It might not be unreasonable when known.

The opposition had no mind to wait. Success seemed on the way at last. Their journalists were more effective now; readers waxed in warmth. Active allies spread the fire. Larger merchants stirred the retail shops. Smugglers and honest traders alike were moved by fear. Tobacconists and tavern hosts throughout the land were taught to feel their businesses at stake. The little shops would be invaded; their keepers' wives and daughters made the prey of vicious men. Facts had no weight, and sober argument was useless in the din. The ministerial writers fell to musing on the art that held them fast.

Some disappointed great ones thought their day had come.

Argyll was sulky; Islay now ruled Scotland in his place. They worked together, though they might not speak. Lord Cobham, master of Stowe, a description of whose magnificence had just appeared in print, Clinton and Marchmont, Montrose and Bolton, Chesterfield and Carteret, and even Stair felt that the country suffered because their weight and talents were not used enough. Were they not born to rule as men of family and estates? Who were the Walpoles, newly rich and bunglers when they dealt in great affairs? Perhaps the King would listen to them now. Stair went to take their message to the Queen.

She heard him through. Walpole, he told her, impelled by "rashness" and "wantonness in power" was alienating the affections of her subjects. "Your Majesty," he urged, "knows nothing of this man but what he tells you himself, or what his creatures and flatterers prompted by himself tell you of him." In fact, "in no age, in no reign, in no country was ever any minister so universally odious." The army hated him, thinking he supported it "against his will." The clergy hated him for having to "earn his help at a dear rate." The City hated him because he did nothing for trade; the Scots "to a man," because he had opposed favors the King intended for them. The "odium" earned by the Minister was now imputed to the crown, his only "hope for protection." The excise was a last straw, and people would not submit.

That Walpole "absolutely governs your Majesty," her monitor continued, "nobody doubts and very few scruple to say; they own you have the appearance of power, and say you are contented with the appearance, whilst all the reality of power is his, derived from the King, conveyed through you and vested in him." Her Majesty, perhaps even Walpole himself, little dreamed of the defection in prospect which would make it impossible for the bill to pass the Lords. Personally, Stair thought it "so wicked, so dishonest, so slavish a scheme" that he would not support it in policy, if he could in "conscience."

His appeal to conscience stirred a sense of humor in the nettled Queen. She did not know who taught him his lesson, she said, but his "system of politics" was from the *Crafts-man*, his sentiments were from Bolingbroke and Carteret. He might tell the latter that she was not yet reduced to wanting his protection.

Fighting with facts and arguments, ministerial writers still wondered why they had been overwhelmed. If "Jealousies reigned among the Common People," explained the *Daily Courant* (February 26), and "by an unfortunate Proneness to Infection" began "to spread among Persons of better Rank," it was the work of an intriguing group who had in the past "embarrassed sometimes the Current of publick Negotiations" and had then attributed these embarrassments to the Minister's want of "Skill," boasting loudly thereafter of "foreseeing the Evils" they had caused themselves.

Walpole could not now turn back. He introduced the proposal for an excise on tobacco (March 14) in one of the ablest speeches of his career. Waverers, expecting to oppose, were moved to take his part. Among the abler speakers on his side was the Attorney General, Philip Yorke. London merchants opposed him almost to a man. Processions filled the city streets. Westminster Hall, the Court of Requests, and places round about were filled with "Merchants and Traders" to a degree not seen within the "Memory of Men." Permission to introduce the bill was given in the early morning of the next day, 265 to 204. Their Majesties waited up for the accounts that Henry Pelham and Hervey brought. Walpole went out through the house of Halifax, the Auditor of the Exchequer, to escape the insults of the mob.

In spite of a majority larger than they had thought, the ministers did not share the easy hope of Delafaye that landed men would smooth the way to final passage after Easter. Charles Howard wrote his father, the Earl of Carlisle (March 31), that though he saw no reason for it, the "Clamours and Spirit of opposition" were "inconceivable." The same day Osborne urged merchants and traders of the metropolis to "restrain their Passions and not . . . run into the wild Extravagances of Bigots and Enthusiasts, burning Books and Papers" that they did not like.

The ministers carried three votes on April 4, but their majorities decreased, while noise outside was louder still. Leave to print the bill was refused the next day. Walpole confessed fatigue and asked postponement of the bill for wines, appointed for the sixth. Members began to be afraid that the ferment might outlast the year and hinder their elections in the next. Since men in place opposed unscathed, perhaps the sun of Walpole was about to set.

Sunday, April 8, observers found the City all aflame with plans to march on Tuesday to the House to demonstrate against the bill. A show of coaches would be seen, all shops be shut, apprentices turned out to gather at St. Stephen's Chapel door. Had Walpole had his way, Chesterfield and Clinton would have been dismissed as a deterrent to the rest in place, but Wilmington and other timid Lords replied that in that case they would quit themselves.

Monday Walpole went to see the King and Queen. There were two ways from which they had to choose. To drop the Minister would still the clamor out of doors. To drop the bill and keep the Minister would bring less sure relief. The choice was easy for the King. Walpole's courage in the fight had won his heart. The bill had been intended for the public good. "He is a brave fellow; he has more spirit than any man I ever knew," George had exclaimed when told of the proceedings in the House. Regretfully, the word was given to the Minister to drop his bill.

Tuesday, the City merchants staged their show. The statement of the question in the House left all precedents on the ministerial side. Should the petitioners be heard by counsel and also in person? The point was carried, but by a narrow vote. The joyful opposition left the House with noisy cheers. Walpole remained behind, "leaning against the table, . . . his hat pulled over his eyes," perceiving little comfort in the "melancholy countenances" of the small group of faithful friends that gathered round.

Pelham and Hervey went to tell the King and Queen. "Discipline," they remarked, was as "necessary in an administration as an army." Walpole dined that night with a small circle of his friends. After the servants left, he slowly shook his head while speaking with an "unpleased smile." "This Dance, it will no farther go." "Tomorrow," he would "sound retreat." [3]

III

BOLINGBROKE RETREATS

Feeling an offensive to be the best defensive move, Walpole on Wednesday asked that the Excise Bill be postponed to a day in June when he thought Parliament would be up. He would not leave through Halifax's house that day as friends advised. To meet such "dangers" boldly was a wiser plan. The crowd in the Court of Requests was courteous as he passed. Outside, the friends accompanying warded off attacks. Edward Walpole was struck in the arm and Hervey, in the forehead. The latter was afraid to tell the story to the Queen that night, uncertain of the version Walpole wished to spread.

The next day ministers were indignant in the House. Behold the "spirit of liberty," they said, the opposition had aroused. By resolution, without dissent, the tumult was denounced in strongest terms. Chesterfield heard the next day of his dismissal from his place at court. Clinton learned that he was out. In polysyllables, Chesterfield affected hurt surprise. If under the King's "displeasure" it was from an effort to serve the King. He had pursued his "duty" without regard to "interest." He thought as "the whole nation did" about the excise. His "Majesty's Interests and those of the nation, when fairly and disinterestedly represented," would always be "inseparable."

[3] In addition to files of periodicals cited in the text, see *Political State*, XLI. 174ff.; XLII. 19ff.; XLIII. 208ff.; XLIV. 73ff.; XLV. 137ff.; Dobree, *Chesterfield Letters*, II. 144ff.; Hist. Mss. Com., *Egmont Diary*, I. 106ff.; *Carlisle*, pp. 85ff.; *Dartmouth*, p. 327; *Stopford Sackville*, I. 147; Coxe, *Robert Walpole*, III. 88ff.; *Horatio Walpole*, I. 301ff.; Williams, *Atterbury*, II. 427ff.; Harris, *Hardwicke*, I. 216ff.; *Parliamentary History*, VIII. 864ff.; IX. 1ff.; *Marchmont Papers*, II. 416ff.; Hervey, *Memoirs*, I. 164ff.; Stanhope, *History*, II. Appendix, pp. cxiiff.; Legg, *Diplomatic Instructions, France, 1727–1744*; E. R. Turner, "The Excise Scheme of 1733," *Eng. Hist. Rev.*, XLII. 34ff.; Paul Vaucher, *La crise due ministère Walpole, 1733; Robert Walpole et la politique de Fleury, 1731–1742*.

The opposition had another card to play. If the customs revenues suffered from fraud, as Walpole said, there ought to be an investigation by a committee of the House. The man responsible should be impeached. In Walpole's absence, Pelham accepted authorization (April 19) of a committee chosen by secret ballot. Success, however, brought embarrassment too. If excises were wholly bad, why not remove those levied on coffee, tea, and chocolate? "Druggists" and dealers urged that it be done. Ministers forced a vote, which the proponents of repeal did not desire. Only a hundred and fifty were for it in a full House. But the *Craftsman* rejoiced that Saturday (April 21). The "Spirit of Liberty" was not "extinct." "The original Power of the People in their collective Body . . . without any ridiculous Adherence to *Old Party Names*" had shown its weight. "Traders" and "Country Gentlemen" joined together had banished a "gloomy Prospect" and made the "Sky . . . serene." The excise had been "universally opposed by the *Voice of the People* without Doors and . . . gloriously defeated by . . . worthy Representatives within." Its "Projector" should learn a lesson and use a little "Caution for the Future" as the "only effective Way for him to sleep in quiet without being haunted by continual Dreams of Murder and Assassination."

When Lord Perceval returned to town on Sunday he found that dropping the excise did not mean the court's defeat. That question was on the ballot for a committee to investigate the frauds. Confident of success, with members giving secret votes, the opposition list omitted all of Walpole's friends. The Minister avoided that mistake. More than half the House was at the Cockpit Monday night to hear his side. His speech was critical in his career. It was a scheme of Bolingbroke, he said. The welfare of the country was at stake, whatever they might think of him. Pelham, Yorke, and Onslow joined his plea. The spirit of their followers was revived. The names they sponsored carried the next day with good effect. "From the highest expectations," a member wrote, "the disappointment on this occasion has altered the scene quicker than anything I ever saw." Walpole had met a test "no minister besides himself could have" come through. The story went, that Pulteney wished a fairer list, but Wyndham for Boling-broke would not consent.

Ministerial journalists agreed that the spirit of the mob had caused the excise to be laid aside. The *Craftsman* now complained that Chesterfield and Clinton were turned out. At any rate, an "insolent, domineering Minister . . . after all his Defiances" had been reduced "to the wretched Necessity of recanting his abusive Reflections and giving up his ignominious Project, with Tears in his Eyes, which seemed to flow from an equal Mixture of impotent Rage and Pusillanimity." His "Character and Actions" had been "branded with such popular Marks of Indignation, Derision, and Contempt in all Parts of the Kingdom" as to deserve the anathemas of Cicero on Catiline. In reply, Osborne could only explain (May 12) that the *Craftsman* defamed the ministers, corrupting the people "by false Representations, vile Insinuations, and impudent Assertions."

Five days later Pelham thought that "by the steadiness of the party in the House of Commons and the firmness of their master" the ministers were "firmly in their seats again." But Horace Walpole complained that Chauvigny, the French Minister in London, still habitually consorted with Boling-broke. And even while the tempest over the excise raged, French intervention in the choice of a successor to the vacant throne of Poland offered a variety of openings for embroiling Britain in a question that Walpole felt it better to avoid.

In the House of Lords in the last days of the session the ministers barely defeated a motion for the investigation of the disposal of the forfeited estates of South Sea directors. A protest, bearing among other names those of Cobham, Stair, Montrose, Chesterfield, Carteret, and Marchmont, alleged the possibility of protecting "flagitious frauds" by a "corrupt and all-skreening minister" and boasted that the signers were not "under the influence of any man whose 'safety' might depend on the protection of fraud and corruption." In his concluding speech (June 11), the King remarked the recent efforts "to inflame the minds of the people and by most unjust misrepresentations to raise tumults and disorders that almost threatened the peace of the kingdom." He hoped members returning to their homes would "undeceive . . . deluded" subjects and "make them sensible of their present happiness and the hazard . . . run of being unwarily drawn by specious praters into their own destruction."

Cobham was deprived of his regiment; Stair, Montrose, and Marchmont, of the places that they held. With these recruits to the side of Carteret and Chesterfield, Newcastle would need assistance in the Lords. Hervey, the son of a peer, was summoned thither by a writ, a personal spokesman for Walpole and the King. Before another session met, Yorke as Baron Hardwicke, Chief Justice in Raymond's room, and Charles Talbot as Lord Chancellor more than compensated all the losses suffered in the peers dismissed. Newcastle and Hardwicke were already friends.

At Hampton Court that summer Hervey by her carriage amused the Queen, while "galloping" crowds were entertained by "barking dogs." Her son had entertained himself diversely hitherto. Denied a wife to qualify his children for the crown, he chose their mothers where he found a will. Ambitious to achieve a place and name, Dodington was buzzing at his door. His royal sister was about to make an inauspicious match. The time had come for him to settle down. Walpole proposed in June that he should take one of the women mentioned for his wife and have the naming of his court, with eighty thousand pounds a year to spend. The Prince accepted, but would not be friends with the Minister.

The *Craftsman* thought (July 4) that the Minister's brother had "neither Head nor Heart." "Laughed at as a Buffoon" in earlier years, now he "became still more ridiculous by attempting to be grave." He was "saucy and insolent when merry and absurd when serious; long a Joke for being dirty and ten times more so for endeavoring to be clean." The *Daily Courant* could only note (July 18) that when Sir Robert went to Norwich, thirty coaches and a thousand horse conducted him to town. He stayed with the Bishop and was given the freedom of the city in a gold box. As for Horace, his jests were seasoned with a "good Nature" that took away their "Sting." The stale "Joke of his being sloven" was too ridiculous to note.

Both sides made ready for elections soon to come. The *Craftsman* (July 21) had a platform for the fight. Government was "originally ordain'd for the Good of the Governed," who in their "collective Capacity" were superior even to the "supreme Magistrate." "Arbitrary Governments" were "tyrannical Usurpations on the natural Rights of Mankind," established by "Force" and "Fraud." Though called a monarchy, the British government was in fact a "regal Commonwealth," partaking "very much of democratical Principles." Since preserving a "Balance in the Legislature" was fundamental, the "Freedom of Election out of Doors" and the "Virtue of Representatives" within should be secured. "Alteration of Persons" was not the "only Point." Walpole was doubtless getting ready to retire, but that would not suffice. No mere "Patching and Screening" would satisfy the "Nation" or cool the "present Heat."

Thus, as the summer came and went, the rival writers plied their quills. They held an inquest on the Excise Bill. Why had the noise grown so loud? Walpole's defenders wrote in greater numbers and with equal skill. Why did their art have less effect? Osborne marveled (July 21) that former projectors of the Schism Act now championed the "royal Family and the Cause of Liberty." A writer in the *Daily Courant* (August 2) could only moralize that noise was not enough. With the same effort on the other side, there might have been as many addresses for as against the excise. If the people were "fairly polled," he neither knew nor cared what the result would be. A mob, suiting its "Patron's Humour," would always "holloa" on whichever side.

The question was whether or not, as in Sacheverell's time, the clamours could be kept alive through elections just ahead and cause the choice of members pledged to turning Walpole out. Such was the plan, and at the moment there was noise enough. But Newcastle and Walpole were realists and knew the game they had to play. As ever, Bolingbroke was a theorist, unmindful of the seats of power. In lucid moments he saw, perhaps, the handicaps he had to overcome to gain his point. In 1710 he was in office. The prestige of the Sovereign was on his side as was the skill of Harley and a frightened Church. The case was different now. Walpole had the King and had the Church in part. Perchance Dissenters might be won.

In that field Bolingbroke had to work with care, from fear of losing in the Church more than he gained in the Dissenters. A celebration of the repeal of the Schism Act, recalling its patron in an earlier day, was not an ineffective ministerial countermove. Still, in early autumn, Chesterfield thought the ministers could not "hold it long" without another "miracle," such as hitherto a "crisis" always brought. He was in no state of mind to see the worldly energy that helped to work these miracles in time. None would deny the need for effort now. The *Craftsman,* reflecting (October 20) "on the Industry and Activity of Agents for a certain Gentleman in every Part of the Kingdom," was moved almost to despair.

Fog's printers were arrested again, October 22. In that month Horace Walpole went to The Hague to help enlist the Dutch in case of failure to avoid participation in the Polish war. The naïve Perceval, now Earl of Egmont, tried to obtain from ministers help for the *Weekly Miscellany.* But Walpole was less sure than he had been of Gibson's coterie. That Egmont thought the writers in the *Free Briton* and the *London Journal* to be "atheists" disturbed him not at all. The Irish peer tried also to enlist government support for his family influence in Harwich to return his son to Parliament in his own seat. But the son would not promise the help the father gave, and Walpole felt another member would better serve his cause, though Egmont might feel that he had been wronged.

It was more serious in December when Gibson opposed the nomination of Thomas Rundle, Talbot's protégé, to the see of Gloucester. The new Lord Chancellor would not give ground; the Bishop was as adamant. He felt that Rundle was an heretic. Walpole's concern was that his two lieutenants should agree. Perhaps he cared not whether Rundle was an heretic or not. There would be noise enough when the elections came without a wrangle with the Church.

In November Bolingbroke began to publish in the *Crafts-*

man essays to show that ancient party names should be ignored. These artful dissertations gave the weekly life. Osborne admitted (November 24), that their author was a "Gentleman of Wisdom and Experience . . . well skilled in History and human Nature," although his cause was bad. Consequently, his "excellent Parts and great *Abilities*" served "only to make his *Crime* the greater."

Bolingbroke spoke truly the next week. An English leader needed both a native capacity for "Discernment of Spirits" and "that *acquired publick political* Sagacity flowing from Nature too, but requiring more to be assisted by Experience and form'd by Art," which made possible foreknowledge of the effects of events and "much more" of the acts of the leader himself "on the Sentiments and Passions of Mankind." The greater marvel, that in the next two weeks he interrupted his *Dissertation on Parties* and admitted to the *Craftsman* essays ascribed to Shippen. The first dealt with Walpole and the King and Queen.

What was to be "expected from a Prince hated by his Subjects but Violence and Oppression, Rage and Resentment?" "Fears" of a people might subside, but "Hatred never," and the "Fate of a Nation in such Circumstances" could not be "long in Suspense." "It must soon be decided either by enslaving the People or by the Overthrow of the Prince." Another writer was quoted, who said of an "unpopular Queen" that "she loved her Minister only because she knew he was as much hated as herself and that his Refuge was only her; and the Minister accepted her Favour upon those Terms." This minister "laughed at Opposition," saying: "The Queen will protect me. I have done her such Service that she cannot abandon me." A "first Minister universally hated," the writer thought, was "certainly a Being inconsistent with the Liberties of any Country." An "honest Minister" would not struggle against "publick Aversion," but would resign, scorning the protection of the Prince and would rather be "executed in reality than hanged in Effigy."

The next Saturday Horace Walpole and Newcastle felt pricks from the same pen. The first was "so formed by Nature for Dirt and ill Manners that they almost became him; and he grew ridiculous by putting on Civility and clean Linnen." Newcastle was "born with Talents below the Vulgar, and those puzzled and perplexed, not improved by a laborious Application; advanced to high Station only by Birth or some whimsical Concurrence of Circumstances; rather bewildered in the Mazes than engaged in the Despatch of Business; wallowing in Papers," of which he "neither comprehended the Substance nor understood the Language"; his "Eloquence" was only a "Profusion of misplaced and unconnected Words." With such persons pretending to the "Conduct of Affairs the Dignity of Employments, or the good Breeding of a Court," their high posts were a "sort of political Pillory," inviting "Passengers to club their Lump of Dirt at Heads so ridiculously exposed."

To these screeds Walsingham could simply oppose the truth (December 20). Walpole "as a private Man" had "hardly an Enemy, and as a publick Minister . . . more personal Friends than any Man in Power was ever blest with before him." Friends made no such claim for Bolingbroke. Few in England wished him to have Walpole's place. As to the references to their Majesties, a "Minister whose Enemies spoke to the Throne in this Language" would not be sorry that they were "his Enemies." No doubt it was better to be "executed in Reality than hanged in Effigy," but Bolingbroke had chosen rather "to suffer an Attainder for high Treason than take his Tryal and answer to an Impeachment for Maladministration."

A writer in the *Daily Courant* (December 26) was more sarcastically severe:

To behold a Man who bravely fled from the Justice of his Country, which he had seen raised to the highest Pitch of Glory and Terror; and afterward as it were in a Moment of Time by his unparalleled Skill and Address reduced to the lowest Degree of Infamy and Contempt, to behold this Man poorly and basely cringing for Pardon, which was no sooner extended to him, but he thinks himself qualify'd to write Dissertations on Parties, to read weekly Lectures on Politics, and to spread his Rage against a certain Person as a "sorry Creature of Fortune, whom she raised in the Extravagance of her Caprice," this is much such another Scene as it would be to see a Carted

Whore, who had been whipt out of her native Town or County; and upon Promise of Amendment of Life suffered to return, take it upon her to read Lectures upon Morality and Chastity; and in her scolding Fits to rave against the good Women of the Neighbourhood as *saucy Creatures of Fortune.*

In that month also Pulteney, Marchmont, and others were busy trying to concert means of regular private communication between Scotland and the capital. While Bolingbroke in his interrupted *Dissertation* turned to the Popish Plot, Walpole was worrying about the Polish war and the reluctance of the Dutch to be involved. New Year's Day, Dodington induced the Prince to attend the King's levee. Hervey spurred the Queen to urge the father to greet his son amid the bowing crowd. Chesterfield and Cobham remained away from court; Marchmont took their cue and meditated a bill to confer on army officers tenure for life. After a talk with Dodington (January 5), the last was unsure of affairs and blessed "God he was a single man."

Chesterfield was afraid (January 11) that Stair would be tolled off. Carteret doubted (January 11) whether "anything to the purpose" could be done in "Scot affairs." Marchmont and Stair began to be suspicious of Carteret. Nevertheless, the opposition Lords united in the Rump Steak Club, so named to show resentment of a peer on whom the King had turned his back. Carteret, however, disliked a tavern dinner and would not attend. Pulteney doubted whether that Lord or Chesterfield would carry on the fight. Dodington saw that the ministers would win, but meant to trade upon his friendship with the Prince. Bolingbroke could only write and wait. At the first meeting of the Rump Steak Club Cobham was in the chair.

Two days later (January 17) Parliament met. The King was troubled at the Polish war. As always, he hoped the session would be "free from heats and animosities." Thereafter, he would "take the sense of the people" in a new election. Both in and out of doors attention turned to this event. On both sides appeals were made in weekly essays and in pamphlets. The excise was replaced by fears of war. Bolingbroke and Pulteney offered argument that for this danger Walpole was to blame. His blundering treaties had involved the country. Those who had "intangled" England in these "Difficulties" would be "most unlikely to work" her out. The ministers had "dealt with and . . . disobliged" every country in turn.

Osborne replied (February 16), that England had no obligation to go to war except to protect her "Trade or preserve the Balance of Power in Europe." Walsingham cherished the optimistic hope (February 14), that the crisis had restored the unity of the country. If any treaty had caused the current trouble, it was that "of Utrecht"; "no honest or reasonable Man would willingly see" the ministers "embarrassed or distressed." If England would only "show the World that Faction" could not "gain the Ascendant" in her "Councils," other countries would "have that Deference" which British "Interest" and "Power" deserved.

On the Polish question, Walpole had to thwart the King as well as France. Hatolfe, the Hanoverian Minister, was active on the Emperor's side. In consequence, the Minister came empty-handed from the closet when he went in to get the little sops that smoothed the way in an election year. A war was on; George was a military man; his interests were at stake. Even the Queen on this point was not sure.

In February Samuel Holden persuaded his fellow Dissenters to delay again their hopes against a better day that was to come. But Gordon in March, supporting Talbot's cause, addressed *A Letter to the Reverend Dr. Codex on the Subject of his Modest Instructions to the Crown inserted in the Daily Journal of February 27*. Nomination to the bench, he said, was with the crown, and not "a proud assuming Priest," who threatened not to come to court unless his "Creatures" were advanced. No "Service to a Court" could "palliate the Growth of such alarming Encroachments upon the Power of the Crown." Walpole, however, found a compromise. Rundle had to wait and take an Irish see, where heretics, apparently, would do less harm. In Gloucester, Gibson had his way.

Sometimes the fight took little, petty forms. Clinton in

March flung off his garter as a Knight of Bath, pronouncing it unfit for "a gentleman to wear." Coached by Dodington not to join his father or to break with him, the Prince canvassed openly for the opera in Lincoln's Inn Fields and against that in the Haymarket, for which his Majesty subscribed a thousand pounds. Uncertain where to go, some, like Lady Betty Germanin, made an excuse and stayed at home. Even the royal marriage did not pass without mishap. Hervey, in charge, did not consult the Herald's Office, and Irish peers, with Egmont at their head, not given the place they thought they ought to have, refused to go. Walpole could not induce the King to yield. The following Sunday, being St. Patrick's Day, Egmont was asked to take the sword before the King. The Bishop of Chester preached a sermon to the bride and groom. "Blessed are they that mourn, for they shall be comforted," was the curious text. The bride was not to find the prophecy come true.

In March, advocating the repeal of the Septennial Act in the House of Commons, Wyndham supposed "a gentleman at the head of the administration, whose only safety" depended upon "corrupting the members" of the House. From this beginning, he drew the picture of the Minister familiar in the opposition prints. A slower wit than Walpole's might have made reply: "Sir, let me too suppose, and the house being cleared, I am sure no person that hears me can come within the description of the person I am to suppose; let us suppose . . . an anti-minister, who thinks himself a person of so great and extensive parts, and of so many eminent qualifications, that he looks upon himself as the only person in the kingdom capable to conduct the public affairs of the nation. . . . We will suppose this anti-minister to be in a country where he really ought not to be, and where he could not have been but for the effect of too much goodness and mercy." Traversing thus the earlier speech, he painted with bold strokes the Bolingbroke with whom he felt he had to deal, until he came to ask at last: "Can there be imagined a greater disgrace to human nature than such a wretch as this?"

City mobs were out again the night of Thursday, April 11, to break unlighted windows and celebrate the anniversary of the defeat of the excise. For trying to preserve order, the Lord Mayor of the year had his windows broken. Osborne and Bolingbroke divided coffee-houses in a constitutional debate. The session was prorogued, April 16. The next day the *Daily Courant* proclaimed that the choice was between Walpole and Bolingbroke. Osborne confessed (April 20) that a war seemed to be inevitable. The *Craftsman* (April 27) reprinted "Of Elections," a piece from *Cato's Letters*.

In general, the well-informed knew in advance what the result would be. Ministerial candidates in London had opposed the excise in the previous year. There were some county upsets, where families were at odds. Sir Charles Wager, after "totaling up" at Walpole's house, congratulated Horace (May 6) that the majority might be too great. Knowing better how the trick was turned, Newcastle wrote (May 24) in a soberer tone: "Our Parliament is, I think, a good one; but by no means such a one as the Queen and your brother imagine. It will require good care, attention, and management to sett out right and keep people in good humour." By success in Holland, Horace could give help. The *Craftsman* (June 8) felt the result to be evidence of the "Power of the Ministers," not "Proof of the Sense of the People."

Hoadly was translated to Winchester that year. Gordon published the last installment of his Tacitus. Stirred by the attack on Gibson, Webster criticized its scholarship. But the author was to be a Commissioner of the Wine Licenses for the rest of his life. He was also a journalist who understood the art of politics, and the ministerial defense that summer would need a practiced hand.

The *Craftsman* was repetitious. Such victories as Walpole won were by corruption. The popular voice was on the other side. Freeholders in the counties had voted as they felt. Opposition even tried to hope that half the House would join in making Samuel Sandys its Speaker. Unfortunately for that plan, Marchmont, Stair, and other Scottish peers, omitted from the elected list, were bent on making that election the point of test. Islay had used corruption and ought to be impeached. Chesterfield, Carteret, and Pulteney urged the need of "proof," or such a charge could not be made to hold. When Marchmont would not be appeased, Chesterfield thought (June 15), "some of the lowest" of the "venal peers" might well confess. In fact, "it would be worth while to make them lusty promises and even give them some little money in present; for two witnesses who have actually taken money and voted for it are worth ten who have only been offered and refused." Pulteney observed that if the evidence did not come out, the case would better be allowed to drop. In the late summer (August 21), even Queensbury felt that it would be enough to make an open attack on Islay, which "might give the Minister no small disturbance and might prove a weight too great for even his shoulders," though they were "pretty broad ones."

Osborne discussed the *Craftsman's* charges in papers running several weeks (June 22–July 27). The methods in the elections were the same on either side; each used the strength it had. The "Voice of the People . . . ; that is, the Mob with oaken Boughs in their Hats, and no Ideas in their Heads, holloaing about the Country, Liberty and Property! No Excise!" was not the "Sense of the People of England about the Administration of public Affairs." "Noise made by a Pack of ignorant Fellows drunk with Sounds" and "Brandy" was merely the fruit of what the *Craftsman* called "a proper Application to their Passions." The truth was, a majority of the "country People" had been "against the Court since the Revolution, unless in the last four Years of Queen Anne." Perhaps they would remain so until there was "a more general Change among the country Gentlemen and Clergymen, . . . their sole Guides and Leaders."

"Men of Property in Estates and Trade ever did and ever" would "choose the Parliaments of England." Men would not shake off "mutual Dependencies," by which subsisted the "moral and political World." It was unreasonable "to expect that an Elector should vote against the Man to whom he and his Family" were "obliged, unless his Conscience or Judgment" told him "that the other Candidate would make a better Representative of the People." This was human nature, not "Corruption." Two thirds of the members supporting the ministry were "Independent as to their Seats in Parliament"; that is, "Persons who could be chosen by a mutual Interest, . . . their own Relatives and Friends, though the Court stood neuter." More than a fourth of the ministerial members had above four thousand pounds a year; a half, two thousand; the rest had "very good Estates in Land and Money."

The *Craftsman* (July 13) admitted greater wealth to be on Walpole's side, but said that the money had been "squeezed out of the Blood and Bowels of the Kingdom." Osborne the same day went on: The current strife was not between "the Government and the People, or between the King and the Nation, nor between the Minister and the People; but between the Gentlemen in Power and certain Gentlemen out of Power." The ministers were not to be tried by the "Number of Voters," though the result of this trial was in their favor, but "by their Actions . . . only." *"Vox Populi"* was always on the side of Charles II and would have sent William back to Holland, recalling James. What the *Craftsman* called the "Sense of the People" was not to the point, "for the same People, encouraged by proper Authority and having reverend Divines and venerable Judges on their Side, would believe in Witches as well as Patriots and attest the Story of Devils riding on Broomsticks through the Air as strongly as they attest Falsehoods . . . retailed to them every Week in publick Papers . . ."; this was not the "Sense of the People," but "their Passions; not their Judgment, but their Prejudices."

The *Craftsman* replied that Osborne wrote like an "old Woman" and labored the point arriving at "Mother Osborne" as an identifying epithet for the future. Similarly, when an enthusiastic admirer called Walpole the "Father" of the people, Pulteney's wit pronounced him to be "political Daddy" of the nation. Osborne in turn (August 24) denied that either Pulteney, the "Patron," or Amhurst, his "Client," in the *Craftsman* showed "the least Ability for Reasoning"; their strength was "Satire and Ridicule." Pulteney excelled in the "Force and Archness of his Ridicule and the Vigour of his Expression." Amhurst's "Compositions" were "little Pertnesses, cloath'd in smooth, easy Words."

Their paper had "occasional Writers . . . of very different Abilities . . . particularly the Author of the Dissertation on Parties." He had "Knowledge got by Study and the Pursuits of Business and Pleasure." He understood "History and human Nature." His pieces had "Unity of Design and End, Method and Order"; they were "full of Sentiment, strong and masterly Reflections on Men and Things." For all that, these writers had not made their point, and for that reason called their opponents names: "Ministerial Scribbler," "low Creature," "Pedagogue," "an Attorney," "Son of a Potato Man in Ireland." A writer with argument on his side did not resort to tactics such as these.

In autumn Walsingham was still saying that there was "no Medium" between Walpole and Bolingbroke, a "Protestant Succession" and a "Popish Pretender." If a "Faction" were suffered to take "the Choice of Ministers" from the King, it had "full Power to take away his Crown" (October 10). The next day Horace Walpole penned an impressive letter to the Queen. She and the King should warn the Emperor in time. He must not expect the support against France his country had in Marlborough's day. Britain could not give it unless the Dutch would help. The States had not the credit, if they had the will. Contrary assurances sent by agents in England deterred the Emperor from seeking peace. A week later, Horace suggested that his brother lay conditions frankly before the Cabinet in order to win members sympathetic with the King.

Opposition Scot Lords kept up their fight. Out of Parliament, they were of less account. Islay should be impeached. They campaigned to enlist the ·body of their peerage on their side. Cobham with George Lyttleton (recently elected to the lower House) and Chesterfield vied with Dodington in seeking favor from the Prince. The latter's mother finally asked Horace Walpole (October 18) to make inquiries concerning a woman desired for his wife.

Ministerial journalists tried their pens at advocating peace. "The Genius of Britain," said the *Daily Courant* (November 6), smiled "upon the Ocean" when she saw "her Navies

crowding to the Ports with Peace for their Pilot and Preserver," but turned "away her Eyes with Horror" from
"rapacious War, . . . the last Resort of Policy, . . . never
to be put in Practice till the utmost Extremity of Injury"
made "it a Deed of Prudence and Honour." A fortnight later
another hand took up the theme. "Peace" was the "Nurse
of Commerce and the Parent of Plenty; War, . . . the Sire
of Want and the Bane of Industry." "Peace" was the "Health
of the Nation and War a "Disease," preying on "its Vitals."
"Peace" was the "mildest Breath of Heaven"; "War," the
"Thunder of the Almighty's Voice" awaking "Poverty, Woes,
and Death." "Peace" was the "good Man's Hope, the wise
Man's Endeavour; War, . . . the Wish of the Needy and the
Delight of the Cruel." "Peace" was the "Genius of Mankind, its Friend and Preserver; War, . . . a Demon that
frowns upon its Happiness and longs for its Destruction."
In order to retain this blessing, it was worth while to conquer
"Passions," struggle with "Faction," and forbear "Resent-
ment."

While Walpole was at Houghton in November, Mrs. Howard
left her place at court, alleging "unkind usages" by the King.
In the summer she had gone to Bath. Reports were that she
had been with Bolingbroke. Feeling safer since her husband's
death, she was now making ready to wed again. The Queen
was ill, and Newcastle was in charge. Walpole's letter to
Horace, the Duke thought (November 13) the "best" he ever
read. The King and Queen approved and, he believed, would
follow it. But the Secretary of State wished that the Minister
would return and see the King or send advice on foreign letters. Meantime, he hoped to prevent anything that Walpole
would not like.

By a bustle "beyond all Expectations" the opposition made
ready in December for the first session of the new Parliament.
Their "Orators" spared "neither Pains nor Horseflesh to
propagate the Doctrines of their Party." They published an
optimistic roll of strength. Bolingbroke brought his *Dissertation* to an end. When the defeated Scot Lords threatened to
petition, Islay bade them do it. Their successors were chosen

in the same way that they themselves had been before. The first test was to be between Sandys and Onslow in the lower house.

Travelers that summer had noticed a new scheme of gardening in vogue. Kent's plan of working without level or line was used in town on the twelve acres at the Prince's place. It made variety, leaving an "Appearance of beautiful Nature." "Without being told, one would imagine Art had no part in the finishing." The gardens of Claremont, Chiswick, and Stowe were "full of labourers to modernise the expensive works finished in them even since every one's memory."

Thinking of other things in the last days of Christmas week, the Master of Stowe counseled Marchmont that, though the case of Scotland was bad enough, it seemed to him to be "without Redress." Chesterfield wished to help, but knew not how; Carteret and Wyndham promised to be in town. Pulteney was still at Bath, "as uncertain in his motion as his mind." Not knowing these uncertainties in the opposition camp, Walpole in the first week of the new year urged a supporter to come to town. Extravagant rumors were at large, he said; "threats about the Scot peerage" exceeded "all the bounds of reason."

There were also rumors on his side. *The Grand Accuser; the Greatest of all Criminals,* Part I, sold for a shilling and was dispersed by the ministers, Sir Thomas Robinson said. It was alleged that the *Craftsman* was the *Examiner* revived; the author had "Ability in writing," but "pernicious Principles." For many years he had "set himself up for an Accuser and Demolisher of Ministers and Ministries." He had returned to his old "Methods of Virulence and Malice, of Calumny and Slander" in an effort to turn the present ministers out. His case being "peculiar," it deserved to be "proceeded against in a peculiar Manner." Should he be "permitted to seduce the People again and pervert them from their lawful Allegiance?" Not so. It was "high Time to reckon with him" for the "Debt" he owed.

Writers in the *Daily Courant* (January 4) took up the

charge. A "Rabble at a County Election, the peevish, shallow Declaimers on Newspapers in Coffee Houses, or even a London Mob" should not be allowed to "subvert the Constitution." To talk of the "Majority of the People of Great Britain" was "either to talk Nonsense" or indicated "a Design to change the Government." The *Craftsman* replied two weeks later that Oxford was impeached for being "the Prime if not the sole Minister and engrossing to himself the absolute Direction and Management of all Affairs." Walpole was one of his accusers and thus should beware himself.

Sunday, January 12, the opposition Lords at Cobham's heard what Marchmont and his colleagues had to say. Tuesday, when Parliament sat, Onslow was reëlected to the chair. The King confessed that affairs in Europe were in a serious state. After several meetings, opposition peers could not agree. Carteret would not support the Scots, though Cobham did. After a warm assembly February 4, the group broke up, and members of the Rump Steak Club went "heavily" to dine. Two days later the Scots met by themselves. Bedford brought their cause up in the Lords (February 13), and there was talk, but nothing more. The vote of credit was carried the next day in the lower house, 167 to 109. Carteret reflected that a ministry could not stand unless it had a larger vote.

But Walpole was not idle in these weeks. The *Daily Courant* (January 21) thought the personal morality of the ministers to be better now than when Bolingbroke was in place. The next day a series of essays began on "The Reasonableness and Necessity of driving Bolingbroke out of the Kingdom." If he were "once banished," the writer thought, "Faction would crumble and die away; for this Apostate" was "their Life, their Soul, their Support, their sole Counsellor and Director." One who had "ridiculed, reviled, and condemned the Revolution" and other things held dear should not be tolerated in the land. From time to time this charge was made again. Perhaps an act of Parliament might be had, since respite had been granted thus. No "Friend of the present Establishment," the writer said again the day before the Scot petition came up in the Lords, would think the

"Banishment" undeserved or that the country was "secure whilst he" resided there.

The trick was turned. There were good reasons not to wait for Parliament to act. The self-appointed exile struck one final blow before he went. Since he was going, he could say more boldly what he had in mind. It was in part a tribute to the man who made him go. Perhaps there was a glance at Pulteney too. The *Dissertation on Parties* was published as a book. A dedication to Walpole made the author's points.

In lofty tones he used at length pathetic eloquence. In his papers he had tried to vindicate the "Principles of the Revolution," even as Walpole had aforetime at "Sacheverell's Tryal." He meant to "extinguish Animosities and even the Names of those Parties that had distracted the Nation so long." A minister with "no Refuge but in Faction" was in a "Desperate State." Not that it was improper for Walpole to defend himself against writings in the *Craftsman*. The public would judge in that matter. The "Laughers" would be for those with "Wit"; the "Serious," for those with "Reason on their Side." "As to Affairs of Peace or War, publick Occurrences, domestick Management, formed Negotiations, in short, the News of the Day, and the current Business of the Time, weekly and daily Papers" were "properly employed." This was "fair War."

His own papers in the *Craftsman* had pled the constitution's cause. Thrice he repeated it. "The Cause of the Constitution hath been *pleaded;* for the *Constitution* hath been attacked, and is so every Day by those against whom the *Craftsman* so often employs his Pen." Walpole's defenders, not content with praising his "Conduct at Home," his own and that of his brother abroad, went to the roots of "British Liberty." He did not impute the scurrility of these writers to their "Prompter"; the journalists themselves had *"ill Manners, Impudence,* a *foul Mouth,* and a fouler Heart." But in menacing they took a higher note.

A pamphlet "lately published" called for "vigorous proceeding in Parliament" against himself. In it the writer spoke the will of those for whom he wrote. Therefore the "Person

. . . against whom all the Virulence of their Malice" was directed addressed himself to Walpole and observed: "It is possible that you may have very strong Resentments against this Person and he, against you. It is possible that you may have shewn *yours,* and he may have shewn *his* according to the different Circumstances you have had." It was "too certain" that at times the "Publick" had been engaged "in private Quarrels," but the "bare Suspicion of any private Interest . . . in a publick Prosecution" would prejudice it at once. A British Parliament would not tolerate the thought.

But suppose that "this obnoxious Man . . . wrote from his Heart," feeling "for the British Constitution" the "same Warmth" he "laboured to infuse into the Breast of every other Man." Would such a man "be ashamed to avow in the Face of his Country the Contents of the following Sheets?" "Would his Endeavours to reconcile all *Parties* and to abolish odious Distinctions; would pleading for *all the Ends* proposed by and promised at the *Revolution;* for securing the Independency *of the two Houses of Parliament* and the Freedom of Elections as effectually against *Corruption* as they are already secured against *Prerogative* . . . make him pass for the greatest of Criminals? No, sir, . . . his *Accusers,* and his *grand Accuser* in the first Place would pass alone for *Criminal."* If the writer fell at all, it would be as a "Victim to Power."

The author felt his persecution as he wrote. He thought the argument was sound. But "weary of the World," he was preparing "totally" to "retire." He would return to "face the Persecution," although the "Persecutors" might not think he would. Different judgments would attend the character of every man on a "divided Stage." Not all spoke well of any one, but "rarely, very rarely" was there one of whom all spoke "ill except those . . . hired to speak well."

Some said that the writer went away because he was afraid. His wife was ill and had to stay in France. His father had not died as soon as he had thought he would. Without his wife, without the means to live as he desired, without his restoration as a peer, his zest for life in England had declined. Pulteney thought his very presence harmed their cause. Within the year Dawley was up for sale. Perhaps he later told the simple truth himself: His "Part" was "over," and "he who remains on the Stage after his Part is over deserves to be hissed off." Other and younger men would carry on.[4]

[4] *Marchmont Papers,* II. 12ff.; Hervey, *Memoirs,* I. 203ff.; II. 36ff.; Hist. Mss. Com., *Carlisle,* pp. 107ff.; *Various,* VI. 14; *Mar and Kellie,* p. 259; *Egmont Diary,* I. 359ff.; II. 9ff.; *Stopford Sackville,* I. 150ff.; *Townshend,* p. 242; Coxe, *Robert Walpole,* II. 333ff.; III. 133ff.; *Horatio Walpole,* I. 328ff.; Sykes, *Gibson,* pp. 136ff., 154ff.; Torrens, *Cabinets,* I. 420ff.; *Parliamentary History,* IX. 1ff.; Ball, *Correspondence of Swift,* V. 3ff.; Basil Williams, "The Duke of Newcastle and the Election of 1734," *Eng. Hist. Rev.,* XIII. 448ff.; *Political State,* XLVI. 411ff.; Harris, *Hardwicke,* I. 255ff.; Robert P. Phillimore, *Memoirs and Correspondence of George, Lord Lyttelton,* I. 67ff.; Cartwright, *Wentworth Papers,* pp. 502ff.

Chapter XII

VICTORY IN DEFEAT, 1735-1742

> Every Party hangs together by Interest, and every Particular means his own. It is impossible to gratify all; and all that are not gratified are disobliged. Whoever, therefore, is Head of a Party has but an uneasy Station. Whatever Blaze he may take and however absolute he may seem, his Disappointments often equal his Triumphs; and when we say that he carries all before him, it is because we see his Successes but not his Difficulties.
>
> GORDON in the *British Journal*, November 30, 1723.

I

A CHILD IS BORN

OSBORNE was almost sorry Bolingbroke had quit. "I love to argue with you," he said (March 15). "If you go, I go too, for the Ministry will not have an Adversary left worth contending with." Soon, however, another cause invited his support. A writer in the *Daily Courant* had said (January 10), that to revive the question of the repeal of the Test Act and the dispute concerning the see of Gloucester would engage the attention of the public and embarrass the government. These questions and others of like kind were now to be revived.

The campaign was for social as well as ecclesiastical change. The poor should be relieved. The use of alcoholic liquors should be curtailed. The Church should not become too rich again, acquiring from laymen near to death property better left to natural heirs. To save expense, Quakers should be made to pay their tithes by justices of the peace without recourse to other courts.

Two days before Osborne paid his parting tribute to Bolingbroke, appeared the first number of a weekly in the usual format of the *London Journal* and the *Craftsman.* The *Old Whig and Consistent Protestant* was not a party sheet. Supporters of the ministers and of the opposition had soothed Dissenters with vague promises in the months just past. The *Craftsman* was to be neutral in the fight.

A writer in the first number of the new weekly wondered at the elevation to the Irish bench of a clergyman excluded in England. The exclusion seemed to imply "inquisitorial Powers" and the "Subjection of the Crown itself to the lordly Claims of the more sacred Priesthood." Hence an appeal: "Awake ye Whigs, in Defence of injured Majesty, the Honour of your Church thus impudently aspersed and your own and your Fellow-subject's Liberties thus insolently invaded." The old "ecclesiastical Favourite" seemed to be losing ground at court; perhaps there would be a new one. At any rate, the new Bishop of Winchester on the previous Sunday had preached in the royal precincts on, "Here we have no continuing city."

Pulteney sympathized in part with this campaign. He agreed, as he wrote to Swift (March 11), with the comments on Rundle. On the question of opposition in general, he was "heartily tired of struggling to no purpose against the corruption" always likely to "prevail." He might help in repealing the Test Act. It was too late to agitate it that session, but the "merits of the Dissenters were greatly acknowledged," and there would be no "doubt all proper assistance at the proper time."

Walpole was not so sure. He would repeal the Test Act if he could, but recent experiences with churchmen made him hesitate and wonder whether he would ever live to see a "proper time." Perhaps there was a more expedient way. Hoadly, the Bishop of Winchester, tried his hand in *A Plain Account of the Nature and End of the Sacrament of the Lord's Supper.* Using quotations from writers in the New Testament, "who alone had any Authority to declare the Nature of it," he described the sacrament as a "memorial" rite, depending for its usefulness upon the participant rather than the officiating priest. Thus dissenting communicants might by implication partake properly under the auspices of the Established Church without violence to their own consciences.

The *Old Whig and Consistent Protestant* insisted (March 27) that writers in the *Weekly Miscellany,* though professing friendship for the ministry, were in fact by their attacks on Rundle impinging on the royal prerogative and exalting the Church above the State. It thought the Scriptures "plain and easily to be understood" and that the national Church was in accord therewith. An individual, however, might conform to it while believing "many Things contrary to the established Orthodoxy of the Nation, . . . the System of Priests, the Religion of the Prince, or the implicite Faith of the disciplined and ductile Multitude." And none was too sacred to be subject to the civil government. The claim of "Independency in the Clergy" was "Insolence and Sedition." When a writer in the *Daily Courant* (April 17) questioned an immediate reason to fear an infringement of the liberty of private judgment, the new weekly cited (April 24) the *Weekly Miscellany,* "set up and dispersed . . . to vilify the best Men."

Routine legislation and the usual round of opposition moves filled up the days in Parliament. Denied the instructions of the Minister to Poland, Chesterfield failed also to obtain documents concerning the Treaty of Seville. Barnard wished to restrain abuses in the playhouses, which were corrupting City youths. There was a bill against bribery in elections and a resolution concerning the maintenance of the poor. A place bill was rejected in April by a smaller majority than usual. Supporting it were young protégés of Cobham, George Lyttelton and William Pitt, who were said later in the coffeehouses to have made distinguished speeches. With this new blood, the opposition in the House of Commons seemed to be stronger than before. Henry Fox, Hervey's young friend, was a newcomer in that Parliament too. The King ended the session in the middle of May with commendation for prudent conduct in a difficult time.

Against the wishes of his ministers, he meant to go to Germany again. Horace still labored at The Hague, supporting his brother at home in efforts to save Britain from participation in the Continental war. That winter he had appealed directly to Fleury, who had dealt with him secretly behind the back of his own agent. He cared little whether it was by his own mediation of by direct negotiation between France and the Emperor, so he gained the point. Harrington and Newcastle were not wholly sympathetic with his views. There was danger that the King and Harrington in Hanover might wreck the hope of peace. But his Majesty would not have Horace accompany him, nor would he stay at home, as Sir Robert urged.

In the closing days of the session (May 1 and 8) Walsingham defended publicly the country's policy abroad. England would take the part of neither, unless the power of France or the Emperor should become too great. In that case, the danger would be from factionalism at home, though fortunately "this unreasonable Animosity" was not so "violent" as hitherto. The "Business of Parliament" had been transacted "with less Heat" that session than for many years. Only Pulteney was still "peevish without Cause and passionate without Provocation." At the same time the *Old Whig* denied the charge that it was anti-ministerial, professing "political Orthodoxy" and a resolution not to "meddle with great Things," concluding that those not against were for its causes.

Horace Walpole lamented that in a "great crisis" the King would make his journey. "How business" could be "carried on in a practicable manner between the distance of the King at Hanover and his Council in England, especially if there should be difference of opinion" was "incomprehensible." But there was "noe help for it"; Harrington must go, though the Minister at The Hague would like to know what the Secretary of State would say in passing through in order to conduct himself "accordingly."

Pious writers in the *Weekly Miscellany* (May 10) lamented evils of the time, tracing their ancestry from a marriage between "Free Will and Evil Genius" to the more immediate union of "Ignorance" and "Corruption," whose progeny were "Pride, Folly, Fear, Lewdness, Luxury, Cruelty," and finally

"Sickness and Death." In a world so peopled, the stage was naturally not to be compared with that in days of yore, and dress was "contrary to Nature and even Decency." A lady shivered in January with "her Sleeve tucked up to her Shoulder, and no Covering for her Arms besides a transparent Linnen." Was it "useful"; was it "becoming"? No, but it was "new."

Saturday, May 17, George II "passed over Blackheath on his Way to board the Yacht at Gravesend." London was full of rumors the next week that "Sir Robert would not long hold his station." Some said that Henry Pelham would succeed. It was known that the King had refused to take Horace to Hanover. Even loyal supporters, such as Hervey, complained of the Minister's failure to punish his enemies or to reward his friends enough. The disappointments of the younger men encouraged opposition in the lower house. Hervey had in mind especially the brothers, Stephen and Henry Fox. Walpole in reply lamented the small number of places in his gift, hinting when he dared the failure of the King to understand.

The *Old Whig and Consistent Protestant* had already found (June 12) that its campaign in "Favour of Liberty," against an authoritarian Church, caused an "Outcry that Religion, Truth, Government, and every Thing valuable" was "going to Wreck." Its authors were "charged with Atheism, Deism, and republican Principles." A commendation of Hoadly's pamphlet (June 26) as by an author "to whom the Publick" was more "obliged than perhaps to any Person living for his Writings in Defence of civil and religious Liberty" did not mitigate this charge.

Walsingham did not approve of the *Old Whig*. He had a scheme for unifying Walpole's defense. The *London Journal,* the *Daily Courant,* even the *Free Briton,* should disappear. A single ministerial daily would take their place. There would be no duplication of the *Daily Courant's* news. Osborne, as the ablest of the group, would still have the choicest day; his weekly essay would come out on Saturday as before. Walsingham would write for Thursday, when his weekly had appeared. The *Daily Courant* writers would come four times a week. A title was chosen "with a View to the Intelligence" the journal would "contain," its staple being news.

Walsingham, the general manager, announced the plan Thursday, June 26. Saturday, Osborne in his last essay in the *London Journal* discoursed on private judgment against "Authority over Conscience" and referred his readers to the *Old Whig and Consistent Protestant.* On the same day the *Daily Courant,* established in the first years of the reign of Anne, forerunner in a field of which the possibilities were yet unrealized, sent its last issue to the press. Monday, June 30, the *Daily Gazetteer* appeared.

The newspaper was growing up. No other ministers had ever had support by such a press. It was a new experiment. The same goods would be offered, but at less expense and to a wider public, it was hoped. The coffee-houses would have a single paper to take in. The quantity of news purveyed would be the same. The advertisements would not be much less. Essays in comment, as before, would be what the contributors sent in, provided always they were on the ministerial side. The hope was, by uniting in "the same Paper and by the most extensive Circulation to publish . . . faithful Endeavours in support of the general Interest." It was economy for the ministers, but as an enterprise it would not float itself. The opposition, thus, could not compete on equal terms.

The magazines were handicapped that summer in getting news that had become an item of their stock in trade. Hitherto, they had depended in part on reports in the *Political State,* now drawing to an end. That publication explained in July that interest in the European war left little space for debates in Parliament, "in most Cases" limiting them to "the Substance . . . by Way of Argument, Answer, and Reply." In fact, the Master of the Rolls had in the previous session moved that "the House be cleared and the Doors locked up every Morning," and the Serjeant at Arms was ordered to enforce the rule.

As usual, the press campaign was less intensive in the summer's heat. Writers had recourse to history. Unwilling to give up the profit of the venture, the printer of the *London Journal* revived it for a while with an author who volunteered to help the *Old Whig and Consistent Protestant*. Neither the *Craftsman* nor the *Daily Gazetteer* would openly support that cause. Amhurst remarked the "frank Indecency of uniting an abandoned Crew of Scribblers" to make a daily sheet. The latter boasted in reply that they had put to silence "Bolingbroke," the other side's "chief Strength." The *Proper Reply* had left Pulteney self-condemned. The *Weekly Miscellany* tried to provide an antidote against "Deism" to "obviate the wicked Principles" circulating in "Conversation and in publick Papers." Ministerial writers hoped for quieter times.

Quiet was disturbed again. By the end of August Harrington's house near St. James's was said to be filling up to greet the Princess of Saxe-Gotha, intended consort to the Prince of Wales. Lyttelton cautioned the Prince to try "to gain the affection of the public." To ask additions to the Civil List would help toward "universal discontent." The King had arranged the marriage, which would not come too soon. Walpole's advice had not been asked. Indeed his Majesty sent home that summer commissions which Talbot, Hardwicke, and Walpole thought not legal, power having been delegated to the Queen. But she knew better than to raise the point.

Her husband entertained her in those weeks with accounts of fresh delights he found in Madame Walmoden. Caroline herself was ill and growing old. She knew that the mistress could not take her place as Queen, and worldly wisdom closed her eyes to things she could not help.

The King came back to Kensington that autumn in such haste that he was ill and peevish for a month. Leaving his mistress pregnant, he had promised to return in spring before her time. Attendants noticed that he ceased remaining in the Queen's chamber of mornings, writing to her he left behind. When Walpole returned from Norfolk, Hervey reported his Majesty still in an "abominable humour" to the Queen. Chiefly, he talked of "scenes of his happy loves . . . at Hanover" and details of his "amorous amusements" there. The Queen appeared "a little angry, a little peevish, a little tired."

When Horace Walpole thanked her for "instructions and commands" on foreign affairs, she wished Hervey to let him know that instead of giving commands herself she had "during the whole summer been only writing in pursuance and obedience" to his own. France and the Emperor came at length to terms. Bolingbroke again saw in Walpole fortune's favorite. If the English ministers "had any hand in it," they were "wiser" than he thought, if not, "they were luckier than they deserved to be."

Events between the return of the King and the meeting of Parliament revealed the changed complexion time had brought. Pulteney was discouraged. The Queen, he wrote to Swift (November 22), was not so "well beloved" as he could wish; the "Minister, . . . as much hated and detested as ever." But a new Parliament chosen just after the failure of his "odious scheme" went on as before. "After this, what hopes" could there "ever possibly be of success?" The King could never "fail of a majority in both houses of Parliament." He made "all in one house" and chose "above half in another." He was himself feeling the want of Daniel Pulteney's help. He missed also a lesser, lately dead, who performed the "drudgery" of collecting information he had used. Though he would act the same part; lacking aid, it would be with less effect. Bolingbroke would not return from France even though "his father died."

The perspective of distance did not give that leader added hope. Were his father as "likely to die" as he seemed "likely to live," he wrote Wyndham (January 5, 1736), it was still prudent to sell Dawley as "no longer desirable." In England he was "an alarm to the Whigs." His friends should say that he did not desire power and was indifferent as to "restoration." If the Duchess of Marlborough would provide materials, he would write a defense of the late Duke. If Wyndham could not "do much good," perhaps he might "prevent at least some evil."

With Parliament about to meet, the *Craftsman* defended (January 10) Rapin's history from Walsingham's attack. None was ever "so universally read by all Degrees of People in the Kingdom." The press campaign was taking other turns. Osborne and the *Old Whig* engaged in friendly argument, wherein the former, writing for a ministerial organ, was at a disadvantage. Eschewing personalities, he would take the side of neither Rundle nor Gibson in their dispute. Though favoring a Church dependent on the government, he was not sure that the English Church was yet too rich. Perhaps the lesser livings should be raised to fifty pounds a year. The "dreadful Independency of the Church with all its Train of dismal Consequences" was "at an End," as were the "theological Scarecrows, Heresy and Schism." A gradual change had been apparent in the English clergy since the Revolution. They were now the best preachers and the most learned in Europe.

The *Old Whig and Consistent Protestant* (November 13) thought he might exaggerate. There was a "great Increase of Wealth and Land in Mortmain and Advowsons daily purchasing by Spiritual Corporations." Had Gibson given up the plan stated in the preface to his *Codex?* Had not a tithe bill recently been "thrown out" and an "ecclesiastical Court Bill amended by it?" Was Rundle Bishop of Gloucester? Had he not gone to Ireland? Perhaps so, but the *Daily Gazetteer* (November 20) defended Gibson as "one who for more than forty Years in an uninterrupted Series of uniform Conduct" had "appeared upon all Occasions and in all Junctures an Enemy of *Tyranny and Persecution* and, as such, a constant Friend to the Revolution and Protestant Succession." But the *Old Whig* found an "Inquisition" under way "into the State, Members, and Circumstances of all Men whatsoever, Dissenters from the Church." With a "Sword" drawn, any "Man . . . not a *very honest Gentleman*" would be "apt to think the Assault begun."

Osborne (December 6) pled the services of Hoadly, who, supplementing Locke, "went to the Bottom of the Arguments relating to the common Rights of Subjects and convinced more Clergymen by his cool, decent, and strong Way of Reasoning than any Layman or perhaps any Number of Laymen tho' of equal Ability could have done." He had been the "great Apostle and Converter of the Clergy to the Principles of the Revolution and to Sentiments of Liberty worthy of Men and Christians." The *Old Whig* was not convinced. If the Church acquired "Inheritances without the Power of Alienation" only to raise all livings to fifty pounds a year, it would take a tenth of the revenue of all the kingdom's land. No minister could withstand a power thus intrenched.

This was not the only question raised. A group of ministerial supporters thought something ought to be done in behalf of the colonies as well as to enhance the benefits they brought. There were projects for a court to consider "matters of trade and navigation" and for further settlements of the poor. More urgent was a restriction of "intoxicating Liquors." Apothecaries and chemists were said to sell them "under the salubrious Titles of Gripe and Cholick Waters." For months Hogarth's cartoons had emphasized the evils of this vice. The Justices of Peace in Middlesex petitioned Parliament to act.

The King announced to this body (January 15) a restoration of peace in Europe, which he hoped would banish "discord" at home. The army might be reduced. But the opposition said that England could have had no hand in making peace, or France would not have got Lorraine. Pitt was teller for the ministers when Pulteney moved a reference of the navy estimates to a select committee. Argyll had become a British Field Marshal, and Dodington a Lord of the Treasury before Parliament met. A versifier in the *Daily Gazetteer* observed (January 20) that the *Craftsman* alone "with Grief" surveyed the scene. "Are thus my Toils repaid?", he asked the "witless Herd."

> Is Britain's Peace at last to mine preferr'd?
> Ye ragged Rascals, ye are hir'd to this;
> Be incorrupt like me, and give a Hiss.

The hiss would come. Now the *Craftsman* (January 24) could only complain that Walpole and the Queen ruled the country, guarding the King so closely that he was a stranger in his own dominions and knew not what was done. Not so felt those who saw his Majesty's haste to have the session done and be away. The Queen delayed the marriage of their son to hold the father on at home. Harrington's house had been got ready for its master, not the bride. Walpole and his supporters began to dine together at the Bell in King Street to make their plans. The opposition flagged within the House. Pulteney was ill and seldom took a part. With Bolingbroke away, Wyndham did not seem to care.

The King would not delay. In February he sent a message to his son. The wedding must be hurried up, or he would not attend. Knowing little of the fate awaiting her, the Princess came to Greenwich Easter Sunday, April 25. Lady Irwin, Carlisle's daughter, was her companion, having made the quickest passage to Holland and return "ever known." Walpole had warned her that she had a "ticklish post." The Prince was at the boat to meet his bride, not yet eighteen. Within a week, she went to court and had been wed. Handel composed an anthem which was poorly sung. The omission of a procession prevented Hervey from ruffling Irish peers a second time. His Majesty began to give his son a niggardly fifty thousand pounds a year.

The Princess made a good impression where she went. Walpole thought the pleasing of her husband and his father both the measure of no slight success. She undertook at once to learn the language of the country where she was to live. Given half a chance, she meant to do her part. The curious approved her looks. Lady Irwin found the Prince effusive with embraces when they met. Ten times they kissed before she left the room. Hervey had helped him get release from Henrietta Vane. Her child already dead, its mother did not linger long. The Queen advised indulgence of her son's "amours." "Jealousy" chiefly wounded those who felt the hurt.

There were other things to think about if Parliament was to rise in time. A motion to repeal the Test Act was introduced and lost. The Mortmain and Tithe bills were pending when the Princess came. Gibson went to Walpole and urged him to oppose. But the Minister had yielded on the Test Act merely to keep peace and meant to see these measures through.

The Bishop was as warm upon the other side. Summoning his colleagues on the bench, he urged that they arouse the clergy of their dioceses. His partnership with Walpole could not stand this strain. Arousing the clergy to "put the whole nation in a ferment" was not a little matter for a minister who recalled Sacheverell.

The Mortmain Bill was passed after the universities were excepted by the Lords. The Tithe Bill failed. Hardwicke was sympathetic with the end to be attained, but found fault with the procedure it proposed. There was not time to iron the matter out. An act to prohibit strong drink by the use of high licenses and taxes passed. Egmont found a parson of Teddington who had written the previous year on the "poison-ous qualities of spiritual liquors" with tears of joy in his eyes. Walpole had to find another seventy thousand pounds to make up the loss to the Civil List. Pulteney admitted that "nothing but a total prohibition" would cure the evil, but had some fears for the distilling trade and the "poor families" thus distressed. Furthermore, the act might "produce such riots and tumults" as would "endanger" the "present estab-lishment." He had heard of "sumptuary laws" prescribing clothes for certain groups, but not prescribing food or drink.

The *Craftsman* complained again, that the King had not changed ministers when the "People desired it." Osborne in-quired (February 28), who the "People" were and how his Majesty would ascertain their will. Should he read country journals and listen in at coffee-houses? Might not the "People assembled in Parliament" be wiser than scribblers for the press or a "Mob huzzaing with Clubs in their Hands, oaken Boughs in their Hats, and no Sense in their Heads?" It required "no Art" to govern by force, he reflected the next week, "but the greatest to govern by Management of other People's Opinions, Prejudices, Passions, and different Views of Life." Such was the task a British minister had to face.

Others besides the ministers were appealing to the crowd. Egmont went Thursday, March 25, to a theater in the Hay-market to see Henry Fielding's *Pasquin* and found the house still crowded after a fortnight's run. The author was a protégé of Lyttelton and the Cobham group. A character in the play was "Queen Common Sense." Some of the lines were pertinent to the pending bills; others made the usual points against the court.

By early spring (March 27) Osborne was sorry he had not kept his word to quit with Bolingbroke.

> He engaged our Attentions; he exercised our Reason and commanded our Passions; he had a fine Genius; great Knowledge of Men and Books; his Discourses were full of Sentiment; his Diction nerv'd and sinew'd; strong, yet polite; bold, yet delicate; so that had not the Iniquity of his Heart engaged him against his Country, he would have been justly counted one of the best Writers of the Age. It was an Honour to wrestle a Fall with him; besides he afforded Matter to discourse about for he wrote upon all the great Arguments relating to Politicks.

The writers left used only "a little low Wit and Humour upon Persons and Names." Again, Osborne thought it time to "have done." The *Daily Gazetteer* "being chiefly designed for ministerial Subjects," he would appear again if opponents said anything worth while. Until they did, he would cease "impertinently troubling the Publick."

The *Craftsman* complained (April 3) that the Dissenters were "bubbled." The ministers had not performed their promises. He had himself "purposely" kept "neuter." Walsingham denied (April 16) the promise. Walpole would have "exposed" both the "Safety" of Dissenters and "his own had he revived the Spirit of Division; . . . fired the Nation with religious Animosities, and this too with no Probability of attaining the Good for which he should risque so much Evil."

The *Old Whig* noted (April 8) *Pasquin's* "Panegyrick," as Mr. Fustian called it, on the English clergy, "so different from" that satire's "heathen Priest." He wondered that Queen Common Sense had no "Minister" on the stage. Although she did not, the strokes of the piece were so "strong" that if audiences held up as they had done "for twenty Nights together" its blows might hurt more than a series of pamphlets would. The *Weekly Miscellany* (May 15) was moved quite otherwise. It had not realized until lately how systematic the efforts to lessen the prestige of the Church and clergy. That a "modern Audience" in a theater "could with Pleasure behold the Religion" of the "Country represented as inconsistent with Common Sense" was a fact to be deplored. "Thank God, the Legislature had not yet come into the Plans of these designing Men."

Twitted with "Prostitution," if he wrote again, "Ingratitude," if he should quit, Osborne returned to say (May 15) that of the Church he wrote his "honest Sentiments." "All ministerial Writing must be defensive." But why defend if none attacked? The "Devil of the Party" had gone into "voluntary Exile." As for the rest, some were "Converts and others half converted, or waiting for the Moving of the Waters by some courtly Hand" that they might "step in and be healed of all their Discontent." If the *Craftsman* favored the Dissenters, why not publish on their side? Believing the race "at present over," Osborne meant to "breathe a little."

But an episode in the House of Commons before the session closed betokened what the next year had in store. Pitt and Lyttelton were heard on the address upon the marriage of the Prince. Not relishing remarks the former made, the King turned him out as Cornet of Horse. He was a "young man of no fortune," Lady Irwin wrote, but "a very pretty speaker," one the Prince was "particular to, and under the tuition of Lord Cobham." He had now become "a distinguished Friend of the Liberty of his Country," a writer in Fog's *Journal* said (May 29). But by that time the King was on his way to keep his tryst. Horace went that year, Harrington being ill.

The *Old Whig and Consistent Protestant* did not yet despair. Progress made gave room for hope. The *Weekly Miscellany* was as sure the Church must stand its ground. Writers in the *Daily Gazetteer* insisted that both the circulation and the influence of the *Craftsman* had declined. Fog's weekly was now dragging toward its end. By early autumn ministerial versifiers thought the "Shafts of Malice" to be "spent," since "fierce Ambition" learned "to be content."

Throughout the summer, one point gave rise to fear. The *Craftsman* (June 5) would have imposed restraints on "Mother

Gin," but was "not for having her knocked in the Head." The *Daily Gazetteer* replied (June 23) that Walpole's preference was to come more gradually to the task, but in the past few years excessive drinking had been "complained of by all sorts of People as an Evil which cried aloud for Redress." Consumption of spirits could not be redressed without curtailing it. The Minister owned privately the apprehensions that he felt.

In riots in Spitalfields in July, caused by a flood of Irish laborers willing to work for a third less pay, the Gin Act was a shibboleth for the mob. The several thousand discontented did not heed a reading of the Riot Act. The Tower guards were called to help. The Proteus mob at Edinburgh raised the point again. The *Daily Gazetteer* explained (September 14) that though "private Property must always give Way to public Convenience," when laws affected the "Interests of particular Bodies of Men," the sufferers would complain, be the "Regulations . . . never so just and reasonable in themselves." A fortnight later Walpole was chiefly afraid of a "very riotous and mobbish Application" at the next session of Parliament. A member of the ministerial circle in mid-November thought that in spite of "inconceivable" and various ways of evading the act, by Christmas the drinking of gin would be entirely broken up.

As autumn waned, the *Craftsman* (November 23) replied pointedly to ministerial writers who charged him with failure in the cause he undertook. He knew but "three possible Methods of getting rid" of an "ignorant or a wicked and tyrannizing Minister": by "the Wisdom and Goodness of the Prince himself, the Interposition of the Legislature, or the general Complaints and Cries of the People for Redress." Surrounded by flatterers, Princes seldom had "a good Servant unless by Accident." An "honest Parliament and a good Prince" could bring relief only when there was no "unwarrantable Influence" by a corrupt ministry. The sole remaining hope was for cries of the people to awake a "deluded Prince" and a "mercenary Parliament."

Not on this line was the fight that year. The royal birthday came and went before the King returned. Tradesmen lamented loss of patronage. The birthday of the Prince was celebrated all the more. Affable beyond most scions of his house, he had the instincts of a demagogue and learned increasingly the art of winning crowds. Cobham's group had taken him in tow, though Dodington still lingered in his entourage. At the opera indignant people hissed the Queen. A woman quack, not recognized within her carriage on the Kentish Road, was greeted as she passed with: "No Hanover Whore."

Complaints were heard openly about the town. Walpole and Hervey urged the Queen to write and hurry up her recreant spouse, inviting him to bring his mistress if he must. She wrote and got a tender letter in reply some thirty pages long. With the contents of the missive, she confessed herself to be "reasonably pleased"; but of it, "not unreasonably proud." Her husband followed it impetuously to make amends.

He got to Helvoetsluys Friday, December 11. Sir Charles Wager would not risk his royal passenger in a storm. Never having "seen a storm" at sea, the King would sail. For several days they thought him lost. Ministers at the Duke of Devonshire's considered the proclamation of the Prince. While she was at church a message came to tell the Queen, her husband was back at Helvoetsluys. While he stayed, a fire in London gave the Prince a chance to shine before the crowd. Not until Saturday, January 15, did the King, returning, pass through London streets. None pulled their hats off as he passed. "Some of the Vulgar" by the way were heard to hiss.

Perhaps his fright had stirred alive a better self. Perchance he had not understood the human feelings of his wife. He greeted her with warmth and smiles. "No man," he said, "ever had so affectionate and meritorious a wife or so faithful and able a friend." But a cold contracted in the storm grew worse for several days, and he was not able to read his speech to Parliament (February 1). The Prince was designated on the commission, but did not go.

Nine days after the King's return the Archbishop of Canterbury died. Denied a voice in choosing a successor in London, Gibson did not wish the place. With the patronage of the Queen, Sherlock had opposed the ministers in the previous session and was advised by his mistress to retire to his diocese. Walpole would have liked his own old tutor, Francis Hare. Hervey and the Queen finally supported Potter of Oxford, whose "capacity was not so good, nor his temper so bad as to make the ministry repent" of giving him the place. With Gibson in opposition, the Church might still be difficult. Certainly it could not be defied.

In the week that Parliament met, appeared the first number of a new journal, *Common Sense,* named for the character in Fielding's play. It was designed to supplement the *Craftsman's* work, speaking the mind of Lyttelton and the Cobham group. Its announced purpose was "to rebuke Vice, correct Errors, reform Abuses, and shame Folly and Prejudice without regard to anything but Common Sense." Amhurst's paper henceforth was of less account, save that it earned pittances for those who sent it forth.

Monday, two days after the birth of the new weekly, hearing that the Prince was ill, Dodington went next morning to inquire. This Lord of the Treasury was thus apprised of a secret kept as yet from other servants of the crown. His Royal Highness meant to apply to Parliament for a hundred thousand pounds a year. Walpole learned the news the next week-end. Two days later it was in "everybody's Mouth."

With this news came also on St. Valentine's Day the sudden death of Talbot, the Lord Chancellor. Hardwicke was the man in line, and a week later got the price he asked to take the place. He and Newcastle were thus left the dominant leaders in the Lords. The Cobhams with the Prince's project might well call for all the skill of both. Confronted with this question, leaders heeded little the *Old Whig's* wish (February 10) for "locally chosen Guardians of the Poor." Such men as Egmont and his brother thought (February 18) the Prince's application fit only "for young men . . . ambitious and inconsiderate"; those older, with "something to lose," desiring "peace and quiet," were "troubled." Charles

Howard was of opinion the next day that it was the "most unlucky and the most unfortunate measure . . . that ever came into Parliament." It seemed to Islay that those who advised the step "had a mind to shake the King's hour glass and spill the sand."

As best he could, Walpole made haste to be prepared. Using every persuasive effort at his command, he urged the King to settle a jointure on the Prince's wife and to make permanent to the husband his fifty thousand pounds a year. Monday, February 21, when Hardwicke went to get his seals, he and some colleagues in the Cabinet were sent to bear this offer to the Prince. He felt aggrieved to go on such an errand to the Heir Apparent, making his first call as the Lord Chancellor. The Prince was enigmatic in reply. He was "sorry," but the matter was "in other hands."

It was the Cobhams' plan, and Pulteney did not quite approve of it, though he made the motion, February 22. The prestige of his name was the chief weight of any argument the mover used. Walpole was cool and sensible in reply. "Let us stop in time," he said, "this widening gap which may make way for an inundation to drown us all." Members were in distress to know which way to vote. Hopes for the future challenged the uncertainty of mounting age. Cobham and Chesterfield were active on the Prince's side, but Wyndham and his remnant stayed away. The move was lost, 234 to 204. Carteret made the motion in the Lords, where it was lost by twice as many votes. His Royal Highness joined openly the canvass for support. Horace Walpole feared that he was in "hands" that would "endeavour to bring all things into confusion." Egmont heard that had the Prince succeeded, the next move would have been to send Walpole to the Tower.

Other moves in Parliament taxed the Minister's ingenuity that year. The long debate on the Edinburgh mob had to be ended in a way to punish the city for the disorder and yet leave Islay able and willing to keep control. *Common Sense* took up the *Craftsman's* cry against the King's prerogative, instancing the national debt as an unhappy source of royal power. The current interest rate was low, and Sir John

Barnard introduced a bill reducing that on public debts from four to three per cent. It was a clever move to embroil Walpole with either the landed or the monied men.

With more insight than some of his followers, the Minister opposed the move. National obligations were held, he knew, by landed men. Adopting a lofty resolution to keep faith with South Sea annuitants, he won support from those who had financial as well as from those with political interests involved. A mob inspired from Garraway's Coffee-House shouted, "Long Live Sir Robert Walpole," in the streets. The more enthusiastic had to be restrained from burning Barnard's house. The measure was lost, 244 to 134.

At the theater in the Haymarket, which even his friends knew as "Mr. Fielding's Scandal Shop," that author repeated that season his success in the *Historical Register for the Year 1736* and *Eurydice Hissed,* and began to rehearse another piece representing Horace Walpole holding in one hand a balanced scale while tugging with the other at his breeches. Friends of the ministers thought it time to call a halt. The *Daily Gazetteer* demanded that they act. The new pieces wanted *Pasquin's* sprightly lines. One so little Walpole's friend as Egmont found *Eurydice Hissed* a satire on the Minister, an allegory on the Excise Bill. The Prince was there, applauding when the actors made the author's points.

Chesterfield in speeches in the House of Lords and by essays in *Common Sense* affected indignation at the curtailed freedom of the stage. Thenceforth, by the Licensing Act all theatrical entertainment was placed under the supervision of the Lord Chamberlain. The *Daily Gazetteer* alleged (June 9) that the measure was passed because "by a most wicked Design . . . the Royal Family and the King upon the Throne were made the Object of . . . Attack." The act would not work as its opponents said. Pieces "lately exhibited" at the Haymarket with success would have been damned at Drury Lane. The two regular theaters would be free as before, always taking Orders from the Lord Chamberlain and barring "political Medleys."

Given their way, some of the ministerial writers (July 7)

would have placed restrictions on the press. But their patron "after Victory" would not adopt a measure he had "scorned . . . during the Heat of Battle." However, when the *Craftsman* commented (July 2) that Shakespeare's *Julius Caesar* might be suppressed because in it a king was "insnared by a foreign Mistress," and made also other points with similar design, that issue was suppressed, and Haines, the printer, placed under arrest. So was John Kelly, reputed author of Fog's *Journal* (July 16), for insinuating that the Queen by acting as procurer for the King "kept him at Home."

In these same months Lyttelton and his group puffed a long, dull poem, *Leonidas,* by Richard Glover, a City pamphleteer and partisan of Barnard's group. Other critics called it a creditable first effort, acclaimed beyond deserts because of "party Politics." "Poetry" it was not, wanting the "Manner and Style peculiar" to that art. However that might be, Glover reaped a passing fame on which he built the slight career he later had.

Again the ministers seemed to have a breathing spell. Bolingbroke thought (June 9) that it had been plain "for some years that nothing but the hand of fate could shake the men" in power. Wyndham had written that the affair of the Prince troubled Walpole chiefly because of the King's poor health. Bolingbroke thought an organized opposition might have made it trouble more. Amhurst collected another seven volumes of the *Craftsman's* essays, omitting those that gave offense. The *Daily Gazetteer* doubted in verse (May 20) whether one who had eluded St. John's "Pen," laughed "each Day at Pulteney's Spleen," and shook "his Sides at Barnard's Spite," would be moved much by Lyttelton's "pert Pen" or beg him "not to print again."

Within the ministerial circle all was not so calm. Walpole finally obtained for Henry Fox a place as Surveyor of the Works, but not a peerage, and lamented that the King was as "reluctant to bestow honours as money." True, at the Minister's behest, he began to appear more frequently at levees to greet the crowd, but his son was using greater art.

Two things Walpole made clear. He would not yield to

Carteret's overtures. He told Newcastle and the Queen that they must choose between them to the end. When Hervey warned him that Newcastle was trying to make a party with Hardwicke to stand alone, Walpole agreed that it might be so. Perhaps he thought, the Duke did only what he might have done himself in the same case. But he had made his choice. He would not now discard the Pelhams if he could. "He was too old to form new schemes"; therefore, he "must rub on with" the hand he held until it "would last no longer" and then "throw up his cards." When Lady Walpole died (August 20), her husband lacked the time to grieve had he been so inclined.

The pregnancy of the Princess was known in her circle by the middle of March. The public was told in April that she was four months gone. July 5 the hopeful father wrote to the Queen, but would not tell her the expected time. The royal family spent the summer at Hampton Court. The Prince wished his child to be born in London. Had not a man the right to manage the accouchement of his wife? His parents preferred the summer residence and so informed their son. The birth of an heir to the crown was not a small event. The Queen was ill, but wished to witness the labor in order to be sure that no tricks were played.

Sunday, July 31, the Princess dined in public with the King and Queen. That evening she was ill. Against her wishes and the entreaties of attendants, her husband secretly called a coach. By ten o'clock with speedy driving they were in town. Nothing was ready, St. James's being closed. Table-cloths had to serve her bed for sheets. Within an hour after she arrived a child was born. At the same time at Hampton Court the royal couple finished cards and went to bed. Two hours later a message said, the Princess was in labor. Asking a robe in order that she might attend, the Queen was told that she would need a coach as well. Getting off at half past two, she and Hervey were in town by four. Walpole and Harrington came in. The Minister thought it prudent to reflect, but Caroline was in a hurry to return.

The child, it seemed, was born before its time. Hervey saw

it as "a little rat of a girl about the bigness of a good large toothpick case." But his obstetrical experience was insufficient to make his judgment of a newborn babe of much account. In his excitement, the Prince was voluble, explaining the events. He meant to go to Hampton Court that day to ask his father to have a part in the christening. The Queen advised him not to go. The King would be displeased at all the "bustle" he had made. After a conference with Walpole at Hervey's lodgings, that Lord and Caroline were back to greet the angry King at eight o'clock. Henry Fox was left behind to urge that Walpole, when he came, should speak with Hervey before he saw the King.

The Minister followed as soon as he had evidence to authenticate the birth of one who might be heiress to the crown. Hervey reminded Walpole that both the King and Queen blamed him for setting up the Prince with fifty thousand pounds a year. A breach would come between the royal parents and their son. Why put it off, now that the Prince had challenged public ridicule? Walpole was not convinced. The Prince himself began to wonder how the world would take what he had done. Carteret, Chesterfield, and Pulteney came to St. James's, and he began to hedge, changing the story told to Walpole and Harrington on the morning of the birth. He wrote to make submission to the King and Queen. The truth was dimmed, as groups began to spar for place. A family incident became an issue in the party strife.

Nine days later the Queen drove in to call a second time. Her son was cool within the Palace, but followed her outside and knelt to kiss her hand before the crowd. As Walpole wished, she and the King were sponsors for the child. But reluctantly the ministers were convinced; the break must come. At length, September 10, the Cabinet agreed. The Prince and Princess should not go to court. Courtiers must choose between the father and his son.

Lyttelton felt that (August 18) "no submission" had been wanting on the "Prince's side." He took a place made vacant in his Royal Highness' court. The poet Thomson wrote an ode. He hoped to live to sing the Prince's reign when France would "insult" and Spain "rob" no more. Monday, September 12, the nurse with the Princess Augusta in her lap was seen to leave for Kew. The Prince and Princess followed. The guards were ordered not to stand at Carlton House. As summer passed, the opposition thought there might be hope. Reconciliation would not come. Marchmont wrote to Stair (September 28) that Carteret and Pulteney would be moved to act. Appeals were made to justify the Prince and answered on his father's side.

To Bolingbroke abroad (October 13), the case was not so clear. He thought the break was overdue. He hoped advisers of the Prince would make its pretence not only "plausible but popular." Both "plausibility" and "popularity" were now wanting, as it seemed to him. He assumed that it affected Wyndham as "a scene from Tom Thumb would have done." One on the "stage" no doubt "must keep the countenance" his part required; one off of it could "laugh" his "fill."

The royal family came back from Hampton Court, October 28. In mourning, Walpole skipped the birthday and went to Norfolk for a rest. Partisans of the King filled up the room to show that the quarrel had no bad effect. Uncertain what the winter's cause would be, the *Craftsman* glanced a week (November 5) at Spanish depredations, and remarked again "corruption" by a Minister who "filled a certain Bench with Persons of mean Learning and worse Morals" and sent abroad "Buffoons," exposing the "Country to the Contempt of foreign Courts."

In her new library in St. James's Park on Wednesday morning, the next week, the Queen was taken ill. She had complained twice at Hampton Court of similar pains. Thursday she was better, and the King attended his levee. Friday, Andrew Stone, Newcastle's Secretary, wrote to Horace Walpole that if she did not improve relays of horses would be sent to bring Sir Robert back to town. Saturday her doctors learned that for two years she had concealed a ruptured abdomen. "Oppressed with sorrow and dread," Sir Robert, back in town, wrote at noon Tuesday to say her Majesty was losing ground.

The news appealed to some quite otherwise. Chesterfield

from Bath, Saturday, November 12, urged Lyttelton to have the Prince make personal advances to the King and Queen. If the Queen died, Walpole should be looked upon as out whether he really was or not. The Prince's faction must not treat with the Minister. He might retain some power with the King, but would not dare "to mention many things" he might have compassed "by her means." By Tuesday that optimistic Lord was even more convinced. They might expect that Hardwicke, Compton, Argyll, and other men in Walpole's group would now increase their demands. The Prince should make public the "resentment" that he felt. The contest would be "very unequal between the next heir to the crown and a minister whose favour, whose fortune, and possibly whose life" depended upon "the precarious protection of a passionate and changeable Prince, who into the bargain never loved him."

But there were troubles in his party too. The "sallies and extravagances of Pulteney" were changing "oftener than the wind." His occupation seemed to be to "pick up a few pennies at whisk," his ambition to "get as much power and as much money as soon" as he could "upon any terms," which revealed perhaps as much about Chesterfield as about the man of whom he wrote.

The King revealed his feelings for his wife throughout the painful days she lingered after hope was gone. Attendants heard pathetic, tender passages between the two. Some of them stir a smile in calmer times, with tragedy behind. But those who waited knew what they would lose in Caroline. Walpole scarcely saw how to go on. He lacked the time or patience to persuade the King. Hervey volunteered to help. Perhaps that plan might work, though Hervey would not help for naught. She died on Sunday night, November 20, while the waiting husband held her hand.

The Prince was not allowed to capitalize his grief. A precedent was found that made his sister the chief mourner when between the hours of twelve and one at night, December 17, the body was taken from St. James's to its final resting place. The King was overcome when greeting the attendants of his Queen. But the next week he went to see some horses brought from Turkey by the Lord Kinnoul. The cynical remarked that, having gone thus far, he might be looking at fine women soon. Within two months he was attending his levee.

During these weeks the *Craftsman* hammered on at inroads made by Spain on British trade. The *Daily Gazetteer* replied that ministers supported all the merchants' rightful claims. A costly war would not enlarge their privileges. Keene at Madrid thought the merchants never willing to confess that they might be wrong. The Spanish claimed the right of searching ships they did not seize.

Fog's *Journal* being now defunct, its printer was engaged for *Common Sense*. The previous printer did not like the change, and for a while two rival weeklies used the name and did not help their cause. For one number, the *Craftsman* was suppressed.

The Prince's faction questioned whether they should mourn the Queen. Frederick gave orders that his coach be hung with black. The timid, dilettante Chesterfield at Bath (November 28), afraid of "singularity," would not conform "if any number of peers" would bear him company. December 12 he had not gone to town. With a "supream contempt for fools and an extreme aversion to knaves," he did not wish to be an "actor" on the "public stage," where both of these would always shine. Yet he would come to London in the hope of "seeing Cobham." As for mourning, he would do as he had done in 1727. He was sure that if the Lord President had proposed the "deification of her late Majesty" and the bishops had been ordered "to perform the ceremony of her apotheosis in the true pagan manner" it would have been obeyed. Nothing went on at Bath. Pulteney was still there, but did "not know it." Chesterfield would come to London, "which after all," was "England."

Hervey assured Walpole (December 1) that he could help to greater strength than ever with the King. His Majesty told Horace in the month that Sir Robert was "his chosen minister," superior in that office and "preferable to all his subjects." The opposition had to nurse the Prince. New Year's Day, Stair wrote to Marchmont that if "all the different pieces" could be joined "Sir Robert could not stand" against the weight. If by word and deed the Prince would strictly oppose an increase of the royal power, all "true lovers of the country" would be united on his side. Once Walpole was in a minority, all the "enchantment" that deluded the King would fade. The Minister was weaker since he lost the Queen; his health was worse. Cobham was "a man."

Whatever else he did, the Prince corrected one mistake. In January he notified the King that his consort was with child again. This time Archbishop Potter attended at the birth. Wednesday, May 24, nine months and twenty-three days after her ordeal of the previous year, the Princess bore a son. From infancy his breath was English air. He suckled at a Chelsea woman's breast of the plebeian name of Smith. He used the English language when he spoke. Otherwise, his blood and name were German as the predecessors in his line.[1]

II

A WAR BEGINS

Amhurst had lost his zest. "Necessity shoves him on; set out he must, matter or no matter, like a stage coach." So said the *Literary Courier of Grub Street* (January 19), in which the *Grub Street Journal* approached the end of a dull and fruitless life. The *Weekly Miscellany* droned on, now defending the Church, soon about to arouse itself in a feverish fear of George Whitefield and John Wesley. *Common Sense* dwelt on a hackneyed theme, the liberty of the press. The King still mourned the loss of "his best adviser in public matters, . . .

---

[1] In addition to periodicals and pamphlets mentioned in the text, Hist. Mss. Com., *Carlisle*, pp. 144ff.; *Egmont Diary*, II. 171ff.; (14 Rept. Appendix, Pt. 9), pp. 2ff.; Torrens, *Cabinets*, I. 447ff.; Coxe, *Robert Walpole*, II. 333ff.; III. 250ff.; *Horatio Walpole*, I. 363ff.; *Marchmont Papers*, II. 57ff.; Ball, *Correspondence of Swift*, V. 146ff.; Sichel, *Bolingbroke*, II. 537ff.; Straus, *Unspeakable Curll*, pp. 154ff.; *Parliamentary History*, IX. 615ff.; X. 1ff.; Ilchester, *Holland*, I. 39ff.; Hervey, *Memoirs*, II. 161ff.; III. 1ff.; *Political State*, L. 55ff.; LII. 269ff.; LIII. 11ff.; LIV. 1ff.; Yorke, *Hardwicke*, I. 118ff.; Sykes, *Gibson*, pp. 169ff., 402; Cartwright, *Wentworth Papers*, pp. 522ff.; H. P. Wyndham, *Diary of George Bubb Dodington*, pp. 439ff.; Phillimore, *Lyttelton*, I. 78ff.; Harris, *Hardwicke*, I. 361ff.; Cunningham, *Letters of Horace Walpole*, I. cxixff.; Dobree, *Letters of Chesterfield*, II. 307ff.

his most agreeable companion in private ones." The *Daily
Gazetteer* lamented ironically (January 25, 1738) that *Leonidas,* though praised by Lyttelton, did not sell.

The Bishop of Chester, in London to attend Parliament, regaled his son about the weather, its "very sudden changes," the "wind and rain." Turck Pelham, he said, had drunk himself to death. The opposition threatened, but was disconsolate. There were rumors that the King would make up with his son. Members were at the Cockpit in larger numbers to hear the speech read than at any other time save one within the reign.

His Majesty urged members again to "lay aside all heats and animosities" that might "protract the session." The *Daily Gazetteer* descended to lament (January 27) "excessive Feastings, profane Embroideries, wide and wild Spaces of Green and Gravel under the Name of Gardens." The next day *Common Sense* ruminated that, since the "Distinction of Parties without Doors" arose "wholly from the different Opinions espoused by Numbers within," it followed that if all "within Doors" were "upon the same Side of the Question, all Hands and Hearts in the Country would be so too." But no sooner were "the Noses" within "divided upon a Question," than word was given dividing the "whole Nation."

Half-heartedly the same day the *Craftsman* hoped, though ministerial writers encouraged the Spanish depredations, that "Merchants of London, Bristol, and other Ports of the Kingdom, . . . very justly alarmed," would not "suffer themselves to be amused by the sophistical Arguments of those groveling Wretches," who would "sacrifice even their native Country to their private Interest or Advantage." Within doors, opposition leaders found even less room for hope. A correspondent condoled Marchmont (February 3) that he had a "sad pack to deal with." All their "consultations" would "come to nothing," and "Sir Robert outwit" them "every one." Bolingbroke at a distance hoped that the Prince, if "properly used," might become "a center of union," enabling "men of different characters and different views . . . to draw better together." Walpole depended wholly upon the "power of the purse," and if Hardwicke and the Pelhams could be drawn away, he might be overthrown.

The *Daily Gazetteer* (February 3) complained that the merchants took their cause to the people through the *Craftsman* at the same time that they took it to his Majesty. A member in the House of Commons observed the same day that one who flattered "the vanity of a mob" would always have it on his side. Another thought the people to be governed by the "press." Weekly papers were read with "greater reverence" than "acts of Parliament." For all that, Horace Walpole wrote (February 14) that the work of the Commons moved "so fast and glib" that members went to dinner "every day at 3 o'clock." He thought the session would be up in early spring.

February 11 the *Craftsman* complained again that ministerial journalists, not content with defending "the Vices and Misconduct of their Masters," were "daily throwing Dirt at . . . injured and distressed Merchants, . . . colouring the most flagrant Acts of Violence and Rapine that were ever committed by the Subjects of one Nation on another in Peace and Friendship with them." There was, for example, the case of "Captain Plater and his Mate." Had poor mariners "forfeited their Liberty because they happened to belong to a ship that had 8 or 10 Tons of Logwood on Board, which perhaps was shipped as Freight and produced at Jamaica?" Thus encouraged, West India merchants met, February 24, at the Ship Tavern behind the Royal Exchange and resolved to apply to Parliament for redress. The King had offered to grant letters of marque against the Spanish, but merchants had not applied.

While this bit of cloud began to spread, Walpole dwelt on thoughts that pleased him more. He sent abroad for pictures to decorate his walls. By marriage, he legalized relations with the woman whose society he enjoyed most. The Duchess of Newcastle or of Richmond would have sponsored her at court had not the wife of Horace claimed the rôle. The brother thought her "a very sensible, well behaved, modest woman," knowing Sir Robert's "happiness . . . very deservedly wrapt up in her." The Dowager Duchess of Marlborough did not wonder at the match. Though prejudiced against the husband and only a casual acquaintance of the bride, she nevertheless "liked her behaviour very well," allowing her a "great deal of sense."

The groom's old tutor, Bishop Hare, covered a mild disapproval with the thirty thousand pounds reputed to be her wealth. "Everybody," including a Mrs. Williams as fond of "scandal" as of "her eyes," said she was "a woman of an extreme and good understanding and . . . very agreeable." Notices in the press appraised her wealth at eighty thousand pounds. "Everybody," said Sir Thomas Robinson, "gives her a good character both as to her understanding and good nature." Was "everybody" wrong?

Her husband would soon need any good nature with which he was endowed. The opposition had found another issue. Beginning the session with a motion to reduce the army, the proposal now was to go to war with Spain. A list was published of British ships the Spanish had attacked for nine years past, including the *Rebecca*, Captain Jenkins. In early March the merchants took the case to Parliament. As usual, they claimed and were denied the right to come both by attorney and themselves. Wyndham thought, at least, they might give testimony. Walpole alliteratively wished action to be based on "facts fairly presented, not artfully aggravated." But opposition weeklies were using all the arts they knew.

Frustrated by this new diversion, after an essay against slavery and the slave trade, the *Old Whig and Consistent Protestant* was coming to a close. Two volumes of its collected essays were announced, carrying the names of subscribers in order to show that "Friends of Liberty" had "Patrons whose Power and Prudence" might "give Success to any reasonable and virtuous Undertaking." Primarily, the venture had been designed to "check the Vices" of those attributing exaggerated importance to the Church, such as "a Doctor Sacheverell." It had "answered its End" if it had given "Insight into the Weakness of their Reasoning; the Formidableness of their Power, and the Wickedness of their Endeavours."

The *Weekly Miscellany* now confessed a want of the encouragement promised in its outset. Warburton was added to Wesley and Whitefield among the number that felt its little blows.

Thomas Fitzgerald, known as Geraldino, represented Spain in London and urged the opposition to go on with its work. Sufferers from "Spanish depredations," including Captain Jenkins, were summoned to appear and tell their tales. Jenkins was otherwhere engaged and did not go. Pulteney cited "amazing instances of cruelty, barbarity, and injustice," urging a resolution that would immediately provoke a war, appealing for the use of a "little of the spirit and courage of Oliver Cromwell." But Walpole felt that British rights might be secured by using "general words"; Spain would not specifically give up the right of search. The opposition cried "no Search" the more.

"One would imagine," said the *Craftsman* (March 18), "that the Depredations of the Spaniards and their Barbarity to our Seamen required only a full and clear Representation to raise the antient British Spirit, and fill every Breast with the highest Indignation and Resentment against all our Adversaries, their Aiders and Abettors." Instead, there was a "want of publick Spirit," a "Wretchedness of Spirit," a "mercenary, low Way of Thinking," due to "false Brethren" at home. It was "amazing to think that any Part of the Nation" could be "unmoved at the Groans and Complaints of . . . fellow Subjects . . . unjustly deprived of their Liberty, loaded with Irons, and fed with Provisions neither sufficient nor wholesome, being nothing more than salt Fish and dry'd Beans full of Worms." So great was the "Barbarity," said the *London Evening Post* (March 25), that "several Members of the House of Commons . . . could scarce refrain from Tears at hearing of such unparalleled ill usage and barbarous Treatment." The gallery of the House became a "greater Resort of Ladies" than was ever seen before. Said *Common Sense* within a month (April 22), "the Nation calls loud for War."

Henry Fox gained a point by winning the Duke of Marlborough, who accepted a regiment and bade the Prince farewell. The end of the session approached, when the magazines, following their custom, would assume that the standing order did not hold and publish speeches made in Parliament. The question was brought up, and Wyndham asked if members were ashamed of what they said. No, replied Pulteney, but if the publication was not stopped, members would be accountable out of doors for what they said within. Walpole remarked that he had been reported as saying the opposite of what he meant. Thus a resolution forbade the printing while the House was up as well as when it sat. Offenders were informed that they would be proceeded against with "the utmost severity," whatever that might mean. Had publishers of the magazines collected their reports that year in vain?

Hearing noise again, the *Daily Gazetteer* (April 28) began to wonder about the art with which the ministry was opposed. Those unacquainted with methods used in "raising Esteem and Reputation to One's self" might think "that all the greatest Wits and Geniuses of the Kingdom were against the Ministry, and that none but the greatest Idiots and Blackguards . . . were for them," this despite the difficulty of explaining "how so many great and wise Men could be baffled and kept out of Place so long" by those having as supporters "such a Parcel of Fools." A man enlisting on the "Side of the Patriots" was "trumpetted about . . . as possessed of the highest Qualifications. . . . Thus every little Verse Maker" was "immediately cry'd up as a great Poet; every little Speech Maker as a great Orator; every little Joker as a great Wit; and every little Scribbler as a fine Writer."

Walpole still strove within the House for peace. "I remember," he said (May 5), "when I was a young man, nothing gave me greater pleasure than voting for a war with France; I thought that it sounded well, that it was heroic and for the glory of my country. But, sir, how fatal in some respects have the consequences of that war, just and necessary though it was, been for Britain." Though "absolutely bent" on war again if satisfaction could not be otherwise obtained, his preference now was "honourable peace." This in opposing the first reading of a bill to tempt officers and seamen with all the

Spanish prizes taken, against which the Minister cast a solitary vote. Pulteney redoubled his zeal on the third reading ten days later. It was England's business "to command Justice" when denied, he said. Lacking other allies, the "story of Jenkins" would raise up "volunteers." Thomas Winnington thought this story might be told in vain if London was faced with the prospect of increased taxes. The bill was lost, 106 to 75.

Marchmont informed a fellow Scot (May 12) that the opposition leaders would not work together and could scarcely be induced to meet. They lacked "patience" and acted from no common "principle." The excuse was "want of right points to preach, and that points must arise from the other side." If one mentioned Spanish depredations, he was told that "merchants must take the initiative." The same was true of the affair of the Prince and the freedom of the press. He, Cobham, and Chesterfield agreed that opposition was "at an end." Proroguing Parliament (May 20), the King congratulated its "moderation" and lack of "heat." He hoped for a peaceful settlement with Spain.

A week earlier Haines, the *Craftsman's* printer, was sentenced for a year and fined two hundred pounds. The paper complained, at that "Rate" there could be "no Mentioning the eminent Rascals of Antiquity" but some would say the Minister was meant. The *Daily Gazetteer* (May 26) marveled again that there were "none but Heroes, Demi-Gods, and Angels of Light on the one Side, and none but Fiends, Furies, and Devils incarnate on the other." In truth, were the matter "thoroughly canvassed and the Characters . . . exactly delineated, . . . hardly any other Difference" would appear "between the Patriot and the Courtier" but that the former wanted what the latter had.

The prorogation of Parliament brought conductors of the magazines to a question which taxed their ingenuity. Readers had complained the previous year of the scant space given to debates. The prospect now was loss of this desirable item of the stock in trade, which furnished substance to the summer issues and made them worth the shilling that was asked. The

London Magazine was ready to evade the House's rule. An "unknown Correspondent" (Gordon it was said) sent in the "Journal" of a "learned and political Club," which was purveyed in monthly issues after May. After experimenting for six months, the editor could not think that "having published or continuing to publish such a Journal" would be "disagreeable to any Party in the Kingdom." If any who complained of lack of "Justice to their Side" would submit material, it would be used if it could be "safely" done. Speakers were given Roman names, but they talked of matters Parliament had discussed.

The *Gentleman's Magazine* could not permit its rival this advantage without an effort to compete. It began to run the next month "Debates in the Senate of Magna Lilliputia," prepared by William Guthrie if reports were true. With a nose for news and thinking to atone for timidity and loss of time, the first issue carried the debate on "Spanish Depredations." Jenkins, it said, when summoned, attended at the bar. His recommendation of his soul to God and his cause to his country, "these words and shewing the Piece of his Ear which wrapt in Cotton he carries about with him in a Box, made a great Impression on the whole Assembly." Some license, even fiction, was permissible when a periodical was in a pinch.

Walpole was in no state to care. He lost his second wife, June 4; she died "of a Miscarriage succeeded by a Fever." "His dauntless Spirit languish'd o'er her Tomb," said one report, "and for a while forgot there was a Rome." Horace was "inexpressibly" concerned at the "deplorable and comfortless condition" in which he found his brother. The best hope seemed to be to "divert his melancholy by business." But not till the end of June could the Minister be induced "to take a resolution to dissipate his sorrow thus." In the same weeks Lord Townshend, partner of his earlier years, passed from the scene.

Meanwhile, on christening the royal heir, a "most elegant and magnificent Fireworks was played off," showing among other things, "Minerva educating the young Prince." None foresaw that fourscore years would be required to tell how well her task was done. The proud father gave to the nurses ten guineas each. In the same month Madame Walmoden, arrived in town, attended at a royal drawing room. The host approved with a salute on both her cheeks, an honor, the Duchess of Marlborough thought, "never any lady had from a King in public." Harrington presented the ministers and foreign ministers in turn. This also seemed to Sarah a thing "quite new." Hervey remembered the Queen and was not there.

The parties labored out of doors that summer to complete the work begun within. The *Daily Gazetteer* complained (June 29) that those having "the Direction of publick Affairs" were "oblig'd thro' Clamour and Importunity to follow the Tide of popular Opinion," which was "seldom or never formed upon a true Judgment of the State and Nature of Things," but was "generally the Effect of a blind Prejudice and unreasonable Resentment and of Passions artfully worked up and fomented by restless and ambitious Men." *Common Sense* insisted (July 1) that "the Merchant, the Sailor, the money'd and the landed Men" all cried "aloud for War." Only courtiers and soldiers were on the other side.

The *Daily Gazetteer* (July 6) thought the sound "Art of Government" to be the "Rule of the Many by the Few," and was fearful at the prospect of the "wild State of Nature" if the many should be suffered "to sway, direct, and lead." It would set up "a fourth Estate consisting of the People," rivaling the King, Lords, and Commons. *Common Sense* entreated again a war with Spain, interrupting this refrain (July 15) to commend the King's personal morality as an example to his subjects. The "Evil of Adultery," the "Indulgence of a Lawless Passion for the Wife of another," was an offense tolerated in a King of France, but not in one who wore the British crown.

More serious than the carpings in the press was the Duke of Newcastle's feeling that the cause of the merchants called for the use of force, which he thought the noise in the city would ultimately compel. Hardwicke and Henry Pelham had to soothe the Duke; Horace prevented his brother from "being in a passion." The *Daily Gazetteer* thought (August 10) that Britain, as "a Christian Nation," should not make war on every provocation, even when the cause was just. The "Credit of Grotius" was "as well established as that of Caleb D'Anvers." By the end of August, Newcastle and Walpole, thanks to the intervention of Hardwicke and others, were more nearly agreed. The Duke had a conference with Geraldino; Walpole spoke "with all the firmness imaginable," which seemed to mark the "end of the whole affair."

Common Sense denied (August 26) that the ministers had ever followed public opinion, as the *Daily Gazetteer* alleged. Having the representatives of the people, it was unnecessary to do so. In twenty years the people had gained but one point, the defeat of the excise scheme. But within a fortnight Newcastle and Fitzgerald reached an agreement which, it was hoped, would prevent war. Walpole, hunting at Richmond, suffered an attack, September 2, which almost cost his life. Not for three weeks was he able to take his place at the Treasury board.

Within these weeks *Old Common Sense* claimed the right to reprint debates in Parliament and expressed the hope that they would "continue to be published as long as Parliament" had a "being." The *Daily Gazetteer* was afraid (September 23) that such publication would do more harm than good. *Old Common Sense* found it "inconvenient," after several weeks, to go on. The *Daily Gazetteer* felt (October 5) that if a war could be avoided, soon the "good old Cause of Minister Hunting" would not be "worth following." Now, the opposition thought a war would do its "Business," and therefore "a War! a bloody War!" it would have, "right or wrong."

Walpole did not work to avoid war wholly because he thought its advocates chiefly after his own scalp. He felt that the very merchants induced to support the cause would suffer an immediate loss of trade and a greater burden of debt, not likely to be compensated by remedial terms on making peace. He saw, too, that in this war England must largely stand alone. France was growing strong again and was allied with Spain. Neither the Emperor nor the Dutch would give the grudging help of Marlborough's time. Furthermore, the Minister felt the weight of years. He would rather take the chance of riding out a storm at home than launch the country in a foreign war, with little hope that unity would ensue and even less that allies would give aid.

The younger Newcastle, intimidated by the noise, was readier to fight. He hoped for peace, provided that domestic quiet would ensue. Neither minister meant to give the merchants up without support. From Houghton in November Henry Pelham wrote his brother that Walpole had gone through the Duke's dispatches and approved them all. He never saw the Minister better pleased, proof of what a "willing mind" could always do. The host was on his horse again, but could not ride as hard as was his former wont.

Bolingbroke was back in England and never "more disgusted with politicks" in all his life. "Every man" talked "of them and . . . nothing else," but none talked "sense." The ministerial press alleged that he wrote again, and Osborne's name was signed to pieces in the *Daily Gazetteer*. But a message came from Keene, Saturday, December 9, to say that the Convention would be signed. The ministers hoped the crisis had been passed. *Common Sense* (December 16) was sure that the treaty did not grant the right of search. If so, it was "dishonourable." Parliament had voted "no Search," and the ministers must "respect the Word," or "no Search" would be "reëchoed through the Kingdom." If the press would "print the Story of Captain Jenkins and have it cried in market Towns," there would not be an "honest John Trot in all the Country whose Fingers would not itch" for Spanish ears.

Hopeful of peace, the *Daily Gazetteer* (December 23) rejoiced. War would have helped the French and hurt the English, even though the French had not come in. Once started, it would last till "1748." War was not Britain's "Business any more than Conquest." The country throve by "Trade." "Being aggrieved, it was right to seek Redress, but wise to seek it only by Negotiation"; nothing was to be gained by war.

The press returned to essays on the repeal of the Test Act

or the enforcement of the laws against spirituous liquors. The *Gentleman's Magazine* found the weekly essays worth less space. It explained that to "single out any Man for a perpetual Mark of Reproach or Theme of Panegyrick" was "to the last Degree shameless and profligate." Only the long division of men "by Party Rage could make Caution necessary against such open and undisguised Artifices." With Parliament up, the problem of the writers was, "to say Something" with "Nothing to say."

Parliament was prorogued to February 1, to await the arrival of the Convention of Pardo, finally signed in the early days of the new year. The City was uncertain in those weeks. The Convention was still on every tongue. Orrery found Pope "lost" in it; the "very dunces" forgot him in their thoughts of "politics." "All the old Trojans" were "divided and despaired." Bolingbroke was in England, but lived privately. Bathurst was currying favor with the Prince.

Newcastle began to be afraid. Walpole seemed to withhold accustomed confidence; even Hardwicke appeared to be reserved. The same week, in an Oriental sea, the *Harrington*, Captain Robert Jenkins, returning from a China voyage, was attacked by pirates "along the Shore of Goa Road to Bombay." The courage of the Captain saved the ship. The papers said that the Prince of Wales would ask again his hundred thousand pounds. The Quakers and Dissenters might appeal to Parliament too.

The Convention was received and ratified (January 22). Marchmont found (January 27) the opposition ill prepared. There were "no meetings"; "all the members" had not "come to town." But that very day a writer in the *Craftsman* had a plan. If the Convention should be withheld from Parliament, "Nobility of high Rank and Station" should claim an "ancient Privilege" and give advice. If "discountenanced . . . by any Minister or Favourite," let them "absent themselves from Councils where Experience" showed, "their Votes and Influence" would have "no Effect." The Earl of Oxford had been impeached for negotiating a treaty in a perfectly "legal Manner." Whatever came, Britain must insist upon "no Search in any Latitude." Let the Spanish on "no Account presume to visit any English Ship or maltreat Mariners in any Part of the Sea or under any Pretence what so ever." Walpole was responsible, and his would be the blame if things went wrong.

A more serious matter, even as Parliament met, Cobham and Chesterfield were afraid that Carteret and Pulteney would "get the Prince into their hands." Again, there was a rumor that the son and father might make friends. Marchmont reminded his Royal Highness of the "hurt" that would ensue. Even the report of a negotiation with Carteret and Pulteney had done harm. To call at the royal court on his birthday would cost him favor in the "hearts of the People." Thus besought, Frederick promised not to go to court unless ordered to do so; "he never would speak to Sir Robert Walpole," though he might to other courtiers if they came to him. Carteret told Egmont, a Trustee for Georgia, that the giving up that colony to make peace with Spain would "hang" Walpole.

The King and his ministers offered the Convention as a means of obtaining justice for the merchants "without plunging the nation into a war." Chesterfield hoped it would be "censured," and Carteret agreed. Bathurst called it a "piece of paper." Argyll knew not what was in it, but would not support an article. Petitions were presented against it by London and West India merchants. Pamphlets and journals out of doors reflected what went on within. Lyttelton wrote on one side, and Horace Walpole on the other. Amhurst was less active, since his eyesight was impaired. A masquerade at Drury Lane (February 8) saw sailors using dangling ears as ornaments. The Prince of Wales was "hearty," Marchmont wrote; all his servants voted "to a man" against the ministers.

As the month went on, the *Daily Gazetteer* confessed (February 23) that "tho' the Clamours . . . artificially raised against the . . . Ministry" had not "wrought" its "Expulsion from Power," they had "visibly operated on the Minds of the common People and prejudiced them, not only against the Government, but against Government in general."

On all "Occasions" were "Marks of a seditious Spirit and manifest Distrust, not of the Ministry, but of the Legislature, and a visible Tendency to Anarchy, . . . the Rule of the People." The opposition did not try to "convince the Judgment," but to stir the "Passions."

Common Sense (February 24) was not surprised at so poor a treaty, considering the "mean" family and character of Keene. But the fault was at Walpole's door. Indeed, he had "been a Disease upon the Nation." But the world was now "sick of him," and he was almost at the "End of his Race," having "filled up the Measure of his Iniquity." Perhaps he might gain a "slight Reprieve," but he was "in the Toils." No gift of prophecy was needed to foretell his fall, and those willing to depend on him adopted "his Guilt and must share in his Ruin." The same issue noted in its news that "Bob Booty, a very old Offender," was of "late closely pursued and in great Danger of being taken." He had been seen "about Town with a large Bag of Guineas tied to his Waste."

The *Daily Gazetteer* replied in kind (February 26). To have exacted more than the Convention obtained "would have embittered a Nation it was wise to be friendly with." The treaty would "satisfy good Subjects," though not the "confederated Incendiaries." On the day appointed for debate in the Lords (March 1), a number of ladies sought admittance at the door at nine in the morning and persisted with noisy demonstration until at five in the afternoon, when a door was opened at the side. Within, they laughed at some, but cheered when Carteret or Chesterfield made points. Hoadly thought those seldom successful who practiced to be "bullies of mankind." Trade might be ruined by a "successful war, and secured by an indifferent peace." Argyll would not hear this argument. He spoke no longer as a Privy Councillor, but as a "citizen of the world." Hardwicke, as always, was convincing, clear, and cool. Chesterfield thought the Convention the "most pernicious the nation ever made." If it dared not seek "revenge" from "fear of France," nothing was left to do but "lie down and die." Pointing to an historical tapestry in the hall, he hoped that none was weaving then. The Prince was in the House and voted with his friends. The ministers won, 71 to 58.

Daily, frantic ministerial writers pled their cause. Members of the opposition would have "looked more like Patriots" had criticism been withheld until terms of the treaty were made known. Would supporters of a good cause be "in a Passion"? The precedent was bad. If "Clamour" could "destroy one Ministry," it might "as well destroy another." This method of procedure revealed things "least fit for the Eyes of Foreigners." It was an "easy Thing to inflame the Passions and work up a popular Ferment." "Long Harangues" and "labored Invectives" were not always necessary; sometimes "a bye-Word, or a cant Term" would suffice. Men alive had "seen the Multitude run mad with the Danger of the Church"; some of the very same persons then responsible were now "endeavouring to make them so again with a Jargon full as unintelligible and ridiculous, that of *no Search.*" "No Art" had been "left wanting . . . to raise the Torrent of popular Fury and make it overflow all Bounds." There had been "private Meetings with Party Clubs to form Plans and deliberate a Scheme." A "false Alarm" had spread through the kingdom, based on a "thousand Phantoms" without the "least Foundation in Fact."

As the lower house came to vote, the journalists told the sober truth. It was a fact that the Spanish had taken several British "trading Vessels in America contrary to the Terms of Treaties." But it was "no less true" that natives of British plantations drew "all their Wealth from an illicit Traffic with Spanish Colonies . . . particularly for Pieces of eight." Was it arguable that it was "lawful for an Englishman" because he "was an Englishman" to engage in illegal trade, but "unlawful for a Spaniard to prevent it because he was a Spaniard?" Suppose British seamen had been wronged; British buccaneers inflicted wrongs in turn, and that in time of peace. Villages had been burnt and sacked, men "slaughtered in cold Blood . . . Women ravished, Virgins deflowered, and Churches plundered." These excesses had been tolerated, even "supported by Commissions from the Governors of

. . . American Plantations, notwithstanding the continual Remonstrances of the Court of Spain." Finally, a war ought to be judged by the probable event; admitting all possible success, England had little to hope from one with Spain.

These were scarcely arguments to stem the tide that ran. Merchants were at the doors of Parliament with reënforcements to add morale to members on their side. The Prince was in the gallery to cheer them on. But stubbornly the ministers stood their ground. Walpole announced his resolution to "let no popular clamour get the better of what" he thought to be the "country's good." Pulteney made an imflammatory speech. A vote in favor of the ministry would yield all that was "dear among a free people in order to support one man in his power." Pitt was violent. The Convention was "nothing but a stipulation for national ignominy; an illusory expedient to baffle the resentment of the nation; a truce without a suspension of hostilities on the part of Spain." Walpole patiently reviewed the case again; it was well known, he said, "with what views all the clamours against the Convention had been raised." The House agreed, 244 to 214.

Pulteney and Wyndham announced a resolution to attend no more. Walpole was afraid that they would change their minds. The *Daily Gazetteer* (March 8) could not deny that "there never was a Time when the People or Nation in general were more unanimous and eager to enter a War." Egmont thought that Walpole had "put off the evil day to another session"; it was universally believed, "he could not stand his ground next year."

Marchmont was not so certain (March 10) that the opposition leaders in the lower house had helped the cause. The "City was in a flame," but people were "at a gaze and doubtful how it" would "turn out." Walpole was "constantly distressed," but almost none was "pleased." *Common Sense* observed the same day that the Minister had acted his part "miserably ill." And with "the whole People . . . calling for Justice against" him, those "in Employments" would better "behave . . . in a Manner" to "vindicate their Reputations from the Suspicion of having accepted them upon infamous

Conditions," and to convince the world that they did not "dread Enquiry into their Conduct." With that threat were lists by name of officeholders who voted with the ministry. There were reasons for Egmont's apprehensions of "strange violences before next year."

But the same Lord thought the secession from Parliament by opposition leaders "very injudicious for that party." Lacking "heads to conduct them," members of the minority would vote with those in power. Opposition leaders might succeed if the purpose was to arouse the populace, but they might also "raise a spirit" they could not "lay." Bishop Hare described it to his son (March 14) as the "greatest party struggle . . . since the Revolution." The treaty was condemned without its contents being known. People were urged to expect that which "could not be obtained," nor coulu be after "twenty years of war." A war with Spain now meant a war with France. The "Patriots were so enraged to find that they could not demolish the ministry, which they reckoned upon with the greatest certainty, that their speeches were filled with the rudest appeals and the most opprobrious language, such as no man had ever heard in that House before." It was surprising that Walpole had borne up so well.

The day the Bishop wrote, the Tower guns announced that the Princess had another child. Thus in one session Parliament congratulated twice that she bore sons.

Newcastle was now surer that he had been right. The war would come as he had said. But Hardwicke labored still to "soften things" on points which, left alone, would solve themselves. Writing to Trevor, whom he had left in Holland, Horace thought (March 16) his brother spoke in a "more masterly, dextrous, and able manner" than he had ever heard before. True, a war with Spain was "inevitable, but that" was "not the question. Ambition, avarice, distress, disappointment, and all the complicated vices that tend to render the minds of men uneasy" had "got out of Pandora's Box," filling "all places and all corners of the nation." The Prince was active in the fray. Nothing was left to the *Daily Gazetteer* (March 16), but to urge a "Vigourous Unanimity" to "incline the whole Body of the Nation to turn its whole Force on foreign Enemies and not waste its Strength in domestick Disputes." The country waited to see what Spain would do.

Chesterfield commended *Common Sense* to Lyttelton (March 24) and urged that the "secession" be "writ up as much as possible." He rejoiced that it did "Cobham so much good." Addressing the merchants (March 25), the *Daily Gazetteer* regretted that "Heats and Animosities" deprived them of a capacity to "judge rightly." The opposition had cried "no Search," as formerly they had done other things, and then left the merchants and their "Trade to go which way" they would. Even Marchmont was still uncertain (March 28). "People knew not what to think or say," though none thought Walpole could "stand" through another session. Fortunately for the opposition the Minister had "insulted" the Prince. Carteret condemned what had been done, but "could not dissuade even Mr. Pulteney" from doing it.

In April Wyndham was blackballed when a hundred "noblemen and gentlemen of the best figure" organized a club at White's Chocolate House. Cassandra-like, *Common Sense* (April 7) kept on crying that "Ruin" hung on Walpole; "all the World" saw it; "all the World" said it; "Mankind" would "no longer endure his Corruptions and his Blunders." Throughout Europe, the "general Talk" was of the expectation "that every Post would bring News of the Overturning of this Man and his Mercenaries." Horace was "distinguished by low Habits and Brutality of Manners." "Every Quality of his Mind, every Gesture of his Body contributed to render" him "contemptible." Sir Robert could allege "no Scandal" against another which might not with "Truth be returned upon" his "own Family." The "Resentment" against him was no "Start of popular Fury," but "a considerate and sober Conviction . . . hoped for and expected by ten Million of People." *Old Common Sense* (April 14) cautioned that to "reason" might be more effective than to "rail," but *Common Sense* went on to identify the Minister that week as a "Wretch" it was needless to name, "the Cur-Dog of Britain and Spaniel of Spain."

Tuesday of the next week, after a chill at his levee, Walpole was blistered and bled. Some said that his trouble was "the insolent memorial returned by the court of Spain and the discovery of an alliance between that court and France," putting Gibraltar in peril. While he lay ill, much as in the previous autumn, the *Daily Gazetteer* remarked the "extravagant and unparallel'd Insolence display'd on the one Hand" and the "extreme Patience and Forbearance with which they were borne on the other." The opposition described the majority in Parliament as "a Faction, . . . under the corrupt Influence of the Ministry, . . . in a Conspiracy against the Country," when it was known to include "many Gentlemen of the best Families and the greatest independent Fortunes in the Kingdom." This was done in a paper conducted by an "infamous Miscreant" (Charles Molloy), who had "spent his whole Life in the very Sink of Scandal," had "wallowed in the Mire of Calumny and Defamation ever since he left the Bogs where he was engendered and came naked and starved to seek his Fortune" in England "as a Knight of the Post, a Bully to a Brothel, a Puff to a gaming Table, or a Hackney Writer, as Chance and Time should direct."

With companies in the coffee-houses feeding on this pabulum, Whitefield in the Moorfields easily moved his frantic crowds to penitence and tears. Webster in his *Weekly Miscellany* (May 12) could have understood such performances in a "medical Mountebank," but Whitefield had a "liberal Education," was "accustomed to the Discipline in the University," had "received a regular Ordination in an Episcopal Church," had "subscribed to its Articles." Yet he and the Wesleys were "bold Movers of Sedition and Ring Leaders of the Rabble." There was nothing that such an "Enthusiast" might not "bring himself to undertake." A writer in the *Daily Gazetteer* (May 25) observed an epidemic of a "kind of Insanae, whereby the Passions and Principles of Men" were "highly distempered and overheated, as well in a civil as a religious Sense." The disease was of "a most pestilent Kind," arising from "an ugly Habit . . . of being wise over-little and righteous overmuch." "Sound" would "gather a Mob as well as . . . collect Bees," and was naturally used by a party that wished decisions to be by "a Plurality of Hands rather than Heads."

But Bishop Hare observed that the seceders had not made the noise they hoped. If they had continued to come and "tease from day to day," they would have "killed Sir Robert" with "fatigue"; thanks to them, he was now well again. Parliament ran more smoothly after they were out. On the last of May, however, Bathurst moved an inquiry, whether Spain had made the payments promised. Newcastle found a certain pleasure in the answer he had to make. Carteret thought the subject fitter for "meditation than discourse." Within a fortnight the session was prorogued. The King was thankful for augmented forces and supplies, but fearful of the "fatal consequences," to the "nation divided within itself, inflamed and misled by all the wicked arts and insinuations that falsehood" could "suggest."

Whitefield, preparing to go to Georgia, still preached on. But even before Parliament rose, Hardwicke could write to Newcastle with better cheer (June 2). He had tried to show Walpole that his "difficulties arose chiefly from a fixed opinion . . . and . . . suspicion of some of his friends that nothing would be done against Spain." Now that Spain had "broke the Convention," it was a "new event," and the Minister could act as "vigourously" as he desired. Walpole agreed that either he or Newcastle should propose a scheme to the Cabinet. The *Craftsman,* on the other hand, thought the same day that "a War managed by such an Head would certainly be ridiculous." Lady Egmont heard Whitefield preach that week. In a sermon two hours long she found little that she "had not heard before." Partly for that reason, perhaps, the "people were very attentive" when he spoke. The *Daily Gazetteer* (June 6) observed that his success made him a public character.

Printers of both the *Craftsman* and *Common Sense* were in prison at this time. When their weeklies defended the secession as lessening the prestige of the victory of "Bribery and Corruption . . . over Honour and publick Spirit," the

Daily Gazetteer replied (June 29) that "Enthusiasts and Madmen" were the "only Enemies" the ministers should "justly fear." Actually, the opposition leaders were losing hope. Now that Parliament was up, nothing appeared to vindicate the secession "except a letter in some of the weekly papers; and everybody expected more."

A manifesto against Spain was published July 10. Walpole had gone to Houghton several days before, and his name was not affixed. Edward Vernon kissed hands as a Vice Admiral. In violent opposition he had made his boasts, and now he had a chance to make them good. The coming war inspired *Common Sense* to say (July 14), that Walpole was "more ignorant, more cowardly, and composed of baser Qualities than the ill bred Clown who makes a Riot in the Streets." If affairs had been properly managed and in better hands, there would have been no war. Under the name of "Falstaff," the *Craftsman* paid the Minister its respects: "He was merry and a Buffoon; and though he was not brave, he could bully; if he did not care to speak Truth, he could swear to a Lye; if he was not vigourous, he was treacherous, constantly robbing the Publick; a great corruptor of Manners and loved to talk bawdy."

Perhaps this was an effort in advance to live up to Bolingbroke's advice to Wyndham (July 23), that public attention be centered on Walpole in an effort to discredit him and to justify the secession of his opponents. But Bolingbroke marveled at the same time that Pulteney wished him to write, having so lately thought his presence in the country harmful. Others complained that Pulteney did not provide a promised pamphlet.

However, the aging Stair in Scotland thought he saw "daylight" in breaking the "neck of Sir Robert Walpole's power," if Cobham and Argyll would agree. The Prince was not "overfond of money or power." Scots might be aroused to instruct their members against one who had "been for many years sole and absolute Minister, a thing little known and never liked" in that country. This, together with the old dissatisfaction with the election of peers, might produce "the strongest machine . . . employed to advance the cause of liberty."

A chorus of doubt and disagreement was the answer. Winchelsea thought Scotland "apt enough to be put in a flame," but Walpole held the "purse and sword," and the suggested moves would "not operate in the manner" expected. Carteret felt that, since the ministers were "at present in all appearance pursuing the sense of the nation and acting toward the Spaniards as they should have done long ago," if things could not be made "better, for God's sake" let them not be made "worse." Chesterfield found Argyll not ripe for the plan and doubted whether it would help. Learning of the scheme through Cobham, Argyll thought it of no use to prove what all knew of Walpole's unpopularity. Queensbury was of opinion that petitions from all parts of the kingdom asking for a dissolution might do good. Pulteney postponed again his pamphlet, finally pleading reluctance "to give advice"; "perhaps it were better to say nothing, lest future events should necessitate the retracting of what had been advanced." Wyndham complained that there was no "dependency on anybody so changeable." Cobham concluded in a paradox that the "folly and wickedness" of Walpole had "turned so much to his advantage" that those "not bribed to hold their tongue" were "ashamed to talk of them for fear of repeating what everybody" knew. A kinsman of Marchmont felt that leaving the House "and doing nothing on it but running up and down a-sporting like a parcel of the silliest school boys who were playing truant" was "ridiculous and indeed criminal."

The ministers were having troubles too. The King refused to appoint Trevor at The Hague with full powers in order that Horace Walpole might help his brother at home. Horace was persuaded by Hardwicke to keep his post, but warned Sir Robert that Europe would "soon be in a general combustion and that France must be absolutely master unless some plan of united measures" could be found. The King as Elector would claim a share in such a plan, but that could not be helped.

Aided and abetted by Harrington, as Newcastle thought, the King was making trouble about Haddock's expedition. How was business to go on, the Duke inquired of Hardwicke, if a minister who seldom spoke in "Council" and never said "one word in Parliament" could intermeddle thus? Walpole intervened to set the matter right. Fortunately, the Minister was in a "good humor" with the Lord Chancellor and the Duke.

But not for long. Hervey demanded his reward for services, which Walpole needed more than ever now. With a war in prospect, the King would scarcely listen to his recommendations of officers in the army, claiming for himself superior wisdom in that field. But Newcastle objected to Hervey as Lord Privy Seal and pled with Hardwicke to resign if the appointment should be made. Feeling that time had justified him on the war with Spain, the Duke was vexed the more at a move which he thought to be personal against himself. He might not resign unless his brother and Hardwicke would agree, but he would have "nothing more to do with Sir Robert Walpole." He confessed that, because of his "temper," he was "often uneasy and peevish and perhaps . . . wrong-headed" to his "best friends," but for him and Hardwicke to share the leadership in the Lords with Hervey was more than he would bear.

Others had cooler heads, whether or not they understood the vital part that Hervey played. Horace persuaded his brother to postpone the appointment to the following spring. Bishop Hare wrote frankly to the Duke. As long as Walpole was in office, Newcastle would have to be content with second place. Should the Minister's "death or any other incident" make it prudent to take in some of the "patriots," they would not "suffer" him "to be first." The moral was, his "Grace should again unite heartily with Sir R[obert] with the same intimacy as formerly for the common cause." The Bishop urged this as the opinion of all of his friends.

In the midst of these bickerings the *Gazetteer* carried the declaration of war with Spain (October 23). The *Craftsman* noted (October 27) that on its public proclamation the crowd "assembled between St. James's and the Royal Exchange . . . was so great, that you might have walked on the People's Heads," the while they shouted "the loudest Acclamations of Joy." But *Common Sense* was not to be diverted from its constant theme. If "one Man" directed all, he was answerable "for all Mismanagements." "Power exercised by a First Minister" was inconsistent with a free government; nay, "it would hardly be endured in Constantinople." Whatever happened, the blame was his, and "overarming" would be a "Mark of Fear and Cowardice."

Now that war had come, the *Daily Gazetteer* (October 30) thought it to be "necessary by the strictest Laws of Reason and Humanity" and "founded only upon a Claim and Privilege" which could never "be invaded without Violence." The *Craftsman* (November 3) remembered that it had foretold twenty years before, negotiation would not keep the peace, and war would come. *Common Sense* began to doubt whether money ought to be provided for the war unless the number of placemen in Parliament should be first curtailed, since they were bulwarks of the "Man" who would "ruin the Interests of the Kingdom." Glover at this inauspicious time published his *London,* with which the *Daily Gazetteer* found fault (November 10), in spite of "artful Stories whispered about Town" by some of the poet's friends.

When Parliament met in mid-November, the King complained once more of "heats and animosities . . . with greatest industry . . . fomented throughout the kingdom" as the "chief encouragement" to Spain, making it necessary to have "recourse to arms." Chesterfield denied the charge. The division was between all the people on one side and the ministers on the other. Hervey and Hardwicke helped Newcastle to create discord by advocating unanimity in the face of war.

Pulteney, back in the House of Commons, claimed that the secession was justified by the declaration of war. The next week, Wyndham raised the real issue in a different way. After twenty years, the ministers had not known how to keep the peace. "We have been negotiated into an unnecessary but expensive war," he said. Asserting that the gentleman's long speech wanted only "the necessary forms" to be an impeachment of himself, Walpole made the frank reply: "I have lived long enough . . . to know that the safety of a Minister lies in his having the approbation of this House. Former Ministers, sir, neglected this, and therefore they fell; I have always made it my first study to obtain it, and therefore I hope to stand."

Perhaps he would. Chesterfield condoled Stair (December 3) that Argyll was "by no means ripe"; he needed to be "stroked, . . . not spurred." Boroughs might be induced to "instruct" members on the place bill. After its rejection and publication of the names of its opponents, it might help to get "fresh instructions from every county and borough in both England and Scotland" where they could be had. The crown was in control of both houses of Parliament, a thing "unfortunately" wished by "many People." Walpole's health was bad, however. This might be a "melancholy case," but little improvement would come unless they got together among themselves, a thing unlikely with their views "so widely different."

Common Sense that week had its same specific: All the divisions in the country might be healed by "the Dismission of one Placeman from all Publick Engagements whatsoever." When writers in the *Daily Gazetteer* defended by what shifts they could a war whose coming was against their patron's will, the *Craftsman* called them (December 8) "Dunghill Hens set to hatch Eggs brought from other Nests." *Common Sense* interrupted its usual theme a week later to complain of the current mode of making gardens. There were no longer "fix'd rules, founded upon Reason, and originally deduc'd from Observations made upon Nature." Instead, "one large Room, a serpentine River, and a Wood" had become "absolute Necessaries of Life" without which a "Gentleman of the smallest Fortune" thought he made no "Figure in the Country."

For a month after Christmas the whole country was frozen, and Horace Walpole understood why some peoples were worshippers of the sun. Newcastle was worried in these weeks. Hardwicke had talked with Walpole without reporting what was said. The opposition began its campaign with a motion by Sandys (January 29) for a place bill to prevent "criminals" from being "their own judges." Pulteney asked (February 21) for a secret committee to investigate the authors and advisers of the Convention. There was so much popular discontent that there must be "some fault in the administration," "weakness or wickedness" perhaps; Parliament should make inquiry and set it right. He hoped his Majesty's "Cabinet Council" did not consist solely of Walpole. The Prince attended, applauding the abuse of Walpole and canvassing the members for votes. Pitt made a speech which Winnington pronounced the "prettyest words and the worst language he had ever heard." The words of *Common Sense* (March 15) lacked that saving grace: "The World will not be right while such Fellows remain unhanged. What a Pity it is that so many honester Gentlemen should be sent from the Old Bailey to Tyburn once a Month in London, while this Fellow gets an Estate by his Roguery in the Country."

News of Vernon's victory at Porto Bello inspired addresses from both houses, but the Admiral was just another piece to help the opposition game. The ministers had done nothing right, said *Common Sense* (March 29); Vernon had exposed "their Ignorance." What could the "Mercenaries say to hide the Shame of their Chief?" All who had suffered loss should go to Walpole and demand repayment. He was rich enough, and "his Estate ought to be sold for that Purpose."

The *Daily Gazetteer* (April 23) was almost justifiable in saying that in no "Age" was "scurrilous Abuse . . . so much in Fashion." But Chesterfield still doubted whether it was of any use. The "court" might very well think that there was "no opposition." The only hope was "from the spirit of the nation in the next election." Looking forward to that hope, there would be a "general meeting."

There were at least two reasons, however, for taking a more optimistic view. When Argyll asked to be made Commander in Chief with the title of Marshal, the King refused "with indignation" and removed the Duke "from all his employments." This might be the needed spur. His Majesty himself proposed to go abroad again. In vain Walpole urged, that to do so was almost to abdicate his throne. The Countess of Yarmouth (the English title of Madame Walmoden) was induced to help. Newcastle asked the Cabinet to join in a memorial, but Walpole feared that it would irritate the King and do no good.

Not only did he mean to go; he would take the pliant Harrington instead of Horace when he went.

The latter found his brother (May 13) "so fatigued with business and chagrin on account of the journey and having encountered many disagreeable shocks and reproofs in opposing it, that he was a good deal out of order." His own best hope was that the King of Prussia might die, and this event be used to "stop the sound of clamour." It was a rash hope, fated to come true.[2]

III

WALPOLE GIVES WAY

Hardwicke exerted himself while the King was abroad to preserve harmony among his ministers at home. The suspicious Newcastle tended to see slights where his friend saw only normal differences of opinion among men faced with trying tasks. The Duke became more anxious when the Lord Chancellor took needed rest at Wimpole, which he had purchased that year from the Earl of Oxford, Harley's son. Walpole dissented frankly concerning ships to be dispatched on Haddock's expedition, yielding to the judgment of his colleagues in a petulant speech that vexed Newcastle more. The conciliating influence of Hardwicke, Horace, and Henry Pelham held the group together through it all.

Horace was beginning to wonder whether the Duke and his brother could go on indefinitely, but urged Hardwicke (June 16) to help "save appearances for one year at least." The death of the King of Prussia and the accession of his son in the spring did not bring the anticipated relief, and by early

---

[2] In addition to citations in the text, Hist. Mss. Com., *Carlisle,* pp. 192ff.; *Egmont Diary,* II. 462ff.; III. 16ff., (14 Rept. Appendix, Pt. 9), pp. 12ff., 237ff.; *Marchmont Papers,* II. 96ff.; Cunningham, *Letters of Walpole,* I. cliiiff., 31ff.; *Parliamentary History,* X. 365ff.; XI. 1ff.; Yorke, *Hardwicke,* I. 183ff.; Coxe, *Robert Walpole,* I. 572ff.; II. 701ff.; III. 513ff.; *Horatio Walpole,* I. 416ff.; *Administration of Pelham,* I. 11ff.; Sichel, *Bolingbroke,* II. 555ff.; *Political State,* LIV. 9ff.; LX. 526ff.; Ball, *Correspondence of Swift,* VI. 107; Phillimore, *Lyttelton,* I. 130ff.; Dobree, *Chesterfield Letters,* II. 358ff.; Torrens, *Cabinets,* I. 500ff.; Hervey, *Memoirs,* III. 367ff.; H. V. W. Temperly, "The Causes of the War of Jenkins's Ear, 1739," *Trans. Royal Hist. Society,* III. 197ff.; J. T. Hillhouse, *The Grub Street Journal.*

autumn Horace lamented that Harrington was at Hanover chiefly "to make his court" and was not seeking the needed alliance with the new King necessary to counterbalance France and Spain. He saw no "possibility of ending the war with honour and satisfaction by gaining the ends proposed."

The case of the opposition was not more cheerful. Although Dodington had gone wholly over to the Prince and had been replaced at the Treasury board, Chesterfield saw (September 6) "a possibility," but "very little prospect" of "doing any good." He looked chiefly to the "chapter of accidents"; "even death, . . . hitherto . . . very partial," might "at last prove just." "Remote and improbable" events, he thought, should be "attended to," and it was "in some degree criminal to withdraw from the possibility of improving them." The death of Wyndham left Bolingbroke's old party leaderless in the lower house.

Out of doors *Common Sense* had for some months had the help of a triweekly, the *Champion,* in which Fielding and later James Ralph wrote as "Captain Hercules Vinegar of Pall Mall." The tone was not much different. For all its troubles, the country was (May 22) "indebted to the Craft, Power, and Insolence of one Man; a Man more obnoxious to the Resentments of the Public than any Minister who preceded him," who had "gone beyond them all in adding Weight to Prerogative and in enslaving and impoverishing the People." Agreed, said *Common Sense* (July 26). "The Crown for several Years past hath been making such large Acquisitions of Power and having the Disposal of such immense Revenues . . . that it may make the long Continuance of the same Administration dangerous to Liberty." If one man should "usurp that Power, which ought to be divided amongst Many," his party would become so formidable that it might not "be safe to call him to Account."

The *Craftsman* was less prosperous. Henry Haines had taken over Francklin's shop when the latter was prosecuted for the publication of "The Hague Letter." Bickering came later between Amhurst and both printers. Francklin had lately seized his shop again, and Amhurst, being in his debt, had deserted Haines. With these disputes the paper had declined and now had little of its former weight.

Webster was tiring of his *Weekly Miscellany,* but gave a literary puff which showed that he still understood the feelings of his clientele. Commenting on the manuscript of Samuel Richardson's *Pamela* (October 11), he could not see why the author would "hesitate a Moment as to the Publication of this very natural and uncommon Piece." Between political essays, the *Daily Gazetteer* reflected the same prevailing spirit (October 22): "Of all the Vices" the most "inexcusable in a Gentleman" was "Drunkenness." Whoever wished "to be thought above the Vulgar and a Degree better than the *Canaille* must upon all Occasions show an Abhorrence of this Vice, which Custom very hardly excuses amongst the Dregs of the People." "Excess in Drinking" made the "Strong weak; the Wise, foolish; and the best Men, Beasts." Besides, it injured health.

But *Common Sense* was seldom diverted from its point (October 25): "What a contemptible Opinion the World entertains of the Abilities of our present Ministers; the Bulk of Mankind are prepared to condemn every Measure without waiting for the Event." In the same month Jenkins returned with news of his victory over the pirates in an Eastern sea, for which his company later voted him three hundred pounds. In his absence came the war that gave him fame.

The King, back at home, was in a cheerful mood. He did not fear the opposition if all his ministers would act a single part, and told Newcastle so. The Duke concluded that Walpole inspired the thought and taxed the Minister therewith, alleging failure to support the measures they agreed upon. Walpole was petulant again. "This war is yours," he said, "you have had the conduct of it. I wish you joy of it." Thus Harrington and the Minister, the Duke wrote Hardwicke, would outweigh their own "credit with the King," and "one" would "govern all." So what would the Lord Chancellor have him do?

Opposition leaders were even less agreed among themselves. The Duchess of Marlborough announced her purpose of rewarding the work of Chesterfield and Pitt. The former wrote to Lyttelton from Bath (November 5). Pulteney was there and sure as usual that Walpole and his colleagues would soon be out. Hardwicke, "in particular, was very angry at" the Minister. Chesterfield was "weary of hearing the same story for more than seven years." Pulteney nodded, "he would see," but thought it "very dangerous" and likely "to shake the King's throne" to refuse supplies. Carteret and Pulteney wished a milder course. Argyll probably agreed. Cobham should be told. Argyll should be "inflamed and flattered as much as possible" and shown that he might be leader of the opposition in the House of Lords. A meeting should be called, though, Wyndham being dead, if Pulteney would not call it, no other leader was in sight.

The approaching session would find many old hands out. Pulteney was ill, but came. Shippen was too ill to come at first. Barnard came, but did not mean to stand again. The King announced the Emperor's death, though what it meant, none as yet foresaw. Argyll opposed a motion to address the King, preferring to greet the speech with simple thanks. He was defeated, as was Pulteney's motion in the lower house. So were the other moves the opposition made. Within a fortnight debate was centered on the press (December 2). Pulteney said that if Walpole would read the papers that he subsidized, he would withhold the writers' pay. Walpole observed that recent journalists were finding little new to say. The "Wit and spirit in a Satire" depended on the point of view of him who read. Later, the "spirit" would evaporate, leaving the "malignity" alone. Men with knowledge seldom had the time to write.

The *Daily Gazetteer* appealed for unity (November 24), without which it was "easy to foretell" things it would "be sad to see." *Common Sense* responded (December 6), that if the country was unable to carry on the war, Walpole was to blame. All in the kingdom were poor save the Minister and his friends. Word came also that the new King of Prussia was out to win more territory for his house. As Horace Walpole saw, this meant a British obligation to help the Queen of

Hungary with the Dutch unwilling to come in and France and Prussia on the way to making common cause with Spain. Soon again an Austrian minister was listening to opposition leaders, uncertain whether the King's ministers or they could help his country more.

On Vernon's birthday the City was illuminated and Walpole hanged in effigy. With the new year opposition leaders to a man were brought to town. Chesterfield wished the Heir Apparent mentioned in the public prayers. His Princess had another child that year. A secret committee was moved again to investigate the war. The real question, as Argyll thought, was whether the "liberties and property" of the country should be given to Walpole "in absolute trust" to enable him to procure the return of another favorable Parliament.

On the contrary, the *Daily Gazetteer* saw (February 2) "in the British Senate" only that which "would" and "should" "naturally happen . . . in popular Assemblies." Members of "great natural Abilities and much Experience" became the "leading Men." But Samuel Sandys gave notice in the House of Commons (February 10), that three days later he would move that Walpole be dismissed. Carteret made the motion in the Lords. Chesterfield came in too ill to speak. Hardwicke, Newcastle, and Hervey joined in the Minister's defense. The Prince of Wales was in the House but did not vote. In the Commons, Shippen refused to play the opposition's game. He and thirty friends withdrew; others, remaining, voted on the ministerial side. Returning to town Sunday afternoon (February 15), Egmont found that the motion had "entirely disunited the minority among themselves, . . . so that Sir Robert Walpole" was "more firmly established in his administration" than before.

A place bill passed the lower house, but was defeated in the Lords. The Prince of Wales attended these debates also. When the Minister chid Pitt for using declamation instead of argument, the orator pledged obscurely his best "endeavours at whatever hazard to repel the aggressor and drag the thief to justice whoever may protect them in their villainy and whoever may partake of their plunder." The *Craftsman* complained (February 28) that ministerial journalists were supported by "Money and Power" and by a "Bully Back." *Common Sense* alleged (March 28) that Walpole prolonged the war just as he had negotiated the Convention. In fact, he took "it upon himself to command in every Province of Business more absolutely than ever any Man before did in that which was peculiarly his own." He was supported by a "servile Crew," who would "do anything to save his Bacon." Not knowing "any other Use of Words but to lie," it was not now possible for him to "impose on the Publick unless he should happen to speak the Truth." Not "even one of his own Gang . . . would take his Word for a Farthing."

In this abusive chatter the King dissolved the Parliament. The *Daily Gazetteer* appealed (April 17) again for unity to fight, if not avert, a general war. In order to "secure her own Liberties," Britain was "bound to preserve those of Europe," which could be done "no other Way than by preserving the Balance of Power." "Scarce ever was a more critical Juncture" than the country faced. The sword was "ready to be drawn" in the north; in the south were "Preparations for Camps and other Tokens of Hostilities." But the day that Parliament was dissolved (April 25) the *Craftsman* confirmed its faith that of "all wicked Men a wicked Minister" was "worst." *Common Sense* granted that Walpole might win because of the "Pack of low, scandalous Fellows he sent about the Country to bribe the poor Electors and returning Officers" and the "impious and wicked Practices of several Ecclesiasticks" who had apparently "renounced Jesus Christ to worship the Corruptor."

Little wonder a correspondent of the *Weekly Miscellany* (May 2) could think "Wesley and Whitefield privately set on by Popish Emissaries to . . . take Advantage" of the "War abroad to raise Disturbances at Home" with a view to bringing in the Pretender and subverting "Church and State." The *Daily Gazetteer* saw (May 4) a "Spirit of Commotion . . . stirring." "Malecontents" of the previous century, lacking precedents, inflamed people with the "Dictates of their Passions." "Modern Factions" pled the example of the earlier time, thus giving "the most extravagant Attempts an Air of Authority."

Fearful for his electorate, even while the elections were in progress, the "King took Water at Whitehall" (May 6), to go to Gravesend on his way to Hanover. Even though his ministers had been agreed among themselves, affairs abroad required time which in prudence ought to have been given to contests at home. Pitt and his brother Thomas helped the Prince win twenty-seven of Cornwall's more than twoscore seats. Argyll labored in Scotland with effect. Ministerial candidates in Westminster suddenly and unexpectedly found themselves opposed. Pulteney had objected to the move, and Carteret refused his help, but it promised some success even before the fear of disorder caused the use of troops and the termination of the poll after six days, while householders were still dribbling in to vote. The *Craftsman* at once (May 23) lamented, that in the only place where the "natural undistinguished Sense of the People" could be seen, the ministry had interfered. Less was to be expected "of those little, corrupt Boroughs, which Bishop Burnet too justly" called the "rotten Part of the Constitution."

Horace Walpole went to Norfolk (May 27), "quite weary of the weak, absurd, distracted, and contradictory councils and motives of those whose steadiness and union" were needed "for the preservation of the whole." Dodington felicitated Argyll (June 18), that whereas "Cornwall gave the first foundation for any reasonable hope," Scotland had "brought the work to such a degree of perfection that it would be now as criminal to despair of success as it would have been before presumptuous to have expected it." He urged the organization of clubs and meetings of the members before the time for Parliament.

Common Sense and the *Craftsman*, meanwhile, were eulogizing Vernon, whose name had been used in Westminster and other places to help the opposition cause. Walpole, it was said, "meant him no Good at the Bottom" and sent him out a "Sacrifice" as Hosier had been sent before. Then came news of Cartagena, and Newcastle confided to Hardwicke (June 19) that things were almost as bad as they could be. He thought Vernon "plainly" to be "concerned for nothing but what" related to himself and his fleet. The Duke and Walpole agreed that reënforcements should be sent. The Lord Chancellor felt that the matter would "require all possible attention, deliberation, and prudence; and all possible temper and union too amidst the chagrin and ill humour" that such an "ill-success" would raise.

The *Craftsman* meditated at the same time (June 20) the result of the elections. There were "many new Members," but none could "answer for their Sentiments or Conduct before" they were "try'd." *Common Sense* was occupied with reprinting from the *London Magazine* the speeches made in Parliament on the motion to dismiss the Minister. The *Daily Gazetteer* (July 3) was uncertain too. A "Parliament terrified by the Many" was as "much to be dreaded" as one "dependent on the Prince." In either case, the members were "Creatures of the Crown" or "of the Crowd," and not the country's "Representatives."

Pulteney was now less sure that he wished to help arouse the crowd. Dodington learned that day that he would not summon members-elect to meet. He might attend if some one else would do it, but preferred that friends bring word of what was done. He was "weary of being at the head of a party; he would rather row in the galleys, and was absolutely resolved not to charge himself with taking the lead." Dodington awaited Argyll's word.

But the ministers now faced another matter more serious for themselves and for the war. France and Prussia having joined against Maria Theresa, George II as Elector saw no alternative but neutrality in that war, unless his British subjects would send an army for defense. Newcastle thought the Queen should be supported and urged that Hardwicke come to town to help. The Cabinet would not be responsible for the King's proposed electoral act. Horace Walpole found the ministers impeded by "narrow," Hanoverian views. All this in secret yet.

The opposition press defended Vernon. Walpole was to blame for his failure; the Admiral would have deserved the credit for success. The *Craftsman* listed members of the new Parliament (July 25), estimating that a majority might oppose the ministers. Chesterfield was not so sure. "I think," he wrote to Dodington (August 8), "we can but just be called the minority." But Walpole knew how to gain men. Carteret and Pulteney, who should lead the opposition, would "make it their business to break and divide it" and would "succeed." They wished "to get in with a few by negotiation, and not by victory with numbers." Chesterfield favored "meetings to concert measures" before Parliament met, but if Pulteney should attend, he would know in advance how to defeat the plans. Nevertheless, Argyll should take the lead. Argyll agreed that he would act and, if he failed, "retire."

The ministers were occupied with other thoughts. Harrington at Hanover might "act and talk agreeably" to his Majesty, said Newcastle, but "we must think how we can serve the King in Parliament and defend there what is done elsewhere." Even Hardwicke began to see troubles in the way. "It looked last year," he wrote (August 17), "as if the old world was to be fought for in the new, but the tables are turned, and I fear now that America must be fought for in Europe."

The time demanded leadership such as the *Daily Gazetteer* described (August 25), a "prudent Man," who waited for "Opportunities" and improved them, who foresaw "Difficulties" and avoided them, who exercised "his Sagacity not in providing for the Future, but in making the best Use of the Present." This leader should be a man who

seldom boasts, but never complains. If he chances to make a false Step, he repairs it as soon as he can and takes care to get more by the Experiment than the Accident cost him. His single Maxim is to follow Providence and not to take unnecessary Pains to get before or to provide against it. . . . He proposes many Things, but resolves on few; he makes Time his Privy Councillor, and draws Intelligence from Events; he pushes every favourable Occurrence and declines every cross one. He is more of the Willow than the Oak, and by prudently yielding sometimes secures Victory always. Rationally attentive to the Rectitude of his Conduct, he is absolutely indifferent whether the many applaud or condemn; provided on a fair Inquiry he can acquit him to himself.

But the leader whose life inspired these comments was now ill and tired with age, wanting the zest that won his earlier fights. Most of life was behind him. And his brother, Horace, thought (August 22) that Harrington wrote with the "art and skill of an old courtier," discovering "his master's desires without explaining them fully . . . or giving his opinion upon them," leaving to the ministers at home the dilemma of disobliging his Majesty or giving advice contrary to their judgment. A week later, this inner group whom the King had left in charge—Walpole, Newcastle, Hardwicke, and Wilmington —felt that he should come home, since they could not advise in his absence on events with which they had to deal. And the *Daily Gazetteer* complained again (August 31), that in a dangerous European juncture England's hand was weakened by divisions known to exist at home. On this plea the Spanish King had justified his decision for war.

September came; electoral neutrality was a fact. Horace Walpole was sorry, but not surprised. France would now do as she pleased. Harrington blithely wrote that obligations to the Queen of Hungary had been fulfilled. Newcastle shook his head the more. As Secretary of State, he was responsible. "We may tell our own story as we please," he said, "and endeavour to deceive ourselves, but the truth will undoubtedly come out, and I think it will be impossible to prevent a parliamentary inquiry into this conduct." He did not blame his colleagues. His own view was so well known that the King disliked him for it. He found it as difficult to quit as to support his Majesty.

Hardwicke admitted that the case was hard. But if they had all done as Newcastle asked, it would not have helped. True the opposition in Parliament would find fault, but few would think that England should have gone to war to save the Queen of Hungary. At least the Duke could quote: "Thou canst not say I did it." As to the neutrality of Hanover, "the conduct of Great Britain ought to be the same as if it had never happened." Writing from Horace Walpole's "most agreeable place" (September 13), Henry Pelham advised his brother to talk as though the King had done his best to keep together the Queen of Hungary's friends. But the Duke still thought the act "disgraceful," and if something was not done, the "electoral neutrality" might become a "royal neutrality" as well.

The weeks brought no relief. The more Newcastle pondered it, the more he doubted whether he should go on. Indeed, the King's partiality for his electorate might be reason for the whole ministry to quit. The Duke was sure his brother understood (October 2) that he was disturbed by "measures," not by "men." He had ways of "thinking and acting" which seemed to him to be right. He had a "natural love for politics" and no wish for "private life." If he should quit, he must "avoid the imputation of leaving the King" and his colleagues in a "time of danger and distress."

The Minister was ill again in those days, near to death, a circumstance inspiring part of what the brother of the Duke made haste to write (October 8). He was satisfied that Newcastle's troubles were due in part to "things," but also to "persons" too. Winter would be time enough to decide what to do about the King's neutrality. "A partiality to Hanover" was nothing new; all who had served the house had suffered from it; none familiar with the Duke's career would now believe, "on that account" alone he "quit the service of the King." The problem was, to "secrete their weaknesses," and if nothing was "required to give any sanctions to their indiscretions," honour and conscience need not scruple at doing that. Besides, once out, Newcastle would find himself an "opponent, as Lord Carteret or Mr. Pulteney" was. If Hardwicke did not think it necessary to go out, why should the Duke? Finally, a thing might "happen in the course of nature very soon" that did not seem "improbable" within the week.

Not knowing what went on behind the scenes, the opposition press continued its abuse. *Common Sense* (October 17) "could name a Man that hath laid out in the Article of Italian Pictures three times as much as the Estate he was born to is worth and hath the same elegant Taste in Pictures as his Coach Horse." But those within the family circle began to see a change. "I have frequently known him," wrote his son (October 19), to "snore ere they had drawn his curtains; now he never sleeps above an hour without waking; and he, who at dinner always forgot he was minister and was more gay and thoughtless than all his company, now sits without speaking and with his eyes fixed for an hour together." Even a mere acquaintance, such as Egmont, thought he seemed "a little cloudy and less smiling" than his wont.

The King returned, and the new Parliament had to meet. Appealing to posterity, the *Daily Gazetteer* tried (October 29) to oppose abuse with ridicule: "In the mild Reign of George II, when Scaffolds were out of Fashion and the Prerogative was scarce heard of, there flourish'd two great Men of whom, after twenty Years whetting their Wits, the very worst their Enemies could say with Truth was, that one wanted a few Teeth before, and the other could not keep his Breeches up Behind." But by the beginning of November young Horace Walpole noted that the "neutrality" began to "break out" and threatened to become "an *Excise* or *Convention.*"

Common Sense (November 7) summoned those tempted to stay in the country and "hunt a Hare" to come to town and help "run down a Wolf." The *Craftsman* discoursed on the "Fall of the House of Austria, how Accomplished." The *Champion* alleged as usual that Walpole perverted good to evil, "admitting none to his Confidence but the Profligate, Rapacious, Betraying, Time-serving, Crafty, and Abandoned," calling every "dirty Job" they did "the Act and Deed of the Nation." Another week, and *Common Sense* blamed Walpole for "all the Disgraces" that had "fallen upon the Nation abroad as well as the Grievances at Home." "Consider," it remarked a fortnight later, "what continual Terrors must he live in when it shall be in the Power of any eight or ten of his own People that understand each other to deliver him up."

As the time for Parliament approached, the *Daily Gazetteer* marveled (November 28) that Scottish members "grew Heroes in Probity of a sudden, and the World was called upon to attest the Virtue and Honour of Cornish Boroughs." Conferences had been called in town; "Cabals held at all the Horse Races in the Country"; every "Village Assembly" had become a "Council of Malecontents." The King's speech announced (December 4) impending dangers in Europe due to the attack on Austria. Chesterfield belabored the ministry in the Lords, and Carteret followed suit. Argyll chimed in. Newcastle defended the ministry in general. Harrington explained the neutrality as declared by the Elector of Hanover and not affecting England.

A little later in the lower house Pulteney asked a day to "consider the state of the nation and Sir Robert Walpole." That Minister agreed, suggesting January 21. The *Champion* was sure (December 12) that England would not tolerate a "Prime or Sole Minister," an office "pernicious and incompatible with that due Balance of Power" necessary to preserve the "national Liberties." Four days later the opposition stole a march and won the chairmanship of the Committee on Privileges and Elections in the House of Commons by a vote of 243 to 238. Cheers of victory echoed from the lobby to footmen in the Court of Requests and thence to coffeehouses and the streets. "You have no idea of their huzzas," wrote young Horace Walpole to his friend, "unless you can conceive how people must triumph after defeats for twenty years together." Each party's members met that night to dine and plan.

Tuesday, December 22, the House of Commons sat from ten A.M. to five the morning after, when the Westminster election was voted void, 220 to 216. The Prince sat up all night awaiting news of the event. The *Daily Gazetteer* that day knew not how to answer "downright Calumny and Falsehood." Christmas Eve, the House recessed to January 18. Young Horace Walpole sat down to write that day. Sir Robert was still sanguine. A Patriot, observing him the day before, remarked: "Damn him, how well he looks." But his family wished him to end his ministry if he should win the fight and seek a last respite from "envy" and "ill will." Other friends who observed him in those days did not "like his countenance." Sunday at court his Majesty was "disturbed and serious."

The *Daily Gazetteer* could not understand (December 30) "with what View, or to what Purpose Men of Fortune should endeavour to lessen their own Security by distressing an upright Administration." Perhaps they acted as "Men do most idle Things, for Want of considering what they do." Opposition candidates were returned from Westminster the next day unopposed. Walpole had suggested Harrington's son, but that Minister would not let him stand. New Year's Day, appeared a pamphlet, *The Expediency of One Man's Dying to save the Nation.*

Walpole saw that the time had come to look for help. Overtures were made to Carteret and Pulteney. Young Horace gave a musicale to entertain Lord Hervey, who was "too ill to go to operas." The Minister enjoyed the music. One last effort was made. Bishop Secker went to see the Prince to offer fifty thousand pounds additional a year and payment of his debts. Frederick replied that "he would listen to no proposals of any kind till Sir Robert Walpole was removed." His Royal Highness held the whip.

A new weekly had appeared in the last days of the previous year, the *Westminster Journal,* which added its emphasis to the thought (January 9) that "of all the odious Characters that ever debased the human Species, none . . . has been so universally detested as that of a wicked, overgrown Prime Minister; none, not that of a Tyrant itself, has been spoke and writ against with such Vehemence, has been attacked with such repeated Efforts of Wit, Learning, and Eloquence by the wisest and most virtuous of Mankind." The same day *Common Sense* compared the incidents in the short meeting of Parliament before the recess with "the first Sight of Land to a Crew of half starved Mariners after a long Voyage," and cautioned against "Efforts making to divide the Patriots," threatening those who yielded with the "Odium" Walpole had "drawn upon himself" and all who followed him.

The Minister was reluctant to retire. The King was loyal and even less disposed to give way to his son. Newcastle thought (January 10) "all might have been easy, quiet, and *safe* had it not been for the fatal obstinacy of one single man." He would attend the King the next day and lay "before him the state . . . his affairs" would "be in and where they might have been had other measures" been adopted. Perhaps Hardwicke's "strong remonstrances" might do more good. The Duke "most heartily pitied" his own "poor brother." Would not the Lord Chancellor comfort "him a little"? Two days later another observer thought Henry Pelham to be the "excellent mortar" binding "my Lord President, my Lord Steward, my Lord Chancellor, and even his Grace of Newcastle himself."

The *Champion* carried a rumor the day that Parliament reassembled that Walpole would retire to the upper house. The Prince was obdurate. His father's Minister must be removed. Pulteney made a surprise motion (January 21), on which the opposition had got ready all its strength. By the hardest, the ministers held their ground, 253 to 250, postponing the main question to another day. A week later the vote on the Chippenham election went against the ministers. But by that time a settlement was already on the way.

Walpole was a realist. The Prince, he saw, must win his point. The *Craftsman* agreed with undue hopes (January 30): "If his Hour is not come, I believe it will soon, for surely Justice will at last overtake him. . . . What a terrible Companion must a guilty Conscience be. I would not have his dreadful Apprehensions but for the Space of one Week for twenty times his Wealth. Poor Man. I almost pity him."

But pity was not needed yet. Hardwicke, Newcastle, Carteret, and the host met at Pulteney's house. Walpole wrote to Devonshire February 2 that the King would approve the Malt Act the next day and direct that the houses adjourn for a fortnight "to give time for setting a new administration." He would become Earl of Orford. The "panick" among his friends had reached a point where they declared his "retiring . . . absolutely necessary, as the only means of carrying on the public business." He was to quit with "honour and security." This was "fixed with the Duke of Newcastle, lord Chancellor, lord Carteret, and Mr. Pulteney." By the King's designation, Wilmington was to head the Treasury, leaving the Presidency open. There was a scheme to force Newcastle into that place, making way for Carteret as Secretary of State, but Walpole had prevented it. The Prince had been told of the arrangement that morning and took it "in a proper manner." Argyll, Cobham, and Chesterfield had not been told. How either to satisfy them or to go on without it, Walpole did not see. Those who "thought they had but one obstacle to remove to make all things easy" would now encounter "difficulties." The King had behaved with "grace and steadiness" and had not yielded to the change until Walpole made it his "desire."

Walpole's levee, February 4, was the "fullest that ever was," but still a "melancholy scene," with everybody showing great "concern." There were some who "did not yet despair of having" Walpole's "life." Within an "overflowing" house, young Horace wrote to Horace Mann. The crowd was no "prelude to victory." Sir Robert would be Earl of Orford, his "other envied name" expiring with "his ministry." "Never was a fallen minister . . . followed" thus. Henry Pelham would accept no office that his chief had held. Some came "crying"; others, to wish joy. Horace's own half-sister was the one he pitied most. She "must be created an earl's daughter," else her birth would "deprive her of the rank."

As Walpole foresaw, sailing was not smooth ahead. One problem was to fill his place, a place that none as yet quite understood. The King had designated Wilmington, but leaders were not chosen thus. Each had to win his way, improving time and circumstance. Pulteney had a momentary chance, but lacked the will to try.

The Patriots were still at odds when the new Earl of Orford gave up his seals. The Prince and King were reconciled, but little else was done. Argyll thought it "impudence" for Orford to be "driving about the streets." The Earl and his daughter planned to go to Richmond for a week, but the press warned of a coming fight. The *Champion* described (February 6) the new peer's execution in advance, reporting that Hosier's ghost was heard to cry for "Justice." *Common Sense* that day thought him less deserving than the Roman Emperor's famous horse. The *London Evening Post* alleged that he burnt his papers the day he kissed hands for his peerage and prophesied that he would be impeached. The *Champion* was convinced (February 9) that those who could not or would not "convict him before God and his Country" had "neither Right nor Pretence to set themselves forth in his Spoils." "The Hog of Noah," said the *Champion* again (February 11), "was not more sensual, Eve's Peacock more gaudy, or Solomon's Horse more proud; no Fox was more subtle, no Wolf more voracious, no Dog more fawning, no Hare more timorous, and no Cat more desperate." The *Westminster Journal* thought him (February 11) "one of the boldest, wickedest Mortals that ever infected a Nation, a Disgrace to his Prince, a Curse to his Country," and asked, "shall a poor Pickpocket swing for stealing a few Pence, and wholesale Thieves who rob a Nation be esteem'd and honour'd?" These preachers had apparently convinced themselves.

Wilmington, who suffered from a "stone," told Egmont (February 9) that he did not aspire to be Prime Minister, feeling that "every great office should be immediately dependent on the King and answer for itself." To that time, he had become First Lord of the Treasury; and Samuel Sandys, Chancellor of the Exchequer. Other arrangements waited to be made. Wager quitted the Admiralty, remarking, "We shall not die, but be all changed." Itching to have a hand in foreign affairs, Carteret was to succeed Harrington instead of Newcastle; Harrington would be Lord President. But Argyll and Cobham's group were clamoring for "justice."

Three hundred of the old opposition met at the Fountain Tavern, February 11. As usual, Carteret would not go. Argyll attacked all that had been done. The party ought to have acted as a whole. But Carteret had warned Pulteney that the King would not accept the opposition as a group. "Upon consideration," he thought, the taking of places by a chosen few would be found "a prudent act." Some said already that Carteret meant "to be Chief Minister" and was a "false man," as bad as Walpole. The country party, or what was left of it, would oppose again.

There was a truce within a week. Argyll and the Prince were pacified. There was another meeting at the Fountain

Tavern. Wednesday, February 17, the Prince and Princess were at the royal Palace. In the father's drawing room the son kissed the paternal hand "with tears trickling down his cheeks," which made attending "ladies" cry. Other leaders of opposition also went to call.

But that very evening at Dodington's Argyll warned a hundred lords that he would not accept the proffered places unless affairs were "upon so broad a bottom that the nation might be satisfied and every person qualified to serve his country without distinction of party" was given a chance to do so. Pulteney agreed to move a secret committee to proceed against Walpole, denying any intention of letting that Minister escape. Wilmington was disconsolate, knowing that the King would not accept such terms. The Prince came down with measles. When Orford was introduced as a peer, some of those attending would not bow, though Chesterfield was of those to wish him joy.

The *Daily Gazetteer* reminded readers (February 18), that there was a war. If not attended to at once, a "Coalition" might not come in time. In the opposition press, the war on Walpole was still more to the point. The *Champion* alleged (February 20) that he had contributed to a Jesuit college. *Common Sense* observed that day that for "any Gentleman or set of Gentlemen to engage to stand betwixt publick Justice and any Man who must, who certainly will be pursued by the Vengeance of these Nations" was a "Thing" surpassing "all Belief." Would those "who by persevering in an Opposition . . . attended with the Labours of Hercules" had "at last worked Things up to this present happy Situation destroy their own Work?" There was no precedent for procedure, since no other man had ever brought "the Tricks of Newgate into the Politicks of the State."

Orford at Richmond tried to feel at ease. "You see, I hunt whilst others hunt me," he said. David Hume was reputed author of an essay on him widely published, which concluded: "I would give my Vote for removing him from St. James's, but should be glad to see him return to Houghton Hall to pass the Remainder of his Days in Ease and Pleasure." But the

Champion still surmised (February 27) that "those who wish his Destruction think he hath furnish'd them with sufficient Matter to do his Business within the last Month." The *Champion,* however, had heard that the "truly great Man to whose unwearied, disinterested and virtuous Opposition" the country was "so inexpressibly obliged" would be "honoured with the Title of Earl of Bath."

Carteret thought this patriot behaved "like a dog in a manger." Unwilling to "act himself," he would not "suffer another to act." But Pulteney appreciated better than Carteret how hard it was to keep Argyll and Cobham in line and also to carry out the promise they had made to Walpole's friends. It was already charged that he had no "zeal" in prosecuting the fallen Minister. A committee waited on him to say that they would not be "satisfied" till "he went brisker on." He answered that he "intended it." The *Craftsman* said the same day, "the Nation justly" cries "aloud for Vengeance."

Pulteney's daughter having died, he was absent three days later when by the narrow margin of two a motion was defeated for a committee to inquire into the conduct of affairs for the past twenty years. Argyll resigned the next day. The day following, another meeting was held at the Fountain. Some said that Carteret had inspired Pulteney's friends to stay away from the debate. Cutting short his grief, the latter was back in the House March 15 to retrieve his lost prestige. A week later he moved a committee to investigate the conduct of affairs for ten years past. He was victorious, 252 to 245. Though he confessed that his own thought had been only to dislodge the Minister from power, not to punish him, he now saw that the nation wished for something more.

Remembering the early days of George I, Walpole used what weight he had against the motion Pulteney made. Young Horace, who the day before had purchased pictures at the Earl of Oxford's sale, was in the House to speak. Having turned his father out, they now wished to inquire the reason why. The Secret Committee was chosen March 29.

Yet a little longer the opposition papers cried for justice. Orford was dragged about the streets in effigy and burned.

Petitions against him were brought in. But the game drew rapidly to a close. In May the Committee confessed itself unable to find out what it sought unless Parliament would indemnify witnesses who refused to testify for fear of incriminating themselves. Carteret thought that such an act would make "legal" that which was not "right." Hardwicke was able on the same side. The most important item brought to light was information concerning Walpole's subsidy of the press. The fact had been well known. Opponents would always criticize, but not for generations would shame attach to ministers who used this method in defense. Sandys opposed a revival of the Committee in December, telling friends the night before that it was the royal wish.

Pulteney, as the Earl of Bath, retired in the summer to the House of Lords. Charles Hanbury Williams and others began to pour out odes in ridicule. "Oh, my poor Country," asked one, "is this all you've gained by the long labour'd fall of Walpole and his Tools?"

> He was a Knave indeed—what then,
> He'd Parts—but this new Set of Men
> Ai'nt only Knaves but Fools.

The *Daily Gazetteer* subsided to a mere newspaper, without party preference. Amhurst in his last days was "taken up in ungrateful Reflections and melancholy Presages." He died without reward except the living he had made as journalist and any satisfaction found in carrying on the fight. John Oldmixon died also at the ripe age of sixty-nine. Bolingbroke's father died at last, but there was little compensation for the son. Plainly, some persons, he said, "meant that the opposition should serve as their scaffolding, nothing else." He was glad that Argyll and his cohorts would keep up the fight.

The Earl of Orford had not many months to live. He had preferred to hold on to the end, and he had never had a chance to serve his country as he wished. But he found consolation in these days; his work had stood the test. Pulteney scarcely signified. Carteret would overreach himself. Hervey, in poor health, had lost his place. But Newcastle, Hardwicke,

Henry Pelham, and their younger followers were men the opposition could not match. In them the fallen leader passed his mantle on.[8]

[8] [James Ralph], *The Case of Authors by Profession or Trade; Political State*, LX. 211ff.; *Parliamentary History*, XI. 610ff.; XII. 1ff.; Ball, *Correspondence of Swift*, VI. 163ff.; Yorke, *Hardwicke*, I. 238ff.; *Marchmont Papers*, II. 237ff.; Dobree, *Chesterfield Letters*, II. 437ff.; Hist. Mss. Com., *Egmont Diary*, III. 164ff.; *Carlisle*, pp. 197ff.; *Stopford Sackville*, I. 36ff.; (14 Rept. Appendix, Pt. 9), pp. 55ff.; Coxe, *Robert Walpole*, III. 554ff.; *Horatio Walpole*, II. 7ff.; *Pelham*, I. 20ff., 473; Basil Williams, *Life of William Pitt, Lord Chatham*, I. 40ff.; Ballantyne, *Carteret*, pp. 239ff.; Phillimore, *Lyttelton*, I. 205ff.; Torrens, *Cabinets*, I. 547ff.; Hervey, *Memoirs*, III. 390ff.

INDEX

437

Cato's *Letters* in, 237, 239, 240, 241, 244, 246, 247, 248, 251, 256, 258, 260; function of, 238; blamed, 246; circulation of, 256; Hoadly contributes to, as Britannicus, 262, 264, 265, 266, 267, 273, 278, 280; Walpole contributes to, 296; at death of George I, 300ff.; on shibboleths, 305; on public opinion, 311; and Gordon, 315; defends ministry, 316; Francis Osborne (*i.e.,* James Pitt and others) contributes to, 318ff.; writers in, thought atheists, 349; suspended, 369f.

London Magazine, 337, 397, 423

Londonderry, Lord. *See* Pitt, Thomas

Louis XIV, King of France, and Charles II, 2; and Spanish succession, 16; seizes barrier towns, 23; recognizes Pretender, 25; negotiates for peace, 93ff.; and Pretender, 179; ill, 180; dies, 181

Louis XV, King of France, 285, 291, 320

Lumley, Lord, 230

Lumley, Richard, Earl of Scarborough, 191, 262

Lyttleton, George, and the Prince, 358; and Cobham, 367; cautions the Prince, 371; and Fielding, 377; and marriage of the Prince, 378; and birth of Princess Augusta, 386f.; and death of Caroline, 388; and Glover, 391; and Convention of Pardo, 402; and secession, 407

McCartney, George, 119

Macclesfield, Earl of. *See* Parker, Thomas

Mackinnon, James, *Union of England and Scotland,* cited, 42

Mackworth, Sir Humphrey, *The South Sea Scheme,* 239

Macpherson, James, *History,* cited, 28; *Original Papers,* cited, 168

Madan, F., *Bibliography of Sacheverell,* cited, 66

Madox, Thomas, 148, 150

Maidenhead, 45

Mainwaring, Arthur, 80, 121, 123

Maitland, William, *London,* cited, 285

Manchester, A. K., *British Preëminence in Brazil,* cited, 130

Manchester, Earl of. *See* Montague, Charles

Manley, Mrs. Mary, offers services

to Harley, 77; *True Narrative,* 88; *New Vindication,* 97; *Learned Comment,* 97; pamphleteer, 99; *True Relation,* 101; ill, 109; and *Examiner,* 124f.; dies, 278

Manly, Roger. *See* Arnall, William, *and* British Journal

Mann, Sir Horace, 431

Mansell, Thomas, 55

Mar, Earl of. *See* Erskine, John

Marchmont, Earl of. *See* Campbell, Alexander

Marchmont Papers, cited, 302, 344, 364, 390, 416, 436

Maria Theresa, Queen of Hungary, 423

Marlborough, Duchess of. *See* Churchill, Sarah

Marlborough, Dukes of. *See* Churchill, John; Spencer, Charles

Mary of Modena, 186

Masham, Abigail, relations with Anne, 43; mediates between Harley and Anne, 53f.; question of dismissal of, 58; and Sacheverell's trial, 66ff.; difficulties with Anne, 69ff.; Cofferer, 81; and Swift's preferment, 122ff.; consulted by Oxford, 131; dissatisfaction of, 143; and Assiento Contract, 146; opposes Oxford, 147; object of sympathy, 152; blamed, 169

Masham, Samuel, 43, 54, 104

Mead, Dr. Richard, 244

Medley, 80, 96, 115, 119

Mercator, 128, 130, 134

Merchant Taylors' Hall, 234

Meredith, William, 23

Mesnager, agent of Louis XIV, 93, 95, 98

Methuen, Paul, 192, 207

Michael, Wolfgang, *Englische Geschichte,* cited, 205

Middleton, Viscount. *See* Brodrick, Alan

Miege, Guy, *New State of England,* cited, 13

Mist, Nathaniel, *Weekly Journal,* 211; Defoe and, 216, 218f.; imprisoned, 248; fined, 278, 307; suspends journal, 314. *See also* Weekly Journal, Mist's

Mob, influence of, 35; at Sacheverell's trial, 65; aroused in London, 118, 177; danger of, 213; the Sacheverell, 253; power of, 313; and the excise, 342; attacks Walpole, 344;

269; opposes Bolingbroke, 271;
leader of Jacobites, 283; professes
repentance, 313; and Mist's *Journal,* 314
Wharton, Thomas, Marquess of, 6;
and the war, 18; Lord Lieutenant of
Ireland, 50; and Sacheverell's trial,
66; comment of, 76; on reward for
Pretender, 130; charges Swift with
libel, 140; dies, 175
Whig Examiner, 80
Whitefield, George, 390, 408, 409, 421
Whitehall Evening Post, 216, 218, 254
Wilkins, W. H., *Caroline,* cited, 168,
189
Will's Coffee-House, 4, 280
William III, King of England, comes
to England, 2; and Anne, 4; in 1700,
16ff.; speech to Parliament, 22;
negotiates Grand Alliance, 25f.; addresses Parliament, 26; dies; 27
Williams, Basil, *Stanhope,* cited, 168,
189, 223, 228, 251; "Election of
1734," cited, 364; *Chatham,* cited,
436
Williams, Charles Hanbury, 435
Williams, Dr. Daniel, 339
Williams, Folkestone, *Atterbury,* cited,
168, 169, 285, 302, 322, 344
Willis, Richard, Bishop of Salisbury,
262; Bishop of Winchester, 268
Wilmington, Earl of. *See* Compton,
Spencer
Winchelsea, Earl of. *See* Finch, Daniel
Winchester, Bishop of, 262. *See also*
Willis, Richard
Winnington, Thomas, 396, 415
Wolsey, Thomas, Cardinal, 323
Wood, William, 273ff., 284f.
Wren, Sir Christopher, 3, 59
Wright, Nathan, 38
Wright, Thomas, *Georges,* cited, 189
Wyndham, H. P., *Dodington's Diary,*
cited, 390

Wyndham, Sir William, Chancellor of
Exchequer, 133; speaks in Parliament, 173; Bolingbroke writes to,
179; in Jacobite rebellion, 181f.;
warned by Bolingbroke, 188; makes
motion, 208; loses in South Sea
crash, 244; confers with Bolingbroke,
271; and opposition to Walpole, 292,
294; and Bolingbroke, 303; and
Dunkirk debate, 319f.; opposes war,
326; and Bolingbroke, 346; on Walpole, 354; and Bolingbroke, 372;
declining interest, 375; and the
Prince's application, 382, 384; secedes from Parliament, 405; blackballed at White's, 407; Bolingbroke
advises, 410; on Pulteney, 411; and
war with Spain, 413; dies, 417

Yarmouth, Countess of. *See* Walmoden, Amalie Sophie Marianne
Yonge, Sir William, *Sedition and Defamation,* 324
Yorke, Philip, Earl of Hardwicke, Solicitor General, 267; advises Newcastle, 331; Attorney General, 342;
on defeat of excise, 345; Chief Justice and Lord Hardwicke, 347;
opinion of, 371; Lord Chancellor,
381; and the Prince's application,
382; and Newcastle, 385; and death
of Caroline, 388; and Newcastle,
398; and Convention, 403; on break
with Spain, 409; conciliates colleagues, 412, 416; on war with Spain,
413; defends Walpole, 420; on neutrality of Hanover, 425; and retirement of Walpole, 430ff.; and investigation of Orford, 435; *Miscellaneous State Papers,* cited, 25, 26,
86, 172, 189, 223, 228, 251
Yorke, Philip C., *Hardwicke,* cited,
390, 416, 436